FRAUD EXAMINATION: INVESTIGATIVE AND AUDIT PROCEDURES

Fraud Examination: Investigative and Audit Procedures

JOSEPH T. WELLS

Foreword by
GIL GEIS

Q

QUORUM BOOKS
Westport, Connecticut
London

Library of Congress Cataloging-in-Publication Data

Wells, Joseph T.
    Fraud examination: investigative and audit procedures / Joseph
T. Wells ; foreword by Gil Geis.
        p.   cm.
    Includes bibliographical references and index.
    ISBN 0-89930-639-X (alk. paper)
    1. Fraud investigation.   2. Fraud investigation—United States.
I. Title.
    HV8079.F7W45   1992
    363.2'5963—dc20   91-32818

British Library Cataloguing in Publication Data is available.

Library of Congress Catalog Card Number: 91-32818
ISBN: 0-89930-639-X

First published in 1992

Quorum Books, 88 Post Road West, Westport, Connecticut 06881
An imprint of Greenwood Publishing Group, Inc.

Printed in the United States of America

The paper used in this book complies with the
Permanent Paper Standard issued by the National
Information Standards Organization (Z39.48-1984).

10 9 8 7 6 5

For Judy

Contents

Tables and Figures

TABLES

FIGURES

Foreword

Decent human relationships depend upon trust and conformity to the law. Unless people behave honestly, do what they are supposed to do, and do these things the way they agreed to do them, others will have to spend a great deal of time and emotion protecting themselves and what they have. It is not a pleasant way to exist, and if fraud and other illegal tactics are not effectively combatted, in time life comes to resemble a battlefield. We must be able to rely upon others' integrity in order to be comfortable and productive.

The need for mutual trust is particularly important in business and commercial relationships. Crimes such as robbery, burglary, rape, auto theft, and murder—those matters that preoccupy the media—have the curious tendency to draw a society together in condemnation of such acts. The result is much like what happens when there is a popular war against a foreign enemy: Americans unite in a common cause to defeat a despicable alien. Street crimes also convey a lesson to each of us, pointing out the kinds of behavior that are not acceptable to people who desire to be regarded as good and respectable citizens.

The response to fraud is different from that to the usual run of street crimes. Americans tend to be so intrigued and respectful of wealth that they often harbor a secret admiration for the successful middle- and upper-class offender who "beats the system," perhaps by trading on the stock market with insider information, embezzling company funds, or by peddling trade secrets, or through the bribery of a member of Congress for a vote for special-interest legislation. When those who commit fraud are caught, many of us turn cynical, shrugging our shoulders, as if we knew all along that we are living in a world riddled with deceit. We anticipate that these white-collar offenders will fare no worse than a brief sentence to a country-club prison where with patience they might be able to improve their tennis backhand. They can then emerge, sun-tanned and healthy, pick up the ill-gotten loot that they had stashed away in some foreign bank account, and live splendidly ever after. Would that we ourselves had been so shrewd.

The control of fraud is a matter of vital importance to the health and well-being of any society. Corruption sucks at the strength of many third-world countries, where any transaction has an under-the-table cost, where doctors and nurses have to be bribed to deliver adequate medical care, where the proposed price of building has to factor in payoffs to inspectors, and where so much attention is devoted to security that ordinary and routine operations become awkward and much more expensive than they need be. In the United States, high shoplifting rates inflate prices, the stealing of trade secrets discourages research and innovation, and embezzlement as in the terrible savings and loan scandals, ultimately has to be paid for by the ordinary taxpayer.

The great virtue of Joseph T. Wells's *Fraud Examination: Investigative and Audit Procedures* is that the author thoroughly understands both the larger philosophical issues associated with fraud and the dirty-hands, day-to-day aspects of working to control the perpetration of crookedness in the business world. The book descends from the ethereal clouds typically occupied by academic and legal writers who address issues of business fraud, yet it translates and incorporates the most important results and insights of work in these realms, so that it will be useful to persons who have to deal on a regular basis with matters of fraud. *Fraud Examination* primarily is a handbook for practitioners, but it also includes intelligent analysis of ethical and philosophical issues involved in enforcement of the law against fraud.

Social scientists usually generate findings and theories about fraud and the manner in which it is handled in the courts from what they call ''data sets,'' which are large, often computer-generated banks of numbers. But they almost never spend time truly learning what it means to pore through a mind-boggling pile of invoices for the few that include incriminating evidence against a suspect, and they never are personally acquainted with the problems of successfully interrogating persons who are belligerent because they are afraid that their crime has been discovered. Lawyers for their part come into fraud cases late in the game, when things often have been prettified, and by the nature of their charge they spend more time trying to advance a particular viewpoint than to discover the facts and only the facts.

While *Fraud Examination* absorbs the best that the academics and the lawyers have contributed to the understanding of its subject, it uniquely adds to that information the results of the author's wide experience and thorough understanding of the mechanics of handling the investigation of fraudulent activity. The book is written so that persons with years in the fraud control business will find helpful advice, while those starting out in the field will have before them useful information on virtually any problem with which they are likely to be confronted in their work.

The author of *Fraud Examination* draws upon a background that has thoroughly acquainted him with all aspects of the problem of fraud. Joseph Wells is a certified public accountant, and a graduate of the business school of the University of Oklahoma. He worked as a Special Agent for the Federal Bureau of Investigation, handling fraud investigations, and in 1988, Wells formed the National Association of Certified Fraud Examiners, based in Austin, Texas. The Association at this writing has 4,000 members, mostly auditors, accountants, and financial advisors. Wells draws deeply upon this group for material for this book: he knows what their work entails, the problems they face, the information they require, and the skills that are necessary for successful completion of their assignments.

Although he was not formally trained as one, Joseph Wells is a criminologist in every sense of the word. His constant lectures to fraud examiners throughout the United States have honed his understanding of the important practical issues in the field, and at the same time he has drawn upon the work of other criminologists—especially Donald Cressey, who before his death was the leading figure in the study of white-collar crime and a close friend of Wells's—to put his work into a broader context.

I have always felt that fraud examination is a noble calling. Nobody should be allowed to commit assaults and perpetrate other street crimes, but the enforcers against such offenses surely know that they are dealing with people who, for whatever reason, very often have gotten the short end of the stick: they usually are poor, ill-educated, and without access to health care or other things necessary to live a decent life. Persons who carry out fraudulent practices do so for a wide variety of reasons, but greed and not need, an inability to be satisfied with what they have and to resist temptation, often lies at the core of their illegal behavior. Those who combat fraud are fighting against an activity that eats into and erodes the guts of American society. Theirs is a vital mission, and *Fraud Examination* by Joseph Wells will add immeasurably to their understanding of the nature of their work and how best to accomplish it.

Gil Geis
Professor Emeritus, University of California, Irvine;
former President of the American Society of Criminology

Introduction

Fraud is the crime of choice for the 21st century. It is easy to see why. Compared to other crimes, fraud pays better, there is little risk of apprehension, and even less risk of serious punishment. By all accounts, fraud and other white-collar crime outstrip the cost of traditional offenses by ten to one. In order to cope with this problem, a new discipline has emerged: the fraud examiner.

Fraud examination is a term for the methodology required to resolve allegations of fraud from inception to disposition. Fraud examiners gather evidence, interview witnesses, write reports and take statements, and assist in the detection and prevention of fraud. In reality, fraud examiners have been around for quite some time under different names: forensic accountants, fraud investigators, and fraud auditors, to name a few.

Because of the scope of fraud, the examination of these issues can be indeed far-ranging. This book concentrates primarily on one type of fraud—internal fraud committed by employees, managers, officers, and executives of governmental and business enterprises. There are two reasons for this. First, in terms of sheer numbers, internal fraud is a significant problem. Because of its clandestine nature, internal fraud is a good learning model; an examiner who can understand and resolve internal fraud will doubtless be able to apply this knowledge to other frauds. Second, internal fraud is a key concern to fraud examiners. How is it detected? How is it investigated and resolved? What will help prevent it? Some of these questions are answered in the following pages; some still require study and research.

Fraud examination, regardless of its nature, consists of four principal steps. First, the examiner must be skilled in the scrutiny of documents. This involves traditional audit functions such as tracing documentation and testing accounting systems. Furthermore, he or she must have the ability to trace funds, draw inferences from documents, and to spot suspected forgeries and alterations.

Furthermore, the fraud examiner must know the legal ramifications of evidence and how it is maintained for evidence purposes.

The second step is the observation. This could involve observing the target's movements and activities, or observing witnesses, documents, fruits of the fraud, or other physical evidence. The third step is interviewing. This consists of obtaining relevant information regarding the alleged fraud from persons other than the suspect or target of the examination. The fourth and final step is interrogation, whose purpose is to obtain a voluntary and legally binding confession of guilt from the target and/or co-conspirators. These procedures are discussed in detail herein.

Dealing with fraud issues requires a variety of disciplines. Knowledge of accounting and auditing concepts is necessary to understand the complexities of business systems. Knowing the personal motivations of this special type of criminal helps the fraud examiner understand why one person will turn to crime while another will not. Being able to gather evidence and interview witnesses is vital to resolving fraud allegations. And a knowledge of the law is essential to successful litigation and recovery of fraud losses. Recognizing these special disciplines, this book is divided into four parts: criminology, law, fraud auditing, and investigation.

Criminology, Part I, starts with the theories of traditional (non white-collar) crime. It helps explain the tremendous body of research that delves into the criminal mind. Once the traditional crime and criminal is understood, the white-collar criminal is described. Similarities and differences are compared and contrasted. An overview of the criminal justice system helps explain the theories behind crime and punishment. Finally, Part I gives some clues as to what might prevent these offenses in a larger, sociological context.

Part II, Law, begins with a description of the legal elements of fraud and an overview of the legal system. It attempts to explain how our laws came to be, and how criminal and civil laws differ. It describes, in detail, the myriad of federal statutes covering fraud and white-collar crimes, and summarizes the state laws used to litigate these issues. It further describes the requirements necessary for qualification as an expert witness, and offers helpful hints on how to testify.

With this knowledge, Part III summarizes basic accounting and auditing theory, then explains the steps required in gathering audit evidence, as well as determining its sufficiency and competency. Next, techniques of financial statement analysis are set out: ratio, vertical, and horizontal analysis, as well as other methods for understanding fraudulent financial reporting. Statistical sampling and its role in fraud detection are explained, and the special applications of computers are discussed. A review of the role of internal controls and how to evaluate them for fraud situations provides the reader a basis for assessing fraud risks within an organization. Finally, this part sets out the methodology for proving illicit financial transactions.

Part IV, Investigation, introduces the reader to the theory of fraud examination. This methodology helps the fraud examiner plan the examination of complex fraud issues. The reader is then introduced to interview techniques. An explanation is provided of the types of witnesses likely to be encountered in fraud investigations, and how to most effectively develop information from them. Key techniques in dealing with obstacles to interviews are discussed in detail. A section on evaluating deception through verbal and nonverbal clues provides a basis for dealing with untruthful witnesses. Interrogation, the art of obtaining confessions, is introduced to provide the fraud examiner with a powerful tool in resolving fraud issues. This section next explains how to take a signed statement, as well as the statement's legal implications. Next, the reader is advised how to obtain information from public records, and finally, how to write up the results of investigation in formal reports.

A book such as this, by necessity, is written largely on the experiences of those whose profession involves examining fraud issues. I am deeply indebted to many colleagues who were patient enough to teach me their art. I am especially grateful to Dr. Steve Albrecht, Director of the School of Accountancy at Brigham Young University; G. Jack Bologna, Professor of Management at Computer Protection Systems; Dr. Gil Geis, Professor Emeritus, University of California at Irvine; W. Michael Kramer, J.D., CFE, President of Kramer and Associates; Dr. Jack Robertson, Professor of Accounting at the University of Texas; Kathie Green and Desda Hilliard, respectively, Vice President and Assistant to the Chairman of the National Association of Certified Fraud Examiners. Without their assistance and the patience of my loving wife Judy, this book would have not been written.

Fraud is a complex sociological and accounting issue. It does not lend itself to simple solutions. But for those who are determined to find it and deal with it, this book is a start.

I Criminology

1 Theories of Traditional Crime

INTRODUCTION

In order to cope with fraud, one must first recognize that in most circumstances fraud is a crime, and fraudsters are criminals. It is therefore necessary to understand theories of crime: why people commit crimes, how they are prevented, and what happens to people who perpetrate them.

Accordingly, we will look first at how crime information is gathered, how it is analyzed, and what conclusions are drawn from the data. We will begin by studying the so-called "traditional" criminal—the person who robs, murders, and assaults. Then we will compare those characteristics with those of the fraud perpetrator. Finally, we will discuss the justice system: the police, the courts, and the prisons.

Official Crime Statistics

The FBI compiles statistics in the Uniform Crime Report (UCR), which collects information from more than 15,000 police departments. It tracks reported index crimes in two categories. Murder and non-negligent manslaughter, forcible rape, robbery, aggravated assault, burglary, larceny, arson, and auto theft are known as Part I offenses. Part II offenses include all others, except for traffic violations.

In addition to the above statistics, UCR provides information on arrestees and on police assaults. It includes all known offenses, resolved or not. The data is classified in three ways. First, crimes reported and arrests made are expressed as a raw figure. Second, the percentage change from year to year is computed. Third, crime rates per 100,000 people are computed.

Crime Trends in the United States

In the 20th century, crime in the United States increased gradually from the 1930s to the 1960s, when the upswing of crime became greater. It peaked in 1981, dipped slightly, then started up again. In 1987, the police reported more than 13 million crimes, near an all-time record.

There are several explanations for recent crime trends. These trends refer generally to crime, and not specifically to white-collar crimes. Violent offenses and fraud have marked differences, discussed later.

Most experts think changes in age distribution are the largest contributing factor to crime trends. The majority of traditional criminals and their victims are between the ages of 18 and 25; therefore, peaks and valleys in those age groups will cause corresponding differences in crime rates. As the population ages, many experts see a rise in white-collar crime, since these offenses are usually committed by older individuals.

In the early 1980s, crime decreased slightly. Conservatives attribute this to the "get tough" policy of former President Ronald Reagan. However, this policy does not explain the apparent recent increases in reported crimes. Bad economic times, drug use, and school dropouts are thought to be causal factors for many crimes. The methods of reporting by citizens also has an effect on reported crime trends. Some experts attribute increases to greater citizen involvement.

Nature of Crime

Regardless of the periodic fluctuations of the crime trends, many experts believe the trends of crime overall to be very stable. Several factors affect the nature of crime. Traditionally, crime in the United States is normally more prevalent in the summer months. This is thought to be because more people are outside, and teenagers are out of school. In the last few years, the southern states have led the country in overall crime rates. The south also has the highest violent crime rates. Rural areas traditionally have much lower rates of crime overall than cities. Large urban areas have the largest crime rates by far. About 10 million people are arrested annually for all categories of crime except traffic violations. About one in five is cleared through arrest. Violent crimes are much more likely to lead to an arrest.

The National Crime Survey (NCS) consists of a statistical study of 60,000 households and 136,000 individuals. Only about 45 percent of violent crimes, 24 percent of thefts, and 38 percent of household crimes are brought to the attention of the police. The NCS does not accurately measure the extent of fraud and embezzlement. It shows a downward trend of victims reporting offenses. The overall victimization rates show declines since the early 1980s. Most declines have been in the rates of household burglary, rape, personal larceny, and robbery. The reasons for these declines are not clearly known.

Self-report studies allow persons to describe criminal activity with guarantee of anonymity. About 90 percent of teenagers in self-report studies have admitted violations of the law. The most common are truancy, alcohol abuse, false identification, shoplifting or larceny under $5, fighting, marijuana use, and damage to property. One study by Franklyn Dunford and Delbert Elliott, found that only a quarter of all serious chronic juvenile offenders were apprehended by police, and only eight percent of youths admitting delinquency were ever arrested (Dunford and Elliott 1983: 57–86).

Crime Patterns

Many experts believe that the greatest amount of crime occurs within the lower classes. This is because of the belief that the people on the bottom of the social scale have the greatest incentive to commit crime in order to acquire goods and services beyond their reach.

Some authorities also believe that those living in poverty areas commit the greatest portion of what are called expressive crimes—rape and assault. These individuals are thought to be expressing rage at society.

Although official statistics indicate higher crime rates in high-poverty urban areas, criminologists have been unable to come up with a definitive link. However, Charles Tittle, Wayne Villemez, and Douglas Smith conducted a study in which they concluded that there is little if any support for concluding that class has any real relation to crime (Tittle, Villemez, and Smith 1978: 643–56). In another study, however, Delbert Elliott, Suzanne Ageton, and David Huizinga found that lower class youths are more likely to engage in criminal activity (Elliott, Ageton, and Huizinga 1980: 95–110). The weight of evidence does seem to indicate a connection between class and crime, but it is not a certainty.

Age and Crime

Most criminologists agree that there is an inverse relationship between age and crime; young persons (specifically males) commit the great proportion of traditional crimes. According to Siegel (1989: 71), while youths 15 to 18 make up only about six percent of the population, they account for about 25 percent of the index crime arrests, and 15 percent of all arrests. The peak for property crime is about 16 years; violent crime peaks at about 18 years old.

There are numerous theories as to why young persons account for so much crime. Some research indicates that rates decrease with age because young persons are able to develop a long-term view of life and resist the need for immediate gratification. Some crimes, such as embezzlement and fraud, are less likely to decline with age, and in fact, may increase.

Gender and Crime

Data indicate that males between 18 and 25 commit about ten times the crimes committed by women. The overall ratios show that women account for one-quarter of the arrests for property crime, and nearly one-tenth of the violent crime.

Why women commit less crime is a hotly debated criminological topic. Early hypotheses tended to portray women as an underclass. In the 70s, Freda Adler's study, *Sisters in Crime*, concluded that women committed less crime because of their second-class economic and social positions. Adler (1975) theorized that as the economic growth of females continued, they would account for more crime. However, criminologists conclude that at the current time, crime rates for women are remaining stable.

Race and Crime

Race and crime is an extremely sensitive issue. The UCR and NCS both agree that blacks commit a disproportionate percentage of crime. While blacks make up about 12 percent of the population, they commit about 46 percent of the violent crime, and about 30 percent of property crime.

At one time, it was believed that at least part of the difference was caused by selective arrests; that is, police were more likely to arrest blacks than whites. Research has generally not supported this proposition. Most theories explain the phenomena of black crime by economic depravation, social disorganization, subculture adaptations, and discrimination and racism. In his book *American Violence and Public Policy*, James P. Comer (1985: 63–86) believes that black crime is best accounted for by an inability of the black to identify with the large white society or with white leaders and institutional achievements.

Career Criminals

Researchers have found generally that offenders can be divided into two groups: those who commit crime occasionally, and a much smaller group of chronic offenders. In a 1972 study Marvin Wolfgang, Robert Figlio, and Thorsten Sellin (*Delinquency in a Birth Cohort*) found that 52 percent of the offenses studied were committed by six percent of the offenders. In violent crime, the same group accounted for between 70 and 80 percent of these crimes. Peter Greenwood of the Rand Corporation (1982) did a study of career criminals. He states that they are likely to have the following characteristics:

- Incarceration for more than half of the two-year period preceding the most recent arrest
- A prior conviction for the crime that is being predicted
- Juvenile conviction prior to age 16
- Commitment to a state or federal juvenile facility
- Heroin or barbiturate use in the two-year period prior to the current arrest, or use as a juvenile
- Employment for less than half of the two-year period preceding arrest

Additional research has indicated that the more severe the sentence for chronic offenders, the greater the likelihood that they will repeat offenses. Current U.S.

policy is being developed to seek out career offenders and incarcerate them for long periods of time. Approximately half the states now have career criminal statutes.

Victim Characteristics

Victimization patterns studied from the NCS have been remarkably consistent. The average victim has the same characteristics as the criminal: young, male, uneducated, and poor. A surprising conclusion regarding victims is that as wealth increases, the likelihood of being a victim of violence or burglary decreases. However, as wealth increases, so does the likelihood of being a victim of personal thefts or larcenies.

CLASSICAL CRIMINOLOGY

Classical criminology is rooted in the belief that man is a rational being, and therefore makes rational choices. It has several basic elements:

- People have the will to choose crime versus non-criminal behavior.
- Criminal behavior may be more attractive because it usually requires less work for a greater payoff.
- A person's choice to commit criminal acts may be controlled by fear of society's reactions to these acts.
- The more certain, severe, and swift the reaction, the more likely it is to control behavior.
- The most efficient crime-prevention device is punishment sufficient to make crime unattractive.

As a part of classical theory, it is assumed that all persons have the potential to be criminals, if it were not for sanctions and fear of punishment. Two persons, Cesare Beccaria and Jeremy Bentham, are largely responsible for developing classical criminology.

Cesare Beccaria

Much of classical theory of criminology derives from the practice in the 17th and 18th centuries of punishing severely any criminal offense. In England, for example, as late as the early 1800s there were literally hundreds of crimes punishable by death. Torture, dismembering, and disemboweling criminals was common. In Beccaria's view, punishment should be severe enough only to deter the action. Certainty of punishment, not its severity, was the key in deterring other potential offenders. In addition, crimes should receive different punishments. Beccaria's reasoning was that if two different crimes are punished the same, the more severe crime will not be deterred. For example, if a bank robbery and murder have the same sentence, a bank robber would not be deterred from committing murder.

Jeremy Bentham

Jeremy Bentham was an odd human being. Indeed, his body can be viewed today by any curious passerby because, in accord with his will, it was mummified and sits staring benignly at persons coming into University College, London. Since he was a man of exceptional intellect, Bentham reasoned, his remains ought to be publicly exhibited to inspire future generations of thinkers. He called the body an autoicon and decreed that it should be seated, as if in thought, in a favorite chair in his own clothes. He also insisted that he be placed at the table from time to time during University meetings.

Bentham believed that he had the answer to total reform of the law, which at the time was both chaotic and mercilessly brutal. As late as 1833, for instance, a boy of nine was hanged for stealing. The law was so barbarous that juries often would declare offenders innocent rather than permit them to undergo the harsh punishment mandated for what was deemed to be a minor offense. Bentham tried to introduce some logic into the process of determining how serious an offense might be, and he insisted stoutly that certain behaviors that harm no one but their perpetrators ought to be eliminated from the concern of the criminal law.

Bentham undoubtedly was correct when he harangued against the inefficiency of certain punishments; after all, extracting and burning the bowels of a traitor after he has been hanging seems rather beyond the point of necessity. Bentham attempted to find a simple formula by which to order human behavior. In this regard, he may have done as well as it is reasonable to do. Note, for instance, that the proposals in 1988 by the U.S. Sentencing Commission for the punishment of organizations, such as business firms which violate the law, were based almost totally on utilitarian or classical principles: the monetary penalties were to be calculated at that level which would induce the companies to calculate that lawbreaking was not a financially sound endeavor.

Bentham believed that punishment had four objectives. First, to prevent all crime; second, if crime is not prevented, punishment can convince the offender to commit a less serious act; third, to convince the offender to use the least force necessary; and finally, to prevent crime as cheaply as possible. He derived six rules of punishment:

- The value of punishment should be at least severe enough to outweigh the profit of the offense.
- The greater the crime the greater should be the punishment.
- When two offenses are in competition, the punishment for the greater offense must be sufficient to induce a lesser offense.
- The punishment must be severe enough to deter others.
- The punishment should only be severe enough to act as a deterrent.
- The punishment should be similar for similar offenses. (Rennie 1978: 22)

General Deterrence

General deterrence is the inhibiting effect of sanctions on criminal activity of people other than the sanctioned offender. In general deterrence, the factors of severity, certainty, and celerity are interrelated. Partial deterrence is not intended to eliminate the act but to curtail it. Absolute deterrence, on the other hand, is intended to eliminate a particular criminal act. Absolute deterrence is thought not to be possible, except in a theoretical sense. Deterrence assumes that persons who are contemplating the commission of a crime will be aware of the punishment. Otherwise, it has no deterrent effect. In one study, the public was aware of the criminal penalties for certain offenses only about one-quarter of the time.

Although the classical theory assumes others will be deterred by the punishment received by a miscreant, data surprisingly shows that does not appear to be the case. According to Siegel, few studies show that perceptions of deterrence actually reduce the crime rates. This may be because of several factors. First, traditional criminals can be a desperate bunch, acting under the influence of alcohol or drugs. Second, many criminologists believe that criminals are simply not calculating enough to be deterred; they are spurred on to criminal activity by sociological factors. After reviewing more than a decade of deterrence research, Paternoster found little hard evidence that people who fear the law will also forego criminal activity.

Another reason for the lack of effectiveness of deterrence is that many traditional criminals are a part of the "underclass" and cannot achieve their objectives by legal means. Finally, in order for deterrence to be effective, the public must perceive that punishment is swift and sure. That certainly cannot be said about the American criminal justice system, which is slow and uncertain.

Special Deterrence

Special deterrence is the inhibiting effect of punishment on the convicted criminal. Many experts believe that, like general deterrence, special deterrence does not work. Even the most severely punished offenders are likely to repeat their offenses. One recent study found that 72 percent of prison releases were rearrested within two years of their discharge (Petersilia, Turner, and Peterson 1986).

The apparent failure of special deterrence may be related to several factors. First, our current system of punishment may further embitter offenders. Punishments which are severe enough to deter criminals may be so brutal as to shock the conscience and violate the constitutional provisions against cruel and unusual punishment. Another reason is that the criminals are seldom punished severely and certainly.

Corporal Punishment

Corporal punishment in generally prohibited by the Constitution. However, some criminologists believe it is warranted in today's society. One of the more provocative theories of special deterrence is advocated by Graeme Newman in his book, *Just and Painful* (1983: 139–43). He argues that society should return to the use of corporal punishment. Newman suggests electric shocks because they are quick, have no lasting effect, can be adjusted to fit the severity of the crime, and are inexpensive.

Incapacitation

Incapacitation is the favored method in America to punish wrongdoers and take dangerous criminals out of circulation. James Q. Wilson, in his landmark book, *Thinking About Crime*, makes the argument for incapacitation by pointing out that the career criminal, small in number, accounts for the greatest amount of crime, and these persons should be vigorously sought out and incapacitated (Wilson 1975). He notes that the career criminal is not deterred by fear of punishment. He argues forcefully that rehabilitation of hardened criminals does not work.

Wilson advocates the following measures to reduce crime:

• Create uniform sentencing.
• Make at least some incarceration mandatory for all but petty offenses.
• Let deprivation of liberty also make use of community-based programs for criminals to work and receive treatment.
• Use progressively stiffer sentences for subsequent crimes committed by the same person.

He sums up his attitude as follows: "Some persons will shun crime even if we do nothing to deter them, while others will seek it out even if we do everything to reform them. Wicked people exist. Nothing avails except to set them apart from innocent people. And many people, neither wicked or innocent, but watchful, dissembling and calculating of their opportunities, ponder our reaction to wickedness as a cue to what they might profitably do" (Wilson 1975: 235).

The Effects of Incapacitation

Studies indicating the effect of incapacitation are mixed. A few researchers have concluded incapacitation has a deterrent effect. Still more have found it has no measurable benefit. David Greenberg concluded that if prisons were entirely eliminated, the crime rate would go up by only eight percent (Greenberg 1975: 541–80). One study by Lee Bowker found that increased incarceration actually increases the crime rate rather than decreasing it (Bowker 1981: 206–12).

Many criminologists feel that only career criminals should be incapacitated, while others are punished by other means. Incapacitation is likely to increase rather than decrease recidivism. According to a federal study, the more prior incarcerations inmates had, the more likely they were to return to prison within 12 months. Other studies have confirmed the same results. Classic criminological theory holds that criminals should be punished for basically two reasons: punishment and retribution. This is because violators bring the wrath of society on them for their offenses. J. D. Mabbott (1939: 152–67) holds that retribution is the most logical reason to punish criminals.

Routine Activities Theory

A variation of the classical theory, routine activities theory holds the view that both the motivation to commit crime and the supply of willing offenders are constant; there will always be a certain number of people motivated by greed, lust, and so forth. The determining factor in predatory crimes (violent and theft-related crimes) are the activities of the potential victims. There are purportedly three variables:

• The availability of suitable targets
• The absence of capable guardians (such as homeowners)
• The presence of motivated offenders (such as unemployed teenagers)

In sum, the theory holds that if there are more plentiful and valuable items to steal and they are unguarded, thefts are more likely to occur. In the case of violent crimes, if more persons put themselves in jeopardy, more attacks will occur.

BIOLOGICAL THEORIES

In order to explain criminal behavior, certain social scientists have turned to the examination of biological traits. These criminologists hold the view that criminal behavior is caused by physical characteristics rather than as a matter of choice.

The Born Criminal

Cesare Lombroso, a physician and psychiatrist and professor of forensic medicine at the University of Turin for most of his career, is generally credited with being the first to regard criminal behavior within a modern scientific framework. Lombroso, as noted by Mannheim (1955: 70–71), "saved criminal science from the shackles of merely academic abstractions and fertilized it with the rich treasures of the natural sciences."

In 1876, when the first edition of Lombroso's treatise on crime, *L'uomo* delinquent (*The Criminal Man*), was published, it drew upon major aspects of the 19-century scientific revolution in biology and physics. The primary intellectual climate of the day had been supplied by the work of Charles Darwin, who had rudely shaken theological suppositions. Prior to Darwin, man might aspire to be one of the angels; now he became a higher form of ape. Darwin's theory of evolution was an instrument not only to examine the modification of the species but also to look into all phases of human behavior. In keeping with the evolutionary doctrine, Lombroso thought he could identify physical characteristics of offenders in the form of facial, cephalic, and bodily anomalies (referred to subsequently as the "Lombrosian stigmata"), suggesting that criminals were a primitive or subhuman type, characterized physically by a variety of inferior morphological traits reminiscent of lower primates, occurring in more simian fossil men and to some extent preserved in what Lombroso called modern "savages," that is, members of preliterate tribes (Wolfgang 1960:183). Criminals "talk differently from us because they do not feel in the same way; they talk like savages because they are veritable savages in the midst of this brilliant European civilization," noted Lombroso.

Corresponding to the lawbreakers' physical characteristics of inadequacy were retarded psychological features, which Lombroso believed rendered such individuals incapable of adapting to more highly advanced social orders and which were crucial in bringing about criminal behavior. The physically retarded types constituted for Lombroso "born criminals," individuals destined by their deficient heredity inevitably to enter into criminal activity. Lombroso granted, however, that not all criminals were "born." He felt that more than half were either insane or criminaloids, that is, individuals who by their physical and psychological constitutions were predisposed toward crime under certain eliciting circumstances.

Body Build Theories

An offshoot of Lombroso's "born criminal" is a school of thought that advocated three types of body builds. Mesomorphs have well-developed muscles and an athletic appearance. Endomorphs have heavy builds and are slow moving. Ectomorphs are tall, thin, less social, and more intelligent.

In one provocative study Sheldon and Eleanor Glueck (1974: 2) found that mesomorphs were disproportionately represented among delinquent boys (60.1 percent versus 30.7 percent). Only 14.4 percent of the delinquents were ectomorphic; as compared to 39.6 percent of the non-delinquents. Notwithstanding this study, most criminologists discount the notion of being able to discern any clues to criminals by their physical appearance.

Biocriminology

Sociobiology stresses that biological and genetic conditions affect the perception and learning of social behaviors, which in turn are linked to existing environmental structures. According to sociobiology, crime can be viewed as a means of survival for people who perceive few other alternatives.

Some biologists and criminologists hold the view that crime can be in part explained by diet and environmental conditions. As an extreme example, Dan White, the confessed killer of San Francisco Mayor George Moscone and Councilmen Harvey Milk, claimed his behavior was linked to sugar-laden junk foods. This became known in legal circles as the "Twinky Defense"; ultimately White was convicted of manslaughter rather than first-degree murder. Researchers have in fact found that in some instances diets high in sugar and carbohydrates can indeed lead to violence and aggression.

Researchers have also found a link between some vitamin deficiencies and crime. Several studies have linked antisocial behavior and some of the B vitamins (B-3 and B-6) as well as vitamin C. In males, some research indicates that the production levels of the male hormone testosterone can affect criminal aggressiveness. In a study of women offenders, Katharina Dalton (1971) found that premenstrual syndrome can lead to aggression.

Neurophysiology, or the study of brain functions, can doubtless account for some criminal activity. Minimal Brain Dysfunction, or MBD, is defined as abruptly appearing, maladaptive behavior. It can be linked to serious antisocial acts, including crime. It helps account for some periods of explosive rage in certain persons, including wife beating, child abuse, suicide, and motiveless homicide. One researcher, Lorne Yeudall (1977), studied 60 patients characterized by lateral brain dysfunction. He has able to predict with 95 percent accuracy the recidivism of violent criminals.

Some researchers have tried to link crime with abnormal genetic coding. The typical person has 46 chromosomes; males have an XY makeup; females have an XX makeup. Some males possess an extra X chromosome, the so-called XXY. Richard Speck, who senselessly murdered eight Chicago nurses in the 1960s had the XXY chromosome makeup. It is thought that the influence of the extra chromosome on criminal activity is minimal.

PSYCHOLOGICAL THEORIES

Psychologists generally hold the view that early personality development and personality are the greatest single influence on criminality. Sigmund Freud (1856–1939) is credited with the most well-known personality development theories. Freud believed that the human mind was made up of three functions. The *conscious* mind governs needs such as hunger, pain, thirst, and desire. The *preconscious* mind contains memories and experiences, and the *unconscious* mind contains biological desires and urges that cannot be readily experienced as feelings and thoughts.

Freud also believed that there was a three-part structure to the human personality. The *id*, present at birth, represents unconscious biological drives for sex, food, and other life-sustaining activities. The id follows the pleasure principal—it requires instant gratification without the concerns of others. The *ego* develops early in life and is the part of the personality which tempers the id through social learning conventions. The ego helps keep the id in check by learning that all pleasure demands cannot be immediately gratified. The *superego* develops when an individual assimilates community values. It is the moral aspect of people's personality, passing judgment on behavior. All three of these personality aspects operate in concert to produce behavior. Criminals are thought to have an unbalanced id.

Two mental conditions are thought to be associated with antisocial activity, including crime. A *neurosis* is a disorder characterized by extreme anxiety which may break through and take control, thereby leading to violent behavior. A *psychosis* is a more extreme form of mental behavior which impairs functioning. *Schizophrenia* is one form of psychosis which manifests itself in extreme behavior. Schizophrenics exhibit illogical and incoherent behavior, including split personalities, delusions, and hallucinations. Although one study found that 75 percent of male murderers had some sort of mental illness, there is little evidence to indicate that mentally ill people are violent or criminal.

SOCIAL LEARNING THEORIES

Social learning theorists, among them Albert Bandura, think that people are not born with violent or criminal traits, but rather these behaviors are learned though life experiences (Bandura 1973, 1977). Behavior modeling is thought to be the most influential in criminal behavior. This modeling comes from three sources: family members, environmental influences, and the mass media. On the latter influence, one researcher, David Phillips (1983: 560–68), found the homicide rate increased significantly after a heavyweight title fight. Many theorists are now debating the important influence of television and violence.

Social learning theorists believe four factors are important in violence and aggression:

• An event that heightens arousal, such as physical or verbal abuse

• Aggressive skills, learned from other aggressive persons or the media

• Expected outcomes, such as believing that aggression will be rewarded through financial gain or increased esteem

• Consistency of behavior with values, such as the belief that aggression is justified and appropriate

PSYCHOBIOLOGICAL THEORIES

Psychobiologists seek relationships among changes in brain cells, nervous system activities, and mental processes. They have used research to demonstrate that particular parts of the brain control many activities, including emotional behavior.

Psychopaths are aggressive, dangerous, antisocial persons who act in an unthinking and callous manner. They neither learn from their mistakes nor are they deterred by punishment. They have been described as unstable, transient, and without long-term commitments. Research has concluded that psychopaths are much more violence-prone than other groups. Estimates of the prison population of psychopaths vary from 10 to 30 percent. It is believed that this mental condition develops early in life because of a lack of proper nurturing. One study by Orestes Fedora and Shawn Fedora (1982) found evidence that psychopathy was related to dysfunction of the left hemisphere of the brain.

The IQ, or intelligence quotient, has been studied extensively as a causal factor in crime. The IQ is thought to be a combination of genetics and environment. Hirschi, in one widely published paper, concluded that the IQ was a more important factor in criminality than race or social class. Persons with low IQs, it is believed, do poorly in school, and therefore are much more likely to be delinquents. However, according to Siegel, there is no good existing research that shows a direct relationship between low IQ and crime.

Personality refers to the patterns of behavior, including thoughts, emotions, and feelings that distinguish one person from another. Psychocriminologists believe that personality colors the way individuals view the world, and therefore the personality controls behavior. However, studies regarding the influence of personality on crime have been largely inconclusive.

James Q. Wilson and Richard Herrnstein, in their book *Crime and Human Nature*, argue that personal factors, such as genetic makeup, IQ, and body build may outweigh the importance of social variables in crime. They further argue that all human behavior, including crime, is influenced by the perceived consequences. They state that "the larger the ratio of net rewards of crime to the net rewards of noncrime, the greater the tendency to commit crime" (Wilson and Herrnstein 1985: 148).

Although crime may be a calculated choice, Wilson and Herrnstein find that there is a close link to biological factors as well. These factors include low intelligence, mesomorphic body types, having a criminal father, impulsivity or extroversion, and a nervous system that responds too quickly to stimuli. Choosing between crime and noncrime is often not an easy choice. The benefits of crime—money, sex, and other gratifications—are instantaneous, while the benefits of noncrime—prestige, reputation, and happiness—are longer-term benefits.

SOCIAL PROCESS THEORIES

Social process theories hold that criminality is a function of individual socialization that persons experience with various people, organizations, and institutions. For example, an individual may turn to crime because of poor family relationships, peer pressure, or lack of education. Social process theories hold that people from all walks of life have the potential to be criminals. What decides their fate are the social learning processes they experience. The most formative factors in this learning are the family, peers, schools, and the criminal justice system. There are three principal social process theories: learning or differential association, control, and labeling.

Differential Association

The theory of differential association is undoubtedly the best-known among all explanations offered in the United States to account for crime. The theory first appeared in 1939 in the third edition of Edwin H. Sutherland's *Principles of Criminology*. Later, Sutherland would make his best-known contribution to criminology by coining the phrase white-collar crime and writing a monograph on the subject.

The theory of differential association begins by asserting that criminal behavior is learned. Explicating that idea, Sutherland (1883–1950) specifies as a second point that criminal behavior is learned in interaction with other persons in a process of communication. If individuals acquiring criminal habits or propensities were exposed to situations, circumstances, and interactions totally of a criminal nature, it would be relatively easy to comprehend how this process of communication operates. In view of the enormous variation in standards and personalities to which any individual in our society is exposed, it becomes exceedingly difficult to discern the elements that induce criminal behavior without some additional principles.

Sutherland's third point is that criminal behavior is acquired through participation within intimate personal groups. This suggests that the roots of crime are in the socializing experiences of the individual. Unfortunately, the process of socialization is far from being adequately understood. Sutherland's fourth point indicates that the criminal learning process includes not only techniques of committing crime but also the shaping of motives, drives, rationalizations, and attitudes. Crime techniques often can involve a high degree of skill: picking pockets (and not getting caught at it) demands considerable adroitness.

Fifth, Sutherland stipulates that the specific direction of motives and drives is learned from definitions of the legal codes as favorable or unfavorable.

And sixth, he establishes the principle of "differential association." According to this postulate, a person becomes criminal because of an excess of definitions favorable to violation of the law over definitions unfavorable to violation of the law.

Sutherland states his seventh point, that differential association may vary in frequency, duration, priority, and intensity. But there is no suggestion regarding which of these elements is apt to be more important than the others.

Sutherland's eighth point is that learning criminal and delinquent behavior involves all the mechanisms that are involved in any other learning.

As his next to last proposition, Sutherland stressed that learning differs from pure imitation. His last point is a worthwhile reminder that while criminal behavior is an expression of general needs and values, it is not explained by these general needs and values, because noncriminal behavior is an expression of the same needs and values. This means that the generalizations sometimes employed to account for crime—that people steal because they crave "esteem" or are "greedy" or kill because they are "unhappy"—have little scientific merit. Criminals and noncriminals are motivated by much the same needs and values. They become or do not become criminals on the basis of their unique responses to common drives for prestige, happiness, success, power, wealth, and other human aspirations. One person with a pressing need for money may take an extra weekend job pumping gas, or try to borrow from a friend. Another person, feeling the same need, may hold up a fast-food outlet.

Control Theory

Control theory takes its cue from a classic of sociology, Emile Durkheim's *Suicide*, in which the French theoretician wrote: "The more weakened the groups to which the individual belongs, the less he depends on them, the more he consequently depends on himself and recognizes no other rules of conduct than what are founded on his private interests" (Durkheim 1951: 209).

Essentially, control theory argues that the institutions of the social system press those with whom they are in contact into patterns of conformity. Schools train for adjustment in society, peers press for success and conventional behavior, and parents strive to teach law-abiding habits to their children. The theory rests on the thesis that to the extent a person fails to become attached to the control agencies of the society, his or her chances of violating the law are increased.

Four aspects of affiliation are addressed by the theory: (1) attachment, (2) commitment, (3) involvement, and (4) belief. Attachment refers primarily to ties with persons such as parents, teachers, and peers. Commitment refers to cost factors involved in criminal activity. People are committed to conventional behavior and probably have invested something—fiscally and emotionally—in their ultimate success, an investment that they are wary of risking by a criminal act. Commitment might involve things such as obtaining a better job or seeing one's children succeed. Involvement concerns matters such as time spent on the job, participation in activities related to future goals and objectives. Belief refers to a conviction about the legitimacy of conventional values, such as the law in general and criminal justice in particular.

Hirschi insists that there is no important relationship between social class and crime. Control theory stresses strongly the bond of affection for conventional persons. "The stronger this bond, the more likely the person is to take it into account when and if he contemplates a criminal act" (Hirschi 1969: 83). What happens essentially, the theory suggests, is that persons confronted with the possibility of committing a crime are likely to ask themselves: "What will my wife—or my mother and father—think if they find out?" Other people whose opinions are important to them will be disappointed or ashamed, and to the extent that they care deeply about these persons, they will be constrained from engaging in crime.

Differential Reinforcement

Popularized by criminologist Ronald Akers (1977), differential reinforcement begins with the notion of operant conditioning: behavior controlled by stimuli that follow the behavior. Under this theory, social behavior is acquired through direct conditioning and modeling of others' behavior. Behavior is reinforced when positive rewards are gained, and discouraged by negative rewards. Whether criminal conduct occurs depends on the degree to which it has been rewarded or punished.

Conditioning Theory

H. J. Eysenck, working with what he calls conditioning theory, argues that the failure of a person to incorporate satisfactorily the dictates of society represents the major explanation for criminal behavior. Eysenck maintains that extroverted persons, both normal and neurotic, are more difficult to train than introverted persons, and that therefore extroverts get into more trouble than introverts.

Another psychological theme is that frustration causes aggression. Frustration is defined as an interference with the occurrence of an instigated goal-response at its proper time in the behavioral sequence. The theory suggests that the expression of aggression, such as a fraud perpetrator's "getting back" at his or her employer, will alleviate the frustration and allow the person to return to a more satisfactory state.

Operant-Utilitarianism

More recently, in what has been called operant-utilitarianism, James Q. Wilson and Richard J. Herrnstein (1985) have updated what essentially is the utilitarian position of Bentham and put it into contemporary language. Their theoretical statement reads as follows:

The larger the ratio of rewards (material and nonmaterial) of noncrime to the rewards (material and nonmaterial) of crime, the weaker the tendency to commit crimes. The bite of conscience, the approval of peers, and any sense of inequity will increase or decrease the total value of crime; the opinions of family, friends, and employers are important benefits of noncrime, as is the desire to avoid the penalties that can be imposed by the criminal justice system. The strength of any reward declines with time, but people differ in the rate at which they discount the future. The strength of a given reward is also affected by the total supply of reinforcers. (Wilson and Herrnstein 1985: 61)

Labeling Theory

Labeling theory essentially rests upon the proposition that human beings respond to the definitions placed upon their behavior by others, especially those who possess power. A young male called a "bad boy" and treated as such comes to believe in that label and acts accordingly. There are two major criticisms of labeling theory: first, that it fails to explain why the original offense occurred, before any criminal justice labeling took place; and second, that persons do not necessarily respond by becoming more criminal when they are labeled: many take the label to heart and make efforts to overcome it by behaving in most acceptable ways.

Shaming

Almost diametrically opposed to the labeling approach is the recent theoretical focus on "shaming," which was outlined by John Braithwaite (1988). Braithwaite draws upon the experience with crime in Japan and China to argue that the best explanation of crime lies in the absence of sufficient shame in the perpetrator regarding what he or she is doing. He points out that Japan, though heavily industrialized and urbanized, has a strikingly low rate of criminal behavior. Braithwaite also notes that in China the tactic used to reduce recidivism is to instill in offenders a sense that the behavior has brought disgrace upon them and upon their families. This idea of learned social responsibility, Braithwaite maintains, lies at the root of an understanding of the genesis of criminal activity.

Techniques of Neutralization

Gresham Sykes and David Matza (1957) have classified the rationalizations that they believe are essential to allow a person to violate the law and yet retain self-respect and self-esteem. They suggest five self-justifying techniques. Criminals are said to: (1) "condemn the condemners," that is, to insist that those who denounce their behavior themselves really are no better than they are: look at white-collar criminals, such as tax evaders, the robber says; (2) deny responsibility for the behavior, claiming that their act was due to forces beyond their control, such as drug use or unloving parents; (3) deny injury, maintaining that what they have done has really harmed no one; after all, the store they robbed has insurance and, besides, it will pass on the loss to the customers in the form of increased prices; (4) deny the victim, claiming that whoever was robbed or hurt only got what that person deserved; and (5) appeal to higher loyalties, stating that support and assistance for friends are more important than anything else.

Integrated Theories

Integrated theories attempt to integrate aspects of various theories into a comprehensive model of crime and delinquency. One early attempt, by Daniel Glazer

(1978), is the differential anticipation theory. Under this model, Glazer asserts, "A person's crime or restraint from crime is determined by the consequences he anticipates from it."

Pioneered by criminologist Delbert Elliott (1985), integrated theory shares points of the strain theory, social learning theories, and control theories. Elliott believes that the perceptions of strain occur when persons believe they cannot achieve success by traditional means. This condition is more likely to produce criminality in situations where family bonds are weak or nonexistent, and where the person lives in a socially disorganized situation. These weak bonds lead to the potential criminal's seeking out other peers, often criminals.

Interactional theory holds that crime can be traced, in many instances, to a deterioration of social bonds developed during youth. These young persons growing up in underclass areas will suffer the greatest risk of a weakened social bond and subsequent delinquency. This theory holds that criminality is a developmental process that changes with maturity.

Social Conflict Theories

Karl Marx, the so-called "father of socialism," believed that laws were primarily made for the benefit of capitalists. Under the Marxist theory, capitalism would concentrate the power and wealth in the hands of a few, the "bourgeoisie" (the owners of the means of production, or ruling class). Marxist analysts believe that laws are a reflection of the interest of the ruling class against the working class. In other words, under the so-called "golden rule theory," he who owns the gold makes the rules. Much of Marxist criminological explanation is devoted to why the poor commit crime. Another explanation of some of the laws passed can be attributed to Marxist theory. Passage of anti-trust and thefts of trade secret laws benefit the ruling class, and are therefore capitalistic.

Group Conflict

Criminologist George Vold wrote that the struggle among group interests and the compromise of their conflicts were at the heart of many laws. For example, the group that has the greatest number of votes in a legislative body will vote for laws favoring its interests. Vold's group-conflict conception explains why certain actions of corporations are considered as civil rather than criminal offenses.

Austin Turk's Theory of Criminalization

Turk does not concentrate on how a group came to power and what laws were passed, but rather what laws were enforced. He believes that the extent to which law enforcement considers behavior serious is the most important factor in determining prosecution. Turk differentiates between high- and low-level enforcement. If a low-level enforcer (i.e., police officer) considers the law has merit and the high-level enforcer (i.e., prosecutor) believes it does not, then there will be many arrests but few convictions. Conversely, if the high-level enforcer believes the law important and the low-level enforcer does not, then arrests will be low but convictions will be high.

Strain Theories

Strain approaches, based on the work of Robert Merton (1968), stress that individuals often become "strained" because they cannot achieve their financial goals. Because their financial goals cannot be achieved through legal opportunities, these individuals elect to employ illegal means. Unfortunately strain theories do not explain why one individual turns to crime while another similarly situated will not.

VIOLENT CRIME

Violent crime includes murder, rape, robbery, assault, and political violence. The United States is an extremely violent society when compared to other countries. Numerous theories attempt to explain violent crime. Some criminologists suggest that there is a subculture of violence that stresses violent solutions to interpersonal problems.

Other theories of violence suggest that humans are instinctively violent, while still other theories hold that violence is related to economic inequality. Some violent crimes, such as rape, are significantly underreported because of the personal nature and the shame of the attack. Further, rape is a very difficult crime to prove, therefore discouraging some victims from coming forward.

Murder, the unlawful killing of a human being with malice aforethought, involves different degrees. The overall murder rate in the United States has declined in recent years. Numerous reasons are suggested for this decline; no one really knows why. Currently, about eight in 100,000 people are murdered. However, these rates differ significantly with race, economic status, and location.

Assault is a serious personal crime, with some estimates suggesting that assault among family members is one of the most significant type. Estimates conclude that at least two million children a year are abused by their parents. Some projections state that about 16 percent of families report abuse between husband and wife.

Political violence has come into vogue within the last half of the 20th century. Many terrorist groups exist in the United States and internationally. These groups are usually motivated by criminal gain, psychosis, and grievances against the state or some ideology.

Robbery involves theft by force, usually in a public place. Offenders are usually amateurs, but other groups engaging in robbery include professionals, opportunists, drug addicts, and alcohol abusers.

2 White-Collar and Economic Crime

ECONOMIC CRIME

White-collar and economic crime are not legal terms, but rather refer criminologically to a wide variety of offenses, such as antitrust violations, advertising fraud, insider trading, and the offering or acceptance of bribes. The major common element of such behaviors is that they grow out of legitimate occupational efforts in business, politics, and the professions. Perpetrators typically do not seek out their jobs in order to commit crime: their lawbreaking occurs after they are confronted with temptation or faced with what they believe are circumstances that they cannot satisfactorily resolve in any other manner.

Economic crimes can be defined as acts in violation of the criminal law and designed to bring financial rewards. In the United States, the range and scope of economic crimes is enormous. Studies indicate that more than 30 million household and personal thefts occur annually, nearly one theft for every eight citizens.

Most criminologists have noted that, compared to violent crime, property crimes are treated with indifference by the average citizen. Part of the reason is that self-reporting studies suggest that nearly every person has participated in a theft of some sort: petty thefts, cheating on income taxes, stolen a book from a college bookstore, or pilfered from their place of employment. Another reason for the public's tolerance is thought to be because economic crimes "really don't hurt anyone." Mild punishment for economic crimes is not at all unusual.

Professional and Amateur Criminals

Much of economic street crime is caused by occasional criminals. Their decision to steal is largely related to opportunity, and their thefts are not well planned or executed. In addition, included in this group of amateurs are the millions of occasional thieves who earn their incomes legitimately, but engage in such activities as shoplifting, pilfering, and tax fraud. These crimes are believed to be caused by situational inducement or opportunity, and because the perpetrators are not professional, it is believed that they respond best to the general deterrent effect of the law.

Professional thieves make the bulk of their income from law violations. Most are not deterred by the law, and many are very skilled at their craft. Not a great deal is known about the professional thief, except that three patterns emerge. One group is young people who are taught the craft of theft by older professionals; another is gang members who continue their thefts after maturing out of gang activity; and the third category includes youths who are incarcerated for minor offenses and later learn the techniques of professional theft.

Commercial Thieves

Commercial thieves can be categorized into two areas: burglars and hijackers. The main goal of the burglar is to acquire cash. As a result, they use establishments that favor cash rather than credit card businesses. Examples include supermarkets, bars, and restaurants. They frequently work in teams, and spend a great deal of time and effort planning their heists.

Hijackers specialize in stealing goods in transit from trucks, trains, and other commercial carriers. These targets are selected because they contain large quantities of goods, the goods are ready for transport, and the commercial carriers are usually less secure than warehouses. In general, commercial thieves do not specialize in one kind of merchandise, but rather pick the best opportunity. There are several theories on commercial thieves, but many, it is believed, started their careers young as incarcerated youths.

Larceny

The common-law definition of larceny is the taking and carrying away of the personal property of another with the intent to steal. Today, common larceny crimes include shoplifting, auto theft, passing bad checks, and other offenses that do not involve forcible entry. The offenses are divided into petty larceny (for small items) and grand larceny for more serious thefts. Larceny is probably the most common criminal offense.

False Pretenses

The law of false pretenses and the law of fraud are generally interchangeable terms. Fraud involves misrepresenting a fact to cause a victim to willingly give his or her property to the wrongdoer, who keeps it. Some states retain the crime of false pretenses, while others have combined it with larceny into a general theft category.

Bad Checks

For a person to be guilty of passing bad checks, the bank the check is drawn on must refuse payment and the check casher must fail to make the check good within a certain period of time, commonly ten days. There are two common types of bad-check passers. The amateurs, sometimes called naive check forgers, believe their actions are harmless. They cash bad checks because of some financial crisis. This is referred to as *closure*. Some criminologists have categorized these amateurs as being socially isolated people who have been unsuccessful in their interpersonal relationships. Professional forgers, sometimes called systematic forgers, make a living by passing bad checks. These are thought to constitute a very small portion of bad check passers.

Confidence Games

Confidence games are perpetrated by professional fraud artists, usually on elderly or ignorant victims. There are countless variations, but most depend on enticing a "mark" or victim into a get-rich scheme. The extent of confidence games is difficult to measure, but they are thought to be extensive.

Credit Card Theft

Most theft involving credit cards is perpetrated by amateurs who acquire the cards through thefts or muggings, and use the card for only a few days. However, sophisticated rings involving bank insiders have been discovered. These schemes, because of the mobility of some of the fraudsters, are difficult to control.

Shoplifting

Shoplifting is an extremely common form of theft; losses are estimated into the billions of dollars annually. Some criminologists claim shoplifting has increased dramatically in the last 20 years or so, but no simple explanation has been offered for the rise. Some studies estimate that one in nine shoppers steals from department stores. In one study, Mary Owen Cameron (1964) found that about ten percent of shoplifters are professionals who derive the majority of their livelihood from shoplifting. The remainder are amateurs with no previous criminal records. Notwithstanding admonitions by stores about prosecuting shoplifters, only about one in 20 is actually reported to the police. In general, criminologists view shoplifters as a group who are likely to reform if apprehended.

Automobile Theft

Automobiles are usually stolen by relatively affluent, white, middle-aged teenagers for joyriding. About 40 percent of all auto thefts are committed by people under 18. Of the arrests, 60 percent are white, and 91 percent are male. About a million cars are stolen annually, and they fall into four categories, in addition to joy riding. Some autos are stolen for short-term transportation; others are stolen for longer-term needs; still others are stolen for profit; the last category includes autos stolen in the commission of another crime.

Arson

Arson is the willful and malicious burning of a home, public building, vehicle, or commercial building. There are around 100,000 arson arrests annually in America, most of them young persons; about 63 percent of the arrestees are under 25. There are several reasons for arson. Some are committed by mentally deranged people, and still others are simple, wanton acts of vandalism. Arson for profit, or arson fraud, is usually committed to collect insurance money under the following circumstances:

• To obtain money during a period of financial crisis
• To get rid of slow-moving or outdated inventory
• To pay off illegal and legal debts
• To plan bankruptcies to eliminate debts
• To eliminate business competition
• To solve labor/management problems
• To conceal other crimes

WHITE-COLLAR CRIME

Notwithstanding some of the more traditional explanations for criminal behavior, Charles R. Henderson (1901: 250), an early 20th century criminologist, wrote: "The social classes of the highest culture furnish few convicts, yet there are educated criminals. Advanced culture modifies the form of the crime; tends to make it less coarse and violent, but more cunning; restricts it to quasi-legal forms. But education also opens up the way to new and colossal kinds of crimes, (such) as debauching of conventions, councils, legislatures, and bribery of the press and public officials."

Although scholars differ widely in their definition of white-collar crime, the Dictionary of Criminal Justice Data Terminology, published by the Bureau of Justice Statistics, defines white-collar crime as "non-violent crime for financial gain committed by means of deception by persons whose occupational status is entrepreneurial, professional or semi-professional and utilizing their special occupational skills and opportunities; also non-violent crime for financial gain utilizing deception and committed by anyone having special technical and professional knowledge of business and government, irrespective of the person's occupation."

Public Perception of White-Collar Crime

Criminologists have long advocated that part of the explanation for the apparent rise in fraud is the lack of seriousness with which it is treated by the public. However, some studies have shown that the public perceives some fraud-related offenses with as much or more seriousness than more traditional crimes, especially those that have harmful physical consequences, such as a toxic waste site that leads to the "accidental death" of innocent citizens.

In 1977, the National Survey of Crime Severity polled 60,000 people 18 or older, and presented them with a list of 204 offenses, and asked the respondents to rate the severity of the crimes and assign a value to each (See Table 2.1). From the table, both occupational and "common crime" are viewed as serious behavior. There are, however, some interesting comparisons noted: fraud by a grocer and a ten dollar embezzlement are viewed with the same seriousness as an obscene phone call. A bribe accepted by a city politician is viewed with the same seriousness as a $1,000 armed robbery.

Some white-collar crime involves businesses that are established for the purpose of committing fraud; other white-collar crimes committed by businesses are incidental to their legitimate enterprises. In addition to individual crimes, some businesses engage in white-collar crime to improve market share or the profitability of their companies.

Criminologists have attempted to classify white-collar crimes by a number of means. Herbert Edelhertz (1970: 73–75), for example, divides white-collar crimes in four broad categories:

- *Ad hoc violations*—committed for personal profit on an episodic basis; for example, welfare fraud and tax cheats.
- *Abuses of trust*—committed by persons in organizations against organizations; for example, embezzlement, bribery, and kickbacks.
- *Collateral business crimes*—committed by organizations in furtherance of their business interests; for example, false weights and measures, antitrust violations, environmental crimes.
- *Con games*—committed for the sole purpose of cheating clients; for example, fraudulent land sales, bogus securities.

Stings and Swindles

Stings and swindles involve frauds ranging from bogus door-to-door salesmen to fraudulent stock swindles. One of the most famous of all stings was the Equity Funding Case, whose officers, in 1973, created bogus policies to support their failing insurance business. The resultant losses were estimated at over $2 billion, becoming one of the largest single white-collar crimes of all time.

Chiseling

Chiseling involves cheating consumers on a regular basis. These frauds can involve bogus auto repairs, shorted weights and measures, and home-repair frauds. Offenders range from the "get rich quick" types to major corporations. For example, in 1988, the Hertz Corporation acknowledged cheating customers on inflated repair bills. The Chrysler Corporation's executives rolled back the

Table 2.1
National Survey of Crime Severity Ratings: Selected Offense Stimuli
(occupational crimes are in boldface)

Ratings	*Offense Stimuli*
1.9	**An employee embezzles $10 from his employer.**
1.9	**A store owner knowingly puts "large" eggs into containers marked "extra large."**
1.9	A person makes an obscene phone call.
3.1	A person breaks into a home and steals $100.
3.2	**An employer illegally threatens to fire employees if they join a labor union.**
3.6	A person knowingly passes a bad check.
3.7	**A labor union official illegally threatens to organize a strike if an employer hires nonunion workers.**
5.4	**A real estate agent refuses to sell a house to a person because of that person's race.**
5.4	A person threatens to harm a victim unless the victim gives him money. The vicim gives him $10 and is not harmed.
5.7	**A theater owner knowingly shows pornographic movies to a minor.**
6.1	**A person cheats on his federal income tax return and avoids paying $10,000 in taxes.**
6.1	A person runs a prostitution racket.
6.2	A person beats a victim with his fists. The victim requires treatment by a doctor but not hospitalization.
6.2	**An employee embezzles $1,000 from his employer.**
6.4	**An employer refuses to hire a qualified person because of that person's race.**
6.5	A person uses heroin.
6.9	**A factory knowingly gets rid of its waste in a way that pollutes the water supply of a city. As a result, one person becomes ill but does not require medical treatment.**
6.9	A person beats a victim with his fists. The victim requires hospitalization.
8.0	A person steals an unlocked car and sells it.
8.2	**Knowing that a shipment of cooking oil is bad, a store owner decides to sell it anyway. Only one bottle is sold and the purchaser is treated by a doctor but not hospitalized.**
8.6	A person performs an illegal abortion.
9.0	**A city official takes a bribe from a company for his help in getting a city building contract for the company.**
9.0	A person, armed with a lead pipe, robs a victim of $1,000.
9.2	**Several large companies illegally fix the retail prices of their products.**
9.4	A person robs a victim of $10 at gunpoint. No physical harm occurs.

Ratings	*Offense Stimuli*
9.4	**A public official takes 1,000 of public money for his own use.**
9.6	**A police officer knowingly makes a false arrest.**
9.6	A person breaks into a home and steals $1,000.
10.0	**A government official intentionally hinders the investigation of a criminal offense.**
10.9	A person steals property worth $10,000 from outside a building.
11.2	**A company pays a bribe to a legislator to vote for a law favoring the company.**
11.8	A man beats a stranger with his fists. He requires hospitalization.
12.0	**A police officer takes a bribe not to interfere with an illegal gambling operation.**
12.0	A person gives the floor plans of a bank to a bank robber.
13.3	A person, armed with a lead pipe, robs a victim of $10. The victim is injured and requires hospitalization.
13.5	**A doctor cheats on claims he makes to a Federal health insurance plan for patient services. He gains $10,000.**
13.9	**A legislator takes a bribe from a company to vote for law favoring the company.**
14.6	A person, using force, robs a victim of $10. The victim is hurt and requires hospitalization.
15.5	A person breaks into a bank at night and steals $100,000.
15.7	**A county judge takes a bribe to give a light sentence in a criminal case.**
16.5	A person, using force, robs a vicitm of $1,000. The victim is hurt and requires treatment by a doctor but not hospitalization.
17.8	**Knowing that a shipment of cooking oil is bad, a store owner decides to sell it anyway. Only one bottle is sold and the purchaser dies.**
19.5	A person kills a victim by recklessly driving an automobile.
19.7	**A factory knowingly gets rid of its waste in a way that pollutes the water supply of a city. As a result, 20 people become ill but none require medical treatment.**
19.9	**A factory knowingly gets rid of its waste in a way that pollutes the water supply of a city. As a result, one person dies.**
20.1	A man forcibly rapes a woman. Her physical injuries require treatment by a doctor but not hospitalization.
33.8	A person runs a narcotics ring.
39.1	**A factory knowingly gets rid of its waste in a way that pollutes the water supply of a city. As a result, 20 people die.**
43.9	A person plants a bomb in a public building. The bomb explodes and one person is killed.
72.1	A person plants a bomb in a public building. The bomb explodes and 20 people are killed.

Source: *The National Survey of Crime Severity* by Marvin Wolfgang, Robert Figlio, Paul Tracy, and Simon Singer (1985). Washington, D.C.: U.S. Government Printing Office (pp. vi–x).

odometers on demonstrators and sold them as new. Pharmacists frequently substitute generic drugs and charge a higher price for name brands. Another common chiseling crime involves "churning" stock sales. Unscrupulous brokers engage in the repeated, excessive, and unnecessary purchases and sales of stock in order to earn commissions.

Exploitation of Positions

Public and private officials sometime exploit their own power for personal gains through taking kickbacks and bribes. In the majority of cases, this type of offense occurs when the offender uses his or her power to ask for an additional payment for services when they should be expected.

Illegal Lobbying

Illegal lobbying occurs when persons receive favored treatment because of payoffs or other subtle bribes to government officials. Under some federal laws, executive branch officials who leave the government are subject to lobbying controls, while former legislators are not.

Embezzlement and Employee Fraud

Employee fraud can reach all levels of the organization. Pilferage is estimated to account for 30 to 75 percent of all shrinkage, and losses from $10 to $20 billion annually. Common techniques for pilferage include:

- Piece workers who steal garments and secrete them inside their clothing
- Cashiers who ring up a sale at a lower price than the merchandise, and keep the difference
- Clerks who sell sale merchandise at regular prices and pocket the difference
- Receiving clerks who obtain duplicate keys to the warehouse and come back and steal merchandise
- Truck drivers who make fictitious purchases of fuel and split the difference with truck-stop owners
- Employees who hide items in the trash and come back later and retrieve them

According to Hollinger and Clark (1983), about a third of all employees engage in pilferage. Most of the time the thefts occur not out of economic circumstances, but rather job dissatisfaction.

Causes of Corporate Crime

Corporate crime are those various crimes perpetrated by corporations in furtherance of their goals, usually to maximize profits. According to Ronald Kramer (1978), the causes of corporate crime involve three structural factors:

- Businesses will engage in criminal conduct if they encounter serious difficulties in attaining their goals, especially profits.
- The internal structure of an organization can influence decisions to break the law. For example, if the organization's profit-making goals include the reduction of costs, this can have an impact on whether fraud is committed to reduce those costs.
- Outside influences, such as market conditions, combined with intense competition and lax law enforcement can be contributing factors to a decision to engage in criminality.

Rationalizing White-Collar Crime

Economic offenders are known for providing elaborate excuses for their crimes, and the nature of such explanations may be a major distinguishing mark between them and street offenders. Cressey (1953) found that the embezzlers he studied typically insisted that they were only borrowing the money; that they intended to repay it once they had covered the bills and other financial demands vexing them. Antitrust violators usually maintain they are seeking to stabilize an out-of-control price situation when they conspire with others to fix prices. Psychologists arrested for phony and unauthorized charges against government medical benefit programs are likely to insist that they are being singled out by power-hungry prosecutors and investigators. Rarely will there appear an economic offender with the refreshing honesty to admit that: "I was deliberately engaged in crooked business dealings. I was trying to do in as many people as I could. I am a rotten, dishonest person." If nothing else, malefactors will say that they stole from victims who could afford the loss, such as insurance companies, banks, and department stores, rather than widows and children, or will blame their violations on personal problems, such as alcoholism, drug addiction, or marital difficulties.

Today, the realm of white-collar and economic crime can be said to primarily involve offenses against laws which regulate the marketplace and/or establish standards of conduct for professional and political life. The category includes such matters as false advertising. Claims have been made that shoes for sale are "alligator" when in fact they were made of a plastic product. Department stores often raise the price of a product significantly one day and then the next day drop it back to where it had been, maintaining in their advertising that it now is "on sale" and reduced "by 70 percent." In bait-and-switch tactics, stores will advertise a specific product at a strikingly low price, but then, when the customer tries to buy the item, indicate either that it no longer is available, or demonstrate that it is much inferior to the thing that the store really wants to sell. It is the customer's presence and attention they want to attract: once they have him or her listening, they assume that slick salesmanship can accomplish the rest of the deceit.

In one of the more blatant advertising frauds, a company selling glass "demonstrated" in television commer,cials that its product car window was so perfect that when you looked through it you could hardly believe that there was anything between you and the outside scene. The Federal Trade Commission later proved that the company was using films taken from inside a car with the window rolled down.

In addition to advertising fraud, white-collar crimes include environmental pollution, violations of occupational health and safety laws, and the marketing of drugs that have not been adequately tested or for which the test results have been falsified.

New Focus on White-Collar Crime

Two decades ago white-collar crime received much less media attention, largely being confined to a short paragraph or two in the business section of the nation's newspapers, if it was mentioned at all. Today's front-page stories testify to considerably greater public interest in and concern about economic crime. Scholars attribute this growing emphasis to, among other things, a greater skepticism about the behavior of persons in authority. The splintering of American society during the Vietnam War undoubtedly contributed greatly to a mood of distrust and concern, while the crimes of Watergate, involving the President and his advisors and members of his cabinet established a mood of distrust of the honesty of those in prominent places.

Aspects of White-Collar Crime

If the definition of economic and white-collar crime is confined to persons with power committing offenses in the course of their occupational work, it is obvious that the definition restricts the ranks of possible perpetrators. Anybody with strength, or decent aim, or access to poison can commit murder. But only a limited number of corporate executives are in a position to violate the Sherman Antitrust law. People typically engage in forms of criminal behavior that are the most familiar, and seem to be the easiest and least likely to produce dire consequences. It is not surprising, in these terms, that a bank teller, short of cash, will try embezzling, while an unemployed minority youth, also without adequate funds, turns to armed robbery. An often unheralded bonus of social status is access to opportunities for the less dirty, "more decent" kinds of crime.

Another notable characteristic of most kinds of economic offenses is that their victims generally are not aware that they have been harmed. Death from smog or asbestos poisoning is very likely to be slow and insidious, and its victims will be hard-pressed to relate their terminal illness to its precise cause, given the complicated nature of other possible contributing factors. A factory worker with cancer is not likely to be certain whether it was the toxic chemicals that he handled for 15 years, the fact that he smoked too many cigarettes, or bad genes or bad luck that will shorten his life.

In many white-collar and economic offenses, the harm tends to be widely diffused and, for each person, rather insignificant. But companies can earn millions over the course of a year by charging higher prices for products that do not meet the standards they are alleged to attain. Few people who pay for a package of 100 thumb tacks will take the time and energy to count the contents of the package to be certain that they have gotten their money's worth: it would be an easy and safe venture to put 92 tacks in each package; some merchandisers find the temptation irresistible. Neither will customers likely ever become aware that the gasoline pumps at a service station are calibrated so that they get fewer gallons than those for which they are charged. Even if they come to know about these kinds of peculation, most customers would shrug them off as not worth the trouble it would take to do something to remedy the situation; at most, they might take their business elsewhere.

The camouflaged nature of most economic offenses poses a particular law-enforcement dilemma. Without complaining witnesses, policing has to be proactive instead of reactive; that is, the enforcement officials themselves have to decide where the offenses are being committed and how to go about stopping them. They cannot, as with crimes such as robbery and burglary, rely on victim reports. Enforcers obviously cannot cope with all the violations and must decide on rules to guide their efforts. Should they go after the behaviors which cause the most harm? Should they take on the bigger offenders, or concentrate on the smaller fry, where their chances of success are much better? They can readily accumulate ten convictions in a year against ten insignificant companies, whereas it might take three years to win a victory over one huge corporation. Besides, the resources of the large organization might allow it to win its case, regardless of the lawless nature of its behavior.

Industrial Espionage and Trade Secret Theft

There are three basic elements to a trade secret: novelty, value, and secrecy. The last item has to do with whether an organization handled its alleged "secret" in a protective manner. If it did not do so, it will not win judicial support if it charges theft of that secret by an employee or an executive.

Patent laws seek a compromise between capitalistic self-interest in a trade secret and social well-being by granting a 17-year monopoly to developers of innovative ideas. The U.S. Supreme Court, in its only ruling on trade secrets, Kewanee Oil Co. v. Bicron Corp. (1974), declared the likelihood "remote indeed" that a company would not patent valuable information that it had developed. The Court, however, overlooked the advantage, well-known to most companies, that trade secrets can be hoarded far beyond the 17-year patent limitation, a matter well documented by the success and secrecy of the formulas for Coca-Cola and Kentucky Fried Chicken, among others.

Leakage of trade-secret information is said to be particularly likely from employees who go to work for competitors, careless secretaries, gregarious field sales personnel, and high-tech computer whizzes who often are more loyal to their equipment than to their fellow employees. Temporary help is regarded as especially vulnerable: in-and-out employees do not have any company loyalty and can be planted for purposes of theft. Having at least two persons in an organization cooperate when dealing with sensitive materials is likely to reduce the compromising of such information. Secret mailing lists used by some businesses include at least one decoy address so that, if the list is compromised, whoever uses it will be sending material to a fictional person, at an address that actually is a company drop.

A review of the appellate court cases on trade-secret theft shows the defendants as persons who have been working for a business in the range of six to ten years. Most purloiners obviously did not join the company with the intent to steal information, but rather formed (or were led to form) that resolve after they had been at work for the better part of a decade. The court materials suggest the illegal behavior probably is not predictable from background investigations or from psychological tests.

Typically, the defendants are smaller companies which have hired scientists from larger organizations. There also appears to be an unusual amount of theft from family-owned businesses, with the defendants saying that they believed, as outsiders, that their chances of advancement were hopeless.

Insider Trading

Criminal charges for insider trading have become the trademark of economic-crime enforcement efforts during recent years. These efforts seek to encourage the confidence of investors that they are sharing satisfactorily in the information about the performance of companies.

A surge of prosecutions for illegal insider information transactions began in the late 1980s when stock transactions were first subjected to sophisticated computer review. Federal investigators could learn of unusual stock movements. Soon afterwards, when some meaningful piece of financial information about the company was released, investigators could determine quickly who had traded the stock heavily before the news release. If, for instance, the transaction was made by the firm's president, it seemed likely (though not assured), that he or she had acted on the information before it was publicly disseminated. Cases arose involving auditors selling stock when their examination of a company's books convinced them that it was in financial trouble, and brokerage houses unloading stock they held and advising preferred customers to do the same, while at the same time they pushed the same securities onto their less important clients. In a particularly egregious case, a young columnist for the *Wall Street Journal* conveyed information to a speculator about the content of the column he would be writing. The speculator brought up stocks and made millions of dollars, sharing a small part of his profits with the journalist (Winans 1984). Of course, the notable cases of Ivan Boesky and Michael Milken illustrate the staggering sums of money to be made from illegal stock trades.

The Extent of White-Collar Crime

Clinard and Yeager (1980) found that 1,553 cases had been filed against the 562 Fortune 500 businesses (that is, the largest American companies) whose records were examined for two years, for an average of 2.7 violations for each company. About 60 percent of the companies had at least one case against them; for those companies, the average was 4.4 cases. The oil, pharmaceutical, and motor vehicle industries were the most likely to be proceeded against for violations.

Clinard and Yeager endorse the following remedial steps to deal with corporate crime:

1. The strengthening of consent agreements and decrees (under which companies do not admit that what they were doing was wrong, but agree to stop doing it) to provide substantial remedies for violations and to include systematic follow-ups.

2. Increases in fine ceilings, with fines to be assessed according to the nature of the violation and in proportion to the company's annual sales.

3. Stiff criminal penalties for violations of health and safety or environmental regulations that "recklessly endanger" the public or employees.

4. Stronger statutes to prohibit companies that previously had violated federal laws from receiving federal contracts.

5. Mandatory publicity for corporate civil and criminal violations.

6. More extensive use of imprisonment with longer sentences. Community service in place of incarceration should be prohibited by law, except for unusual circumstances.

7. Convicted corporate offenders should be prevented from being indemnified by their companies.

8. Management officials convicted of criminally violating corporate responsibilities should be prohibited for three years from assuming similar management positions in their company or others.

9. Directors would be liable, but not criminally, for being derelict in their duty to prevent illegal corporate actions.

10. A new commercial-bribery statute should be enacted to help prosecute corporate executives who receive kickbacks from their customers or suppliers.

Gary Green, in honing the white-collar crime concept, uses the term "occupational crime," which he defines as "any act punishable by law which is committed through opportunity created in the course of an occupation which is legal" (1990: 13). Green further delineates occupational crime into four categories: (a) crimes for the benefit of an employing organization (organizational occupational crime); (b) crimes by officials through exercise of their state-based authority (state authority occupational crime); (c) crimes by professionals in their capacity as professionals (professional occupational crime); and (d) crimes by individuals as individuals.

Organizational Occupational Crime

Some scholars debate whether individuals should be held responsible for crimes committed on behalf of their organizations. Although some direct benefit accrues to the perpetrator, far more benefit accrues to the organization. Regardless of whether the organization is held liable, the frauds are a direct result of some human action or interaction. In the words of Parisi (1984: 41), "If (an organization) is like a gun, then there must be someone comparable to a triggerman."

Most criminal statutes require that the guilty person have criminal intent. Organizations can be held liable even though they are unaware of participating in the fraud. The law recognizes two theories, identification and imputation. "Identification" assumes organizational liability when employees and organizations can be viewed as one in the same; i.e., a small business owner who has incorporated. "Imputation" is where the organization is held responsible for the actions of its employees through the doctrine of *respondeat superior*, a 17th-century doctrine which means "let the superior respond." The legal theory was developed from civil lawsuits to prevent employers from denying financial responsibility for their employees.

Criminogenic Organizational Structures

Edward Gross has asserted that all organizations are inherently "criminogenic" (1979: 199) (prone to generating crime), but not necessarily criminal. Gross makes this assertion because of the inherent reliance of the organization on the bottom line. Without necessarily meaning to, organizations inherently invite fraud as a means of obtaining goals. Criminologist Oliver Williamson noted that because of a department's concern with reaching its goals, managers may well tend to maximize their department's own interests to the detriment of the organization.

Organizations can also be criminogenic because they encourage loyalty. According to Diane Vaughan (1982), the reasons are that:

1. The organization tends to recruit and attract similar individuals.
2. Rewards are given out to those who display characteristics of the "company man."
3. Long-term loyalty is encouraged through company retirement and benefits.
4. Loyalty is encouraged through social interaction such as company parties and social functions.
5. Frequent transfers and long working hours encourage isolation from other groups.
6. Specialized job skills may discourage company personnel from seeking employment elsewhere. This in turn causes company personnel to sometimes perceive that the organization might be worth committing crime for, to maintain and further its goals.

Behaviorists generally conclude that one of the single most important factors influencing group behavior is the attitude of management. In one survey conducted by S. N. Brenner and E. A. Molander (1977: 60), about half the sample believed there was pressure from superiors to engage in unethical behavior. One prime example is the famous Equity Funding Case which occurred in the early 1970s. For nearly ten years, massive fraud was perpetrated by the Equity Funding Corporation through manipulation of financial statements. More specifically, Equity Funding falsified more than 56,000 life insurance policies and overstated their assets by $120 million. It was estimated that 50 to 75 employees, who managed to keep the scheme a secret for several years, were involved. The trustee appointed to sort out the massive fraud, Robert Loeffler (1974: 140–41), wrote, "Of almost equal importance was the surprising ability of the originators of the fraud to recruit new participants over the years." The Equity Funding scheme was uncovered when a disgruntled former employee went to the authorities. In sum, although many organizations may have the motivation to commit fraud, certainly not all do.

Irwin Ross (1980) analyzed 1,043 companies that at one time or another had appeared on the Fortune list of large industrial companies. Included in his study were five kinds of offenses: bribe-taking or bribe-giving by high-level executives, criminal fraud, illegal campaign contributions, tax evasion, and antitrust violations. One hundred seventeen, or 11 percent of the corporations, were violators.

Antitrust Violations

Several federal laws prohibit various activities that restrain trade or free competition. Practices outlawed (primarily under the Sherman AntiTrust Act passed in 1890) include: price fixing, bid rigging, discriminatory pricing, rebating, trusts, and related agreements. According to Green, prior to 1970, prosecution for antitrust was rare: only 26 jail sentences were meted out in the 79 years between 1890 and 1969. Of those, 22 included charges for other offenses such as racketeering. Green states then that only four persons were sentenced to prison exclusively relating to antitrust. Since 1970, primarily because of the precedent set by former President Jimmy Carter, antitrust violations have been prosecuted more aggressively.

Organizational Bribe-Giving

Two kinds of bribes benefit organizations. First, bribing politicians and giving illegal campaign contributions; and second, commercial bribery includes most types of purchasing frauds. It also includes paying bribes for industrial espionage—paying someone to reveal trade and other secrets about competing firms.

In his book *Political Corruption and Public Policy in America*, Michael Johnston (1982: 20) defined three conditions that were normally present in political bribe-giving: "(1) The fruits of governmental action are often extremely valuable (or, in the case of penalties and sanctions, extremely costly), with demand for benefits frequently exceeding supply; (2) these benefits and sanctions can often be gotten or avoided only by dealing with the government; and (3) the routine process through which benefits and sanctions are conferred is time consuming, expensive, and uncertain in its outcome." Green says the most common form of political bribe-giving is illegal campaign contributions. The companies he lists as participants at one time or another include some of the country's best-known businesses: Exxon, Standard Oil, American Airlines, Carnation, Firestone, General Tire and Rubber, Goodyear, 3M, and Singer.

Paying foreign politicians and governments abroad was (and perhaps still is) common in order to do business in many countries. In the mid-70s, a scandal erupted when it was disclosed that several airplane manufacturers routinely paid foreign officials huge sums to insure orders. In the wake of these scandals, Congress passed the Foreign Corrupt Practices Act in 1977, outlawing bribes to foreign officials except in cases of national security.

Commercial Bribery

Commercial bribery involves both the paying of firms for purchasing products and industrial espionage. Several federal and state laws address the practice. In some instances, commercial bribery may be a violation in restraint of trade. Certain industries—notably the liquor industry—are outlawed specifically from paying for business. Several major firms, according to Ross, have been guilty of commercial bribery: Anheuser Busch, Beatrice Foods, R.J. Reynolds Industries, and Joseph Schlitz Brewing, to name a few.

Industrial espionage can involve direct payments to third parties to secure valuable competitive information, or indirectly, through the hiring of the competitor's employees. In 1988, several military procurement agents were charged with giving defense contractors information on more than $500 million in Navy purchases.

Professional Occupational Crime

Green (1990) believes crime in the professions is conceptually different from other occupational offenses. This is because (1) professions are distinctly characterized by self-regulation; and (2) most professions require an oath or ethical commitment which requires the profession to have a special trust with persons who rely upon them. This trust is such that the professional is expected to do what is best for his or her client, usually without regard to compensation to the professional.

Green further notes that it is extremely difficult to prosecute professionals for two reasons. First, the nature of the services provided by doctors, attorneys, and others are difficult to quantify, and hence to use to prove criminal intent. Second, the "self-regulation" by professions tends to handle complaints in such a way that they do not come to light: e.g., bar discipline for an errant attorney, which is not normally disclosed to the public.

Fraud by Medical Professionals

Criminal acts by the medical profession include (1) unnecessary surgery and treatment; (2) fee splitting; (3) fraudulent medical insurance claims; (4) fraudulent expert testimony; and (5) income tax evasion. On the latter score, Gross determined that physicians have been more than ten times as likely to be indicted for income tax evasion as the general population. How likely it is that unnecessary surgery is motivated by fraud is difficult if not impossible to estimate, as incompetence and misdiagnosis are motivators as well. Researchers at Cornell Medical School evaluated over 1,300 cases of major surgery and concluded that 25 percent were unneeded.

Fee splitting involves a kickback, usually to a general practitioner, who refers patients to a surgeon or specialist. The referral can be for either necessary or unnecessary treatment. "Pingponging" is the needless referral to another doctor for additional treatment. Sutherland estimated that two-thirds of surgeons in New York City had participated in fee splitting. Whitman (1953: 24) claimed the practice was as high as 70 percent, and noted that "the less skilled the surgeon, the higher the kickback he must give in order to get business (so) split fee cases gravitate to the highest bidders, the worst surgeons."

The six most common medical insurance frauds by physicians include (1) pingponging; (2) family ganging (needless requests to see other members of a patient's family); (3) prolonged treatments; (4) billing for physician services that are performed by unlicensed personnel; (5) double billing of services; and (6) billing for services not rendered (Green 1990: 195–96). Most physicians are reimbursed by insurance companies on the basis of a fee-for-service (not by the hour). As a result, medical insurance fraud is easy to accomplish.

Many methods are used to catch cheats in the medical insurance area. Where doctors and others bill by the hour, computer analysis can often detect excess billings. Investigators have been able to document fraud through sophisticated surveillance techniques: photographing and timing visits in and out of medical offices. Undercover agents feigning illness have sought treatment for themselves.

The Legal Profession

Offenses generally committed by lawyers include overbilling for time, embezzlement of trust funds, and fraud committed for the benefit of their clients (i.e., preparing false documents for admission in legal proceedings). Fraud is easy to commit for attorneys, in large part because of the nebulous nature of the services provided. As Blumberg states:

Legal service lends itself particularly well to confidence games. Usually a plumber will be able to demonstrate . . . that he has performed a service by clearing up a stuffed drain, repairing the leaky faucet or pipe—and therefore merits his fee. In the practice of law there is a special problem in this regard, no matter what the level of the practitioner or his practice in the hierarchy of prestige. Much legal work is intangible either because it is simply a few words of advice, some preventative action, a telephone call, negotiation of some kind, a form filled out and filed, a hurried conference with another attorney or an official of a government agency, a letter or opinion written, or a countless variety of seemingly innocuous and even prosaic procedures and actions. (Blumberg 1984: 196)

Individual Occupational Crime

Green defines individual occupational crime as all occupational crimes other than those committed for organizations by their employees or by persons in their capacity as governmental authorities or by professionals.

Employee Theft

The estimates of the amount of employee theft vary widely, because there is no statistical measurement by a governmental agency or other authority. Estimates of annual losses to employee theft have varied from as little as $6 billion (Adler 1977) to as much as $120 billion. Notwithstanding, losses from business crime are believed to total more than the dollar losses from street crime. Green reported on a survey by the U.S. Chamber of Commerce which asserted that about half of those who work in plants and offices steal to some extent. Broy (1974: 42) reports that five to eight percent of employees steal in volume. Adler says that 30 percent of business failures can be traced to employee dishonesty.

The thefts can be simple, from the taking of supplies, paper clips and pencils, to the more complex and imaginative. Internal theft specialist Harvey Yaffee detailed one example of midwestern supermarket manager who had an extra checkout lane—with his own cash register—built at the store. Each day he would open up the store and take the money paid into that register. He took some $70,000 in just a few months. Some employees steal in volume. A cleaning woman for Neiman Marcus stole 343 dresses valued at $686,000. And a warehouse employee stole 65,000 beer bottles he redeemed at a nickel each.

A great deal of employee theft apparently occurs at an early age. Franklin (1976) conducted an in-depth study of retail theft, and concluded that four-fifths were perpetrated by persons between 18 and 28. It should be noted, however, that retailers typically employ large numbers of young persons. Three-quarters of the thefts involved money or merchandise, while 20 percent involved the alteration of records. Sales personnel accounted for two-thirds of the frauds. Half of the thefts in Franklin's study involved less than $60.

Computer-Related Employee Crime

No firm statistics can measure the extent of computer-related crime, which can be defined as an illegal act for which knowledge of computer technology is essential. The U.S. Army estimates the chances of being detected for computer crime are about one in a hundred, and being prosecuted for it about one in 22,000 (Thornton 1984). Typical computer-related crimes in reality are not much different from more traditional means of employee fraud: embezzlement and false statements. Perhaps the most sinister aspect is the ease and speed with which they can be accomplished. For example, an employee of the City of Phoenix pleaded guilty to stealing $700,000 while working in the city's accounts payable through setting up a phony vendor who did business with the city. His scheme was aided by an ex-convict; both of them hoped to steal as much as $16.3

million. In another scheme, an employee of the District of Columbia caused the computer to generate 608 checks worth $492,138 which were mailed to the employee's sister-in-law. In a 1980 case, two sports promoters, in conjunction with a bank employee, embezzled $21 million through a computer scheme. One must note, however, that computer frauds are widely reported by the media, and in the opinion of one expert, "computer frauds are probably the most over-reported and overblown schemes I can think of."

Why Employees Commit Fraud

There are a number of theories that attempt to explain why employees steal, many of them covered in portions of this text. Sometimes, under tenets of the theory of differential association, fraud perpetrators learn how to steal from others.

The various techniques of neutralization—denial of injury and the victim—are commonly used: "It was a big bank, they had lots of money; I was only 'borrowing' from the company; I don't get paid enough." Benson (1985: 595) said that three-fourths of the embezzlers he studied "referred explicitly to extraordinary circumstances and presented the offense as an aberration in their life history." In other words, the offenders saw themselves as completely law abiding, except for the incident in question.

Cressey's (1953) model for the embezzler—immediate financial need, perceived opportunity, and rationalization—no doubt describes many fraud offenders. However, even Cressey, who pioneered work in embezzlement, later said that the unsharable financial problem was not critical in all instances. Strain theories no doubt account for a percentage who have set financial goals they cannot otherwise achieve. In one interesting study, only a third of 160 employee thefts—most of them by long-term employees—were motivated by financial need. In contrast to actual need, living beyond one's means was a principal motivator. Females apparently commit less fraud than males, for two important reasons. They tend to occupy fewer managerial positions as a percentage of the work force, and therefore do not have as much opportunity to commit thefts. Secondly, they are more closely supervised because of their positions, making the possibility less likely.

Consumer Fraud

Consumer fraud is an individual occupational crime to the extent that its gains accrue directly and knowingly to employees and owners of a business. It has been estimated that consumer frauds account for about one-sixth of the total income derived from crime in the United States.

Schemes and players are practically unending, ranging from home repair frauds to sophisticated schemes; in a nationwide solicitation, 100,000 people purchased light bulbs because they thought the profits were going to disabled workers. They were, but the disabilities—certified by doctors—included such "cripplers" as acne, hay fever, nervousness, and obesity. And those "donating" paid about three times the going price for light bulbs to help these poor folks. Sometimes fraud occurs when you can't fight back: a funeral director in Tennessee was charged with burying people without caskets, and throwing trash in on top of the corpses. One corpse was uncovered with a metal bucket on his head; another was left with an arm hanging out.

Scandals involving the ministry, especially TV evangelism, have become increasingly public knowledge. In December 1988, Jim Bakker was indicted on mail fraud charges stemming from the television sale of lifetime "partnerships" in a vacation hotel at The Heritage USA theme park, which he ostensibly owned. Prosecutors were also able to document that Bakker and his wife, Tammy Fay, received about $3.5 million in "bonuses" from the scheme. In 1989, Bakker was sentenced to 45 years in prison.

In 1985, a two-year undercover FBI investigation netted indictments of pharmaceutical wholesalers who told drug manufacturers that they were making purchases for resale to hospitals, nursing homes, and international nonprofit organizations. After the drugs were purchased, they were then allegedly sold to consumers at retail prices.

Fraud is common in the repair and service industry. Home repair fraud, frequently perpetrated against the elderly, ranges from purchases of substandard materials such as roofing to simply taking the money and not doing the work at all.

A frequent consumer fraud, most of us would agree, involves automobile repairs. In 1979, one study suggested that 53 cents of each auto-repair dollar was wasted because of unnecessary repairs, overcharging, services never performed, or incompetence. Braithwaite (1979) found Australian used car dealers rolled back the odometers on a third of the cars he verified.

Braithwaite interviewed a typical used car salesman who used denial of injury as his neutralization (1979: 119): "People pay too much attention to the mileage reading on a car. There might be a car with a low mileage reading but all sorts of faults, and another perfect car with a high mileage reading. It doesn't matter what the mileage reading is, but how good the car is . . . So if you turn the mileage reading back of a car in perfect order, you're encouraging people to buy a good car."

However, Braithwaite (1979: 119) stated that neutralization of condemning the condemners was the most used technique. One said, "They think because you're a used car dealer you are a liar. So they treat you like one and lie to you. Can you blame the dealer for lying back?"

Income Tax Evasion

During 1987, the following persons were convicted of criminal income tax fraud: 94 for fraudulent tax shelters, 275 for tax protesting, 116 under the bank secrecy act, and 1,391 convicted for "all other" violations. Green (1990) says the conviction rate is about one in 40,000 returns. However, the actual rate of income tax fraud may be much higher. Green says people commonly believe it is easier to justify fraud against the government because "they can afford it."

Securities Fraud

Churning is the practice of a broker's buying and selling stock for a client to generate fees, rather than for what is in the best interests of the client. Broker discretion accounts are especially ripe for churning. In one case, two sisters gave brokers $500,000 each in discretionary accounts. The brokers traded the stocks more than 1,400 times, allegedly giving themselves $400,000 in commissions, and leaving the sisters with $70,000.

Other schemes involve mixing client funds with the broker's. Sometimes brokers will use the client's stock as collateral for personal loans, and even post the winning trades to themselves, while posting the losses to their clients. Brokers also resort to out-and-out embezzlement of their clients' money and stock.

Insider trading involves the use of non-public information to make stock trades on the market. Ivan Boesky, the Wall Street arbitrage king, was sentenced to three years in prison and fined $100 million. Boesky, in his plea agreement, gave information that led to the indictments of so-called junk bond king Michael Milken, who eventually pled guilty to insider trading and was fined $600 million.

Preventing or Reducing Fraud

Three internal personal forces operate to reduce fraud. The first is fear of formal, officially imposed sanctions (conviction and punishment by the government). Second is the fear of informally imposed sanctions, such as the loss of respectability or a career. Third is the internalization of values that discourage violations of legal codes.

Two other factors, incapacitation and rehabilitation, which are generated by formal and informal sanctioning, may also act to inhibit illegal behavior. Green points out that teaching people that certain behaviors are illegal and therefore inappropriate is uncomplicated and extremely effective in reducing crime. Moral education that discourages illegal behavior must be continuous. Simply put, persons must be informed as to what behavior is acceptable and what is not so they can alter their actions appropriately.

White-Collar Law Enforcement

There are two types of enforcement strategies concerning white-collar crime, compliance and deterrence. *Compliance* aims for law conformity without the necessity of detecting, processing, or penalizing violators. Compliance systems attempt to create conformity by providing economic incentives, or by using administrative efforts to control violations before they occur. The core violation in compliance is usually referred to as a technical violation. For example, the SEC has a host of administrative mechanisms to encourage voluntary compliance with their rules. The Internal Revenue Service also uses such measures, along with criminal penalties. Environmental crimes are usually controlled through compliance strategies.

Deterrence strategies are designed to detect violations of the law, determine who is responsible, and penalize them to deter future violations. The core violation deterrence systems try to control is the immediate behavior of individual(s), not the long-term behaviors of compliance systems. In short, compliance strategies are concerned with the violation, while deterrence strategies are concerned with the violator.

Compliance strategies have been criticized by some criminologists. Some experts believe that they have little effect, as they are imposed only after the violation occurs. And since economic penalties are the most common, in the case of large wealthy corporations, these penalties amount to little more than a slap on the wrist.

Deterrence theory assumes that humans are rational in their behavior patterns, seeking profit and pleasure while avoiding pain. The assumption of deterrence is that an individual's propensity toward lawbreaking is in inverse proportion to his or her perception of the probability of negative consequences. Under the deterrence theory, the difference between criminal and noncriminal behavior is that the criminal has lower fear of perceived consequences. That fear may come from a real threat or a perceived one.

Informal sanctions—the loss of job or prestige—can be powerful deterrents to commission of crime, and may even be more powerful than the fear of formal sanctions such as going to prison. In one case of the author's, a bank president, when told he was about to be indicted for fraud, spent most of his time asking whether the charges were going to be made public. When told that indeed the charges would be public, the banker, that evening, committed suicide. In one study (Cameron 1964) middle-class housewives caught shoplifting were more worried about others finding out than about going to jail. Informal sanctions often exist without formal sanctions. However, the imposition of formal sanctions will usually lead to additional informal sanctions.

There are two types of deterrence, general and specific. General deterrence refers to one person or group of persons being deterred from the commission of crime by awareness, through an example, of negative consequences. If A is sentenced to prison for fraud, then B through Z will be aware of the consequences and therefore discouraged from similar actions. Specific (or special) deterrence refers to A being discouraged from committing an inappropriate act because he or she has committed such an offense in the past and is aware of the consequences. To deter an individual generally and specifically, his or her probability of receiving negative consequences need not be realistic, it need only be perceived as realistic. As an example, Green says: "If executions were faked on television and, in fact no person was actually executed, there would still be the possibility of a general deterrent emanating from the program" (1990: 233).

There are three dimensions of perceptions about the probability of suffering negative consequences. First, the punishment must be severe. Certainty is generally thought to impose a greater fear-inducing dimension than either celerity or severity. It is believed that the more severe sanctions must be reserved for the most undesirable behaviors. This is because some people will commit more heinous crimes than they ordinarily would have if they perceive the consequences to be the same regardless. In the area of occupational crimes, most are quite calculated. Potential perpetrators carefully assess the possibility of certainty, celerity, and severity when plotting to commit fraud.

Chambliss (1967) points out that occupational crimes are more instrumental and less expressive than street crime, and therefore should be deterred more easily. In addition, most occupational criminals, compared to more traditional offenders, are more inclined to perceive the informal sanctions of the loss of career and prestige than formal sanctions, and are therefore theoretically more deterred by those consequences.

Some experts believe there are better deterrents to occupational crime than incarceration. They say the most effective deterrence threats are (1) monetary penalties; (2) adverse publicity, and incarcerating executives. With respect to monetary penalties, some argue that these sanctions are limited to a person's own worth and therefore have limited utility.

Punishment of White-Collar Criminals

The public at large believes that white-collar criminals are not adequately punished for their crimes. They point out, in cases like that of Ivan Boesky (who got three years in a "luxury" prison for a $100 million fraud), that the sentence does not fit the crime.

However, Siegel quotes a study by Donald Manson in 1986 and another by Kenneth Carlson and Jan Chaiken in 1987 provide some interesting information. Manson's survey of enforcement practices in nine states found that white collar crime accounts for about six percent of all offenses. Eighty-eight percent of those arrested were prosecuted, and seventy-four percent were convicted in criminal court. Sixty percent were subsequently sent to prison.

Carlson and Chaiken also followed federal white-collar crime prosecutions between 1980 and 1985. During that time, white-collar crime convictions rose by 18 percent. The conviction rate for white collar criminals was 85 percent, while the rate for other federal crimes was 78 percent. Federal white-collar criminals received more lenient sentences than other offenders, with the average period of incarceration being 29 months, versus 50 months for other federal offenses.

Wheeler, Weisburd, and Bode (1982) analyzed only sentences for white-collar offenders, holding constant other variables such as age, harm inflicted, the sentence options available to the court, and previous offenses. They concluded that the following two conditions associated with white-collar offenses will most likely lead to imprisonment. First is the allowed maximum sentence. More than three-quarters of those who could have done 15 years or more were sentenced to prison. Only a third of the persons who could have been sentenced to a year or less actually received time. Second is the financial impact of the crime. Those who take under $500 are less likely to go to prison than those whose offenses create more substantial losses. The sentencing studies have been careful to note their possible shortcomings. Most important is the fact that certain offenses and offenders have been siphoned off much earlier in the judicial process (Pollack and Smith 1983; Shapiro 1985). Judges may get only the most difficult economic offenses and may be responding to these.

Restitution and Other Sanctions

Green (1990) and other criminologists advocate victim restitution for occupational criminals, in addition to other punishment. First, restitution helps the victim recover a financial loss, and second, it precludes perpetrators from using ill-gotten gains to further illegal activities. He believes excessive amounts of restitution (i.e., double and treble damages) have little if any deterrent effects. He also advocates additional publicity for offenders who are punished, saying this is necessary in order to increase the public awareness of certain punishment.

Occupational Disqualifications

One reason special deterrence works is that it removes the offender from the opportunity to commit additional offenses; it is difficult for a bank robber to commit more robberies while in prison. Similarly, it is difficult for a doctor to commit Medicaid fraud when he has been suspended from the practice of medicine. There are two ways to accomplish occupational disqualification. Selective incapacitation involves removing persons from occupations who it is believed will commit additional offenses. The problem, of course, is predicting who will commit such offenses.

Collective incapacitation involves removing all persons from occupations where an offense has occurred. The problem with this approach, however, is that it may unjustly punish those for whom deterrence is not a future problem. Green advocates the use of clearinghouses for professionals and others who have been convicted of past offenses. Someone seeking to employ or utilize the services of doctors, attorneys, and even clerical employees could check a data bank and see if the person had a past conviction. Green believes such sanctions have the advantage of being less expensive than incarceration, and potentially as effective.

Rehabilitation

The thought of rehabilitation is based on the medical model: a problem is diagnosed, treatment is prescribed, and a recovery ensues. Unfortunately, when it comes to traditional criminals, rehabilitation has been a costly failure (Martinson 1974). Although there are no conclusive studies, it is felt that rehabilitation of white-collar offenders might be effective in some instances. One study (Hopkins 1980) found that companies convicted of the Australian Trade Practices Act made some strides toward self-correction. However, most of these improvements were voluntary, and there is no literature to suggest that mandated rehabilitation will work in the fraud area.

Increasing Enforcement

As Green (1990) points out, no crime control method will work unless offenders are sanctioned. Even informal sanctions work when applied. Formal levels of current enforcement, by all measures, are extremely low. Braithwaite advocates a novel approach: enforced self-regulation. Under his idea, the government would compel each company to write rules for themselves or their employees, unique to the particular circumstances. A governmental agency would then be formed to monitor compliance. He points out several successes in the noncriminal area. The Federal Aviation Administration monitors self-regulation for the airline industry; the Federal Trade Commission monitors rules that the advertising industry has largely set for itself. However, there are problems with self-regulation, and the industries which attempt to regulate themselves have a spotty record at best (Braithwaite 1982: 1470–71). One study (Rensberger 1976) showed that of the 320,000 physicians in the United States, an average of only 72 medical licenses per year were revoked.

It is the author's view that increased enforcement can only come at the expense of a complete and total revision of the criminal justice system. In sum, people have little fear of detection because of the constant barrage of information showing the police and courts simply cannot keep up with the pace of criminal offenses. It is not necessary or even desirable to advocate longer sentences in prison for offenders. We do not have the jails or courts to accommodate them. Perhaps a better plan would be to sacrifice certainty for severity. Until potential offenders have the perception that they will be caught and punished, we should not expect a reversal of the crime trend. How the justice system works (and doesn't work) is covered in the following pages.

3 The Criminal Justice System

Criminal justice refers to the formal process and the agencies that apprehend, adjudicate, sanction, and treat criminal offenders. It is frequently referred to as the criminal justice system, implying that there is indeed an integrated network for treating criminals. However, as many critics have observed, there is nothing systematic about treating offenders. They point out that the various agencies involved do not work together as a unified team, but rather in a patchwork fashion. The basic components of the system involve various police, court, and correctional agencies organized at federal, state, and local levels. There are approximately 55,000 separate agencies, most (81 percent) at the local level. The remainder are funded by state and federal jurisdictions.

POLICE

The function of the police is to investigate and apprehend miscreants, and turn them over to the courts for adjudication. Approximately 20,000 law enforcement agencies exist, with the municipal police agencies accounting for about 13,600 of them. Local jurisdictions also maintain over 1,000 special police units, including park rangers, harbor police, transit police, and campus security.

At the county level, there are about 3,000 sheriff's departments. These agencies normally provide police protection in unincorporated areas of the county. In addition, almost every state maintains a highway patrol or state police. Altogether, there are nearly a million people employed in law enforcement—about 700,000 uniformed or sworn officers, along with 150,000 civilian employees.

Although the traditional role of the police is to apprehend criminals, they also now function in a broader role. They are involved in "order maintenance"—patrolling streets and neighborhoods to deter crime. They also provide many human service functions, such as facilitating the movement of people and vehicles, crime prevention and awareness programs, and resolving family conflicts.

COURTS

There are approximately 25,000 court-related agencies in the United States. About 16,000 are criminal courts. Of those, about 13,000 try just misdemeanors, while over 3,000 try felony cases. There are 207 appellate courts. In addition, there are about 8,000 prosecutor's offices at the federal, state, and local level.

The criminal court is responsible for determining the criminal liability of defendants. Upon a finding of guilty, the court is also responsible for sentencing. These duties must be performed without transgressing the rights of the accused. The defendant has certain basic rights during the charging process, including the right to an attorney, the right to a jury trial, the right to a speedy trial, and the right to due process.

Under the rights of due process, the defendant has the right to be treated with fundamental fairness, including the right to be present at trial, to be notified of the charges, to have the opportunity to confront witnesses, and to have favorable witnesses appear. Notwithstanding all these rights, the fact is that about 90 percent of defendants do not go to trial, opting instead for plea bargaining. This is a process whereby the defendant elects to work out a deal for a lesser sentence with the prosecutor. The theory is that the deals made will ultimately benefit the criminal system, since many more persons can be prosecuted. The plea bargain arrangement has been the subject of intense debate and criticism. Many feel this procedure is abused, and leads to the early release of hardened and dangerous criminals.

CORRECTIONS

There are about 9,000 agencies devoted to the treatment of convicted offenders, among these about 3,500 adult and juvenile probation and parole agencies. There are also about 5,700 residential correction facilities, including about 3,500 jails, 800 prisons, and 1,100 juvenile facilities. All these agencies are charged with providing post-conviction care to the offender. This can range from probation to incarceration in a maximum security prison.

The most common sentence is probation, which allows the convicted offender to remain in the community, subject to conditions imposed by the court and administered by the probation officer. More than one-quarter of felony offenders receive probation. Jails are used both to hold certain offenders before trial and to incarcerate short-term offenders sentenced after trial. Many of these short term institutions are administered by county governments, and as a result there is little done in the way of treatment; they simply house prisoners.

Prisons or penitentiaries are designed to hold offenders for longer periods. They are divided into minimum, medium, and maximum security facilities. Although offering some treatment to offenders, prisons can vary widely in size and quality. Federal prisons, with their budgets, are considered the best of the lot. Community-based correctional facilities are the newest type of treatment centers for inmates. These programs emphasize the use of neighborhood residential centers, halfway houses, pre-release centers, and work-release and furlough programs. An inmate can be sent directly to one of these facilities, or can be released from prison to a correctional facility pending reintegration into society.

Parole is the process whereby an inmate selected for early release serves the remainder of the sentence outside prison walls, subject to supervision by a parole officer. The purpose of parole is to help an ex-inmate adjust to society, while still under supervision. If the inmate violates the rules of parole, he or she can be sent back to the institution to serve the remainder of the sentence. The agencies handling criminal justice process more than two million offenders a year, employ more than 1.4 million people, and cost taxpayers more than $50 billion annually in direct costs. This works out to about $200 per citizen, or almost the same amount paid for transportation or health care.

THE JUSTICE PROCESS

The criminal justice process begins with an initial contact with the police, and ends with the offender's reentry into society. At any point in the process, the offender can be dismissed from the system, for such reasons as:

- The case is considered unimportant or trivial.
- Legally admissible evidence is not available.
- The accused is considered not to need further punishment.
- The prosecutor decides not to press further charges.

One federal survey of over half a million cases shows that about 84 percent of persons arrested are prosecuted, 62 percent are convicted, and 34 percent are incarcerated. Interestingly, about one third of violent criminals are not incarcerated, while another third receive a sentence of less than a year. Only the final third are sentenced to prison for more than a year.

Processing Offenders

The steps to processing offenders vary somewhat, but usually commence with an initial contact with the police. This may involve a citizen complaint, or police observation of criminal activity. Once the initial contact is made, an investigation is instituted if appropriate. The investigation may be short, such as in the case of a burglar breaking into a building; or long, in the case of a white-collar crime.

Once the investigation is complete, an arrest is made if the facts so dictate. The arrest may be made on the police's authority only, or a warrant may be issued by a judge after the police provide evidence of probable cause that the person so charged committed the crime described in the warrant. After the arrest, the person is placed in custody. For most offenses, the arrestee can post bail and be released pending trial. During custody, the arrestee can be interrogated by the police (with a lawyer, if the defendant so chooses) for the purpose of obtaining a confession. This confession, if obtained, will be used to further support the charges against the defendant.

Once the police turn over evidence on a case to the prosecutor, a decision will be made regarding how the charges will be filed. A complaint is used for misdemeanors. An information or indictment is employed in felony cases. These terms define the paperwork used to charge the defendant. If charged by complaint or information, the defendant is brought before a judge for a preliminary hearing. This process is to determine if the state has sufficient information to bring the defendant to trial. If so, he or she is ordered to stand trial; if not, the charges are dismissed.

Indictments are issued by a grand jury after they hear the evidence implicating the defendant. Grand juries meet for specified terms and hear a number of cases during their terms. If they believe the evidence is sufficient, an indictment is issued by the grand jury foreman, ordering the defendant to stand trial for the charges. The grand jury process has been heavily criticized for being a "rubber stamp" for the prosecutor. This is in part because the defendant does not have the right to testify or have evidence presented in his or her behalf. In addition, the defendant has no right to be present, nor can the attorney. In short, the grand jury hears only the evidence the prosecutor wants heard.

Once the defendant is charged, he or she is brought before the court. This process is called the arraignment. Here the defendant is informed of his or her rights, has bail considered, and is set for trial. Bail is a money bond insuring that the defendant will show up for trial. If not, the bond is forfeited, and a warrant for the defendant's arrest is issued. Defendants who cannot post bail, or who are charged with capital or heinous offenses, or who the court believes may flee, are held in jail pending trial. Under provisions of the federal Speedy Trial Act, the government must be willing to try the case within a specified time, usually 90 days. Defendants may make motions for delay. This is common, especially with guilty defendants, who want to postpone the trial under the theory that witnesses' memories will dim, or evidence will be lost.

After arraignment, the defendant's lawyers will plea bargain with the prosecutors if appropriate. Should a deal be struck, the defendant will avoid trial and be brought directly before the courts to plea and be sentenced. If the charges are not bargained, the defendant will stand trial. The jury can reach three conclusions: guilty, not guilty, or hung jury. In the latter case, the prosecutors will decide if the charges are sufficient to re-try the defendant. If the defendant is acquitted at trial, he or she is released and the process comes to an end.

If the defendant is found guilty, he or she will be sentenced by the presiding judge. In some states, the jury is involved in setting the punishment; in others, that decision is made solely by the judge. Prior to sentencing, the judge normally orders a pre-sentence investigation to be conducted by the probation staff. This investigation is to determine the defendant's good attributes, and to determine whether the state is likely to be at risk if the defendant is not incarcerated.

CONCEPTS OF JUSTICE

Although many justice systems are influenced by the law, they are also influenced by criminological thought and philosophy. Several models of criminal justice have developed over the years that take into account these various philosophies.

The crime-control model is built on classical criminological theory. That is, crime is a rational choice, and the purpose of criminal justice is to deter criminal behavior and incapacitate known criminals. The crime-control model has been a dominant force in American criminal justice. This model emphasizes protection of society and compensation of victims. Under the crime-control model, rehabilitation does not work.

The rehabilitation model holds that crime is a function of social injustice, poverty, and racism, and that criminals are criminals through no fault of their own. Further, given the proper incentive and treatment, criminals can become law-abiding citizens. The rehabilitation model reached the height of its popularity during the 1960s. In today's climate, many criminologists have abandoned the notion of reforming criminals.

A combination of several thought processes, the due process model advocates individualized justice, treatment, and rehabilitation of the offender. Most important, the civil rights of the accused should be protected at all costs. Further, this model tends to restrict the definition of criminal behavior by eliminating certain offenses, such as traffic offenses, prostitution, and drug violations.

At its roots, the nonintervention model believes that the more government interferes with the rights of people, the greater the harm. This model calls for limits on the intrusions into the lives of people, including those who run afoul of the law. It advocates deinstitution of nonserious offenders, diversion from the formal court process for many offenses, and decriminalization of nonserious offenses. Under this theory, the criminal justice system has a negative impact on offenders, and this theory minimizes the contact with the system.

There is also a radical-conflict view of the justice system. Radical-conflict theorists reject the due process-crime control dichotomy. Instead they view the justice system as a state-initiated and state-supported effort to rationalize mechanisms of social control. The criminologist's role is to expose the aspects of the justice system that are designed to specifically control or exploit the laboring classes.

One of the newer models of criminal justice, the justice model, holds that it is futile to rehabilitate criminals because treatment programs are ineffective. Justice advocates find fault with other crime-control models, as they depend on predicting what offenders will do in the future while deciding their fates in the present. The justice model calls for fairness in criminal procedure, and advocates flat or determinate sentences, thereby removing judicial discretion.

Once, in our justice system, the needs and desires of the victim were ignored. Beginning in the 1960s, victim rights have come into play in the criminal-justice model. Victims' rights advocates argue that the victim should have considerable influence in the criminal process, and should be compensated for their injuries. More than 35 states now have adopted legislation involving victims' rights, including compensation, and allowing the victim to actively participate in sentencing hearings, and to express views.

THE JUDICATORY PROCESS

The judicatory process is designed to provide an open and impartial forum for deciding the justice of a conflict between two or more parties. The courts are the forum for resolving those conflicts. They are generally divided into federal and state courts. The court system hears about 1.5 million felony cases annually.

State Courts

Although the procedure varies from state to state, most states employ a three- or four-tier court system. Lower courts try misdemeanors and the preliminary processing of felony offenses. Superior trial courts have jurisdiction over actual trials of felony cases. Appellate courts review the criminal procedures of trial courts to determine whether the offenders were treated fairly. Superior appellate courts or supreme courts, used in about half the states, review lower appellate court decisions.

Federal Courts

The federal system uses a three-tier model. The U.S. District Courts are the trial courts; appeals are made at the Federal Courts of Appeal, and the U.S. Supreme Court is the court of last resort. The U.S. Supreme Court generally hears only the cases it wants to, or cases it deems important. It must also accept jurisdiction in cases where:

- A federal court holds an act of Congress unconstitutional.
- A federal appeals court finds a state law unconstitutional.
- A state's highest court holds a federal law invalid.
- An individual's challenge to a state statute on constitutional grounds is upheld by the state supreme court.

The Supreme Court can define a legal issue narrowly or broadly. In the latter case, it becomes a landmark decision, and future cases are decided on that basis. It also has the power to reverse a landmark decision.

Court System Personnel

There are three major players in the courtroom: the prosecutor, the defense attorney, and the judge. The role of the prosecutor is to conduct investigations of violations of the law, cooperate with the police, determine charges, represent the government at pretrial and motions, try the case, recommend sentencing, represent the government at hearings, and conduct investigations as necessary. Prosecutors in general have almost unlimited discretion in determining what crimes are prosecuted and what cases are dismissed.

The defense counsel represents the accused in the courtroom. His or her functions include: investigating the incident, interviewing witnesses, discussing the matter with the prosecutor, representing the defendant in pre-trial matters, plea negotiations, preparing the case for trial, filing and arguing legal motions, representing the defendant at trial, providing assistance at sentencing, and preparing the appeal.

The majority of those charged with crimes are indigents who cannot afford legal counsel. In those situations, the defense attorney comes from one of three areas. First, the courts can assign private attorneys to represent indigents on a case-by-case basis. The state in this situation pays the legal fees. Second, the state can contract with a law firm to regularly provide defense services to indigents. Finally, the accused can be represented by a public defender.

The judge is the senior officer in a court of law. During trials, the judge rules on the appropriateness of conduct, settles questions of evidence and procedure, and guides the questioning of witnesses. If the trial is before a jury, the judge must instruct jury members on which evidence is proper and which should be ignored. The judge also formally charges the jury by instructing its members on what points of law and evidence they must consider. The judge is also involved in the sentencing decision. In some courts, the judge also controls the functions of probation agencies and to some extent the prosecutor and the police. Depending on the jurisdiction, judges are either appointed or elected.

Pretrial Procedures

Once a person has been charged with a crime, he or she is brought before a court to plead. There are three possibilities: guilty, not guilty, or nolo contendere, which is equivalent to a guilty plea (see chapter 5). After being formally charged, the defendant has the right to post bail in all but capital punishment cases, such as murder. The bail system has been subject to much criticism, as it tends to favor the wealthy over the indigent. However, in the federal system, the Federal Bail Reform Act of 1984 provides for the automatic release of defendants on their own recognizance unless circumstances otherwise warrant.

Although the great majority of defendants released on bail return for trial, there is considerable crime committed by a small minority. One study indicated that about 15 percent of defendants on bail were rearrested before trial. Those rearrested tend to be on bail longer; have a serious prior record; are drug abusers; have a poor work record; and are disproportionately young, male, and nonwhite. Thirty states consequently have laws which limit bail for recidivists.

Because of the problems with the criminal justice system, pretrial diversion programs have become popular at the local level within the last 20 years. Pretrial diversion means that selected individuals, after they are arrested but before the trial, can be put into treatment programs. If they successfully complete this treatment, a trial and hence a criminal record can be avoided. Usually, the judge, probation officer, prosecutor, and defense lawyer must agree to the program. The person selected for pretrial diversion usually receives services in three areas: counseling, employment services, and human services (health, education, and emergency housing). The defendant can be left in the pretrial diversion program almost indefinitely. If he or she is successful in the program, charges are dropped. If not, the person is tried for the crime charged.

Sentencing

A determinate sentence is for a fixed term of years, set by the legislature, to be served by the criminal. If for example, the legislature determines a sentence of five years for one particular kind of fraud, then under flat determinate sentencing, each person convicted of that crime must serve the entire five years without the possibility of parole.

A variation is for the law to establish a maximum sentence for each offense, and to give the sentencing judge discretion over imposing a lesser period of incarceration. Under this method, inmates who behave can earn good time, which may reduce the actual time served by as much as one half. In addition, inmates can be granted special time off for participating in education or vocational training. Determinate sentencing is widely used in the United States.

Indeterminate sentences impose a short minimum prison stay followed by a longer maximum sentence which can be imposed if need be. The overriding philosophy of indeterminate sentences is that the sentence should fit the offender rather than the crime. For example, the penalty for fraud could range from 5 to 20 years. Whether the prisoner gets out before 20 years is determined by the correction agency, dependent on how the offender behaves during his or her time behind bars. Indeterminate sentences are also widely used.

Legislatures, responding to public pressures, have recently been adopting mandatory sentences for some crimes. This has the effect of reducing judicial discretion. The typical mandatory sentence prohibits parole, for example, for certain violent crimes, as well as for repeat offenders. Mandatory sentences provide equal treatment for those who commit the same crime, regardless of age, sex, or circumstances. The judge is not permitted to place the individual on probation or suspend imposition of the sentence. More than 35 states have now adopted some form of mandatory sentences. Not surprisingly, judges have been critical of the concept because it reduces or eliminates their discretion.

Presumptive sentences give the offender a specific sentence unless mitigating circumstances exist. For example, a fraudster may statutorily be sentenced to five years for a particular fraud. If he or she has a good prior record, that sentence could be reduced by the judge to, say, three years. One with several prior problems might get eight years. Good time and other early releases are not considered. The supposed advantage of this sentence is that it recognizes certain special circumstances while eliminating disparity in a wide range of sentences for the same offense. Forms of this method have been adopted in California, Illinois, and Indiana. Other states are considering versions.

CORRECTIONS

History of Corrections

Corrections is the general term for the administration of punishment following the conviction for a criminal offense. In the United States, the functions of corrections are divided among the federal, state, and local governments. Felony offenses draw prison time, while misdemeanor miscreants are housed in jails, reformatories, community-based corrections centers, and halfway houses. The incarceration of humans has long been the subject of controversy, many saying that prisons create cross-purposes and instead of reforming criminals, incarceration makes them worse. These statements are not without some truth.

The American system of corrections, like our laws, is based in part on the English system. In fact, the word felony is based on the 12th-century term *felonia*, referring to a breach of faith with one's feudal lord. Offenders were required to pay penance. If they were unable to do so, corporal punishment such as whipping or branding was substituted.

As strong monarchs took over England and cities were established, corporal and capital punishment became the favored way of controlling crime committed by the starving poor. It is estimated that Henry VIII executed 72,000 thieves in his reign alone, an astonishing number considering the world's small population at the time. In addition, gruesome punishments—beheadings, debowelings, and amputations, to name a few—were held in full view of spectators, presumably to discourage them from similar activity. By the late 18th century, over 350 offenses could technically draw the death penalty.

Corporal punishment never found its way into U.S. law. William Penn is widely credited with commencing our favored method, incarceration. At first, solitary confinement was preferred; however, this practice was largely abandoned by the middle of the 1800s, as it resulted in excessive suicides and mental breakdowns. Unruly inmates were removed to separate quarters. They were whipped if they refused to cooperate, and reputedly this system worked quite well. Rules requiring silence between inmates were common in prison systems. Inmates were treated harshly. In the opinion of some, corporal punishment had just been moved indoors, where it could not be seen by the public at large.

Gradually reforms were made in the courts, giving inmates rights and establishing standards for treatment. Of course, many critics argue that today the rights of prisoners are too liberal. A period of change and turmoil has marked the recent era of prisons. According to Siegel, three major areas stand out (1989: 503). First, prisoners have used the courts to seek greater rights and privileges concerning religion and speech, medical care, due process, and living conditions. Second, prisons have become much more violent. Finally, the alleged failure of the system to rehabilitate offenders has led penologists to rethink the purpose of incarceration.

Modern Corrections

At this writing, four main components of corrections exist in some form at the federal and local levels: community-based corrections, jail, prisons, and parole. Community-based corrections includes probation as well as a variety of institutional facilities located in the community. They are frequently called halfway houses or correctional centers. These programs cost less, and they are considered a charitable gesture to the less serious offender who can avoid the pains of incarceration.

Probation involves the suspension of the sentence in return for a promise of good behavior. Laws vary from state to state; some sentence the offender to prison and then suspend the sentence. Others delay the prison sentence while the offender is placed on probation. Probation can be revoked if the offender commits certain behaviors—crime, drug use, and other prohibited activities—while on probation. In most jurisdictions, nearly all juvenile offenders are eligible for probation, as are most adults, violent crimes excepted. Probation cannot be granted after prison time has been served; the inmate is instead paroled.

A split sentence can be applied to make a person eligible for probation only after serving some time in prison. The effect of this sentencing method has been criticized. In one limited study, it did not show a marked decrease in rates of recidivism.

Most probation agencies are organized at the estate level. About 30 states combine the administration of probation and parole in one agency.

Probation Procedures

After a person is convicted for a crime, the probation department investigates the person's background to determine the factors relating to the criminality of the offender. It then makes a recommendation to the sentencing judge. On probation, the offender usually undergoes some sort of personality evaluation to recommend treatment. Supervision can be strict or lax, depending on the criminal's background, and normally includes some sort of counseling or psychological services, if needed. Because of budget limitations, most criminals do not get more than minimum supervision, such as an occasional telephone call.

Recently, more innovative probation and punishment, including house arrests and electronic monitoring, have become popular in more than 20 states. With prison overcrowding, the low cost of keeping a person under house arrest while letting him or her continue to work has been an attractive alternative in some cases. The arrestee can also be called electronically at odd intervals as a check. Opponents of electronic monitoring see it as "Big Brother" tactics.

A variation used as an alternative to prison in some cases is called intensive probation supervision. It is used where intense supervision is required, normally five or more contacts a week. In one study, it was about 80 percent effective and cost $7,000 annually—about a fourth of the cost of incarceration. However, other studies have questioned the success of this method.

Most probation rules require that the offender (1) maintain steady employment, (2) make restitution for loss or damage, (3) cooperate with the probation officer, (4) obey all laws, and (5) meet family responsibilities. Special rules, such as not using drugs, may also be added. If the rules are violated, privileges may be revoked by the courts. In those cases, a hearing is afforded the probationer.

A Rand Corporation survey found that 65 percent of probationers were re-arrested, 51 percent were convicted, and 34 percent were reincarcerated. Three quarters of the charges were for new crimes. The study pointed out that because of prison overcrowding, many serious offenders received probation rather than being removed from society. Although probation doesn't work very well, it is used because of the economics of handling so many offenders in the criminal justice system.

Jails and Prisons

Jails are used to house persons both before they are convicted and after. Less serious offenders serving shorter times are normally held in jails. Originating in France in the 1600s, jails have traditionally been considered hellholes of pestilence and cruelty. Over the years, the American justice system has gradually improved jail conditions, and has attempted to reduce jail overcrowding through the use of bail. However, over eight million persons per year are placed in jail, even if for a short period of time. The great majority of those in jail reflect the typical criminal: uneducated, unemployed, poor, and drug-ridden.

There are over 500 prisons in the United States today, housing nearly 700,000 inmates. Of the prisons, 150 are maximum security, 225 are medium security, and 182 are minimum security. Of course, the maximum security prisons are used to house the most violent inmates. They use an elaborate system of fences, alarms, and guards and are therefore the most expensive to maintain. Prison population, reflecting a get-tough attitude of the public, has soared in the last few years. Between 1980 and 1987, the prison population doubled. In 1980, there were 139 inmates per 100,000 in population; in 1987, that figure had grown to 228. Since prison construction has not kept up with the population, prison overcrowding is a serious problem, and over half the states are under federal mandates to reduce overcrowding.

Many believe that prisons are warehouses for the dregs of society. In one study, over four fifths of the inmates had a previous record. Two thirds of the inmates were incarcerated for some violent behavior. More than half were using drugs at the time of their offense, and most used drugs on a daily basis. Blacks make up nearly half of the prison inmates, and 46 percent of all inmates are between the ages of 25 and 34. Prior to incarceration, their median income was less than $10,000 per year.

Aside from the loss of freedom, prison life is harsh. According to some experts, the prison subculture has changed in the last 20 or so years to a more violent system. Part of the reason has been the increase in the number of black gang members, such as the Black Muslims. As a result, many prison cultures are now organized along racial lines. The situation is so bad that some criminologists are now suggesting racially segregated prisons in order to reduce violence.

Some sort of education and correctional treatment is offered by most prisons. These services include therapy and counseling, educational programs, vocational rehabilitation, and even conjugal visits. One researcher, Robert Martinson (1974), found in a national study of prisons that rehabilitation simply doesn't work. As a result of this survey, social policy now in large part tends to keep first-time offenders out of prison, while sentencing recidivists to longer and longer terms.

Parole

Parole is the planned release and community supervision of incarcerated offenders before the actual expiration of their prison sentence. Parole is not the same as a pardon; the inmate can be legally recalled to serve the remainder of his or her sentence if the parole authorities deem the offender's adjustment inadequate, or if the offender commits a further crime while on parole.

Prisoners are paroled under statutory guidelines, and usually a minimum sentence is required. Parole boards, established by the states, are in charge of administering criteria for the parolee, including any specific rules the parolee must obey. Once community release has been authorized, the inmate is closely supervised by a parole officer or equivalent. Parole is considered an act of grace by the criminal justice system, which inmates must earn; it is not automatically granted.

As of 1987, there were over 300,000 persons on parole. Despite longer sentences, the number of parolees grew by a third between 1983 and 1987. This is in part due to the overcrowded prison conditions. The decision to grant parole is made on the basis of several factors, the most important of which is the belief that the offender will not return to crime. To help in the decision, parole prediction tables have been developed which claim to determine which criminals are likely to repeat their offenses. Included in the tables are such factors as age, type of offense, prior parole background and criminal history, use of drugs, and prior employments.

Studies on the effectiveness of parole are mixed. In one study, the Bureau of Justice Statistics in the 1970s found that only one-quarter of parolees returned to prison (National Council on Crime and Delinquency 1981). However, a 1987 study suggested that 69 percent of those paroled were rearrested for a more serious offense, and 49 percent were returned to prison. About 10 percent of those paroled accounted for 40 percent of the arrest statistics.

II Law

4 Legal Elements of Fraud

The materials included in this section are neither intended nor designed to make anyone an expert in law. They are intended mainly to provide a short and simplified view of some aspects of law that fraud examiners are likely to encounter in their work. In dealing with specific legal issues, consult your attorney.

Law is a form of social control. It is therefore intended to guide or direct human behavior toward ends that satisfy the common good. But legal norms vary from time to time and place to place, so law is a cultural and evolutionary process. In that sense, law embodies moral principles and the rights and obligations that members of an organized society have toward one another for their own mutual protection and well-being. Law, in that context, is therefore divinely inspired (natural law) or man-made. Since this is not a treatise on philosophy or morality per se, we will focus on man-made laws.

In the United States our legal system dates back to (1) the English Common-law, (2) our Declaration of Independence, which asserts as self-evident truths our rights to life, liberty, and the pursuit of happiness and (3) our own Federal Constitution, which specifies certain other rights we have as citizens, such as due process and equal protection. Our Federal Constitution, and interpretations of it made by the U. S. Supreme Court, is the supreme law of the land. That is, it supersedes decisions by lesser bodies (state legislatures and supreme courts) and even acts of the U. S. Congress, if they exceed the Congress' own constitutional powers.

As distinguished from law created by the enactment of legislatures, common law comprises those principles and rules of action, relating to the government and security of persons and property, which derive their authority solely from usages and customs of immemorial antiquity, or from the judgments and decrees of the courts recognizing, affirming, and enforcing such usages and customs; and, in this sense, particularly the ancient unwritten law of England. The ''common law'' is, therefore, all the statutory and case law background of England and the American colonies before the American Revolution.

The sources of substantive law in the United States are (1) statutes and ordinances enacted by federal, state, and local legislative bodies and regulations promulgated thereunder, (2) state and federal constitutions, and (3) the so-called common law or case law (previous opinions of state and federal supreme courts of appeal). Criminal and civil legislation is derived from the above.

Procedural law deals with the manner in which substantive laws are passed, administered, and enforced, i.e., according to due process and equal protection standards as set forth in the U. S. Constitution. For example, a criminal law passed by a state legislature that has vague or ambiguous language may be ruled unconstitutional as a matter of substantive due process. Criminal laws must be clear and understandable, so that people can know in advance that a particular act or inaction is a crime.

Criminal statutes may be enacted by all levels of government—federal, state and local. The same act, therefore, may violate a federal statute, a state statue, and a local statute, for example when an interstate trucker violates safety rules. But the elements of any particular crime may vary among these three jurisdictions. Fraud examiners must know under which statute criminal prosecution is intended, so that the appropriate evidence can be collected. (Title 18 of the U. S. Code contains the provisions of many of the federal crimes.)

CIVIL AND CRIMINAL LAWS

Civil law is that body of law that provides remedies for violations of private rights, usually in the form of money damages or court-ordered actions.

Criminal law is that branch of the law that deals with offenses of a public nature; that is, wrongs committed against the state. These laws may be imposed by state or federal statutes and usually provide penalties, fines, and/or incarceration for their breach.

Crimes can also be classified between those offenses made criminal by the common law and those offenses made criminal by statutory law. Most states, however, have chosen to codify their criminal laws, so the distinction between common-law crimes and statutory crimes is generally speaking a moot point today.

As criminal law deals with offenses committed against the state (the general public) and civil law deals with the rights and remedies of individuals, a crime is a public wrong and a tort is a private or civil wrong.

Crimes can also be distinguished between those that are called felonies and those that are called misdemeanors. A felony is a more serious crime. Felonies and misdemeanors provide different punishments. Conviction of a felony can result in a fine, loss of certain civil rights (right to vote and hold public office), and incarceration for a period exceeding one year. Misdemeanors usually provide for incarceration periods of less than a year, but fines may also be imposed.

Crimes and torts can be distinguished by the elements of proof required to sustain them in a court of law. The elements of a crime are those constituent parts that must be proved to sustain a conviction; that is, sufficient to make a prima facie case. For example, in a federal bankruptcy fraud prosecution, the government must prove (1) that there was an estate in bankruptcy, (2) that certain property belonged to that estate, (3) that the defendant concealed or transferred the property in anticipation of a bankruptcy proceeding with intent to defeat the bankruptcy law, and (4) that the defendant did these things knowingly and fraudulently.

The elements of a tort are (1) existence of a legal duty owed by the defendant to the plaintiff, (2) breach of that duty, and (3) damage to the plaintiff as a direct or proximate result.

Crimes can also be classified as to those that are *mala in se* and those that are *mala prohibita*. Crimes that are *mala in se* are said to be evil or immoral in and of themselves; they are offenses against conscience. Some of the more common of these crimes include the common-law felonies of murder, mayhem, rape, robbery, larceny, arson, and burglary.

Crimes that are *mala prohibita* are offenses that are made criminal by statute; in and of themselves they are not necessarily immoral. While crimes that are *mala in se* usually require the proving of criminal intent (*mens rea*) as an element of the crime, *mala prohibita* crimes usually don't require the proving of a criminal intent. *Mala prohibita* crimes include violations of government regulations of businesses, such as violations of the pure food and drug laws, environmental laws, traffic regulations, and the tax laws (but proof of criminal intent may be required for tax evasion).

THE LEGAL NATURE OF FRAUD

Early references to fraud in the English common law define it as cheating or deceit. A common-law cheat was one who, by false pretenses, false tokens, or intentionally false representations, induced another to part with his property and/ or his legal or equitable rights. Common-law cheating or fraud was considered both a crime (a misdemeanor as distinguished from larceny, which was a felony) and a matter for civil redress in courts of law and equity, by way of contract rescission, restoration, restitution, or recovery of damages. So fraud has a historical foothold in the English civil law as well as in criminal law.

Criminal fraud has gone by many names over the years. It has been called deception, fraud and deceit, false pretenses, larceny by trick, and embezzlement. Income tax evasion is another form of criminal fraud. But tax evasion can be treated as a civil fraud as well. Indeed, many frauds are both criminal and civil offenses, and the damaged party can both file a criminal complaint and a civil action for recovery of damages or property.

In many states, fraud now goes by the name "larceny by trick" or "false pretenses." The elements of a criminal fraud usually include (1) an intentional false representation (2) of a material fact (3) that induces someone to part with his property (4) to his financial detriment.

Fraud is a generic term, and embraces all the multifarious means which human ingenuity can devise which are resorted to by one individual to get an advantage over another by false representations. No definite and invariable rule can be laid down as a general proposition in defining fraud, as it includes surprise, trick, cunning and unfair ways by which another is cheated. The only boundaries defining it are those which limit human knavery.

The U. S. Supreme Court, in Southern Development Co. v. Silva (125 U.S. 247, 8 S.C. Rep 881, 31 L.Ed.), decided in 1887, defines civil fraud as follows:

First - That the defendant has made a representation in regard to a material fact;

Second - That such representation is false;

Third - That such representation was not actually believed by the defendant, on reasonable grounds, to be true;

Fourth - That it was made with intent that it should be acted on;

Fifth - That it was acted on by complainant to his damage; and

Sixth - That in so acting on it, the complainant was ignorant of its falsity, and reasonably believed it to be true.

The first of the foregoing requisites excludes such statements as consist merely in an expression of opinion or judgment, honestly entertained; and again, excepting peculiar cases, it excludes statements by the owner and vendor of property about its value.

Fraud versus Larceny and Embezzlement

By ordinary laymen, the words theft, fraud, embezzlement, and larceny are used interchangeably. Breach of trust or fiduciary duty, conversion, false representation, false pretenses, false tokens, false entries, and false statements are rarely used by laymen because they sound legalistic; yet they also relate to fraud. The word with the broadest connotations is theft. Theft and stealing have become so generally understood and so commonly used that they are considered generic terms for a range of crimes. The words themselves are rarely used in criminal statutes. The technical charge for the kind of behavior most of us think of as theft or stealing is "larceny."

Larceny is usually defined as the "wrongful taking and carrying away of the personal property of another with intent to convert it or to deprive the owner of its use and possession." If the taking is by stealth—surreptitiously—the crime committed is larceny. If the taking is by guile and deception, by false representation, or by concealment of that which should have been disclosed, the crime charged may be fraud. Fraud then is any kind of artifice employed by one person to deceive another.

Because of its generic use and applications, the word fraud now means behavior which may be either criminal or civil, actual or constructive (by legal construction), and in a contractual sense fraud may be found in the inducement or in the execution of a contract.

Embezzlement is the "fraudulent appropriation of property by a person to whom it has been entrusted, or to whose hands it has lawfully come." It implies a breach of trust or fiduciary responsibility.

The major distinction between larceny and embezzlement lies in the issue of the legality of custody over the article stolen. In larceny, the thief does not have "legal" custody. He "feloniously" takes the article from the owner. In embezzlement, the thief is legally authorized by the owner to take or receive the article and to possess it for a time. The formulation of intent to steal the article may occur subsequent to the time it came into his or her possession or concurrently with initial possession. If initial possession and intent to steal occur simultaneously, the crime is larceny. If intent to steal forms subsequent to initial possession, the crime is embezzlement.

Samples of typical state statutes on larceny, embezzlement, false pretenses, and forgery are as follows:

Larceny

Any person who shall commit the offense of larceny by stealing, of the property of another, any money, goods or chattels, or any bank note, bank bill, bond, promissory note, due bill, bill of exchange or other bill, draft, order or certificate, or any book of accounts for or concerning money or goods due or to become due, or to be delivered, or any deed or writing containing a conveyance of land, or any other valuable contract in force, or any receipt, release or defeasance, or any writ, process or public record, if the property stolen exceeds the value of $100 shall be guilty of a felony. If the property shall be of the value of $100 or less, such person shall be guilty of a misdemeanor. Elements of larceny:

- Actual or constructive taking
- Carrying away
- Property of another
- Without consent and against the will of the owner
- With intent to permanently deprive the owner of the property
- Value of the property over or under $100

Embezzlement (Felony over $100)

Any person who as the agent, servant, or employee of another, or as the trustee, bailee, or custodian of the property of another or of any partnership, voluntary association, public or private corporation, or of this state or of any county, city, village, township or school district within this state, shall fraudulently dispose of or convert to his own use without the consent of his principal, any money or other personal property of his principal, which shall have come to his possession or shall be under his charge or control by virtue of his being such agent, servant (etc.) shall be guilty of the crime of embezzlement.

Larceny by Conversion (Felony if over $100)

Any person to whom any money, goods or other property which may be the subject of larceny shall have been delivered, who shall embezzle or fraudulently convert to his own use, or shall secrete with the intent to embezzle, or fraudulently use such goods, money or other property, or any part thereof, shall be deemed by so doing to have committed the crime of larceny. Elements of larceny by conversion: delivery of property and fraudulent conversion or concealment

Larceny by False Personation (Felony over $100)

Any person who shall falsely personate or represent another, and in such assumed character shall receive any money, or other property whatever, intended to be delivered to the party so personated, with intent to convert the same to his own use, shall be deemed by so doing, guilty of the crime of larceny.

False Pretenses with Intent to Defraud (Obtaining Money or Goods under False Pretenses) (Misdemeanor/Felony)

Any person who, with intent to defraud or cheat, shall designedly, by color of any false token or writing or by any false or bogus check or other written, printed or engraved instrument, by spurious coin or metal in the similitude of coin, or by any other false pretense cause any person to grant, convey, assign, demise, lease or mortgage any land or interest in land, or obtain the signature of any person to any written instrument the making whereof would be punishable as forgery, or obtain from any person any money or personal property or the use of any instrument, facility or article or other valuable thing or service, or by means of any false weights or measures obtain a larger amount or quantity or property than was bargained for, if such land or interest in land, money, personal property, use of such instrument, facility or article, valuable thing, service, larger amount obtained or lesser amount disposed of, shall be of the value of $100 or less, shall be guilty of a misdemeanor; and if such land, interest in land, money, personal property, (etc.) be of the value of more than $100, such person shall be guilty of a felony, punishable by 10 years or $5,000.

Forgery of Record and Other Instruments (Felony)

Any person who shall falsely make, alter, forge or counterfeit any public record, or any certificate, return or attestation of any clerk of a court, public registrar, notary public, justice of the peace, township clerk, or any other public officer in relation to any matter wherein such certificate, return or attestation may be received as legal proof, or any charter, deed, will, testament, bond or writing obligatory, letter of attorney, policy of insurance, bill of lading, bill of exchange, or other property, or any waiver, release claim or demand, or any acceptance of a bill of exchange, or endorsement, or assignment of a bill of exchange or promissory note for the payment of money, or any accountable receipt for money, goods or other property, with intent to injure or defraud any person, shall be guilty of a felony.

FEDERAL CRIMINAL FRAUD STATUTES

Under our federal system, the prosecution of most common-law white-collar crimes, such as embezzlement, larceny, and false pretenses, is left to the states. The criminal fraud statutes in the U.S. Code require some federal jurisdictional basis, such as an effect on interstate commerce, the use of the mails, or some other federal nexus. The U.S. laws are often used to prosecute the larger and more serious crimes, primarily because of the superior resources of federal law enforcement agencies and their nationwide jurisdiction.

All federal criminal laws are the product of statutes, which come in great numbers and variety, from the trivial to the monumental; from a statute barring the unauthorized use of the Smokey the Bear emblem to the criminal provisions of the Antitrust Laws. The most important of the literally hundreds of federal laws, rules and regulations prohibiting a wide range of fraudulent conduct are cited below.

Mail Fraud (Title 18, U.S. Code, Section 1341)

The mail fraud statute is the workhorse of federal white-collar prosecutions. It has been used against virtually all types of commercial frauds, public corruption, and security law violations. The statute provides:

1341. Frauds and Swindles

Whoever, having devised or intending to devise any scheme or artifice to defraud, or for obtaining money or property by means of false or fraudulent pretenses, representations, or promises, or to sell, dispose of, loan, exchange, alter, give away, distribute, supply, or furnish or procure for unlawful use any counterfeit or spurious coin, obligation, security, or other article, or anything represented to be or intimated or held out to be such counterfeit or spurious article, for the purpose of executing such scheme or artifice or attempting so to do, places in any post office or authorized depository for mail matter, any matter or thing whatever to be sent or delivered by the Postal Service, or takes or receives therefrom, any such matter or thing, or knowingly causes to be delivered by mail according to the direction thereon, or at the place at which it is directed to be delivered by the person to whom it is addressed, any such matter or thing, shall be fined not more than $1,000 or imprisoned not more than five years, or both.

The gist of the offense is the use of the mails; without it, no matter how large or serious the fraud, there is no federal jurisdiction. The mailing does not itself need to contain the false and fraudulent representations, as long as it is an "integral" part of the scheme. What is integral or incidental depends on the facts of each case; generally any mailing which helps advance the scheme in any significant way will be considered sufficient.

"Frauds and Swindles" are not defined in the statute or elsewhere in the U.S. Code. Most of the cases treat any intentional scheme to deceive and deprive another of any tangible property right as being within the statute. Mail fraud counts have often been used in official corruption prosecutions, along with the bribery laws, under the theory that the payment or receipt of bribes deprived the public of the right to the honest and unbiased services of public servants. The Supreme Court in 1987 ruled in McNally v. United States, 107 S.Ct. 2875 (1987), that the statute's language indicated it was not intended to reach such "intangible" rights but was limited to the protection of pecuniary interests.

In 1988, however, in response to the McNally decision, Congress passed a new law, Title 18, U.S. Code, Section 1346, which states: "For the purpose of this chapter, the term 'scheme or artifice to defraud' includes a scheme or artifice to deprive another of the intangible right of honest services." Section 1346 eliminates the grounds on which the Supreme Court based its decision, and permits continued use of this effective prosecution tool.

It is not necessary that the fraudulent scheme succeed or that the victim actually suffer a loss for the statute to apply. It is also not necessary that the predicate mailing travel in interstate commerce; any use of the U.S. postal system provides sufficient grounds for federal jurisdiction.

Wire Fraud (Title 18, U.S. Code, Section 1343)

1343. Fraud by Wire, Radio, or Television

Whoever, having devised or intending to devise any scheme or artifice to defraud, or for obtaining money or property by means of false or fraudulent pretenses, representations, or promises, transmits or causes to be transmitted by means of wire, radio, or television communication in interstate or foreign commerce, any writings, signs, signals, pictures, or sounds for the purpose of executing such scheme or artifice, shall be fined not more than $1,000 or imprisoned not more than five years, or both.

The wire fraud statute is often used in tandem with mail fraud counts in federal fraud prosecutions. Unlike mail fraud, however, the wire fraud statute requires an interstate or foreign communication for a violation.

Interstate Transportation of Stolen Property (Title 18, U.S. Code, Section 2314)

The pertinent part of this statute provides:

2314. Transportation of Stolen Goods, Securities, Moneys, Fraudulent State Tax Stamps, or Articles Used in Counterfeiting

Whoever transports in interstate or foreign commerce any goods, wares, merchandise, securities or money, of the value of $5,000 or more, knowing the same to have been stolen, converted or taken by fraud; or

Whoever, having devised or intending to devise any scheme or artifice to defraud, or for obtaining money or property by means of false or fraudulent pretenses, representations, or promises transports or causes to be transported, or induces any person to travel in, or to be transported in interstate commerce in the execution or concealment of a scheme or artifice to defraud that person of money or property having a value of $5,000 or more shall be fined not more than $10,000 or imprisoned not more than ten years, or both.

Section 2314, popularly known as "ITSP," is often used in fraud prosecutions in conjunction with mail- or wire-fraud counts, or to provide federal jurisdiction in their absence, when proceeds of a value of $5,000 or more obtained by fraud are transported across state lines. The statute is also violated if a defendant induces the victim to travel in interstate commerce as part of the scheme to defraud. Individual transportation of money or other items valued at less than $5,000 as part of the same scheme may be aggregated to meet the value requirement.

Racketeer Influenced and Corrupt Organizations (RICO)
(Title 18, U.S. Code, Section 1961, et seq.)

"RICO" is probably the most well-known and controversial federal statute in use today. Originally enacted in 1970, ostensibly to fight organized crime's infiltration of legitimate business, its powerful criminal and civil provisions have been used in a wide range of fraud cases. The statute outlaws, in general, the investment of ill-gotten gains in another business enterprise, the acquisition of an interest in an enterprise through certain illegal acts, and the conduct of the affairs of an enterprise through such acts. Criminal penalties include stiff fines and jail terms, as well as the forfeiture of all illegal proceeds or interests acquired. Civil remedies include treble damages, attorney fees, dissolution of the offending enterprise, and other remedial measures.

The complex statute provides in part:

1962. Prohibited Activities

(a) It shall be unlawful for any person who has received any income derived, directly or indirectly, from a pattern of racketeering activity or through collection of an unlawful debt in which such person has participated as a principal within the meaning of Section 2, Title 18, United States Code, to use or invest, directly or indirectly, any part of such income, or the proceeds of such income, in acquisition of any interest in, or the establishment or operation of, any enterprise which is engaged in, or the activities of which affect, interstate or foreign commerce. A purchase of securities on the open market for purposes of investment, and without the intention of controlling or participating in the control of the issuer, or of assisting another to do so, shall not be unlawful under this subsection if the securities of the issuer held by the purchaser, the members of his immediate family, and his or their accomplices in any pattern or racketeering activity or the collection of an unlawful debt after such purchase do not amount in aggregate to one percent of the outstanding securities of any one class, and do not confer, either in law or in fact, the power to elect one or more directors of the issuer.

(b) It shall be unlawful for any person through a pattern of racketeering activity or through collection of an unlawful debt to acquire or maintain, directly or indirectly, any interest in or control of any enterprise which is engaged in, or the activities of which affect, interstate or foreign commerce.

(c) It shall be unlawful for any person employed by or associated with any enterprise engaged in, or the activities of which affect, interstate or foreign commerce, to conduct or participate, directly or indirectly, in the conduct of such enterprise's affairs through a pattern of racketeering activity or collection of unlawful debt.

(d) It shall be unlawful for any person to conspire to violate any of the provisions of subsection (a), (b), or (c) of this section.

1963. Criminal Penalties

(a) Whoever violates any provision of section 1962 of this chapter shall be fined not more than $25,000 or imprisoned not more than twenty years, or both, and shall forfeit to the United States, irrespective of any provision of State law—

(1) any interest the person has acquired or maintained in violation of section 1962.

1964. Civil Remedies

(a) The district courts of the United States shall have jurisdiction to prevent and restrain violations of section 1962 of this chapter by issuing appropriate orders, including, but not limited to: ordering any person to divest himself of any interest, direct or indirect, in any enterprise; imposing reasonable restrictions on the future activities or investments of any person, including, but not limited to, prohibiting any person from engaging in the same type of endeavor as the enterprise engaged in, the activities of which affect interstate or foreign commerce; or ordering dissolution or reorganization of any enterprise, making due provision for the rights of innocent persons.

(b) The Attorney General may institute proceedings under this section. Pending final determination thereof, the court may at any time enter such restraining orders or prohibitions, or take such other actions, including the acceptance of satisfactory performance bonds, as it shall deem proper.

(c) Any person injured in his business or property by reason of a violation of section 1962 of this chapter may sue therefor in any appropriate United States district court and shall recover threefold the damages he sustains and the cost of the suit, including a reasonable attorney's fee.

(d) A final judgment or decree rendered in favor of the United States in any criminal proceeding brought by the United States under this chapter shall estop the defendant from denying the essential allegations of the criminal offense in any subsequent civil proceeding brought by the United States.

Probably the most commonly used Section is 1962(c). The elements of a subsection (c) offense are:

1. The defendant was associated with an "enterprise" as defined in the statute, which may be a business, union, a group of individuals "associated in fact"; or even a single individual;

2. The enterprise was engaged in or affected interstate commerce;

3. The defendant conducted the affairs of the enterprise through a "pattern of racketeering activity," that is, two or more illegal acts, enumerated in the statute as predicate violations, such as mail and wire fraud or ITSP violations.

RICO's complexity is due in part to efforts by the draftsmen to avoid constitutional problems which voided attempted antiracketeer legislation in the 1930s. Those provisions were found to be unconstitutional because they punished the mere "status" of being a gangster, rather than any particular wrongful conduct. RICO avoids this impediment by basing its definition of "racketeering" and enhanced penalties on "patterns" of conduct defined in the statute.

The most controversial aspect of RICO is its civil provisions. Civil actions may be brought by the government or any private party injured in his or her business or property. Critics complain that private party suits have been used to reach "deep pocket" defendants, such as accounting firms, which cannot be characterized as "racketeers," and to coerce unwarranted settlements from blameless defendants fearful of possible treble-damage judgments. Supporters contend that a plaintiff cannot recover unless he or she proves fraud or other criminal acts, whoever the defendant, justifying the stigma of being alleged a "racketeer" and the award of treble damages. Several bills to repeal or amend RICO, particularly the civil provisions, have been introduced in Congress in recent years, and some amendment is widely expected.

Federal Securities Laws (The 1933 and 1934 Acts)

There are numerous federal statutes which prohibit false statements and other fraudulent activity in connection with security transactions. The most commonly used are Section 17(a) of the Securities Act of 1933 (popularly known as the "1933 Act"), and Rule 10(b)5, promulgated under the Securities Exchange Act of 1934 (the "1934 Act"). Both contain civil and administrative remedies (such as the power to initiate actions to enjoin further violations) enforced by the Securities and Exchange Commission, as well as criminal sanctions enforced by the Department of Justice. Whether a particular violation is prosecuted civilly or criminally depends in large measure on the degree of willfulness that can be proven.

Section 17(a) of the 1933 Act makes it unlawful to employ fraudulent devices or misrepresentations in connection with the "offer or sale" of securities through jurisdictional facilities (such as the U.S. mails), whereas Rule 10(b)5 prohibits the same conduct "in connection with" the "purchase or sale" of any security by "any person." Because Rule 10(b)5 has the broadest reach—including insider trading—it is the most often used. Found in Title 17, Code of Federal Regulations, Section 240.10b–5, it specifically provides:

240.10b–5. Employment of Manipulative and Deceptive Devices

It shall be unlawful for any person, directly or indirectly, by the use of any means or instrumentality of interstate commerce, or of the mails or of any facility of any national securities exchange,

(a) To employ any device, scheme, or artifice to defraud,

(b) To make any untrue statement of a material fact or to omit to state a material fact necessary in order to make the statements made, in the light of the circumstances under which they were made, not misleading, or

(c) To engage in any act, practice, or course of business which operates or would operate as a fraud or deceit upon any person, in connection with the purchase or sale of any security.

Specific intent to defraud is an essential element of a violation of Section 17(a) and 10(b)5; however, "intent to defraud" is defined more broadly in securities regulation than in other areas of common-law fraud, and includes reckless statements, as well as the knowing circulation of half truths and false opinions or predictions, which elsewhere may be considered nonactionable "puffing."

Good faith is always a defense to a section 17(a) or Rule 10(b) 5 fraud action. Intent is proven by circumstantial evidence, as in any fraud case. Violations of other indirect antifraud provisions of the federal securities laws, such as certain registrations and disclosure requirements, do not require a showing of fraudulent intent.

To be actionable, a false statement must be "material." The test for materiality is the substantial likelihood that a reasonable investor would have considered the misstated or omitted facts significant in deciding whether to invest. Materiality is most often expressed in dollar terms, or its effect on financial statements, but may also relate to serious questions of management's "integrity," regardless of the dollar amounts involved.

SEC civil actions are often settled by "consent decrees," in which the party agrees to stop the offending practice, without admitting or denying that he or she engaged in it in the first place. Violations of such decrees may be punishable as contempt with jail terms or fines.

The Foreign Corrupt Practices Act of 1977 (Title 15, U.S. Code, Section 78m(b)2)

The FCPA amended the 1934 Act to prohibit certain security issuers (publicly held companies) from making corrupt payments to foreign officials or political organizations. Other amendments to the Act, incorporated in Title 18 of the U.S. Code, make it illegal for any U.S. citizen to make such payments. The statute was the result of disclosures from the Watergate investigations of corporate "grease" payments to foreign officials to obtain business overseas. Of more current interest are the separate "books and records" provisions of the FCPA (Section 13(b)2) which require certain issuers to:

(a) make and keep books, records, and accounts, which, in reasonable detail, accurately and fairly reflect the transactions and dispositions of the assets of the issuer; and

(b) devise and maintain a system of internal accounting controls sufficient to provide reasonable assurance that—

(i) transactions are executed in accordance with management's general or specific authorization;

(ii) transactions are recorded as necessary (1) to permit preparation of financial statements in conformity with generally accepted accounting principles or any other criteria applicable to such statements, and (2) to maintain accountability for assets;

(iii) access to assets is permitted only in accordance with management's general or specific authorization; and

(iv) the recorded accountability for assets is compared with the existing assets at reasonable intervals and appropriate action is taken with respect to any differences.

SEC Regulations enforcing these provisions specifically require that:

Rule 13(b)(2)–1:

No person shall, directly or indirectly, falsify or cause to be falsified, any book, record or account subject to Section 13(b)(2)(A) of the Securities Exchange Act.

Rule 13(b)(2)–2:

(a) No director or officer of an issuer shall, directly or indirectly, make or cause to be made a materially false or misleading statement, or

(b) omit to state, or cause another person to omit to state, any material fact necessary in order to make statements made, in light of the circumstances under which such statements were made, not misleading to an accountant in connection with (1) any audit or examination of the financial statements of the issuer required to be made pursuant to this subpart or (2) the preparation of filing of any document or report required to be filed with the Commission pursuant to this subpart or otherwise.

The statute and regulations thereunder effectively give the SEC supervisory authority over the financial management and reporting functions of publicly held corporations.

Violations of the statute may be punished by corporate fines of up to $1,000,000 and fines and jail terms for individuals of up to $10,000 and 5 years, or both. Administrative and civil relief is also available.

Conspiracy (Title 18, U.S. Code Section 371)

The principal federal conspiracy statute provides:

371. Conspiracy to Commit Offense or to Defraud United States

If two or more persons conspire either to commit any offense against the United States, or any agency thereof in any manner or for any purpose, and one or more of such persons do any act to effect the object of the conspiracy, each shall be fined not more than $10,000 or imprisoned not more than five years, or both.

If, however, the offense, the commission of which is the object of the conspiracy, is a misdemeanor only, the punishment for such conspiracy shall not exceed the maximum punishment provided for such misdemeanor.

The essential elements of this deceptively simple but extremely important statute are: (1) that the conspiracy was willfully formed; (2) that the accused willfully became a member of it, and (3) that at least one of the conspirators knowingly committed at least one overt act in furtherance of the conspiracy.

The gist of the offense is a combination or agreement of two or more persons to accomplish an unlawful purpose by lawful means, or a lawful purpose by unlawful means. The purpose of the conspiracy need not be accomplished for a violation to occur; however, at least one of the co-conspirators must have carried out at least one "overt act" in furtherance of the conspiracy. The overt act need not be criminal in itself, and may be as innocuous as making a phone call or writing a letter.

Conspiracy counts are favored by the prosecution because they provide certain evidentiary and pleading advantages. If a conspiracy is shown, the acts and statements of one co-conspirator may be admitted into evidence against all, and each co-conspirator may be convicted for the underlying substantive offense (such as destroying government property) committed by any one of its members.

A corporation cannot conspire with one of its own employees to commit an offense, since the employee and employer are legally viewed as one. A corporation may, however, conspire with other business entities or third parties in violation of the statute.

Aiding and Abetting (Title 18, U.S. Code, Section 2)

The aiding and abetting statute provides:

2. Principals

(a) Whoever commits an offense against the United States or aids, abets, counsels, commands, induces or procures its commission, is punishable as a principal.

(b) Whoever willfully causes an act to be done which if directly performed by him or another would be an offense against the United States, is punishable as a principal.

Under this fundamental tenet of criminal law anyone who induces another to commit an offense, or who aids in its commission, may be charged and convicted of the underlying offense and subject to its penalties. The statute differs from a conspiracy in that, for anyone to be guilty of aiding and abetting, the underlying offense must actually be committed by someone.

Obstruction of Justice (Title 18, U.S. Code, Sections 1503, et seq.); and Perjury (Title 18, U.S. Code, Sections 1621 and 1623)

These statutes all punish efforts to impede or obstruct the investigation or trial of other substantive offenses. Prosecutors are pleased to discover such violations because they add a more sinister flavor to what may be drab white-collar charges, and help to prove underlying criminal intent. In many instances, these charges eclipse the underlying offenses and draw the stiffest penalties.

There are several "obstruction" statutes in the federal code which punish, among other things, the attempted or actual destruction of evidence, tampering with or threatening witnesses, jurors or other court personnel. Perjury is an intentional false statement on a material point given under oath. Under a related federal statute, Title 18, U.S. Code, Section 1623, the government may allege and prove perjury if the defendant makes two irreconcilable contradictory statements, without proving which is true and which is false. False and fraudulent statements, orally or in writing, made to a government agency on a material matter may also be punished as a felony under a variety of statutes, even if not given under oath.

Tax Evasion, False Returns and Failure to File (Title 26, U.S. Code, Section 7201, 7203, 7206(1), et seq.)

Fraud and corruption prosecutions may include tax evasion or false returns. Failure to file counts if, as is often the case, the recipient of illegal payments has not reported them as income, or the payor has attempted to conceal and deduct them as a legitimate business expense. Surprisingly, a company may be able to lawfully deduct commercial bribes and kickbacks as "ordinary and necessary" business expenses if the state has no commercial bribery law, or if such a statute is generally not enforced.

Bankruptcy Fraud (Title 18, United States Code, Section 151, et seq.)

Two related but somewhat different types of criminal conduct fall under the general heading of bankruptcy fraud. The first is the planned bankruptcy or "bust out" scheme, in which the wrongdoer sells off inventory obtained on credit (often through false or inflated financial statements) for cash, usually below cost, and absconds with the proceeds. Formal bankruptcy proceedings are often not initiated and the crime may be prosecuted under general fraud statutes, such as mail or wire fraud.

The second type of bankruptcy offense involves misconduct by a person or entity in a formal bankruptcy proceeding. The federal criminal laws which regulate bankruptcy proceedings are set out below.

151. Definition

As used in this chapter, the term "debtor" means a debtor concerning whom a bankruptcy petition has been filed under title 11 of the United States Code.

152. Concealment of assets; false oaths and claims; bribery

Whoever knowingly and fraudulently conceals from a custodian, trustee, marshal, or other officer of the court charged with the control or custody of property, or from creditors in any case under title 11, any property belonging to the estate of a debtor; or

Whoever knowingly and fraudulently makes a false oath or account in or in relation to any case under title 11; or

Whoever knowingly and fraudulently makes a false declaration, certificate, verification, or statement under penalty or perjury as permitted under section 1746 of title 28, United States Code, in or in relation to any case under title 11; or

Whoever knowingly and fraudulently presents any false claim for proof against the estate of a debtor, or uses any such claim in any case under title 11, personally, or by agent, proxy, or attorney, or as agent, proxy, or attorney; or

Whoever knowingly and fraudulently receives any material amount of property from a debtor after the filing of a case under title 11, with intent to defeat the provisions of title 11; or

Whoever knowingly and fraudulently gives, offers, receives or attempts to obtain any money or property, remuneration, compensation, reward, advantage, or promise thereof, for acting or forbearing to act in any case under title 11; or

Whoever, after the filing of a case under title 11 or in contemplation thereof, knowingly and fraudulently conceals, destroys, mutilates, falsifies, or makes a false entry in any document affecting or relating to the property or affairs of a debtor; or

Whoever, after the filing of a case under title 11, knowingly and fraudulently withholds from a custodian, trustee, marshal, or other officer of the court entitled to its possession, any recorded information, including books, documents, records, and papers, relating to the property or financial affairs of a debtor—

Shall be fined not more than $5,000 or imprisoned not more than five years, or both.

153. Embezzlement by trustee or officer

Whoever knowingly and fraudulently appropriates to his own use, embezzles, spends, or transfers any property or secretes or destroys any document belonging to the estate of a debtor which came into his charge as trustee, custodian, marshal, or other officer of the court—

Shall be fined not more than $5,000 or imprisoned not more than five years, or both.

154. Adverse interest and conduct of officers

Whoever, being a custodian, trustee, marshal, or other officer of the court, knowingly purchases, directly or indirectly, any property of the estate of which he is such officer in a case under title 11; or

Whoever being such officer, knowingly refuses to permit a reasonable opportunity for the inspection of the documents and accounts relating to the affairs of estates in his charge by parties in interest when directed by the court to do so—

Shall be fined not more than $500, and shall forfeit his office, which shall thereupon become vacant.

155.   Fee agreements in cases under title 11 and receiverships

Whoever, being a party in interest, whether as a debtor, creditor, receiver, trustee or representative of any of them, or attorney for any such party in interest, in any receivership or case under title 11 in any United States court or under its supervision, knowingly and fraudulently enters into any agreement, express or implied, with another such party in interest or attorney for another such party in interest, for the purpose of fixing the fees or other compensation to be paid to any party in interest or to any attorney for any party in interest for services rendered in connection therewith, from the assets of the estate, shall be fined not more than $5,000 or imprisoned not more than one year, or both.

The most commonly used of the above statutes is Section 152, which, among other things, prohibits the concealment of assets and false claims in a bankruptcy proceeding. The elements of a typical section 152 offense are:

1. that the defendant contemplated a bankruptcy proceeding,
2. that in contemplation of such a proceeding the defendant transferred or concealed assets which belonged to the bankrupt estate, and
3. that the defendant acted, knowingly and willfully, with intent to defeat the bankruptcy law.

Federal Corruption Statutes (Title 18, United States Code, Section 201, et seq.)

Chapter 11 of Title 18 of the U.S. Code, Section 201, et seq. has 19 separate criminal provisions which define and prohibit a wide variety of conflicts of interest and other corrupt and unethical conduct involving public officials. The statutes of particular interest to fraud examiners follow.

201.   Bribery of public officials and witnesses

(a) For the purpose of this section—

(1) The term "public official" means Member of Congress, Delegate, or Resident Commissioner, either before or after such official has qualified, or an officer of any department, agency or branch of Government thereof, including the District of Columbia, in any official function, under or by authority of any such department, agency, or branch of Government, or a juror;

(2) the term "person who has been selected to be a public official" means any person who has been nominated or appointed to be a public official, or has been officially informed that such person will be soon nominated or appointed; and

(3) the term ''official act'' means any decision or action on any question, matter, cause, suit, proceeding or controversy, which may at any time be pending, or which may by law be brought before any public official, in such official's official capacity, or in such official's place of trust or profit.

(b) Whoever—

(1) directly or indirectly, corruptly gives, offers or promises anything of value to any public official or person who has been selected to be a public official, or offers or promises any public official or any person who has been selected to be a public official to give anything of value to any other person or entity, with intent—

(A) to influence any official act; or

(B) to influence such public official or person who has been selected to be a public official to commit or aid in committing, or collude in, or allow, any fraud, or make opportunity for the commission of any fraud, on the United States; or

(C) to induce such public official or such person who has been selected to be a public official to do or omit to do any act in violation of the lawful duty of such official or person;

(2) being a public official or person selected to be a public official, directly or indirectly, corruptly demands, seeks, receives, accepts, or agrees to receive or accept anything of value personally or for any other person or entity, in return for:

(A) being influenced in the performance of any official act;

(B) being influenced to commit or aid in committing, or to collude in, or allow, any fraud, or make opportunity for the commission of any fraud, on the United States; or

(C) being induced to do or omit to do any act in violation of the official duty of such official or person;

(3) directly or indirectly, corruptly gives, offers, or promises anything of value to any person, or offers or promises such person to give anything of value to any other person or entity, with intent to influence the testimony under oath or affirmation of such first-mentioned person as a witness upon a trial, hearing, or other proceeding, before any court, any committee of either House or both Houses of Congress, or any agency, commission, or officer authorized by the laws of the United States to hear evidence or take testimony, or with intent to influence such person to absent himself therefrom;

(4) directly or indirectly, corruptly demands, seeks, receives, accepts or agrees to receive or accept anything of value personally or for any other person or entity in return for being influenced in testimony under oath or affirmation as a witness upon any such trial, hearing, or other proceeding, or in return for absenting himself therefrom—

Shall be fined no more than three times the monetary equivalent of the thing of value, or imprisoned for not more than fifteen years, or both, and may be disqualified from holding any office of honor, trust, or profit under the United States.

(c) Whoever—

(1) otherwise than as provided by law for the proper discharge of official duty—

(A) directly or indirectly gives, offers or promises anything of value to any public official, former public official, or person selected to be a public official, for or because of any official act performed or to be performed by such public official, former public official, or person selected to be a public official; or

(B) being a public official, former public official, or person selected to be a public official, otherwise than as provided by law for the proper discharge of official duty, directly or indirectly demands, seeks, receives, accepts, or because of any official act performed or to be performed by such official or person;

(2) directly or indirectly, gives, offers, or promises anything of value to any person, for or because of the testimony under oath or affirmation given or to be given by such person as a witness upon a trial, hearing, or other proceeding, before any court, any committee of either House or both Houses of Congress, or any agency, commission, or officer authorized by the laws of the United States to hear evidence or take testimony, or for or because of such person's absence therefrom;

(3) directly or indirectly, demands, seeks, receives, accepts, or agrees to receive or accept anything of value personally for or because of the testimony under oath or affirmation given or to be given by such person as a witness upon any such trial, hearing, or other proceeding, or for or because of such person's absence therefrom—

Shall be fined under this title or imprisoned for not more than two years, or both.

(d) Paragraphs (3) and (4) of subsection (b) and paragraphs (2) and (3) of subsection (c) shall not be construed to prohibit the payment or receipt of witness fees provided by law, or the payment, by the party upon whose behalf a witness is called and receipt by a witness, of the reasonable cost of travel and subsistence incurred and the reasonable value of time lost in attendance at any such trial, hearing, or proceeding, or in the case of expert witnesses, a reasonable fee for time spent in the preparation of such opinion, and in appearing and testifying.

(e) The offenses and penalties prescribed in this section are separate from and in addition to those prescribed in sections 1503, 1504, and 1505 of this title.

212. Offer of loan or gratuity to bank examiner

Whoever, being an officer, director or employee of a bank which is a member of the Federal Reserve System or the deposits of which are insured by the Federal Deposit Insurance Corporation, or of any National Agricultural Credit Corporation, or of any land bank, Federal Land Bank Association or other institution subject to examination by a farm credit examiner, or of any small business investment company, makes or grants any loan or gratuity, to any examiner or assistant examiner who examines or has authority to examine such bank, corporation, or institution, shall be fined not more than $5,000 or imprisoned not more than one year, or both; and may be fined a further sum equal to the money so loaned or gratuity given.

The provisions of this section and section 213 of this title shall apply to all public examiners and assistant examiners who examine member banks of the Federal Reserve System or insured banks, or National Agricultural Credit Corporations, whether appointed by the Comptroller of the Currency, by the Board of Governors of the Federal Reserve System, by a Federal Reserve Agent, by a Federal Reserve bank or by the Federal Deposit Insurance Corporation, or appointed or elected under the laws of any state; but shall not apply to private examiners or assistant examiners employed only by a clearing-house association or by the directors of a bank.

213. Acceptance of loan or gratuity by bank examiner

Whoever, being an examiner or assistant examiner of member banks of the Federal Reserve System or banks the deposits of which are insured by the Federal Deposit Insurance Corporation, or a farm credit examiner or examiner of National Agricultural Credit Corporations, or an examiner of small business investment companies, accepts a loan or gratuity from any bank, corporation, association or organization examined by him or from any person connected herewith, shall be fined not more than $5,000 or imprisoned not more than one year, or both; and may be fined a further sum equal to the money so loaned or gratuity given, and shall be disqualified from holding office as such examiner.

215. Receipt of commissions or gifts for procuring loans

(a) Whoever—

(1) corruptly gives, offers, or promises anything of value to any person, with intent to influence or reward an officer, director, employee, agent, or attorney of a financial institution in connection with any business or transaction of such institution; or

(2) as an officer, director, employee, agent, or attorney of a financial institution, corruptly solicits or demands for the benefit of any person, or corruptly accepts or agrees to accept, anything of value from any person, intending to be influenced or rewarded in connection with any business or transaction of such institution—

Shall be fined not more than $5,000 or three times the value of the thing given, offered, promised, solicited, demanded, accepted, or agreed to be accepted, whichever is greater, or imprisoned not more than five years, or both, but if the value of the thing given, offered, promised, solicited, demanded, accepted, or agreed to be accepted does not exceed $100, shall be fined not more than $1,000 or imprisoned not more than one year, or both.

(b) As used in this section, the term ''financial institution'' means—

(1) a bank with deposits insured by the Federal Deposit Insurance Corporation;

(2) an institution with accounts insured by the Federal Savings and Loan Insurance Corporation;

(3) a credit union with accounts insured by the National Credit Union Share Insurance Fund;

(4) a Federal home loan bank or a member, as defined in section 2 of the Federal Home Loan Bank Act (12 U.S.C. 1422), of the Federal home loan bank system;

(5) a Federal land bank, Federal intermediate credit bank, bank for co-operatives, production credit association, and Federal Land Bank Association;

(6) a small business investment company, as defined in section 103 of the Small Business Investment Act of 1958 (15 U.S.C. 662);

(7) a bank holding company as defined in section 2 of the Bank Holding Company Act of 1956 (12 U.S.C. 1841); or

(8) a savings and loan holding company as defined in section 408 of the National Housing Act (12 U.S.C. 1730a).

(c) This section shall not apply to bona fide salary, wages, fees, or other compensation paid, or expenses paid or reimbursed, in the usual course of business.

(d) Federal agencies with responsibility for regulating a financial institution shall jointly establish such guidelines as are appropriate to assist an officer, director, employee, agent, or attorney of a financial institution to comply with this section. Such agencies shall make such guidelines available to the public.

Section 201 is the principal federal anticorruption statute, and applies to virtually any United States official, juror, or witness. The section actually contains two separate offenses:

201(b) "Bribery," which prohibits, in general:
1. giving or receiving
2. anything of value
3. with the intent to influence
4. an official act

and the 201(c) "Illegal Gratuity" offense, which outlaws:
1. giving or receiving
2. anything of value
3. for or because of
4. an official act

The illegal gratuity statute is a lesser included offense of bribery. A bribe is a payment made with the purpose of influencing (changing) official conduct; a gratuity is a payment made to reward or compensate an official for performing duties he is already lawfully required to perform. Note that bribery is punishable by up to 15 years imprisonment, fine, and disqualification from holding public office, and that an illegal gratuity carries only a maximum two year term, a fine, or both.

Sections 212 and 213 of Title 18, U.S. Code, forbid the giving of any loan or gratuity to a bank examiner. Intent to influence or be influenced does not appear to be an element of the offense; the only reported case construing these statutes held that the prosecution need not prove that the loan or gratuity was given or received with any corrupt or wrongful intent. The strict application of the statute is justified by the public's need for disinterested bank examiners.

Section 215 bars the corrupt giving or receiving of anything of value to influence the actions of any employee or agent of a federally connected financial institution. The statute is aimed primarily at reducing corrupt influences in making loans. Unlike Sections 212 and 213 above, a specific intent to influence or be influenced through the illegal payment must be proven to obtain a conviction. Payments made after a loan has been approved and disbursed may be in violation of the law if made as part of a prearranged plan or agreement.

Embezzlement and Misapplication of Bank Funds (Title 18, United States Code, Section 656, et seq.)

Sections 656 and 657 are the principal federal embezzlement statutes. The statutes provide:

656. Theft, embezzlement, or misapplication by bank officer or employee

Whoever, being an officer, director, agent or employee of, or connected in any capacity with any Federal Reserve Bank, member bank, national bank or insured bank, or a receiver of a national bank, or any agent or employee of the receiver, or a Federal Reserve Agent, or an agent or employee of a Federal Reserve Agent or of the Board of Governors of the Federal Reserve System, embezzles, abstracts, purloins or willfully misapplies any of the moneys, funds or credits of such bank or any moneys, funds, assets or securities intrusted to the custody or care of such bank, or to the custody or care of any such agent, officer, director, employee or receiver, shall be fined not more than $5,000 or imprisoned not more than five years, or both; but if the amount embezzled, abstracted, purloined or misapplied does not exceed $100, he shall be fined not more than $1,000 or imprisoned not more than one year, or both.

As used in this section, the term "national bank" is synonymous with "National Banking Association"; "member bank" means and includes any national bank, state bank, or bank and trust company which has become a member of one of the Federal Reserve Banks; and "insured bank" includes any bank, banking association, trust company, savings bank, or other banking institution, the deposits of which are insured by the Federal Deposit Insurance Corporation.

657. Lending, credit, and insurance institutions

Whoever, being an officer, agent or employee of or connected in any capacity with the Reconstruction Finance Corporation, Federal Deposit Insurance Corporation, National Credit Union Administration, Home Owners' Loan Corporation, Farm Credit Administration, Department of Housing and Urban Development, Federal Crop Insurance Corporation, Farmers' Home Corporation, the Secretary of Agriculture acting through the Farmers' Home Administration, or any land bank, intermediate credit bank, bank for cooperatives or any lending, mortgage, insurance, credit or savings and loan corporation or association authorized or acting under the laws of the United States or any institution the accounts of which are insured by the Federal Savings and Loan Insurance Corporation, or by the Administrator of the National Credit Union Administration or any small business investment company, and whoever, being a receiver of any such institution, or agent or employee of the receiver, embezzles, abstracts, purloins or willfully misapplies any money, funds, credits, securities or other things of value belonging to such institution, or pledged or otherwise intrusted to its care, shall be fined not more than $5,000 or imprisoned not more than five years, or both; but if the amount or value embezzled, abstracted, purloined or misapplied does not exceed $100, he shall be fined not more than $1,000 or imprisoned not more than one year, or both.

Embezzlement is generally defined as the wrongful taking or conversion of the property of another by one who lawfully acquired possession of it by virtue of his office, employment or position of trust. The essential elements of a typical Section 656 violation are:

1. The defendant was an officer, director, agent or employee of
2. a federally insured bank
3. who willfully
4. "embezzled" (as defined above) funds of the bank
5. with the intent to injure or defraud the bank.

The terms "abstract," "purloin," and "misapply" as used in the statutes are largely redundant, and in normal usage simply mean to take or convert bank funds for one's own use or the use of a third party, for improper purposes, without the bank's knowledge or consent.

Section 657 prohibits the embezzlement of funds from designated federally connected lending, credit, and insurance organizations. The basic elements of a violation are the same as in section 656.

False Statements and Entries (Title 18, United States Code, Section 1001, et seq.)

Chapter 47 of Title 18, U.S. Code, contains a number of related provisions which punish false or fraudulent statements, orally or in writing, to various federal agencies and departments. The principal statute is section 1001, which prohibits such statements generally. It overlaps many of the more specific laws, such as section 1014, which applies to false statements made on certain loan and credit applications.

Section 1001 is most often used to prosecute false statements to law enforcement or regulatory officials, not made under oath, in the course of an official investigation, or on applications for federal employment, credit, visa applications, and so on. The statute, a felony, may also be used in lieu of the misdemeanor provisions of the IRS Code for filing false documents with tax returns.

The false-statement statutes of greatest importance to the fraud examiner follow.

1001. Statements or entries generally

Whoever, in any matter within the jurisdiction of any department or agency of the United States, knowingly and willfully falsifies, conceals or covers up by any trick, scheme, or device a material fact, or makes any false, fictitious or fraudulent statements or representations, or makes or uses any false writing or document knowing the same to contain any false, fictitious or fraudulent statement or entry, shall be fined not more than $10,000 or imprisoned not more than five years, or both.

1005. Bank entries, reports, and transactions

Whoever, being an officer, director, agent or employee of any Federal Reserve Bank, member bank, national bank or insured bank, without authority from the directors of such bank, issues or puts in circulation any notes of such bank; or

Whoever, without such authority, makes, draws, issues, puts forth, or assigns any certificate of deposit, draft, order, bill of exchange, acceptance, note, debenture, bond, or other obligation, or mortgage, judgment or decree; or

Whoever makes any false entry in any book, report, or statement of such bank with intent to injure or defraud such bank, or any other company, body politic or corporate, or any individual person, or to deceive any officer of such bank, or the Comptroller of the Currency, or the Federal Deposit Insurance Corporation, or any agent or examiner appointed to examine the affairs of such bank, or the Board of Governors of the Federal Reserve System—

Shall be fined not more than $5,000 or imprisoned not more than five years, or both.

1014. Loan and credit applications generally; renewals and discounts; crop insurance

Whoever knowingly makes any false statement or report, or willfully overvalues any land, property or security, for the purpose of influencing in any way the action of the Reconstruction Finance Corporation, Farm Credit Administration, Federal Crop Insurance Corporation, Farmers' Home Corporation, the Secretary of Agriculture acting through the Farmers' Home Administration, any Federal intermediate credit bank, or any division, officer, or employee thereof, or of any corporation organized under sections 1131–1134m of Title 12, or of any regional agricultural credit corporation established pursuant to law, or of the National Agricultural Credit Corporation, a Federal Home Loan Bank, the Federal Home Loan Bank Board, the Home Owners' Loan Corporation, a Federal Savings and Loan Association, a Federal Land Bank, a Federal Land Bank association, a Federal Reserve Bank, a small business investment company, a Federal credit union, an insured State-chartered credit union, any institution the accounts of which are insured by the Federal Savings and Loan Insurance Corporation, any bank the deposits of which are insured by the Federal Deposit Insurance Corporation, any member of the Federal Home Loan Bank System, the Federal Deposit Insurance Corporation, the Federal Savings and Loan Insurance Corporation, or the Administrator of the National Credit Union Administration, upon any application, advance, discount, purchase, purchase agreement, repurchase agreement, commitment, or loan, or any change or extension of any of the same, by renewal, deferment of action or otherwise, or the acceptance, release, or substitution of security therefor, shall be fined not more than $5,000 or imprisoned not more than two years, or both.

A statement is "false" for the purposes of Section 1001 if it was known to be untrue when made, and is "fraudulent" if it was known to be untrue and was made with the intent to deceive a government agency. The agency need not actually have been deceived, nor must the agency have in fact relied upon the false statement for a violation to occur. The statement must have been "material," however; that is, capable of influencing the agency involved.

The elements of a typical Section 1001 violation are:

1. The defendant made a false statement (or used a false document)
2. which was material
3. regarding a matter within the jurisdiction of any agency of the United States
4. with knowledge of its falsity
5. knowingly and willfully (or with reckless disregard for truth or falsity).

Section 1005 makes it unlawful, among other things, for any officer, director, agent or employee of a federally insured or chartered bank to make any false entries on the books of such institution with the intent to injure or defraud such bank or third parties, or to deceive any bank officer, examiners or government agency. Section 1014 prohibits false statements or reports upon any credit application or related document submitted to a federally insured bank or credit institution for the purpose of influencing the organization's actions. As with Section 1001, the false statements must be willful, but need not have been relied upon or actually deceived the agency involved for a violation to occur.

Bank Fraud (Title 18, United States Code, Section 1344, et seq.)

A relatively new federal statute makes it a crime to defraud or attempt to defraud a federally charted or insured bank. Previously such offenses were prosecuted under the more generic fraud statutes, such as mail or wire fraud. The bank fraud statute and related section 1345, which provides for civil actions by the government to enjoin fraudulent activity, are set out below.

1344. Bank fraud

(a) Whoever knowingly executes, or attempts to execute, a scheme or artifice—

(1) to defraud a federally chartered or insured financial institution; or

(2) to obtain any of the moneys, funds, credits, assets, securities, or other property owned by or under the custody or control of a federally chartered or insured financial institution by means of false or fraudulent pretenses, representations, or promises, shall be fined not more than $10,000, or imprisoned not more than five years, or both.

(b) As used in this section, the term "federally chartered" or insured financial institution" means—

(1) a bank with deposits insured by the Federal Deposit Insurance Corporation;

(2) an institution with accounts insured by the Federal Savings and Loan Insurance Corporation;

(3) a credit union with accounts insured by the National Credit Union Administration Board;

(4) a Federal home loan bank or a member, as defined in section 2 of the Federal Home Loan Bank Act (12 U.S.C. 1422), of the Federal Home Loan Bank System; or

(5) a bank, banking association, land bank, intermediate credit bank, bank for cooperatives, production credit association, land bank association, mortgage association, trust company, savings bank, or other banking or financial institution organized or operating under the laws of the United States.

1345. Injunctions against fraud

Whenever it shall appear that any person is engaged or is about to engage in any act which constitutes or will constitute a violation of this chapter, the Attorney General may initiate a civil proceeding in a district court of the United States to enjoin such violation. The court shall proceed as soon as practicable to the hearing and determination of such an action, and may, at any time before final determination, enter such a restraining order or prohibition, or take such other action, as is warranted to prevent a continuing and substantial injury to the United States or to any person or class of persons for whose protection this action is brought. A proceeding under this section is governed by the Federal Rules of Civil Procedure, except that, if an indictment has been returned against the respondent, discovery is governed by the Federal Rules of Criminal Procedure.

As in the mail and wire fraud statutes, the terms "scheme" and "artifice" to defraud include any misrepresentations or other conduct intended to deceive others in order to obtain something of value. The prosecution must prove only an attempt to execute the scheme, and need not show actual loss, or that the victim institution was actually deceived, or that the defendant personally benefitted from the scheme.

Fraud in Connection with Federal Interest Computers (Title 18, United States Code, Section 1030)

"Computer crime" is a new and somewhat amorphous term, referring both to cases in which a computer is the instrument of a crime and those in which it is the object. As the instrument, for example, a computer may be used to direct calls in an otherwise routine fraud scheme to sell shares in a nonexistent gold mine, or may be used to steal funds from a bank account. As the object of a crime, the information contained in a computer may be stolen or destroyed.

Most computer crimes of either type are prosecuted under traditional fraud, theft, and embezzlement statutes. A statute enacted in 1984, Title 18, U.S. Code, Section 1030, makes certain computer-related activity a specific federal offense. The lengthy statute provides:

1030. Fraud and related activity in connection with computers

(a) Whoever—

(1) knowingly accesses a computer without authorization or exceeds authorized access, and by means of such conduct obtains information that has been determined by the United States Government pursuant to an Executive order or statute to require protection against unauthorized disclosure for reasons of national defense or foreign relations, or any restricted data, as defined in paragraph r of section 11 of the Atomic Energy Act of 1954, with the intent or reason to believe that such information so obtained is to be used to the injury of the United States, or to the advantage of any foreign nation;

(2) intentionally accesses a computer without authorization or exceeds authorized access, and thereby obtains information contained in a financial record of a financial institution or of a card issuer as defined in section 1602(n) of title 15, or contained in a file of a consumer reporting agency on a consumer, as such terms are defined in the Fair Credit Reporting Act (15 U.S.C. 1681 et seq.);

(3) intentionally, without authorization to access any computer of a department or agency of the United States, accesses such a computer of that department or agency that is exclusively for the use of the Government of the United States or, in the case of a computer not exclusively for such use, is used by or for the Government of the United States and such conduct affects the use of the Government's operation of such computer;

(4) knowingly and with intent to defraud, accesses a Federal interest computer without authorization, or exceeds authorized access, and by means of such conduct furthers the intended fraud and obtains anything of value, unless the object of the fraud and the thing obtained consists only of the use of the computer; Shall be punished as proved in subsection (c) of this section.

(5) intentionally accesses a Federal interest computer without authorization, and by means of one or more instances of such conduct alters, damages or destroys information in any such Federal interest computer, or prevents authorized use of any such computer or information, and thereby—
    (A) causes loss to one or more others of a value aggregating $1,000 or more during any one year period; or
    (B) modifies or impairs, or potentially modifies or impairs, the medical examination, medical diagnosis, medical treatment, or medical care of one or more individuals; or

(6) knowingly and with intent to defraud traffics (as defined in section 1029) in any password or similar information through which a computer may be accessed without authorization, if—
    (A) such trafficking affects interstate or foreign commerce; or
    (B) such computer is used by or for the Government of the United States;

(b) Whoever attempts to commit an offense under subsection (a) of this section shall be punished as provided in subsection (c) of this section.

(c) The punishment for an offense under subsection (a) or (b) of this section is—

(1)(A) a fine under this title or imprisonment for not more than ten years, or both, in the case of an offense under subsection (a)(1) of this section which does not occur after a conviction for another offense under such subsection, or an attempt to commit an offense punishable under this subparagraph; and

(1)(B) a fine under this title or imprisonment for not more than twenty years, or both, in the case of an offense under subsection (a)(1) of this section which occurs after a conviction for another offense under such subsection, or an attempt to commit an offense punishable under this subparagraph; and

(2)(A) a fine under this title or imprisonment for not more than one year, or both, in the case of an offense under subsection (a)(2), (a)(3) or (a)(6) of this section which does not occur after a conviction for another offense under such subsection, or an attempt to commit an offense punishable under this subparagraph; and

(2)(B) a fine under this title or imprisonment for not more than ten years, or both, in the case of an offense under subsection (a)(2), (a)(3) or (a)(6) of this section which occurs after a conviction for another offense under such subsection, or an attempt to commit an offense punishable under this subparagraph; and

(3)(A) a fine under this title or imprisonment for not more than five years, or both, in the case of an offense under subsection (a)(4) or (a)(5) of this section which does not occur after a conviction for another offense under such subsection, or an attempt to commit an offense punishable under this subparagraph; and

(3)(B) a fine under this title or imprisonment for not more than ten years, or both, in the case of an offense under subsection (a)(4) or (a)(5) of this section which occurs after a conviction for another offense under such subsection, or an attempt to commit an offense punishable under this subparagraph.

(d) The United States Secret Service shall, in addition to any other agency having such authority, have the authority to investigate offenses under this section. Such authority of the United States Secret Service shall be exercised in accordance with an agreement which shall be entered into by the Secretary of the Treasury and the Attorney General.

(e) As used in this section—

(1) the term "computer" means an electronic magnetic, optical, electrochemical, or other high speed data processing device performing logical, arithmetic, or storage functions, and includes any data storage facility or communications facility directly related to or operating in conjunction with such device, but such term does not include an automated typewriter or typesetter, a portable hand held calculator, or other similar device;

(2) the term "Federal interest computer" means a computer—
(A) exclusively for the use of a financial institution or the United States Government, or, in the case of a computer not exclusively for such use, used by or for a financial institution or the United States

Government and the conduct constituting the offense affects the use of the financial institution's operation or the Government's operation of such computer; or

(B) which is one of two or more computers used in committing the offense, not all of which are located in the same State;

(3) the term "State" includes the District of Columbia, the Commonwealth of Puerto Rico, and any other possession or territory of the United States;

(4) the term "financial institution" means—

(A) a bank with deposits insured by the Federal Deposit Insurance Corporation;

(B) the Federal Reserve or a member of the Federal Reserve including any Federal Reserve Bank;

(C) an institution with accounts insured by the Federal Savings and Loan Insurance Corporation;

(D) a credit union with accounts insured by the National Credit Union Administration;

(E) a member of the Federal Home Loan Bank System and any home loan bank;

(F) any institution of the Farm Credit System under the Farm Credit Act of 1971;

(G) a broker-dealer registered with the Securities and Exchange Commission pursuant to section 15 of the Securities Exchange Act of 1934; and

(H) the Securities Investor Protection Corporation;

(5) the term "financial record" means information derived from any record held by a financial institution pertaining to a customer's relationship with the financial institution;

(6) the term "exceeds authorized access" means to access a computer with authorization and to use such access to obtain or alter information in the computer that the accesser is not entitled so to obtain or alter; and

(7) the term "department of the United States" means the legislative or judicial branch of the Government or one of the executive departments enumerated in section 101 of title 5.

(f) This section does not prohibit any lawfully authorized investigative, protective, or intelligence activity of a law enforcement agency of the United States, a State, or a political subdivision of a State, or of an intelligence agency of the United States.

In brief, section 1030 punishes any intentional, unauthorized access to "federal interest" computers for the purpose of:

1. obtaining restricted data regarding national security

2. obtaining confidential financial information

3. using a computer which is intended for use by the United States government

4. committing a fraud, or

5. damaging or destroying information contained in the computer.

The Electronic Funds Transfer Act (15 U.S.C. 1693n) provides, in part, that whoever:

1) knowingly, in a transaction affecting interstate or foreign commerce, uses or attempts or conspires to use any counterfeit, fictitious, altered, forged, lost, stolen, or fraudulently obtained debit instrument to obtain money, goods, services, or anything else of value, which within any one-year period has a value aggregating $1,000 or more; or

2) with unlawful or fraudulent intent, transports or attempts or conspires to transport in interstate or foreign commerce a counterfeit, fictitious, altered, forged, lost, stolen, or fraudulently obtained debit instrument knowing the same to be counterfeit, fictitious, altered, forged, lost, stolen or fraudulently obtained: or

3) with unlawful or fraudulent intent, uses any instrumentality of interstate or foreign commerce to sell or transport a counterfeit, fictitious, altered, forged, lost, stolen, or fraudulently obtained debit instrument knowing the same to be counterfeit, fictitious, altered, forged, lost, stolen, or fraudulently obtained, or

4) knowingly receives, conceals, uses or transports money, goods, services, or anything else of value (except tickets for interstate or foreign transportation) which (A) within any one-year period has a value aggregating $1,000 or more, (B) has moved in or is part of, or which constitutes interstate or foreign commerce, and (C) has been obtained with a counterfeit, fictitious, altered, forged, lost, stolen, or fraudulently obtained debit instrument; or

5) in a transaction affecting interstate or foreign commerce, furnishes money, property, services, or anything else of value, which within any one-year period has a value aggregating $1,000 or more, through the use of any counterfeit, fictitious, altered, forged, lost, stolen, or fraudulently obtained debit instrument knowing the same to be counterfeit, fictitious, altered, forged, lost, stolen, or fraudulently obtained . . . shall be fined no more than $10,000 or imprisoned not more than ten years, or both.

As used in this section, the term "debit instrument" means a card, code, or other device, other than a check, draft, or similar paper instrument, by the use of which a person may initiate an electronic fund transfer.

Prosecuting Computer-Related Frauds

Federal and state legislatures have moved very quickly to make criminal all manner of computer frauds and abuses, such as hardware theft and destruction, misappropriation of software, unauthorized accessing of computers and data communications facilities to steal data or money or to cause mischief.

The basic federal law on computer crime codified in Title 18 U.S.C. 1030(a)(4) makes it illegal when one "knowingly and with intent to defraud, accesses a Federal interest computer without authorization, or exceeds authorized access, and by means of such conduct furthers the intended fraud and obtains anything of value, unless the object of the fraud and thing obtained consist only of the use of the computer.''

A ''federal interest'' computer, under that code, means (1) a computer owned and/or used by the federal government, (2) one owned by and/or used by a financial institution, and (3) one of two or more computers used in committing an offense in which not all the computers are located in the same state. The elements of that crime seem to include (1) unauthorized access (or exceeding one's authority), (2) an intent to defraud, and (3) obtaining anything of value. Software, as a thing of value, would seem to be included. Certainly money is included.

Section 1030 (1)(5) of that law provides that anyone who accesses a ''federal interest'' computer without authorization and alters information or destroys it and causes a loss of $1,000 or more in one year commits a felony. The penalty for violations of Sections 1030 (a)(4) and 1030(a)(5) of Title 18 U.S.C. is up to five years of imprisonment, and substantial fines for repeat offenders.

The Federal Computer Fraud and Abuse Act of 1984 (as amended in 1986) does not cover the full body of computer abuses. Its language for example, does not make it a criminal offense to copy software or misappropriate computer data. Furthermore, it doesn't cover the unauthorized accessing of computers owned by private businesses nor by state governments. However, most states have now enacted laws that make unauthorized access of computers a crime. And some state statutes, such as New York, forbid unauthorized duplication and possession of computer data.

At the state level, statutes that may be of use in prosecuting computer crimes would include the penal code violations of larceny (in its many forms), false pretenses, forgery, fraud, embezzlement, vandalism, property destruction, malicious mischief, proprietary information, theft, commercial bribery, extortion, etc. But most states now expressly provide penalties for crimes perpetrated by way of computers or perpetrated against computers.

OTHER FRAUD SPECIES

Deceit. A fraudulent and deceptive misrepresentation, artifice or device used by one or more persons to deceive and trick another who is ignorant of the true facts, to the prejudice and damage of the party imposed upon (People v. Chadwick, 143 Cal. 116).

Defalcation. The act of a defrauder; misappropriation of trust funds or money held in any fiduciary capacity; failure to properly account for such funds. Usually spoken of officers of corporations or public officials (In re Butts, D.D., N.Y., 120 F 970; Crawford v. Burke, 201 Ill. 581, 66 N.E. 833).

False and Misleading Statement. Failure to state material fact made a letter a ''false and misleading statement'' within rule of Securities and Exchange Commission (SEC v. Okin, C.C. A. N.Y., 132 F 2d 784, 787).

False Entry. An entry in books of a bank or trust company which is intentionally made to represent what is not true or does not exist, with intent either to deceive its officers or a bank examiner or to defraud the bank or trust company (Agnew v. U.S., 165 U.S. 36).

False Pretenses. Designed misrepresentation of existing facts or condition whereby person obtains another's money or goods (People v. Gould, 363 Ill. 348). (Example: giving a worthless check.)

False Representation. A representation which is untrue, willfully made to deceive another to his injury.

False Statement. Under statutory provision making it unlawful for officer or director of corporation to make any false statement in regard to corporation's financial condition, the phrase means something more than merely untrue or erroneous but implies that the statement is designed to be untrue and deceitful and made with intention to deceive the person to whom false statement is made or exhibited (State v. Johnston, 149 S.C. 138).

False Token. In criminal law, a false document or sign of the existence of a fact—in general used for the purpose of fraud. (Example: counterfeit money.)

Falsify. To counterfeit or forge; to make something false; to give a false appearance to anything. To make false by mutilation or addition; to tamper with, as to falsify a record or document (Pov v. Ellis, 66 Fla. 358).

Forgery. The false making or material altering, with intent to defraud, of anything in writing which, if genuine, might apparently be of legal efficiency or the foundation of a legal liability (People v. Routson, 354 Ill. 573).

Fraudulent Concealment. The hiding or suppression of a material fact or circumstance which the party is legally or morally bound to disclose (Magee v. Insurance Co., 92 U.S. 93).

Fraudulent Conversion. Receiving into possession money or property of another and fraudulently withholding, converting, or applying the same to or for one's own use and benefit, or to use and benefit of any person other than the one to whom the money or property belong (Commonwealth v. Mitchneck, 130 Pa. Super. 433).

Fraudulent or Dishonest Act. One which involves bad faith, a breach of honesty, a want of integrity, or moral turpitude (Hartford Acc. and Indemn. Co. v. Singer, 185 Va. 629).

Fraudulent Representation. A false statement as to material fact, made with intent that another rely thereon, which is believed by other party and on which he relies and by which he is induced to act and does act to his injury; and statement is fraudulent if speaker knows statement to be false or if it is made with utter disregard of its truth or falsity (Osborne v. Simmons, No. App., 23 S.W. 2d 1102).

Malfeasance. Evil doing; ill conduct; the commission of some act which is wholly wrongful and unlawful; the doing of an act which a person ought not to do at all, or the unjust performance of some act which the party had no right or which he had contracted not to do. Comprehensive term including any wrongful conduct that affects, interrupts or interferes with the performance of official duties (State ex. rel. Knabb v. Frater, 198 Was. 675, 89P. 2d 1046, 1048).

Misapplication. Improper, illegal, wrongful, or corrupt use or application of funds, property, etc. (Jewett v. U.S., C.C.A., Mass., 100 F. 841, 41 C.C.A. 88).

Misappropriation. The act of misappropriating or turning to a wrong purpose; wrong appropriation; a term which does not necessarily mean peculation, although it may mean that (Bannon v. Knauss, 57 Ohio App. 228).

FIDUCIARY DUTIES OF CORPORATE OFFICERS AND DIRECTORS

Corporate officers and directors are said to be bound or obligated to act in the utmost good faith, give the enterprise the benefit of their care and best judgment, and exercise their powers in the best interest of the stockholders. As agents of the corporation, directors and officers are held liable as trustees for the corporation and its stockholders.

Fraudulent or tortious acts of corporate officers and directors, or any act beyond their powers that causes a loss to the corporation, will require them to reimburse the corporation from their own estates. They also cannot appropriate corporate property for their own purposes, nor waste, squander, convert or misapply corporate property. These acts also require reimbursement for loss to the corporation.

Corporate officers and directors owe a due care and diligence to the corporation. Any breach of such duties makes them liable for losses and injuries that are the proximate results thereof.

The degree of care and diligence required is difficult to measure. The degree of care depends on the particular circumstances of a case and the customs or usages of business. In general, officers and directors should exercise ordinary care and diligence as required by the so-called "prudent man" theory. (In essence, "what would an ordinary, reasonable, prudent officer or director do under like or similar circumstances?") Generally speaking, an error in judgment is excusable if reasonable care, diligence and good faith have been executed.

A corporate officer or director is not entitled to any secret profit or advantage by reason of official position (insider trading, for example). As a general rule, all secret profit is against the law for an officer or director.

Corporate directors are not sureties (guarantors) to the corporation for the fidelity of an inferior officer or agent appointed by them. They are not liable for embezzlements and defalcations, if they have acted prudently and in good faith and had no knowledge that their agent was untrustworthy.

RULES OF EVIDENCE

In a broad sense, evidence is anything perceptible by the five senses such as testimony of witnesses, records, documents, facts, data, or concrete objects, legally presented at a trial to prove a contention and induce a belief in the minds of the court or jury. In weighing evidence, the court or jury may consider such things as the demeanor of a witness, his or her bias for or against an accused, and any relationship to the accused. Thus evidence can be testimonial, circumstantial, demonstrative, inferential, and even theoretical when given by a qualified expert. Evidence is simply anything that proves or disproves any matter in question.

Witnesses, other than experts, cannot generally testify as to probabilities, opinions, assumptions, impressions, generalizations, or conclusions but only as to things, people, and events they have seen, felt, tasted, smelled, or heard firsthand. And even those things must be legally and logically relevant. Logical relevancy means that the evidence being offered must tend to prove or disprove a fact or consequence. But even if logically relevant, a court may exclude evidence if it is likely to inflame or confuse a jury or consume too much time. And testimony as to the statistical probability of guilt is considered too prejudicial and unreliable to be accepted.

Evidence can be direct or circumstantial. Direct evidence proves a fact directly; if the evidence is believed, the fact is established. Circumstantial evidence proves the desired fact indirectly and depends on the strength of the inferences raised by the evidence. For example, a letter properly addressed, stamped, and mailed is assumed (inferred) to have been received by the addressee. Testimony that a letter was so addressed, stamped, and mailed raises an inference that it was received. But the inference may be rebutted by testimony that it was not in fact received.

Some evidentiary matters considered relevant and therefore admissible are:

1. The motive for a crime
2. The ability of the defendant to commit the specific crime
3. The opportunity to commit the crime
4. Threats or expressions of ill will by the accused
5. The means of committing the offense (possession of a weapon, tool, or skills used in committing the crime)
6. Physical evidence at the scene linking the accused to the crime
7. The suspect's conduct and comments at the time of arrest
8. The attempt to conceal identity
9. The attempt to destroy evidence
10. Valid confessions

The materiality rule requires that evidence must have an important value to a case or prove a point-in-issue. Unimportant details only extend the period of time for trial. Accordingly, a trial court judge may rule against the introduction of evidence that is repetitive or additive (that merely proves the same point in another way), or evidence that tends to be remote even though relevant. Materiality then is the degree or relevancy of the matter. The court cannot become preoccupied with trifles or unnecessary details.

Competency of evidence means that which is sufficient, reliable, and relevant to the case and presented by a qualified and capable (and sane) witness. But competency differs from credibility. Competency is a question that arises before considering the evidence given by a witness; credibility is one's veracity. Competency is for the judge to determine; credibility is for the jury to decide.

Judicial notice is a process by which a judge may, on his own motion and without the production of evidence, recognize the existence of certain facts that bear on the controversy he is trying. For example, he may elect to judicially notice that a state law on a certain subject exists, that mixing oxygen and hydrogen in a certain combination will produce water, or that July 4, 1988, fell on a Monday.

The "best evidence" rule deals with written documents proffered as evidence. The rule requires that if the contents of the document are in issue, the original, if available, and not a copy thereof, must be presented at a trial. If the original has been destroyed or is in the hands of an opposite party and not subject to legal process by search warrant or subpoena, then an authenticated copy may be substituted. Business records and documents kept in the ordinary course of business may be presented as evidence, too, even though the person who made the entries or prepared the documents is unavailable.

Photocopies of original business documents and other writings and printed matter are often made to preserve evidence. These are used by examiners so that original records needed to run a business are not removed. In the event of an inadvertent destruction of originals a certified true copy of the document is still available as proof. The certified copy may also be used by examiners to document their case reports. At trial, however, the original document—if still available—is the best evidence and must be presented.

To introduce secondary evidence, one must explain satisfactorily the absence of the original document to the court. Secondary evidence is not restricted to photocopies of the document; it may consist of testimony of witnesses or transcripts of the document's contents. Whereas the federal courts give no preference to the type of secondary evidence, the majority of other jurisdictions do. Under the majority rule, testimony (parol evidence) will not be allowed to prove the contents of a document if there is secondary documentary evidence available to prove its contents. However, before secondary evidence of the original document may be introduced, the party offering the contents of the substitute must have used all reasonable and diligent means to obtain the original. Again, this is a matter to be determined by the court.

When the original document has been destroyed by the party attempting to prove its contents, secondary evidence will be admitted if the destruction was in the ordinary course of business, or by mistake, or even intentionally, provided it was not done for any fraudulent purpose.

Burden of Proof

The burden of proof in a criminal case is the burden the state carries of proving the guilt of an accused beyond a reasonable doubt. In civil litigation, the burden of proof is on the plaintiff to prove his case by a preponderance of the evidence, which is less than proof beyond a reasonable doubt. In a criminal case, when the prosecution produces evidence beyond a reasonable doubt on each element of a crime to the point where a prima facie case has been made, the defendant can be convicted, unless he or she accepts the burden of going forward and introduces evidence that tends to challenge or controvert the damaging evidence against him.

Presumptions and Inferences

A presumption is a rule of law by which finding of a basic fact gives rise to the existence of a presumed fact, until the presumption is rebutted (Van Wart v. Cook, Okl. App., 557 P. 2nd 1161, 1163). A presumption, therefore, shifts the burden of going forward with evidence to the other side to rebut it. But it doesn't shift the burden of proof.

The presumption of innocence, on the other hand, means that in a criminal case, the state has the burden of proving each element of a crime beyond a reasonable doubt. The defendant, therefore, has no burden to prove innocence.

An inference is a derived truth, i.e., a process of reasoning from other facts which have not been controverted. In essence, an inference is a deduction or conclusion.

Other Rules of Evidence

The chain-of-custody rule requires that when evidence in the form of document or object is seized at a crime scene, or as a result of a subpoena *duces tecum* (for documents), or discovered in the course of a fraud examination, it should be marked, identified, inventoried, and preserved to maintain it in its original condition. This is to establish a clear chain of custody until it is introduced at the trial. If gaps in possession or custody occur, the evidence may be challenged at the trial on the theory that it may not be the original (or is not in its original condition) and therefore is of doubtful authenticity.

For a seized document to be admissible as evidence, it is necessary to prove that it is the same document that was obtained, and that it is in the same condition as it was when obtained. Because several persons may handle it before the trial, it should be adequately marked at the time for later identification, and its custody must be shown from that time until it is introduced in court.

The rule supporting privileged communications is based on the belief that it is necessary to maintain the confidentiality of certain communications. It covers only those communications that are a unique product of the protected relationship. The basic reason behind these protected communications is the belief that the protection of certain relationships is more important to society than the possible harm resulting from the loss of such evidence. Legal jurisdictions vary as to what communications are protected. Some of the more prevalent claims to privileged relationships are:

1. Attorney-client
2. Husband-wife
3. Physician-patient
4. Priest-penitent
5. Law enforcement officer-informant
6. Reporter-source
7. Accountant-client (not recognized in federal courts)

When dealing with privileged communications, the following basic principles should be considered:

1. Only the holder of a privilege, or someone authorized by the holder, can assert the privilege.
2. If the holder fails to assert it after having notice and opportunity to assert it, the privilege is waived.
3. The privilege may also be waived if the holder discloses a significant part of the communication to a party not within the protected relationship.
4. The communication, to be within the privilege, must be sufficiently related to the relationship protected (for example, communications between an attorney and client must be related to legal consultation).

It should be noted that under common law a person cannot testify against his or her spouse in a criminal trial. While married, neither may waive this testimonial incompetence. This witness incompetency must be distinguished from the confidential communications between spouses made and completed during the marriage, which retain the privileged status after the marriage has ceased.

Conversations in the known presence of third parties do not fall within the purview of privileged communications. The protected communications are those that are, in fact, confidential or induced by the marriage or other relationship. Ordinary conversations relating to matters not deemed to be confidential are not within the purview of the privilege.

Whenever a fraud examiner is confronted with the need to use evidence in the nature of communications between parties in one of these relationships, he or she should consult with counsel, especially if the evidence is crucial to the case.

The hearsay rule is based on the theory that testimony that merely repeats what some other person said should not be admitted because of the possibility of distortion or misunderstanding. Furthermore, the person who made the actual statement is unavailable for cross-examination and has not been sworn in as a witness. Generally speaking, witnesses can testify only to those things of which they have personal and direct knowledge, not conclusions or opinions.

But there are occasions—exceptions—when hearsay evidence is admissible. Some examples:

1. Dying declarations, either verbal or written
2. Valid confessions
3. Tacit admissions
4. Public records that do not require an opinion but speak for themselves
5. *Res gestae* statements—spontaneous explanations, if spoken as part of the criminal act or immediately following the commission of such criminal act
6. Former testimony given under oath
7. Business entries made in the normal course of doing business

A confession is the acknowledgment of all the facts upon which a criminal conviction can stand. An admission falls somewhat short of a full confession. A statement against interest is a prior acknowledgment of a material fact relevant to an issue now being litigated, and prior acknowledgment is at variance with the person's current claim. For example, in a tax evasion prosecution, evidence in the form of a financial statement submitted for credit or life insurance that shows a higher net worth than now claimed may be used in evidence against the defendant.

A *res gestae* statement is a spontaneous comment made by a defendant at a time of great emotional strain, i.e., at the time of arrest or at the scene of an accident. The theory is that such a statement made at such a time is likely to be truthful.

The shopbook rule is an exception to the hearsay rule in that books of original entry kept in the regular course of business can be introduced in court by someone who has custody of them but who may not have made the entries therein. However, the custodian must authenticate the records, i.e., testify that he or she is custodian, that entries are original (not copies) and that the entries are made contemporaneously with the transactions described therein.

The official records rule allows the introduction of books, records, reports, and compilations kept as a regular and routine duty by a public official. Testimony as to the character and reputation of an accused may be admissible under certain conditions, even though it would seem to violate the hearsay rule. Such testimony may be admitted when character is an element of the action; that is, when the mental condition or legal competency of the accused is in question.

Evidence of other crimes committed by an accused is not generally admissible to prove character. It may be admitted for other purposes, however, such as proof of motive, opportunity or intent to commit an act.

The credibility of a witness may also be attacked by showing that he or she was convicted of a serious crime (punishable by death or imprisonment for more than a year) or for such crimes as theft, dishonesty, or false statement. Such conviction should have occurred recently—usually within the last ten years.

Expert testimony is opinion evidence given by a person who possesses special skills and knowledge in a science, profession, or business. These skills and knowledge are not common to the average person. The expert's testimony is, therefore, intended to assist the judge to determine a fact in issue.

When an expert witness is called upon to testify, a foundation must be laid before testimony is accepted or allowed. Laying a foundation means the witness's expertise must be established before a professional opinion is rendered. Qualifying a witness as an expert means demonstrating to the judge's satisfaction that by formal education, advanced study, and experience the witness is knowledgeable about the topic upon which his or her testimony will bear. The testimony of experts is an exception to the hearsay rule.

While all of the following characteristics are not necessary to qualify a witness as an expert, they are listed to give the reader a comprehensive view of the matter:

1. Professional licensure, certification, or registration by a recognized professional body in the field of expertise in question.

2. Relevant undergraduate, graduate, and postgraduate academic degrees directly in the field of expertise or a suitable background to it.

3. Specialized training and/or continuing professional education beyond academic degrees that indicates up-to-date familiarity with the latest technical developments in the expert's subject area.

4. The expert's writings and publications that display technical opinions and are available as part of the general body of knowledge in the subject area.

5. Relevant teaching, lecturing and/or other consulting undertaken by the expert which indicates that he or she is held in high professional esteem in the given subject area.

6. Professional associations with which the expert is affiliated.

7. Directly relevant prior experience which the expert has gained through undertaking similar assignments, whether as technical advisor or expert witness, in the given subject area.

8. Special status, or access to privileged information peculiar to the case at hand which renders the individual an expert because he or she is in possession of unique facts.

5 Criminal and Civil Justice

BASIC PRINCIPLES OF CRIMINAL LAW

A defendant in any United States or state court is presumed innocent, has the right to remain silent, to confront accusers, to be advised by counsel, to have a speedy trial in front of a jury of peers, and to other well-known protections. The government bears the entire burden of proving the accused guilty beyond a reasonable doubt. Thus, our system of justice is adversarial, rather than inquisitorial (in which the defendant is presumed guilty, and the evidence to convict him is extracted from his or her own mouth).

The protection afforded an accused in our courts after being placed in custody are extensive. They have been so engrafted on our procedures that it is but a slight exaggeration to say that it takes longer for a judge in this country to determine the legality of an arrest than it does an English court to try, convict, and sentence an accused. Numerous attempts to loosen these rights, usually in response to public dismay over perceived rising crime rates, have failed. Perhaps this is in part because, even with the prosecution's heavy burden, more than 90 percent of prosecutions end in convictions.

The Court System

Criminal cases are heard by courts at virtually all levels of government, from municipalities enforcing their own ordinances to state and federal courts. The power of any court to hear a case and render a judgment is strictly limited to its lawful jurisdiction. This is defined by both geographical boundaries and the specific powers granted it by the legislature. This reflects the basic constitutional principle of separation of powers: the legislature, elected popularly, enacts the laws, the executive (state or federal prosecutors) enforces them (with a great deal of discretion as to when and what to prosecute), and the judiciary interprets and applies them. If a law proves unpopular, the court is obliged to apply it until amended or repealed by the legislature.

Appeals from decisions of the District Courts are heard in the U.S. Court of Appeals for the circuit which covers a particular geographical area. The United States at present is divided into eleven judicial circuits, plus the District of Columbia. The U.S. Supreme Court is the highest appellate court in the federal system, and may also hear certain appeals from state courts, particularly on constitutional grounds.

In the trial court, the jury finds the facts and the judge applies the law, rules on evidence, and generally moderates the proceeding to assure a fair trial. If a jury trial is waived by the defendant and government, the judge decides both the facts and the law.

Appeals may be taken only on questions of law, not questions of fact. Questions of law are decided by precedent; that is, prior decisions of courts of equal or higher authority that have considered similar cases. The reliance on an accumulated body of case law is the principal feature distinguishing the common law of England and the United States. In civil code systems in continental Europe and elsewhere, every case is decided separately and anew, solely by reference to the applicable code provision, by each individual judge.

Generally, because of the double jeopardy provisions of the Fifth Amendment, only a convicted defendant can appeal a verdict. The government cannot appeal an acquittal, no matter how entered or how egregious the decision. The prosecution, may, however, appeal adverse pretrial rulings on the admissibility of evidence and certain other matters which may terminate a prosecution temporarily, but do not result in a decision on the merits in favor of the defendant.

An appellate court will not reverse a conviction unless it finds error that affected the "substantial rights" of the defendant; "harmless error," not affecting the jury's decision, is tolerated. If the appellate court reverses, it will usually order a new trial, but may direct dismissal of the case if there is some clear legal impediment to the charges.

If the appellate court affirms the conviction, the defendant may attempt an appeal to the highest court in the jurisdiction. In the federal system, an appeal to the U.S. Supreme Court is accomplished by applying for a writ of certiorari. Relatively few appeals—writs—are granted. Usually only those cases which present important questions of constitutional law, or which may be used to resolve a split or disagreement on a point of law among the circuits, or which have considerable significance to the judicial systems beyond the interest of the litigants, are heard. If the Supreme Court "denies cert" the lower court decision stands and the appeal process ends, unless the defendant can find some collateral ground, such as alleged constitutional errors in state court proceedings, to attack the judgment. As recent death penalty challenges illustrate, appeals on such points, often brought by persons in custody under habeas corpus proceedings, can in extreme cases consume a decade or more.

Of course, the various state and federal courts operate in separate spheres, confined by their own jurisdictional limitations. State courts are inferior to federal courts only in the sense that they are subject to constitutional and "federal question" limitations. Absent these factors, a federal court will not interfere in state court proceedings. A single criminal act may violate both state and federal law. Generally an offender may be convicted and sentenced, to separate terms, for both violations, although one jurisdiction will usually abstain if the other has already prosecuted.

Investigative Procedures and the Law

The duty of a fraud examiner is to document violations of law with proofs and to gather those proofs in such a manner that the suspect's legal rights are not transgressed. Proofs may consist of confessions given freely by violators, statements from witnesses who observed the criminal act, and physical things which relate to the crime, such as means, instruments, and fruits of the crime— weapons, tools, writings, clothing, money, books, and records.

During an investigation, evidence is gathered of the material elements of the crime (the corpus delicti). That information is then referred to a prosecuting authority who reviews the facts and available evidence and decides whether they are suitable and adequate to justify a conviction. If so, a formal accusation is made in the form of an indictment or information—usually an indictment for a felony charge and an information for a misdemeanor in federal cases. But private citizens may also initiate a formal accusation by filing a complaint with an officer of the court or, in some jurisdictions, an office of the law.

Trials are generally held in the legal jurisdiction in which the crime was committed. A public trial (by jury if so desired by the defendant) is usually accorded in criminal cases in the United States. A defendant also has the right to testify on his or her own behalf. But a decision not to testify cannot be held against a defendant, because the burden of proof is on the prosecution and a defendant cannot be forced to testify against himself or herself.

The powers of the police are sharply limited by the U.S. Constitution, particularly the Fourth, Fifth, and Sixth Amendments, which are applied to the states through the "due process" clause of the Fourteenth Amendment. These amendments provide:

Amendment IV—The right of the people to be secure in their persons, houses, papers, and effects, against unreasonable searches and seizure, shall not be violated, and no warrants shall issue, but upon probable cause, supported by oath or affirmation, and particularly describing the place to be searched, and the persons or things to be seized.

Amendment V—No person shall be held to answer for a capital, or otherwise infamous crime, unless on a presentment of indictment of a Grand Jury, except in cases arising in the land or naval forces, or in the Militia, when in actual service in time of War or public danger; nor shall any person be subject for the same offense to be twice put in jeopardy of life or limb; nor shall he be compelled in any criminal case to be a witness against himself, nor be deprived of life, liberty, or property, without due process of law; nor shall private property be taken for public use, without just compensation.

Amendment VI—In all criminal prosecutions, the accused shall enjoy the right to speedy and public trial, by an impartial jury of the State and district wherein the crime shall have been committed, which district shall have been previously ascertained by law, and to be informed of the nature and cause of the accusation; to be confronted with the witnesses against him; to have compulsory process for obtaining witnesses in his favor; and to have the assistance of counsel for his defense.

Amendment XIV—Section 1. All persons born or naturalized in the United States, and subject to the jurisdiction thereof, are citizens of the United States and of the State wherein they reside. No State shall make or enforce any law which shall abridge the privileges or immunities of citizens of the United States; nor shall any State deprive any person of life, liberty, or property without due process of law; nor deny to any person within its jurisdiction the equal protection of the laws.

The application of these basic constitutional rights, as interpreted by the courts, to the principal components of police investigations—searches and seizures, arrests and interrogations—is discussed below:

Searches and Seizures

The Fourth Amendment contains three broad dictates:

1. "Unreasonable" searches and seizures are forbidden,
2. all warrants (for a search or arrest) must be supported by "probable cause," under oath, and
3. all warrants must "particularly" describe the place to be searched or the person or things to be seized.

Katz v. United States, 389 U.S. 347 (1967), is probably one of the most important of the Supreme Court's Fourth Amendment decisions. The court held that the amendment "protects people, not places" (meaning its provisions extend beyond the property line of the citizen); that the amendment applies wherever there is a "reasonable expectation of privacy"; and that a search without a warrant is "per se unreasonable," absent exigent circumstances. Thus, the police normally need to obtain a warrant not only to search a bedroom, but to intercept calls from a public telephone booth, or inspect the contents of a safe deposit box, or to otherwise intrude into matters which society would reasonably consider to be private.

In another major Fourth Amendment case, Johnson v. United States, 333 U.S. 10 (1948), the Supreme Court ruled that all warrants must be issued by a judge or magistrate (a judicial officer empowered to issue warrants and hear misdemeanor cases), explaining that "the point of the Fourth Amendment . . . is not that it denies law enforcement the support of the usual inferences which reasonable men draw from evidence. Its protection consists in requiring that those inferences be drawn by a neutral and detached magistrate instead of being judged by the officer engaged in the often competitive enterprise of ferreting out crime.''

The "probable cause" requirement of the Fourth Amendment is of critical importance, being the central restraint on the power of the police to arrest or search. It has been defined as those facts and circumstances sufficient to cause a man of reasonable caution to believe that a crime has been committed and that the accused committed it. It requires more than mere suspicion or hunch, but less than virtual certainty. "Reasonable grounds to believe" is probably as good a definition as any. The particularity requirement was intended to prevent "general searches," an abuse which outraged the constitutional draftsmen.

Under the exclusionary rule in effect in all federal and state courts, evidence seized in violation of the Fourth Amendment will be suppressed. That is, may not be used against the accused, with limited exceptions. An unlawful search and seizure does not, however, preclude prosecution or invalidate a subsequent conviction based on other evidence. A person whose Fourth Amendment rights have been violated, whether or not a defendant in a criminal case, may sue for damages through a private civil rights action. The Fourth Amendment applies only to actions by the police or other governmental authorities; searches and seizures conducted by the private parties are not regulated, unless they are substantially directed by public officers.

Exceptions to the Fourth Amendment Warrant Requirement

Searches Incident to Arrest

Police officers may search without a warrant the person of the accused and the area within her or his immediate control incident to arrest in order to protect themselves and to prevent the destruction of evidence. For the search to be valid the arrest must be valid, i.e., based on probable cause, and not merely a pretext to justify a search. If the arrest is unlawful when made, it cannot be justified by the fruits of the subsequent search, and all evidence obtained must be suppressed.

Searches of Motor Vehicles

An automobile, airplane, or vessel may be searched without a warrant if there is probable cause to believe it contains contraband or other evidence of a crime. This is because of the mobility and the lower expectation of privacy associated with such vehicles. The police may also conduct warrantless "inventory" searches of impounded vehicles to secure and protect the owner's personal property, and may seize any contraband or other evidence discovered as a result.

Searches of containers and luggage found within a vehicle may require a warrant, because of the higher degree of privacy. This is particularly true if the containers are already in police custody, and removal is unlikely.

Consent Searches

A valid consent obviates the need for a warrant, although such "consents" are carefully scrutinized, particularly when they lead to the seizure of incriminating evidence. Consents obtained by deceit, bribery, or misrepresentations are held to be involuntary and invalid. Consent may be implied in some circumstances, as when one enters a secured court house, or boards an airplane. Consents may be given by third parties to searches of property over which they have authority, such as a co-tenant to a leased apartment, or an employer to business premises.

Evidence in "Plain View"

Evidence in "plain view" of an officer who has a right to be in position to observe it may also be seized without a warrant. This situation usually occurs when contraband or evidence of another crime is inadvertently discovered during a search or arrest for another offense. The discovery must be truly inadvertent, however; if discovery of the evidence is anticipated, and no other exception applies, a warrant must first be obtained.

Border, Customs and Prison Searches

Border and custom searches are a longstanding exception to the Fourth Amendment and may be conducted without probable cause or a warrant. Searches of prison cells and monitoring of inmates' telephone conversations may also be conducted without a warrant or probable cause because of security concerns and the absence of a realistic expectation of privacy in prison.

Arrest and Investigative Steps

A police officer or private citizen may arrest in public without a warrant for a felony committed in his or her presence. An arrest occurs whenever a reasonable person would feel he or she is not free to leave.

The Supreme Court has declined to require a warrant preliminary to any arrest because of the "intolerable burdens" it would create for legitimate law enforcement. The Court has held, however, that a warrant is normally required before a person may be arrested in the home, and that a person arrested without a warrant is entitled to prompt judicial determination of probable cause before she or he can be detained for any extended period of time.

Not all police stops are arrests requiring probable cause. In Terry v. Ohio, 392 U.S. 1 (1968), the Supreme Court held that the police may briefly detain and question a person for investigative purposes (and conduct a "pat down" search for weapons) if there are specific "articulable" reasons to do so. A valid stop may yield evidence to effect an arrest. If the police arrest or detain unlawfully, any statements or evidence obtained as a result will be suppressed. The suspect may still be prosecuted, however, if other untainted evidence of wrongdoing exists.

Interrogation of Suspects

The Fifth Amendment provides that no person "shall . . . be compelled in any criminal case to be a witness against himself." To assure that every citizen has the opportunity to exercise this fundamental right, the Supreme Court ruled in the landmark case of Miranda v. Arizona, 348 U.S. 436 (1966), that the police must give the following warnings before interrogating any suspect held in custody:

1. that the suspect has the right to remain silent;
2. that any statements can be used against him at trial;
3. that he had a right to the assistance of an attorney, and
4. that an attorney will be appointed to represent him if he cannot afford to retain one.

Once a suspect asserts the right to remain silent, all questioning must cease until counsel is provided. If the defendant thereafter decides to make a statement, the government must show it was the result of a voluntary, knowing waiver of the rights.

Volumes have been written about the Miranda decision. It is sufficient to note here that Miranda warnings are required only if the suspect is (1) held in custody (2) by public authorities. Certain exceptions to the warning requirement apply, such as when immediate questioning is necessary to insure public safety. The warnings are not required at all when a person is being questioned by private parties; however, some fraud examiners may choose to do so as a matter of policy.

Apart from the Miranda requirements, a confession must also be voluntary, not coerced by physical or psychological means. Some inducement is permissible, however, such as informing the suspect that a confession may result in more lenient treatment. Using deceit and trickery to extract a confession, such as telling the suspect an accomplice had confessed when in fact he had not, is treated differently by different courts, some permitting such confessions, others not, depending on the particular circumstances. No confession will be admitted if the circumstances under which it was obtained render it unreliable.

The Charging Process

A person under arrest must be brought before a magistrate without "unnecessary delay." At this time the arresting officer must swear to a complaint, establishing probable cause, if the arrest was without a warrant. The defendant will then be advised of the nature of the complaint against him or her, the right to retain counsel or to appointed counsel, and of the general circumstances under which a pretrial release may be secured.

The Eighth Amendment prohibits "excessive bail." The Supreme Court has held that the amendment does not absolutely require pretrial release. It only requires that if bail is appropriate, it be set no higher than necessary to assure the defendant's presence at trial. Bail may be denied and the defendant held in custody if the judge decides release would pose a serious threat to the safety of the community or any particular individual, or that no amount or conditions of release would prevent the defendant from fleeing.

At the initial appearance a defendant who has not yet been indicted is also informed of the right to a preliminary examination. This is a formal, adversary hearing, before a judge, at which the defendant may be represented by counsel and cross-examine witnesses. The purpose of the hearing is to determine whether there is probable cause to hold the defendant for further proceedings, not to establish guilt or innocence. Because of its limited purpose, hearsay and even illegally obtained evidence can be admissible. Motions to suppress must be made to the trial court.

If the magistrate determines at the preliminary examination that there is no probable cause, the complaint will be dismissed and the defendant released. The government may, however, institute a subsequent prosecution for the same offense, presumably with better evidence.

Preliminary examinations are often used by defense counsel as an opportunity to get free "discovery" facts of the details of the prosecution's case. For this reason many prosecutors prefer to obtain a grand jury indictment before the hearing is scheduled. An indictment is held to satisfy the probable cause requirements of the Fifth Amendment, and preclude the need for the preliminary examination.

The Grand Jury

The grand jury consists of 16 to 23 persons, sworn as jurors. They meet in secret deliberation, usually in biweekly or monthly sessions, to hear witnesses and other evidence presented by prosecutors and to vote on indictments. An indictment or "true bill" must be concurred in by at least 12 jurors, voting without the prosecutor present.

The grand jury is a nonadversarial proceeding. The accused has no right to be informed of its deliberations, to know the evidence, or to confront accusers. She or he also has no absolute right to appear before it. If the accused does appear, he or she may not be accompanied by counsel. The defendant, however, may periodically leave the grand jury room to consult with the attorney outside.

These severe limitations on the rights of the accused are thought to be justified on the grounds that they are necessary to effectively investigate criminal activity. The grand jury has only the power to accuse, not convict the defendant, and the defendant, if indicted, has full constitutional protections at trial. The grand jury's power has been severely criticized by many legal and public-interest groups. The abuse of its processes can do severe damage to innocent parties, particularly public figures to whom an indictment alone would be devastating. For this reason defense counsel in major white-collar cases often begin their defense at the grand jury stage to try to convince prosecutors not to indict, rather than waiting until an indictment is returned.

The grand jury has the right to subpoena witnesses and documents. Refusals to appear or produce may be punishable as contempt. A witness or target of the grand jury retains the Fifth Amendment right against self-incrimination, but this right applies only to individuals and not to corporations or other organizations. Historically, an individual could refuse to produce personal books and papers under the Fifth Amendment, but the Supreme Court may be on the verge of deciding that such documents are not protected, unless their preparation was compelled by the government.

A grand jury may be used only to obtain evidence of possible violations of the criminal law. Its process may not be used as a ruse to obtain evidence for parallel civil actions. The grand jury may, however (with the appropriate court order), make evidence available to the proper government authorities for a civil proceeding, as long as the primary purpose of the grand jury inquiry was to enforce the criminal laws. Access by private parties through court orders to grand jury evidence for use in private civil proceedings is much more difficult and unlikely to be granted. This is because of grand jury secrecy requirements, unless substantial need is demonstrated.

In the course of a grand jury investigation or trial the prosecution may apply for a court order compelling testimony from a witness under a grant of immunity. Since immunized testimony cannot be used against the witness in any criminal proceeding, such an order does not violate the Fifth Amendment right against self-incrimination.

Although it is legally permissible to prosecute an immunized witness on the basis of other testimony and evidence, as a matter of practice this is seldom done. This is because of policy considerations and the difficulty in demonstrating, as the law requires, that the subsequent prosecution was not in any way based on the compelled testimony.

A decision to immunize a witness is solely within the discretion of the prosecution. If the application meets statutory requirements, the court must grant the order. If the immunized witness refuses to testify—out of fear of reprisals or for any other reason—he or she will be found in contempt and jailed until agreeing to testify, or until the grand jury expires. The witness can then be summoned before a new grand jury and the process repeated indefinitely, or until a judge decides that there is no possibility that further incarceration will induce cooperation. Only the prosecution can apply for an immunity order; neither the court nor the defense has any power to do so.

An immunity order protects the witness only from prosecution for past crimes about which his or her testimony is compelled. Other, undiscovered crimes are not covered, nor is the witness immune from prosecution for perjury based on the immunized testimony. Such testimony may also be used against the witness in a civil proceeding.

Indictment and Information

In the federal system, all offenses punishable by death must be charged by indictment; all felonies (crimes punishable by imprisonment for a year or more) must be prosecuted by indictment, unless the defendant waives the requirement, in which case the prosecution may proceed by the filing of an information. An information is a charge signed only by the prosecutor without the involvement of the grand jury. A misdemeanor may be charged by either an indictment or information.

Arraignment

A defendant named in an indictment, if not already in custody, may be arrested on a warrant. More often in white-collar cases, the defendant is summoned to appear before a magistrate at a stated time and place to be arraigned.

The arraignment must take place in open court, and consists of reading of the indictment or information to the defendant and calling on her or him to plead. The defendant may plead guilty, not guilty, or nolo contendere. A plea of nolo contendere means the defendant does not contest the charges, without formally admitting or denying them. A defendant may plead "nolo" only with the consent of the court. If accepted, a nolo plea is the same as a plea of guilty for purposes of punishment, but cannot be used as a formal admission of guilt. This makes it a favored plea for corporate defendants facing subsequent civil litigation.

Before the court will accept a guilty plea, it must follow established procedures to insure that the plea is voluntary and accurate; that is, that there is a "factual basis" for the plea. This usually means that the defendant must admit to committing acts which satisfy each element of the offense. In some circumstances, however, a defendant may be allowed to enter an Alford plea (named after the Supreme Court case which upheld the practice) under which he or she pleads guilty although continuing to assert his or her innocence. This plea may be made to obtain the benefits of a plea agreement and to avoid potentially more dire consequences, such as the death penalty, if the defendant is convicted after the trial. Before the court accepts an Alford plea, it must satisfy itself that there is strong evidence of guilt and that the defendant understands the consequences.

A plea of not guilty sets in motion the adjudicative process, described below.

Pretrial Procedures

After arraignment and before trial the defendant, through counsel, may file motions (formal requests to the court) asking that the charges be dismissed. These motions often ask that illegally obtained evidence be suppressed, that separate trials be granted in multiple-defendant cases, or for other relief.

An indictment may be dismissed on a number of legal grounds, including failure to allege all the elements of an offense, expiration of the statute of limitations, defects in the grand jury procedures, prosecutorial misconduct, and so on. Charges dismissed at this stage for procedural errors may usually be filed again. In many cases motions to exclude evidence, decided at a "suppression hearing," are more important than the trial itself. If the defense is able to exclude illegally seized narcotics, a tainted confession, or critical books and records, the prosecution may be forced to dismiss the charges (at least temporarily) for lack of proof. On the other hand, an unsuccessful suppression motion may be followed by renewed interest by the defendant in a plea bargain.

Both the defendant and prosecution have statutory rights to certain pretrial discovery. The defendant may inspect copies of all relevant statements made by him or her (of, if a corporation, by its employees) in the custody of the government, a copy of his or her prior criminal record, and all documents, items, test results, and other evidence the government intends to introduce at a trial or which are necessary to the defense. The defendant does not, however, have an absolute right to see copies of prior statements made by a witness until the witness completes testimony at trial. In many cases, however (particularly fraud prosecutions in which there is little risk of reprisals or tampering with witnesses), the government may voluntarily produce these statements before trial.

The government must also disclose copies of all "exculpatory" statements or other evidence "helpful" to the defense (known as "Brady material" after a Supreme Court case) or risk dismissal of the charges.

The government may also require the defense to produce before trial all relevant documents, items, test results, and other evidence the defendant intends to offer as evidence at trial. This provision does not violate the defendant's Fifth Amendment rights against self-incrimination, which protects her or him only from compelled production of testimonial statements.

The Trial Process

Under the Sixth Amendment, the accused is entitled to a "speedy and public trial, by an impartial jury, in the State and district wherein the crime (was) committed." In federal courts the Speedy Trial Act mandates that the defendant be indicted within 30 days of his arrest and tried within 70 days of notice of the charges, excluding delays caused by certain enumerated circumstances. If the time limits are not adhered to, the court may dismiss the case.

Jury Selection

The Constitution requires that "the trial of all crimes, except in cases of impeachment, shall be by Jury." In the federal system the defendant may waive the right, with the consent of the court and prosecution. Petty offenses do not require a trial by jury.

Most criminal cases are tried to a jury of twelve, with at least two alternates, but the parties may stipulate to a lesser number. The jury must be impartial. The parties or the court may "voir dire" (ask questions of) the prospective jurors to determine their suitability and impartiality. Each party may remove a number of prospective jurors for cause, such as admitted bias or prejudice. Each side has peremptory challenges (the number depending on the offense charged), under which a party may eliminate a prospective juror without having to give any reason. The prosecution may not use its peremptory challenges, however, in a way solely influenced by racial factors. The defendant may also challenge the entire jury pool—called the venire—if the selection procedures systematically exclude certain groups, such as minorities, women, or young people. The jury that actually hears the case (the "petit jury") is not required to reflect a cross-section of the community or contain individuals of the same race or age as the defendant.

Once the jury is selected and sworn, and after some introductory remarks by the judge to the jury, the actual trial begins with the opening statement by the prosecution. In it the prosecutor usually explains the charges, outlines the evidence she or he intends to produce, and tells the jury he or she will ask for a verdict of guilty at the close of the evidence. The prosecutor is not permitted to argue the cases at this point. That is done at the end of the case. The defense counsel then gives an opening statement, although on occasion she or he will waive the opportunity and save the opening until after the prosecution has rested.

The prosecution presents its case first. As noted above, the prosecution bears the entire burden of proving every element of the offense beyond a reasonable doubt. The defense is under no obligation to produce any evidence at any time.

As a general rule, a witness's testimony must be confined to facts within his or her personal knowledge, rather than conjecture or opinion. A duly qualified expert witness, however, may give an opinion, if the court determines that it will assist the jury to understand the evidence or to determine a fact in issue. Accountants and fraud examiners may be (and often are) called to testify in fraud cases, as lay witnesses or experts or both.

The Sixth Amendment guarantees a defendant the right to confront and cross-examine the witnesses against him or her. This is a principal reason why hearsay evidence is generally excluded. If a judge unduly restricts a defendant's right to probe the prosecution's witnesses' credibility or knowledge of the facts, a conviction may be reversed. Far more defendants are in jail, however, because their counsel asked one question too many (and got a devastating answer) than because the judge allowed one too few.

The admission of evidence, and objections, are ruled on by the trial judge. The rules of evidence can be summarized in an extremely simplified way as intended to limit the evidence presented to the jury to only those matters relevant to the specific charges brought, and to exclude evidence which is unreliable or unduly prejudicial. The same piece of evidence, however, may be admissible or inadmissible depending on the specific reason for which it is being offered. For example, evidence of other similar crimes or wrongful acts by the defendant may not be offered by the prosecution merely to show the defendant is a bad person, and therefore more likely to have committed the crime charged. But the same evidence may be introduced to prove intent, if disputed by the defendant, or to rebut a claim of accident or mistake, or to impeach false testimony by the accused.

At the close of the prosecution's case, the defense may (and usually does) move for a judgment of acquittal, on the grounds that the prosecution's evidence, even if believed, is legally insufficient to convict. If the judge grants the motion, the trial ends and the defendant is acquitted. If the motion is denied, the defendant may elect to present evidence, or may rest.

If the defendant elects to testify, she or he is subject to cross-examination like any other witness, and the prosecution may impeach the defendant's credibility by showing prior convictions. This is usually a death blow to the defense and is the reason many defendants do not testify. The prosecution may not introduce such evidence unless or until the defendant takes the stand. The judge may exclude it even then as unduly prejudicial, particularly if the crime is remote in time or did not involve dishonesty or false statements.

A defendant is entitled to call character witnesses. These witnesses often have no knowledge of the charges or facts in issue, but are prepared to testify to the defendant's general good character. This testimony must be given in the form of the witness's opinion or testimony as to the defendant's general good reputation; testimony as to specific incidents of good conduct is not permitted. This seemingly upside-down rule is justified by the belief that testimony as to specific conduct would prove too confusing and time consuming. And since any character evidence is circumstantial at best, it is considered permissible to limit the testimony to reputation or opinion. The defendant's character witnesses may be asked on cross-examination if they have heard about alleged wrongful or dishonest acts by the accused, including a prior conviction.

Common Legal Issues in Fraud Cases

Two general types of legal issues are often encountered in fraud cases. They are substantive and procedural in nature. The substantive issues involve proving each element of the crime beyond a reasonable doubt, including the element of intent (if intent is an element). The procedural issues include the right to counsel and the manner in which investigators conduct arrests, searches and seizures, and interrogations. Fraud examiners are most likely to encounter legal problems over such issues as the condition, organization, and sanctity of their work papers, and their audit assumptions, if the case is based on an accounting hypothesis (net-worth method, for example). Accounting data used as evidence is often challenged as not meeting the hearsay exceptions. Here the issue is whether proffered documentary evidence is "best" evidence or whether secondary evidence is admissible when the best evidence is unavailable. Questions are often raised about the business-records exception to the hearsay rule; that is, whether a record is made in the ordinary course of doing business or an entry is made in books of account contemporaneously with a business transaction.

Another issue often encountered is the qualifications of a fraud examiner called as a witness to provide expert testimony (opinion evidence). The expert witness's credentials may be challenged by the other side. In the latter case, an expert of comparable skill and reputation may be called to question the opinion of the first expert.

Legal Defenses

A defense is an assertion by a defendant in a criminal or civil suit that seeks to explain away guilt or civil liability for damages. The more common defenses include alibi, consent, *de minimis* infraction (trivial), duress, entrapment, ignorance, mistake, infancy, insanity, necessity, protection of property, self-defense, public duty, legal impossibility, and protection of others. Also pertinent are questions involving statutes of limitations, proper venue, and proper jurisdiction.

In criminal fraud cases where intent is an element of the crime, defense attorneys may advance a number of smoke-screen theories to excuse their clients of guilt, i.e., by alleging some inhibiting factor to the formulation of intent. For example, while ignorance of the law may be no excuse, it can persuade a jury, particularly if the crime is complex and financial in nature. An illustration would be an income tax evasion case in which the net-worth method of income reconstruction has been utilized. Certain of the computerized embezzlements fit into this category too; as do bank frauds, securities frauds, and price fixing conspiracies. While ignorance of the law may be no excuse, ignorance itself sometimes induces pity or sorrow.

Insanity may be used as a defense—and often is in crimes of violence. But notice of that defense must usually be given before trial.

Innocent mistake, advanced age, sickness, and illiteracy may be used to evoke sympathy. And while they may not work as defenses (if they are found to be true), they may persuade the judge or jury to be lenient in sentencing.

But the defenses that cause prosecutions the most headaches are assertions of poor investigative work. Examples include improper arrests, searches, seizures, and interrogations, improper handling and documentation of evidence, privacy invasions, libeling, slandering, and defaming the defendant during the investigation. In fraud examinations, sloppy auditing and mishandling of work papers might be alleged.

The increased use of the undercover approach in criminal investigations today has also led to the increased assertion of entrapment as a defense. Entrapment means that the peace officer or undercover agent solicited, encouraged or incited the criminal act. Without that incitement, the defendant would not have committed the act.

After the defense rests, the court may permit the prosecution to call rebuttal witnesses, and the defense to put on re-rebuttal evidence. At the close of all the evidence, the defense may make or renew its motion for a judgment of acquittal. The court may reserve its decision, submit the case to the jury, and decide the motion before or after the jury returns with a verdict. The motion may be made for the first time and granted even after the jury returns with a guilty verdict.

At the close of the evidence, the jury is usually temporarily discharged and the parties meet with the judge to submit proposed jury instructions. These will be read to the jury usually after closing arguments, and include such matters as the basic elements of the charges, the definition of reasonable doubt, the prosecution's burden. If requested by the defense, the judge will instruct that no adverse inference may be drawn from the failure of the defendant to testify. Some defense counsel do not request this instruction because they believe it merely reminds the jury of the accused's failure to explain or defend his or her conduct.

Each side is entitled to instructions on the law supporting its theory of the case if there is any credible evidence to support it, even if there is substantial evidence to the contrary. If a request to instruct is denied, counsel must state his or her objection and the grounds therefor before the jury retires, to preserve appeal rights. This is an extremely important point for defense counsel, as errors in instructions are perhaps the most fertile grounds for reversals on appeal.

Closing Arguments

The prosecution argues first, the defense follows, and the prosecution has the opportunity for final rebuttal.

The prosecutor is held to a particularly high standard in closing argument. He or she may not misstate the evidence, express a personal opinion as to the defendant's guilt or the credibility of witnesses, or make otherwise prejudicial or inflammatory remarks. He or she is expected to stick to the facts and the reasonable inferences which may be drawn. In most cases the defense argument focuses on attacking the motives and credibility of the government's witnesses, and emphasizes the heavy burden of proof the government bears.

Jury Deliberations

After hearing instructions, the jury retires for its deliberations and selects a foreperson. The verdict must be unanimous; if the jury deadlocks, a mistrial will be declared. The defendant can be retried if the prosecution elects to do so. Double jeopardy does not attach unless the defendant is acquitted after the jury is sworn.

If a verdict is reached, it is announced in open court by the foreperson or the bailiff. Either party may request that the jury be polled, that is, that each juror be asked individually whether he or she concurred in the verdict. If any juror answers no, the jury must return for further deliberations or may be discharged.

Sentencing

Following a verdict of guilty, a sentence must be imposed without unnecessary delay. Prior to the sentencing hearing a probation officer will prepare a presentence report. It will review the defendant's character, background, associates, prior criminal record, and other factors relevant to setting an appropriate sentence.

The report will recommend a particular sentence or range of sentence. Recent amendments to the Federal Rules of Criminal Procedure require that the presentence report contain a "victim impact statement." It is an assessment of the financial, social, psychological, and medical impact upon, and cost to, the victim of the crime. This information may be used to set the proper punishment or to support a possible restitution order. The defendant and his or her counsel are allowed to review all or parts of the probation report, except the sentencing recommendation.

At the sentencing hearing the defendant, counsel, and the prosecutor may be heard before sentence is imposed. The court may impose a fine, a term of imprisonment, or both, or place the defendant on probation for a specified period of time under certain conditions. The court may order restitution to the victims, in addition to a fine or prison term, or as a condition of probation. A federal statute provides that a defendant who has been found guilty of fraud may be ordered to give notice to the victims. This is to protect the public from further fraudulent acts by the defendant, or to alert the victims to the possibility of civil recoveries.

Sentences of imprisonment for two or more offenses may be ordered to run consecutively or concurrently, depending on the nature and severity of the offenses and other factors. The Federal Sentencing Reform Act of 1984 requires a judge to sentence the defendant within narrow guidelines focusing on the nature of the offense, the defendant's background, and other factors. In federal court a defendant may be fined up to twice the pecuniary gain realized from the crime, or twice the loss sustained by the victim, as an alternative to the statutory amounts.

Appeal

The defendant is advised of his or her right to appeal at the sentencing hearing. A notice of appeal must be filed within ten days or the right is lost, absent a showing of excusable neglect.

Generally, an appeal may be made only for errors of law to which the defendant made timely objection at trial or in pretrial proceedings. The failure to object is said to waive any claims of error. A timely objection theoretically would permit the trial judge to correct the error at the time, eliminating the delay and expense of appeal and new trial. Very serious errors, however, which are plain on the record and affect "substantial rights" of the defendant, may be raised on an appeal without the necessity for a timely objection.

An appellate court will reverse a conviction only if it finds error which denied the defendant a fair trial. Procedural errors which do not affect substantial rights are ignored.

THE CIVIL JUSTICE SYSTEM

The Investigative Stage in Private Actions

The right to audit or examine for fraud is implicit in our business, accounting, and legal systems. Although a state may require that a person holding themselves out to be a private investigator be licensed and bonded, these requirements generally do not apply to an individual retained to assist an attorney, and do not apply to audits or investigations undertaken by corporate employees or agents, such as outside accountants, on behalf of the corporate employer. Thus, a private fraud examiner may interview witnesses, collect and review documents (assuming they are lawfully available), and inspect public records in the course of an investigation into possible wrongdoing without the necessity of any special commission or public authority. In the case of Certified Fraud Examiners, their conduct is regulated by the National Association of Certified Fraud Examiners.

Of course, investigations in private actions are subject to certain legal limitations, some of which, such as the laws prohibiting unauthorized electronic surveillance, are enforced with criminal as well as civil penalties. Overzealous or imprudent acts by private parties, even if technically legal, can also result in counterclaims and legal side-shows which can delay, disrupt or even completely derail a meritorious case.

Listed below are the most common torts (civil wrongs) and criminal statutes to which the fraud examiner may be exposed in the course of a private investigation. Each can be avoided if the examiner is guided by common sense and professional standards, and confines himself or herself to measures reasonably necessary to accomplish the legitimate objectives. He or she should always pursue the facts, not people, should ask rather than accuse, prove rather than allege.

Defamation

Defamation is the legal term for the torts of libel and slander. A statement is defamatory if it is (1) untrue, (2) "published" to a third party or parties, (3) on an unprivileged occasion, and (4) tends to damage the reputation of the subject. Libel refers to defamatory statements in writing, and slander to spoken statements, although the distinction is often blurred in the case of the electronic media.

If the person defamed is a public figure, he or she must prove that the defamatory statement was made with "malice." That means the author or speaker knew that the statement was false or disseminated it with "reckless disregard" of its truth or falsity. A private-figure plaintiff—such as a mid-level corporate employee—need only prove falsity and some lesser degree of fault, such as negligence. A plaintiff may recover special damages (out-of-pocket losses), "general" damages to reputation, and punitive damages, which may be substantial.

Truth is an absolute defense to any defamation action. The examiner is also protected by a number of recognized "privileges" in the law of defamation, which virtually every jurisdiction recognizes. Statements made in the course of or preparatory to judicial proceedings are absolutely privileged. That is, even knowingly untrue or malicious statements are protected. The passions of litigation would otherwise fuel endless lawsuits, and witnesses would be reluctant to appear. Statements made to protect a legitimate interest of the speaker or recipient, such as a communication between an employee and his or her employer regarding an important business matter, or the results of an examination into suspected fraud, are also privileged, as long as made in good faith. In short, the examiner who conducts himself or herself in a prudent manner should not be concerned about liability for defamation.

Invasion of Privacy

There are two separate torts of invasion of privacy—"publicity of private facts" and unwarranted "intrusion." A person commits the "publicity" tort if he or she (1) publicizes broadly (2) private facts about another (3) which would be highly offensive to a reasonable person (4) about a matter in which the speaker does not have a legitimate interest.

The gist of this tort is the unwarranted publicity of private facts, not their discovery. Courts have held that the publicity must be broad and pervasive for liability to attach. One case found no liability when a bank gave account information on a customer to a representative of his employer, and another court exonerated an investigator who reported credit information to an insurance company.

The collection of such information may, however, violate the "intrusion" tort. The gist of this action is the unreasonable, deliberate prying into private matters or "seclusion" of another, without a legitimate interest or authority. A person may be held liable for conducting an unwarranted search of another's personal property, intensive physical surveillance, or obtaining private bank account information, absent a subpoena or other court order. Reasonable searches of an employee's office, at least those areas which are open to view by third parties, with the consent of the employer, probably would not give rise to liability.

False Imprisonment

The tort of false imprisonment occurs when there is (1) an intent to confine, (2) an act resulting in confinement, and (3) consciousness of confinement or resulting harm.

The thrust of the tort is the unlawful restraint of freedom of movement. Good faith and "probable cause" to believe the person restrained has committed an offense are defenses. In the private fraud investigation, the examiner will seldom have the need to physically restrain the suspect. Inadvertent or thoughtless acts, however, such as closing or locking the door to an interview room, standing in front of a exit, conducting a lengthy, overbearing interview under circumstances indicating the accused is not permitted to leave, or otherwise physically or psychologically detaining the suspect may result in a false imprisonment claim.

Malicious Prosecution

The tort of malicious prosecution is committed when a party (1) institutes civil or criminal litigation against another (2) without just cause, (3) with malice (i.e., the intent to harm the victim), and (4) the proceeding ends favorably to the victim. To bring an action for malicious civil litigation, the victim must also show some interference or harm to person or property, beyond the expense of defending the suit. In either case, it must be demonstrated that the person instituted legal proceedings solely to vex or harass the victim.

Intentional Infliction of Emotional Distress

To recover for intentional infliction of emotional distress, the plaintiff must prove (1) that the defendant engaged in extreme and outrageous conduct which (2) caused severe emotional distress, resulting in (3) physical symptoms or bodily harm. One of the leading cases is an English decision in which a private detective threatened to charge the victim with espionage unless she surrendered private letters. Harassing telephone calls and letters from collection agencies, of an extreme nature over a prolonged period of time, have also been compensated.

For liability to attach, the offending conduct must "outrage the sensibilities of a reasonable man." Mere angry words or insults, or allegations or implications of wrongdoing (if based on reasonable grounds) are not enough.

Prima Facie Tort

A violation of this tort occurs if a person (1) intentionally commits acts harmful to another, (2) resulting in damages, (3) without justification, by (4) acts otherwise lawful. An example might be a company's terminating an otherwise honest and capable employee as punishment for "whistle-blowing." This cause of action is not recognized in many jurisdictions, and often overlaps other claims, such as defamation or wrongful discharge.

Wrongful Discharge

Wrongful discharge suits by terminated employees are increasing in number, under an expanding number of legal theories. Historically, a person without an employment contract was considered to be terminable "at will" by the employer, without the need for any explanation or grounds. Discharged employees are now suing for damages on creative theories such as "implied employment contracts" or other legal fictions which complicate the liability situation.

As a practical matter, whatever the legal theory, an employee terminated because he or she committed fraudulent or dishonest acts will not be able to recover damages for wrongful discharge. Such an action may still be filed, however, in an attempt to extract a settlement because of the high cost of litigation and the potential for embarrassment to the employer. To reduce this temptation, all noncontract employees should be informed of the "at will" nature of their employment. No representations or promises, direct or indirect, of continued employment should be made to employees in the course of a fraud examination.

Right-to-Privacy Statutes

A number of federal and state laws protect individual privacy rights in employment and financial affairs. Attempts to obtain financial or credit reports by unauthorized private parties may subject them to civil liability for invasion of privacy.

The principal federal statutes and a brief summary of their provisions are set out below.

Right to Financial Privacy Act (Title 12, U.S. Code, Sec. 3401, et seq.)

This act prohibits financial institutions from disclosing financial information about individual customers to government agencies without the customer's consent, a court order, subpoena or search warrant, or other formal demand, with limited exceptions. Although the statute applies only to demands by government agencies, most banks and other financial institutions will also not release such information to private parties absent legal process, such as a subpoena issued in a civil lawsuit.

Fair Credit Reporting Act (Title 15, U.S. Code, Sec. 1681)

This federal statute regulates the dissemination of consumer credit information by consumer reporting agencies to third parties. It prohibits the disclosure of any consumer credit report (the terms are defined in the statute) except in accordance with the act. The provisions of greatest interest to the fraud examiner are set out below:

1681b. Permissible purposes of consumer reports

A consumer reporting agency may furnish a consumer report under the following circumstances and no other:

(1) In response to the order of a court having jurisdiction to issue such an order.

(2) In accordance with the written instructions of the consumer to whom it relates.

(3) To a person which it has reason to believe—

    (A) intends to use the information in connection with a credit transaction involving the consumer on whom the information is to be furnished and involving the extension of credit to, or review or collection of an account of, the consumer; or

    (B) intends to use the information for employment purposes; or

    (C) intends to use the information in connection with the underwriting of insurance involving the consumer; or

(D) intends to use the information in connection with a determination of the consumer's eligibility for a license or benefit granted by a governmental instrumentality required by law to consider an applicant's financial responsibility or status; or

(E) otherwise has a legitimate business need for the information in connection with a business transaction involving the consumer.

Section 1681(d) provides that a person may not obtain an "investigative consumer report" on any consumer, which includes information as to the consumer's character, general reputation, personal characteristics and mode of living, unless the consumer is notified of the requested report. The consumer may then demand additional information about the nature and scope of the requested report.

Civil penalties are provided for willful or negligent noncompliance with the act. Any person who attempts to obtain information on a consumer from a consumer reporting agency on false pretenses may be fined up to $5,000 or imprisoned up to one year or both.

Privacy/Freedom of Information Act (FOIA) (Title 5, U.S. Code, Sec. 552, et seq.)

These provisions regulate, among other things, the type of records which a federal agency may maintain about a person, the conditions under which such information may be disclosed to another government agency, and the circumstances and methods under which an individual may obtain copies of agency records which pertain to him or her.

Generally, disclosing government records about an individual, the disclosure of which would constitute an invasion of privacy, is prohibited. A person may obtain copies of his or her own records by requesting them in writing from the agency which maintains them. Such requests are often denied, in whole or in part, because of numerous exceptions to the disclosure requirements, such as the pendency of an ongoing investigation or national security concerns. A person denied access to records may appeal through the agency or courts. Because of the extremely heavy demand for FOIA material from individuals, lawyers, researchers, and journalists, requests to some agencies are backlogged for years.

Title III, Omnibus Crime Control and Safe Streets Act of 1968 (Title 18, U.S. Code, Sec. 2510, et seq.)

Title III makes it illegal for any person, including a government agent, to surreptitiously intercept oral or wire communications without a court order. The statute authorizes law enforcement agencies to obtain an order to intercept communications for a limited time period, usually no more than 30 days, upon a showing of probable cause that such interceptions will yield evidence of certain specified offenses. Criminal and civil penalties are provided.

Under federal law and in most states it is lawful to intercept a communication if one of the parties consents. California and several other states, however, prohibit even such consensual interceptions.

Employee Polygraph Protection Act of 1988 (Title 29, U.S. Code Sec. 2001, et seq.)

This federal statute makes it unlawful for any employer who is engaged in interstate commerce "directly or indirectly, to require, request, suggest or cause any employee or prospective employee to take . . . any lie detector test," or to discharge any employee for refusing to comply based on the results of any such test. An employer who violates this section is subject to a civil penalty of up to $10,000, and an aggrieved employee is given a private right of action for damages. Certain exceptions apply for government agencies and corporate security matters. Of greatest interest to the fraud examiner is the following provision:

Limited exemption for ongoing investigations

Subject to sections 2007 and 2009 of this title, this chapter shall not prohibit an employer from requesting to submit to a polygraph test if

(1) the test is administered in connection with an ongoing investigation involving economic loss or injury to the employer's business, such as theft, embezzlement, misappropriation, or an act of unlawful industrial espionage or sabotage;

(2) the employee had access to the property that is the subject of the investigation;

(3) the employer has a reasonable suspicion that the employee was involved in the incident or activity under investigation; and

(4) the employer executes a statement, provided to the examinee before the test, that

(A) sets forth with particularity the specific incident or activity being investigated and the basis for testing particular employees,

(B) is signed by a person (other than a polygraph examiner) authorized to legally bind the employer,

(C) is retained by the employer for at least 3 years, and

(D) contains at a minimum
(i) an identification of the specific economic loss or injury to the business of the employer,
(ii) a statement indicating that the employee had access to the property that is the subject of the investigation, and
(iii) a statement describing the basis of the employer's reasonable suspicion that the employee was involved in the incident or activity under investigation.

Recovering Losses Due to Fraud

Fidelity Bond Claims

An often overlooked method of recovery for losses due to internal fraud is the fidelity bond claim. A fidelity bond is simply an insurance policy, issued by many large insurance companies, under which the insured is covered against losses caused by the dishonest or fraudulent acts of its employees. Dishonest or fraudulent acts are typically defined as those acts committed with the intent to (1) cause the insured to sustain a loss and (2) obtain for the employee or for any third party intended by the employee a financial benefit other than his or her proper compensation.

As with any other insurance agreement, fidelity policies have deductibles, a limit of liability (often in the millions of dollars), and certain exclusions. To collect, the insured must submit a sworn proof of loss claim, within specified time limits, together with supporting evidence of liability and amount of loss. Proof of loss is entirely the responsibility of the insured; the carrier will not usually conduct nor assist in the investigation, nor will it reimburse investigative or legal costs incurred in making a claim.

Most policies have express subrogation provisions which provide that if the insurance company pays a claim it will acquire the rights of the insured to sue the wrongdoer. Policyholders are prohibited from interfering with these rights in any way, such as releasing the wrongdoer from liability, at the risk of jeopardizing coverage. Therefore, no settlement agreements or releases would be executed with a dishonest employee or any confederate unless the insurance company consented.

Civil Litigation

Civil actions to recover damages for fraud, or to enjoin further fraudulent activity, may be filed by private plaintiffs in state or federal courts. The difference between criminal and civil fraud is often indistinguishable except for the intent provision in criminal penalties. Most common-law fraud actions, usually styled misrepresentation claims, are filed in state courts. Suits which involve parties from different states and have more than $10,000 in controversy (known as "diversity" cases), or actions brought on the basis of federal statutes, such as the Civil RICO provisions, may be brought in federal court. Federal court is generally preferred by plaintiffs in larger cases because of the easier access to witnesses and documents located in different states which the federal rules provide. The procedures described below are largely drawn from the federal rules and procedures.

Beginning the Civil Action

A civil action begins with the filing of a complaint in the appropriate court, usually in the jurisdiction in which the defendant resides, the plaintiff resides, or where the claim arose.

The rules provide that the complaint should be a "short and plain statement" showing the court's jurisdiction to hear the case (for example, in federal court, that there is diversity of citizenship and more than $10,000 in issue), the grounds for relief, and a demand for judgment. Rule 9(b) of the Federal Rules of Civil

Procedure tightens these requirements considerably for fraud actions, requiring that the facts entitling the plaintiff to relief be stated with "particularity." Thus, whereas a plaintiff in a negligence case may get into court by simply alleging, without any details or supporting evidence, that the defendant operated her or his automobile in a negligent manner at a particular place and time, a fraud plaintiff must plead the alleged fraud in detail: the actual misrepresentations that were made, to whom, how they were false, and so on, depending on the particular type of fraud claim.

The 9(b) requirement often creates a catch-22 for fraud plaintiffs. Officers of a company, for example, may have good grounds to believe they are the victims of a kickback fraud, but may need access to the discovery system (subpoenas for documents and witnesses) to prove the illegal payments. In such circumstances, particularly where the specific information needed is within the sole control of the defendants, the court may relax the 9(b) requirement somewhat.

The complaint and a summons must be served on the defendant according to the rules. The summons advises the defendant that he or she has a certain time to answer the complaint (usually 20 days) or suffer a default. A corporation may be served through any officer, managing agent, or other agent authorized by law to receive process. Process may be served on a defendant outside the state where the court sits if the defendant has significant contacts within the state, such as a corporation conducting business in that state.

A defendant may file an answer to the complaint, denying liability, add counterclaims against the plaintiff, or file motions to dismiss the action on legal grounds. Examples included failure to state a claim, expiration of the statute of limitations, improper service and so on. In major litigation these procedural challenges may consume a year or more and result in six-figure legal fees before the case even reaches the merits.

The Discovery Stage

If the legal hurdles are overcome, the case enters the discovery stage. Discovery is the formal process whereby the parties collect evidence and learn the details of the opposing cases. Under the federal rules, either party may take discovery regarding any matter, not privileged, which is relevant to the subject matter of the action, or which may lead to an admissible evidence.

The principal means of discovery are oral depositions, written interrogatories, and requests to produce documents.

Depositions are probably the most popular and useful form of discovery. A deposition is sworn testimony, given by a party or witness, upon questioning by counsel for one of the parties, before trial and outside of court, usually in a lawyer's office. Opposing counsel and a stenographer, who administers the oath and transcribes the testimony, are also present. Deposition testimony may be used to obtain evidence about the party's own or the opponent's case, or to preserve testimony for trial. In the federal system, a witness outside the subpoena power of the court may be deposed where she or he resides. The transcript is then read to the jury at trial.

Interrogatories may be served only on the opposing party, not witnesses. Interrogatories are simply written questions that the party, usually through an attorney, is required to answer in writing. They are much less expensive than depositions, but usually not nearly as productive, as counsel traditionally finds ways to avoid answering or provide minimal information. Interrogatories are frequently abused by the serving party as well. They may submit literally hundreds of questions, many of them irrelevant or very burdensome to answer, in an effort to grind down the opposition. The court may issue orders protecting parties from such discovery if it is plainly designed to harass the opposition rather than to obtain useful evidence.

Requests to produce documents may be served on opposing parties. Records from third-party witnesses or institutions may be obtained by subpoenas. These often must be accompanied by deposition notices as well, in order to take testimony to authenticate the documents. All in all, discovery can be an extremely expensive and time-consuming process, often taking years to complete, particularly in complex litigation. Proposals to reform and streamline the system are constantly advocated. But they are seldom adopted, in large measure because trial lawyers are unwilling to give up or limit their opportunities to look for weaknesses in their opponent's case.

During or at the conclusion of the discovery process a party may file a motion for summary judgment. This motion will be granted if the court determines that the pleadings and proof clearly demonstrate that there is no genuine material issue of fact involved in the proceedings, and that the moving party is entitled to judgment as a matter of law. Motions for summary judgment are generally not favored, as they terminate the proceedings before trial. And the moving party bears a heavy burden to demonstrate that there are indeed no circumstances, factually or legally, under which the opposing party could possibly be entitled to relief.

If a motion for summary judgment is granted, the case ends, although the opposing party may appeal. If the motion is denied, the case proceeds to trial.

Trial of a Civil Case

Trial procedures in civil actions are similar to those in criminal cases, with several notable exceptions. Juries need not consist of 12 persons, and many civil cases are heard by six jurors. The parties may also stipulate that the verdict need not be unanimous. The burden of proof for the civil plaintiff is much lower than for the criminal prosecutor. In most cases the plaintiff must prove his or her case by only the "preponderance of the evidence," meaning that there must be only slightly more evidence in favor than against. The Fifth Amendment privilege against self-incrimination does not apply in civil proceedings. A party may still refuse to answer questions or produce evidence, but if that is the case, inferences may be drawn and the refusal may be disclosed to the jury. The judge may also enter sanctions against the party refusing to produce evidence, up to and including the entry of a judgment.

Certain privileges are recognized in civil proceedings. Examples include the marital privilege, which prevents one spouse from being compelled to testify against another; the attorney-client privilege, which prohibits the disclosure of communications between an attorney and the client for the purpose of rendering legal advice; and the work-product doctrine, which protects an attorney's notes and certain other materials prepared in anticipation of litigation. Work undertaken by an accountant, investigator or fraud examiner at the direction of an attorney may also be protected by the attorney-client privilege and work-product doctrine.

Civil trials begin with the opening statements by counsel, with the plaintiff's counsel speaking first. As in criminal trials, the opening is devoted to introducing the parties and the nature of the dispute, and outlining the evidence the party expects to produce.

The plaintiff presents evidence first. In many civil trials the proof consists of the witnesses and counsel reading portions of depositions taken in discovery from witnesses outside the subpoena power of the court. The latter is particularly uninteresting for the jury, and may be very prejudicial for a party forced to rely on a great deal of such testimony. Answers to written interrogatories by the opposing party may also be read to the jury. These documents, if extensive, may be even less inspirational.

Civil parties may also call expert witnesses to give their opinion on matters thought to be too technical for the average juror to understand. Fraud examiners and accountants may be used as experts in fraud and other commercial cases to compute and testify to damages. Of course, as with expert psychiatric testimony in criminal trials, each side usually produces a highly qualified expert who disagrees categorically with everything the expert for the other side says. Since the jury usually learns through cross-examination that each expert has been paid handsomely for preparation and trial time, and because jurors generally have a difficult time understanding and evaluating expert testimony, it often has little effect on the outcome of the trial.

The same rules of evidence apply in civil and criminal trials, with certain exceptions, such as the application of the Fifth Amendment privilege against self-incrimination, noted above. Witnesses (except experts) must relate only facts, not opinions, and irrelevant and prejudicial evidence is excluded, as is most hearsay. Both parties may cross-examine and attempt to impeach the other side's witnesses in essentially the same manner as at a criminal trial.

The defendant may make a motion for a directed verdict at the close of the plaintiff's case, on the grounds that even if the plaintiff's evidence is believed, he or she is still entitled to a judgment as a matter of law. Both sides may make such a motion at the close of all the evidence. If such motions are denied, both sides argue to the jury, the plaintiff first. The plaintiff is usually also afforded an opportunity for final rebuttal. The jury is then instructed on the law, as to both elements of liability and damages, and it retires for deliberations. The losing party may move for a judgment notwithstanding the verdict, or a new trial, within ten days of the verdict.

Both sides may appeal from an adverse verdict, as to either liability or damages. As in the criminal system, the appellate court is largely limited to reviewing the legal decision of the trial court rather than the factual determination of the jury. The appeals court may reverse and remand for a new trial, on some or all of the issues, may order that a certain portion of the awarded damages be remitted, or may enter final judgment, if legal grounds are clear, in favor of either party.

A plaintiff who obtains a money judgment must often take additional steps to collect it. This may include garnishing the wages of the defendant or levying against his or her assets. In many instances, particularly in fraud litigation, a judgment may go uncollected because the defendant has already squandered the ill-gotten gains or has secreted them. In the latter circumstances, a plaintiff may conduct post-judgment discovery, including a deposition of the defendant in an attempt to locate assets to satisfy a judgment.

Testifying as an Expert Witness

Accountants, auditors, and fraud examiners are often called upon to provide testimony in criminal and civil prosecutions where their services were utilized to support investigations of financial frauds, embezzlements, misapplication of funds, arson for profit, bankruptcy fraud, improper accounting practices, tax evasion, and others. They may also be utilized as defense witnesses or as support to the defendant's counsel on matters which involve accounting or audit issues.

Qualifying accountants, auditors, and fraud examiners as technical experts is generally not a difficult task. Questions are posed to them concerning their professional credentials, i.e., education, work experience, licensing or certification, technical training courses taken, technical books and journal articles written, offices held in professional associations, awards and commendations received.

Smart defense lawyers do not generally challenge the expertise of well-qualified experts, assuming they meet at least minimum standards of professional competence. To do so may give these experts an opportunity to fully highlight their professional credentials and perhaps make a greater impression on the jury or judge, thus adding more weight to their testimony. So defense attorneys often pass on the opportunity to challenge these expert witnesses.

If called by the prosecution, examiners might testify to their findings, and if called by the defense, they may testify regarding opinions expressed by the prosecution's expert—to create doubt in the jury's mind about the credibility or weight to be given to that expert.

To become a credible expert witness, one must be a member in good standing of the profession, and usually be recognized as an authority in that profession or some specialized aspect of practice within that profession. There are other considerations in making an expert a credible witness. The following are some simple tips in that regard:

1. Speak clearly and audibly.
2. Refrain from using professional jargon.
3. Use simple rather than complex terms to describe findings and opinions.
4. Answer the specific questions. Don't go off on tangents or volunteer more than the question requires.
5. Don't verbally fence with the attorney.
6. Look directly at the question-poser, prosecutor or defense counsel.
7. Maintain a professional demeanor—don't smile gratuitously at the judge, jury, or lawyers.
8. Be calm and deliberate in responding to questions. Think before you speak.
9. Wear conservative clothing. For men, a business suit of neutral tone, gray or dark blue, black shoes (shined) and dark socks, and a conservative tie properly knotted at the collar. Be neatly groomed.
10. Use graphs, charts, and other visual aids if they help to clarify a point.
11. Don't read from notes if you can avoid it. (The opposition lawyer will probably demand to see such notes if you do, and you will then look as if you rehearsed your testimony—and did so rather badly.)
12. If you have documents to introduce, have them organized so that you can quickly retrieve them when asked to do so.
13. Don't hem and haw or stammer. Recover your composure when a tough or complex question is posed.
14. Ask for a repetition of the question or clarification if you don't fully comprehend it.
15. If you don't know the answer, say so. Don't guess.
16. In cross-examination, don't respond too quickly. Counsel for your side may wish to interpose an objection to the question.
17. If the judge or jury elects to ask a question, respond to it by looking their way.
18. Don't stare off into space, at the floor, or at the ceiling.
19. Be friendly to all sides.
20. Don't raise your voice in anger if the opponent's lawyer tries to bait you.
21. Be honest. Don't invent, don't inflate. Don't be evasive.

An expert witness in accounting must have a thorough knowledge of not only generally accepted accounting principles but also the current promulgations. Often the expertise may involve special knowledge of a specific industry. In this case, the expert should be aware of recent development and any important issues within that area.

The expert must also be analytical and possess the ability to work with incomplete data. The expert may, however, not always be able to recognize when data is incomplete. As a result, the expert may make various assumptions that would then be open for interpretation or attack. If all data has *not* been made available, then it is quite possible that the opposing counsel may be able to offer alternate scenarios that are more plausible under the circumstances, thus discrediting the expert.

The expert must have the ability to simplify complex issues. It is helpful if he or she can communicate in a very direct and simple manner. The expert's role includes being able to clarify complex issues and allow everyone to understand them. The question often arises whether being a CFE, CPA, or other professional certification is sufficient to qualify as an expert. Although professional designations are considered in evaluating the credentials of an expert witness, that determination is made on a case-by-case basis; therefore, any professional designation does not automatically qualify. It is most helpful to have prior experience with litigation or criminal matters as an expert, primarily for the awareness instilled during the testifying experience. Further, it is often of assistance to have been accepted as an expert in other matters, thereby easing current acceptance. A danger exists, however, of appearing to be a professional witness.

Often, the counsel introducing the witness will read the expert's qualifications or ask specific questions of the witness to establish his or her credentials. On occasion, the qualifications of the expert witness are read directly into the court record. Although the expert's qualifications are not often contested, it does happen. Over and above being accepted by both parties, the expert witness most importantly must be accepted by the court.

Generally, the expert plays an ongoing part in the litigation team. In particular, the expert may be involved at various stages throughout the development of the case, most notably:

1. case assessment
2. identification of documentation required to support the case
3. evaluation of the scope of work
4. consultation with counsel with respect to legal issues
5. preparation of report and accounting schedules

The examiner may also be called upon to give an opinion different from that reached by an equally credible expert accountant on the other side. This may arise due to different interpretations of the facts of the case. In some situations, given equally plausible alternatives, the case might be decided on whichever side has the most credible expert witness.

One important problem in the preparation of reports and accounting summaries arises from delegation of tasks to subordinates. If the person giving evidence has no direct knowledge or has not examined the specific documents or prepared the accounting summaries, this expert may be trapped under the hearsay rule.

If tasks are delegated, it is important that the review process entail review of all work to original documentation on a 100 percent basis.

It is also important to know the effect of other assumptions on the conclusion or opinion reached in the report. An expert can be led into giving alternate opinions, based upon other assumptions that had not been considered. Generally, working papers supporting the report and accounting schedules should not show conclusions contradictory to the report, as they are producible in court. This caveat does not advocate that working papers should be deleted or amended subsequent to preparation. Rather, it is a caution that these papers should be prepared with the understanding that they could ultimately be submitted to the court and, therefore, should take the appropriate form at the time of preparation.

Another aspect of pretrial preparation relates to the availability of all notes the witness intends to use or rely upon. These notes may be requested in evidence for the court or may be producible during examination.

It may be necessary in some cases to derive information from other witnesses to support the expert's conclusions. This is normally done by reference to earlier proceedings. Unfortunately, the witness cannot refer to these unless he or she has direct knowledge of their contents. If the expert has relied upon opinions or information presented by other witnesses, then he or she must either hear that evidence in court or have the transcript or agreed statement of facts available. Otherwise, that information and any opinions based upon that information would not generally be allowable.

Other pretestimony activities include important discussions with the lawyer and that the expert has a complete understanding of his or her report and all other relevant issues. The expert should ensure that he or she agrees with counsel as to the sequence of evidence and the strategy for presenting it. It is often useful to have a dry run at the direct testimony, with all the questions being posed by the counsel to the expert in order to avoid surprises during trial.

The appearance of the expert witness often lends itself to an assessment of the credibility of that witness. For that reason, it is recommended that the witness be well-groomed and neatly dressed. A fraud examiner is often expected to appear in a dark business suit. This appearance may be used to enhance image to psychological advantage. In the witness box, the witness should maintain a poised, alert appearance, stand firmly, and be ready to take the oath. It is important to keep control of hands and to avoid fidgeting, and to maintain eye contact with the questioner while remaining aware of the judge. As the judge will be taking notes, the witness should speak slowly enough to ensure that the judge does not fall behind. The voice should be strong and directed to the questioner. The witness should enunciate clearly.

Several things should be avoided in giving testimony. These range from drinking five cups of coffee immediately prior to testimony, chewing bubble gum while giving evidence, to small physical mannerisms that may affect your appearance. These physical mannerisms, which might be as simple as rubbing the hands together continually, looking down at the hands, continually moving in the stand, jingling coins in a pocket, all could quickly become irritating to the judge and jury.

The purpose of direct examination is to enable your counsel to draw out the evidence to prove their case. Most likely, this will be only a reiteration of what has been previously discussed with your counsel outside the courtroom. It is still very important, however, to refresh your memory by reference to anything you may have read, written, or given in evidence on the case beforehand.

Direct examination is the most organized aspect of the trial; it is the stage in which the expert's credibility must be established with the judge or jury. According to the concept of the primary memory feature, people remember best what they hear first and last. This is often a useful idea to employ in giving or structuring evidence. A further noteworthy point is that the jury will often have a limited attention span in a long trial, thus, it is often useful to use a "grab/give/conclude" method of presenting evidence.

To a witness, the interpretation of questions and the ability to listen are crucial skills. Even though the witness may have already gone through a mock direct examination, it is critical that each question be carefully evaluated again: the witness should reflect upon the questions asked and not anticipate them (they may have been changed, anyway, since rehearsal). Throughout, one must remember that this aspect of testimony was rehearsed in advance and as such is the easiest aspect of examination.

In answering questions, one must be honest. Less obvious, however, is the need to avoid bias and prejudice in answering. The answers to all questions should be clear and concise and, where complex terms are used, should be clarified. Use of notes should be limited as much as possible in order to maintain eye contact with both the judge and the rest of the court.

Schedules, if any, should be described accurately and succinctly in layperson's terms. Schedules are, by their nature, concise documents and should be described concisely. If opinions are given, they should be given with conviction.

Cross-Examination

Cross-examination is truly the highlight of the adversary system. It is geared to allow counsel to either clarify or make points at the witness's expense. As such, it is generally the most difficult part of the trial process for any witness. Anything unexpected can turn up that might refute or embarrass the witness. The witness's credibility is constantly called into question.

The goals of the opposing counsel during cross-examination are threefold. The first goal is to diminish the importance of the expert testimony just presented. The second is to have the expert testify in support of the opposing position by providing a series of assumptions. The third goal is to attack the opinion itself or to show the inadequacies in the expert's opinion, thereby discrediting the opinion, the report, and the witness in the eyes of the court.

The opposing counsel can attack or question anything that has been said or entered into evidence. This includes notes, working papers, affidavits, reports, and preliminary trial or discovery transcripts. Often, cross-examination is an atmosphere of confrontation and contradiction. At all times, one must remember that the expert witness, however crucial to the case, is merely a piece of the puzzle.

The witness must not take attacks or situations of discredit personally. There are many ways to discredit an expert witness. Throughout the process, it is important for the witness to maintain pride and professional integrity. An adage to remember is that "even mud can be worn well."

In general, proper attitude and demeanor during direct examination are also applicable to cross-examination, except that opposing counsel wants to reduce or limit the impact of the witness's evidence. It is natural to feel a certain amount of apprehension at this state, and this does a great deal to keep the witness alert.

The jury often watches the judge, and therefore the expert can often take a clue as to the tempo and reaction of the jury and the judge to the evidence being presented. Slight changes in style and presentation can be made accordingly.

The opposing counsel usually has a plan of cross-examination in mind, and an expert witness should be able to establish this direction to avoid falling into a trap. A danger of this, of course, is that the witness will spend as much time planning ahead as answering the questions and may not be giving appropriate weight to the immediate questions. Further, in attempting to anticipate, the witness may misunderstand the question.

When being asked questions, the expert should evaluate them carefully and take time to consider the answer. The witness should be calm and pause before answering, and tread very carefully toward the answer, knowing exactly how it relates to both the question and the issues in front of the court.

In giving an answer it is important to be honest and to avoid the appearance of bias and prejudice. It is also equally important not to exaggerate, ramble in answering, allow oneself to be baited, or attempt to be humorous. One of the most devastating blows to litigation is when an expert witness makes a transparent attempt to hide errors or loses his or her temper.

It is a rule of thumb that information should not be given away or volunteered. It may often be extremely difficult to avoid getting trapped in various assumptions, "what if" scenarios, and generalities presented by counsel during cross-examination. If this occurs, retrench by asking for a question to be rephrased in smaller components.

It is critical never to underestimate the expertise of the opposing counsel. Often, opposing counsel will be underplaying their understanding of the issues in order to lull the expert into a sense of security. Obviously, this can lead the expert into a difficult situation.

Opposing counsel's golden rule is to cross-examine only if the cross-examination would benefit a case. In asking questions of the witness, opposing counsel will generally ask either short questions in plain words or leading questions. Usually counsel knows the answers.

The opposing counsel will generally evaluate answers and then take a specific approach that furthers its argument. Normally, the witness will not be allowed to explain or elaborate on the question, as that would allow the witness to alter the thrust of a carefully orchestrated cross-examination. Opposing counsel is continually questioning or evaluating how its last question and answer could be used against the witness. If the question has raised new ground, can it be developed and used to enhance the opposing counsel's position?

Opposing counsel will often prepare by reading all earlier testimony and publications of the witness. They might also ask other lawyers about the witness's capabilities in court if they have had experience with the witness. This may indicate specific weaknesses in the witness. If any are discovered, the questioning of the witness will probably be directed to that area.

Opposing counsel may also attempt to take psychological control of a witness by:

1. use of physical presence to intimidate

2. nonstop eye contact

3. challenging space of the witness

4. fast pace to questions to confuse witness

5. not allowing the expert to explain or deviate from the exact question

Physical domination is often used by opposing counsel. They will quickly discover the response pattern of the expert and might take an aggressive stance to lead the expert to the point where he or she is unsure, with devastating results.

The following strategic methods could be employed by opposing counsel to discredit a witness or to diminish the importance of his or her testimony. These methods could be used singly or in conjunction with one another and are not an all-encompassing list. A good counsel in cross-examination will quickly discover the witness's weak areas and employ any possible techniques to achieve his or her goal. Thus, it is often useful to have an overall understanding of some of the more common methods employed.

Myopic Vision. Myopic vision entails getting the expert to admit to spending excessive time in the investigation of a matter, then selecting an area to highlight where the expert is unsure or has not done much work. This area may not be central to the issues in the case or it may in fact be critical—but it must be relevant to conclusions reached. Then, the opposing counsel will make a large issue of it and prove that the expert's vision is myopic in that the work was limited in extent or scope and, as such, substandard. At the same time, the question of fees could be drawn in to show that large sums were expended to have this "obviously incomplete" work done.

Safety/Good Guy. This approach involves not attacking the expert and hence lulling him or her at first into a feeling of false security. Then, the attorney might find a small hole that could be enlarged quickly. This approach is often characterized by being friendly and conciliatory, whereby the jury is made sympathetic to the cause of the opposing counsel. Counsel may also attempt to achieve a certain alliance with the witness that will make the witness want to help the opposing counsel in bringing out information in the matter. Doing so may result in the witness's giving information that otherwise would not have been given. With this additional information, it may be possible to find a chink or hole in the evidence and develop it further.

Contradiction. Opposing counsel may use leading questions to force the witness into a hard or contradictory position. Alternately, counsel can establish a potentially contradicting document or quote from other articles written by experts in the field. If these documents or articles contradict the expert, then an admission can be obtained from the expert. If the contradiction exists, then the expert might be drawn into an argument as to who is the most appropriate or experienced expert in the circumstances.

New Information. Opposing counsel may introduce new information that the expert might not be aware of and refer to a specific relevance in the conclusions reached by the expert witness. This is normally done in order to confuse the witness.

Support Opposing Sides Theory. This approach establishes and recognizes an expert's qualifications and evidence. The same information is then used and interpreted by opposing counsel in a different fashion to support an alternate theory. By getting the expert to agree to the alternate interpretation of the facts and theory, in effect, the opposing counsel has made the expert the witness for the other side. This technique is useful to obtain concessions from the witness that would damage his or her conclusions and, ultimately, credibility.

Bias. This method draws the expert's counsel and the expert together to show possible collusion as to the evidence being presented in testimony. This can be shown if the opposing counsel can determine that the expert's counsel had instructed the witness as to what to say. This approach can also focus on the question whether or not the expert was told by the client what to do. With this approach, opposing counsel can attempt to show that the expert overlooked important documentation in an effort to assist the client.

Confrontation. This very simple method is the continued use of a confrontation of wills to put the witness into a situation where he or she might lose emotional control and display anger. Once a witness has exploded, credibility normally disappears.

Sounding Board. This method uses the witness as a sounding board to reacquaint the jury with the favorable aspects (to opposing counsel) of the case. This technique often uses the "is it not true" and "would you agree with me" approach. Constant nonstop agreement is useful to browbeat the expert. In the eyes of the judge and jury, agreement with various questions raised by the opposing counsel may also be assumed to be a general concurrence with their position. This is often a very valuable psychological tool.

Fees. This method attacks the witness for having taken an inordinate amount of time for the result given. Further, the attack may indicate a lack of complete work and may be correlated to the fees charged. This method is often related to "bias" and "myopic vision." Citing gross fees or recurring engagements with a client, it may be suggested that the witness and his or her opinion are, in fact, biased to retain the client. This technique often builds to a conclusion by which the opposing counsel shows that the work was superficial and unprofessional, yet a great deal of money was received by the expert. The direct inference is that the testimony was purchased or that the expert was paid to overlook facts contradictory to the conclusions made.

Terms of Engagement. This technique is normally employed by obtaining the original engagement letter and examining the terms. Opposing counsel can then show that the expert intended only to look at various items in support of the client and glossed over any alternative theories, generally to the detriment of the opposition. The witness could then be portrayed as not impartial.

Discrediting the Witness. Discrediting the witness is based on proving that the expert is unworthy to be a credible witness to the court. This can often be accomplished by showing that the expert is currently or has previously been grossly biased, prejudiced, corrupt, convicted of criminal activities, shown to engage in immoral activities, made inconsistent statements, acquired a reputation for a lack of veracity, and/or exaggerated his or her qualifications.

Discrediting could also consist of looking at the quality of the expert's educational background to reveal any other unusual activities that might bias the witness or exclude him or her from the court as an expert.

III Fraud Auditing

6 Accounting and Auditing

BASIC ACCOUNTING THEORY

Accounting accumulates, measures, and communicates economic data about an enterprise to various decisionmakers.

Assets are resources owned by an entity. Examples of assets are cash, receivables, inventory, property, equipment, and even intangible things of value such as patents, licenses, and trademarks. To qualify as an asset, something must be owned and provide future benefit. Liabilities are the obligations of an entity or outsiders' claims against a company's assets. Owners' equity represents the net investment of the owners in the company—assets minus liabilities.

The cornerstone of accounting since 1494, when it was invented by Luca Pacioli, the following equation must always be in balance:

$$\text{Assets} = \text{Liabilities} + \text{Owners' Equity}$$

For example, if a company borrows from a bank, both cash (an asset) and notes payable (a liability) increase to show that cash has been received and that the company now has an obligation. When both assets and liabilities increase by the same amount, the equation stays in balance.

The balance sheet of a company is an expansion of this equation—that is, it is a listing of all assets on one side of the page and all liabilities and owners' equities on the other side.

While assets and liabilities are rather easily understood, owners' equities need further explanation. The owners' equity usually represents amounts from two sources—from undistributed earnings (usually referred to as retained earnings), and from owner contributions (usually referred to as common or capital stock), as in the following equation.

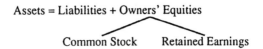

Assets = Liabilities + Owners' Equities

Common Stock   Retained Earnings

The balances in the capital stock account only increase when owners invest in a company. The retained earnings balance increases when a company has earnings and decreases when a company has losses, or when earnings are distributed to the owners in the form of dividends.

In addition to the balance sheet, another major financial statement is the income statement. While a balance sheet shows total assets, liabilities, and owners' equities at a specific point in time (for example, at the end of the year), an income statement shows how much income was earned during a period of time, such as a year, in the form of the following equation.

Revenues - Expenses = Net Income

The accounts on an income statement are temporary. At the end of each period they are all closed (brought to a zero balance), with the resulting net income being added to the retained earnings account of the balance sheet.

Two kinds of accounts are reported on the income statement—revenues, which are gross amounts received from the sale of goods or services, and expenses, which are costs incurred to generate revenues. For example, a sporting goods store would have revenues from the sale of skis and guns. It would also have expenses for amounts paid to purchase the skis, guns, etc. as well as for other costs of operation such as utility expense, wage expenses, tax expense, telephone expense, and other operating costs.

As stated previously, at the end of each period, all revenues and expenses are closed, or brought to a zero balance and the difference, net income (loss), is added to the retained earnings account of the balance sheet. The income statement therefore is tied to the balance sheet through the retained earnings account, as in this diagram:

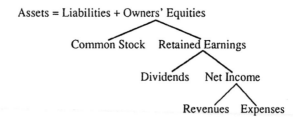

Assets = Liabilities + Owners' Equities

Common Stock   Retained Earnings

Dividends   Net Income

Revenues   Expenses

When an asset is misappropriated, the accounts may be altered to make the equation and resulting financial statements balance. If an asset is stolen, the equation can be balanced by reducing another asset, reducing a liability, reducing an owner's equity account, reducing revenues (and thus retained earnings), or

Table 6.1
Examples of T Accounts

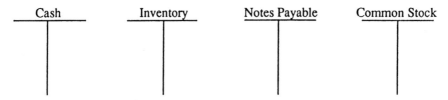

| Cash | Inventory | Notes Payable | Common Stock |

creating a fraudulent expense (and thus reducing retained earnings). Of these, creating a fraudulent expense is most common. A perpetrator, for example, can steal cash, charge the amount as advertising expense, thus making it look as if the money was spent on advertising and the resultant equation in balance. Manipulating of house accounts is less likely to be uncovered because they are closed at the end of the accounting period. If the theft is not discovered in the current period, usually it never will be discovered because the expense will be closed out from the accounting records. If a permanent balance sheet account is manipulated, the account is not eliminated at the end of the period. And the amount stolen must then be concealed as an adjustment of some sort until it is discovered or written off as an expense. Among expenses, certain accounts such as miscellaneous expense, professional fees expense, legal expense, and other service accounts are most often used because these expenses do not call for the delivery of quantifiable goods.

Accounts and the Accounting Cycle

Thus far the term account has been used to indicate specific assets, liabilities, owners' equity, revenue or expense items. In reality, an account is nothing more than a specific accounting record that provides an efficient way of categorizing similar transactions. All transactions affecting the same items can be summarized into assets accounts, liability accounts, owners' equity accounts, revenue accounts, and expense accounts. Accounts may be presented in a number of ways. The simplest, most fundamental format is to use a large letter T, or a T account (See Table 6.1).

Accounts provide a convenient way to summarize all transactions affecting a specific asset, liability, owners' equity, revenue, or expense item. Entries to the left side of an account are referred to as debits (dr) and entries to the right side of an account are referred to as credits (cr). Asset and expense accounts are increased with debits and decreased with credits; while liabilities, owners' equity, and revenue accounts are increased with credits and decreased with debits. (See Table 6.2).

To follow transactions when looking for concealment efforts, the debit/credit process must be understood. For example, when searching for a mysterious $5,000 disappearance of cash, you find that the legal expense account has been

Table 6.2
Accounting Equation in Form of T Accounts

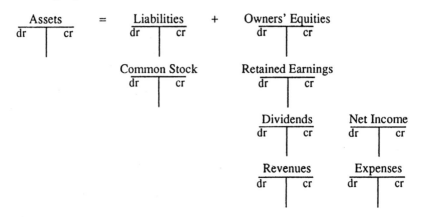

Table 6.3
Flow of Transaction Information

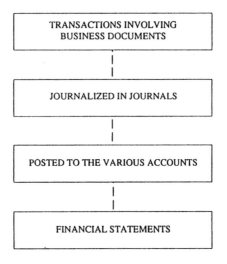

debited for $5,000 and the cash account has been credited for $5,000. If you cannot find a genuine bill from the attorney for $5,000, you can suspect that the perpetrator attempted to conceal the theft by labelling the $5,000 in stolen funds as a legal expense.

Discovering concealment efforts through the accounting records is one of the easiest ways to detect fraud by looking for weaknesses in the various steps of the accounting cycle. Legitimate transactions leave a trail that can be followed (See Table 6.3). Most transactions start with a source document such as an invoice, a check, or a receiving report. These source documents become the basis for journal entries which are chronological listings of transactions with their debit and credit amounts. Journal entries are made in various accounting journals. The entries in the journals are then posted or entered into the accounts. The amounts in the accounts are summarized to become the financial statements for a period.

When fictitious entries are made to the accounting records, source documents are normally absent, fabricated, or altered. These documents, together with the journal entries (debits and credits), accounts, and financial statements leave a trail that can reveal many frauds. When searching for an understatement in the financial statements, one usually begins with the source documents and works forward to the financial statements. If the financial statements are understated, sometimes the information from the invoices will be deleted or altered. When searching for an overstatement, one starts with the financial statements and works backwards to the source documents. True overstatements will not normally have legitimate support documentation. With this analysis, a fraud examiner who thoroughly understands accounting is in a much better position to detect a fraud than one who does not.

An Example of How Knowledge of Accounting Can Help Fraud Examiners

To better illustrate these basic accounting concepts and how an analysis of accounting records can reveal a fraud, consider the following example. Jackson Hardware Supply is a medium-sized plumbing and electrical wholesale distributor. An anonymous tip suggests that the controller is stealing cash from the company. Lately, he has been seen driving a new BMW and has taken expensive vacations. The president of the company wants to follow up on the tip. Although the controller is a longtime, trusted employee, the president asks you to determine if in fact he has been stealing. Although there are several ways you could proceed, you decide to first compare this year's total salary expense with last year's balance. (See Tables 6.4 and 6.5.) You theorize that if the controller is being dishonest, he may be trying to conceal the theft in the salaries expense account. Past experience has taught you to look in the most obvious place first and to search where an opportunity exists. You note that the balance of $220,000 in the salary expense account this year is significantly larger than the $180,000 balance last year. You ask the owner how large across-the-board raises were this year and discover that all employees, including the owner himself, received ten percent raises. You recalculate this year's salaries by increasing last year's salaries ten percent and determine that the balance in the salary expense account should be approximately $198,000 ($180,000 × 1.10 = $198,000). You now believe that excess salaries may have been paid to someone. You next follow the overstatement in salary expense backwards from the income statement through the accounts and journal entries to the source documents—the payroll checks in this case. You find that there are 12 payroll checks payable to John Doe, an employee who quit in January of last year. You compare the endorse-

Table 6.4
Sample Balance Sheet

Jackson Hardware Supply
Balance Sheet
As of December 31, __

Assets		Liabilities & Owners' Equities	
Cash	$2,427,000	**Liabilities**	
Accounts Receivable	300,000		
Inventory	300,000	Accounts Payable	300,000
Supplies	11,000	Salaries Payable	70,000
Prepaid Insurance	44,000	Rent Payable	50,000
Equipment	440,000	Total Liabilities	$420,000
Total Assets	$3,522,000	**Owners' Equities**	
		Common Stock	$2,000,000
		Retained Earnings	1,102,000
		Total Owners' Equity	$3,102,000
		Total Liabilities &	
		Owners' Equity	$3,522,000

ments on John Doe's checks with those on the controller's checks and notice distinct similarities in the signatures. Armed with this evidence, you interview the controller who confesses that he has stolen $22,000 and concealed the theft by issuing payroll checks to a nonexistent employee. He subsequently cashed the checks and converted the proceeds to his own use.

Obviously, this example is simple. In reality, however, most frauds are very simple, especially for an examiner who understands concealment techniques and accounting. There are other detection techniques that could have been used to determine if the controller was stealing. These techniques could include running a computer listing of all employees not electing insurance and other payroll withholdings (withholdings on fictitious employees create additional concealment problems for perpetrators); having someone else distribute the checks; and checking social security numbers of all active employees against amounts paid. Any or all of these methods may have revealed the spurious checks to John Doe. The approach does show, however, that an understanding of accounting can be invaluable when detecting fraud.

Table 6.5
Sample Income Statement

Jackson Hardware Supply
Income Statement
For the Year Ending December 31, __

Revenues

Sales Revenue	$3,470,000	
Rent Revneue	10,000	
Total Revenues		$3,480,000

Expenses

Cost of Goods Sold	$2,100,000	
Insurance Expense	4,000	
Salary Expense	220,000	
Supplies Expense	14,000	
Rental Expense	40,000	
Total Expenses		$2,378,000
Net Income Before Taxes		$1,102,000
Income Taxes		438,000
Net Income		$664,000

AUDITING THEORY

Auditing is the process by which competent, independent individuals accumulate and evaluate financial evidence. Independent financial statement auditors (certified public accountants), for example, accumulate and evaluate evidence about specific companies for the purpose of determining and reporting whether or not their financial statements have been prepared in accordance with generally accepted accounting principles. Internal auditors, on the other hand, who are employees of specific companies working independent of line management, examine and evaluate their company's activities as a service to the organization. Their objective is to assist members of the organization in the effective discharge of their obligations. To this end, internal auditors furnish an organization with analyses, appraisals, recommendations, counsel, and information concerning the activities reviewed. Government auditors gather evidence about governmental programs to establish whether or not they are in compliance with applicable laws and regulations. Internal Revenue Service auditors gather information to determine whether taxpayers are complying with applicable tax laws.

Some persons confuse auditing with accounting. This confusion exists because most auditing is performed on accounting information and many auditors have backgrounds in accounting. This confusion is not reduced by the title most financial statement auditors have, that of "certified public accountant." As defined previously, accounting is the process of recording, classifying, and summarizing economic events about an entity for the purpose of assisting decision-making. While auditing can involve analyzing accounting information, auditing is much broader. One can audit for fraud, audit for compliance, audit for efficiency, or audit for any other reason desired. Auditing for fraud is called forensic auditing. While many auditors possess accounting backgrounds, good analytic and communication skills are probably most important for a successful forensic auditor.

Forensic Auditing

The field of forensic auditing is new and not well developed. Unlike the CPA profession, which has existed for over 80 years, forensic auditing has no generally accepted standards. In fact, most self-proclaimed forensic auditors are certified public accountants or internal auditors specializing in fraud detection. Although there are similarities in forensic ability and fraud examination, the latter is broader. Fraud examiners not only know forensic audit skills, they also know how to investigate and gather evidence regarding fraud.

Audit Standards

While standards do not presently exist for forensic auditors, relevant standards, taken from other types of auditing, would include the following:

1. The audit is to be performed by a person or persons having adequate technical training and proficiency as a fraud examiner or auditor.
2. In all matters relating to the examination, an independence in mental attitude is to be maintained by the auditors.
3. Due professional care is to be exercised in the performance of the examination and the preparation of the report.
4. The work is to be adequately planned and assistants, if any, are to be properly supervised.
5. Sufficient, competent evidential matter is to be obtained through inspection, observation, inquiries, and other means to afford a reasonable basis for an opinion regarding the matter being investigated.
6. The purpose of forensic examinations is to establish whether a fraud has occurred.
7. The results of all examinations shall be clearly communicated to appropriate individuals in a timely manner.

Phases of a Forensic Audit

Forensic auditing can be divided into four phases: (1) problem recognition and planning, (2) evidence collection, (3) evidence evaluation, and (4) communication of results.

In the problem recognition and planning stage, the pertinent facts and circumstances regarding a potential fraud are gathered. Here, examiners learn as much about the potential fraud as possible, without actually gathering evidence. They identify how the potential problem was recognized and communicated, where the fraud was supposed to have taken place, and who the potential perpetrators are. Fraud examiners do not go on fishing expeditions! There must be some indication of fraud for an examiner to become involved. The suspected fraud may have become known because of an anonymous tip, a fraud symptom such as a questionable document, suspicion on the part of an employee, or because of an unusual event or relationship. The important point is that there must be a legitimate reason to believe that fraud exists. This is known as predication. In this first stage, the problem is refined, articulated, and restated. Background checks into the suspects, the environment, and other conditions are conducted. Possible explanations for the potential problem are explored. The problem could be a mistake or unintentional error, rather than a fraud. At this first stage, no one is convicted or incriminated. Indeed, evidence has not yet been gathered.

The problem recognition stage is also when the examination is planned. Proper planning includes determining who will staff the examination, how the examination will be conducted, and when the examination will take place. In deciding the staffing of the examination, the need for specialists or individuals with unique skills is considered. In determining when the examination will take place, it should always be remembered that delaying an investigation can lead to destroyed or lost evidence. Early resolution of a fraud protects both the victim and the perpetrator.

The second phase of a forensic audit is the evidence-gathering stage. The purpose of this phase of the audit is two-fold: (1) to determine whether the initial evidence of suspected fraud is misleading, and, (2) if further action is recommended, to gather sufficient, competent, and relevant evidence to resolve the fraud. Many times missing records, destroyed records, modified records, errors, or omissions can be attributed to human error or accident, and a full-scale investigation should not be pursued.

Several rules must be remembered in the evidence gathering stage. To be effective in detecting fraud, you must attempt to identify the three elements of fraud (act, concealment, and conversion) and work on the easiest element. Most frauds can be resolved by concentrating on the most obvious solutions and the weakest points in the fraud. If someone has an opportunity to commit fraud and/or appears suspicious, he or she probably is the perpetrator.

Another method of obtaining evidence is to search for fraud opportunities by using vulnerability charts and internal control critical combination charts. Fraud cannot occur unless there is an opportunity. The greater or more accessible the opportunity, the more often it is likely to be exploited. Vulnerability charts and critical combinations of controls help examiners arrange risks in order of their probabilities. These charts involve correlating stolen assets with potential thieves, possible methods of fraud, effectiveness of controls around the fraud, possible concealment courses, and possibilities of conversion. These charts are objective ways of homing in on the most likely fraud perpetrators.

Just as critical combinations and vulnerability charts isolate fraud opportunities, document examination is a technique that uncovers concealment efforts of perpetrators by working on cover-up schemes involving documents. Documents can be altered, forged, created, changed, duplicated, or misplaced. Most internal frauds are concealed by manipulating source documents such as purchase invoices, sales invoices, credit memoranda, or warehouse removal slips.

Sometimes the gathering of evidence involves using employee searches. This detection technique involves examining employees' desks, lockers, lunch boxes, and other effects. When searching, it is important not to violate personal rights guaranteed by the Fourth Amendment to the U.S. Constitution, which states, "The right of people to be secure in their persons, houses, papers, and effects, against unreasonable searches . . . shall not be violated." If a search is conducted in an improper way, it can lead to allegations of invasion of privacy, false imprisonment, defamation of character, assault, and/or battery against the examiner. There is an entire case law on the legality of searches, and the law supports searches if conducted in a proper way with adequate notice. However, evidence can be declared inadmissible if obtained illegally.

A seldom-used but powerful method of obtaining evidence is invigilation. Invigilation is the close supervision of suspects during an examination period. It involves imposing such strict temporary controls that during the period of supervision, fraud is almost impossible to commit. Invigilation involves the following steps: *Setting up a test period to be compared to past period(s)*

1. Obtain management's agreement. Top-level support is critical because invigilation can be disruptive to operations and quite costly.

2. Determine the precise objectives of the invigilation. It is very important that it be restricted to discrete and self-contained areas.

3. Decide on the precise nature of the increased temporary controls that are necessary to remove fraud opportunities.

4. Analyze past records to establish the operating norms. These records should include:

   a. The normal rate of loss in the unit.

   b. The number and nature of transactions per day.

   c. The number and nature of exceptional transactions.

   d. The number and nature of movements in and out per day.

   e. Other records necessary to a successful invigilation effort.

5. Impose the temporary controls for a specified period—usually two to three weeks.
6. Check and analyze the results.

Invigilation can be best illustrated by an example. A small, family-owned automobile repair shop began losing money although its volume of business was increasing. The business had been successful for over 20 years and the owners were suspicious. The shop had one office employee who opened the incoming mail and also reconciled the bank statement. Because the employee was a personal friend and had worked for the company for seven years, the owners didn't feel comfortable approaching the employee directly.

To determine whether there were improprieties, the owners hired a fraud examiner to monitor the books each day for one month. They told the employee that they were thinking of selling the company and the buyer insisted on audited cash receipts for the month. Each day, the fraud examiner opened the incoming mail and performed other critical duties such as reconciling the bank statement. Careful records were kept of each day's transactions.

After the 30-day period, the owners told the employee that the sale had fallen through and that nothing would change. Records were examined without the employee's knowledge for a period of two months after the invigilation. It was found that the percentage of cash receipts to total receipts was 18 percent during the invigilation period but only 9 percent before and after the supervisory period. Based on this evidence, the employee was suspected of stealing approximately half of all cash receipts. Armed with this evidence, the employee was interviewed and admitted stealing over $500,000 during a two-year period. The losses had only recently surfaced because the employee was taking an increasingly larger percentage of the revenues.

While this example took place in a small company, invigilation has been successfully used to catch fraud committed by independent suppliers, night watchmen, and warehouse supervisors in both very large and small organizations.

Because invigilation can be expensive, it should be used as a method of gathering evidence only in high-risk areas. For example, invigilation can be used effectively to deal with fraud where inventory is of high value, controls of the handling and receipt of goods or cash are weak, or where accounting controls are inadequate.

Invigilation can also have detrimental side effects on employees. One company, for example, used invigilation to check all employees' lunch boxes as they exited a plant. The practice so upset employees that they staged a work slowdown which proved to be more costly to the company than the suspected fraud.

AUDIT EVIDENCE

Because a legal case is made or lost on the basis of evidence, fraud examiners must understand thoroughly the rules of audit evidence. In this section we discuss

(1) fraud questions to be answered, (2) audit evidence decisions and rules, and (3) kinds of evidence. The section concludes with some cautions to remember when securing evidence.

Fraud Questions to Be Answered

For a fraud case to be resolved, several questions must be answered. Relevant evidence for most of these questions is essential. Facts should be developed concerning:

1. when the fraud was committed
2. where the fraud was committed
3. how the fraud was committed
4. who committed the fraud
5. why the fraud was committed
6. what evidence links the act to the target
   a. whether witnesses to the act are available
      (1) if the witnesses are legally competent, credible, and willing to testify
      (2) if the witnesses can positively identify the suspect
   b. whether documents to prove the offense are available
      (1) who has custody of the documents
      (2) whether the documents will be surrendered voluntarily or whether some judicial process such as a subpoena will be required
      (3) whether the documents are originals or copies *[other document authentication]*
   c. whether other evidence relating to the act is available
      (1) how these evidences were acquired: voluntarily submitted, found at the scene, or obtained by some other means
      (2) whether these items have been marked, identified, and kept in a safe place *[chain of custody]*
   d. whether there is a suspect or target *[obviously, there is.]*
      (1) whether the suspect was questioned
      (2) whether the target's effects were searched
      (3) whether the suspect made a confession

Audit Evidence Decisions and Rules

Every fraud examiner faces the decision of how much evidence to accumulate. Given enough time and money, perhaps more frauds could eventually be resolved. In many cases, however, the cost of gathering additional evidence is more than can be justified. In each fraud case, a tradeoff must be made between the cost and the benefits of additional searching.

The purpose of obtaining evidence is to substantiate or refute specific allegations. There are several guidelines to be followed when searching for evidence described below:

Note: a very small fraud committed
against a high volume of
ACCOUNTING AND AUDITING "transactions" adds up!   155
(4 count by 1% on 10,000 reports)

1. Always search for the strongest possible evidence.
2. Investigate without delay. The probability of resolving the case drops with time, as evidence can be destroyed, lost or forgotten.
3. Don't ignore small clues or leads.
4. Look for facts you can confirm or refute.
5. Be persistent and creative.
6. Concentrate on the weakest point in the fraud.

An examiner must accumulate sufficient objective evidence to establish a reasonable basis for any report rendered, regarding the commission of an offense and the relation of a suspect to it. The three determinants of the persuasiveness of evidence are competence, sufficiency, and timeliness.

A. Competency of Evidence

Competency of evidence refers to the degree to which evidence is considered believable or trustable. If evidence is highly competent, it is persuasive. Competency of evidence deals only with the examination or audit procedures selected. Competency cannot be improved by gathering additional evidence or by gathering the evidence on a more timely basis. It can only be improved by selecting evidence-gathering techniques that increase one of the elements of competency which are: (1) relevance, (2) objectivity, and (3) legality.

Evidence is relevant if it pertains to the objective of the examination. For evidence to be relevant, it must logically help prove or disprove a fact at issue. If a juror or judge can draw a reasonable inference of proof or disproof from the evidence, the evidence is relevant.

Evidence is objective if it does not require considerable judgment to determine whether or not it is relevant or lends proof to a point. Evidence is objective if two or more people would reach the same conclusion when examining it. For example, the testimony of an independent person is more objective than a testimony provided by someone who is related to, or has dealings with, the party at issue.

Evidence is legal if it is capable of answering all legal requirements—that is, it is evidence that is rightfully admissible. Evidence that is obtained by illegal means, evidence that was obtained from incompetent individuals, and evidence that is disqualified because of inadequacies on the part of examiners or others would not be legal evidence.

B. Sufficiency of Evidence

The quantity of evidence obtained determines its sufficiency. In determining whether evidence is sufficient, its nature must also be considered. For example, a small amount of direct evidence (such as eyewitness information) might be sufficient while a larger amount of indirect evidence might be insufficient. Indirect evidence is evidence that deals with a probability of the facts or is circumstantial, such as testimony by character witnesses. Evidence such as, "He was the only one with an opportunity" is indirect evidence; whereas evidence such as, "I personally saw him take the money" is direct evidence. Obviously, the more direct evidence the better.

Sufficiency also relates to the number of pieces of evidence available. If a paymaster was stealing money by using a fictitious employee, many checks payable to the fictitious person would be better evidence than a few checks. The more documents and/or the more witnesses, the more sufficient the evidence. Often, numerous counts of fraud are suspected, but insufficient evidence allows conviction on only one or two counts.

Materiality of evidence is the final aspect of sufficiency. Material evidence is evidence without which the case cannot be fully supported. Evidence is material if it supports the probability or improbability of a significant fact.

C. *Timeliness of Evidence*

The third attribute of evidence is timeliness. Timeliness refers to when evidence was accumulated. Evidence is usually more competent and persuasive if it is obtained as early as possible. Evidence can go "stale" in the fading memories of eyewitnesses, for example. Some evidence, such as perishable goods, may actually disappear. Timely written statements, depositions, photographs, and other means of providing evidence should be employed.

Kinds of Evidence

There are different categories of evidence from which to choose. Financial statement auditors, for example, have seven broad classes of evidence. They are:

1. physical examination, inspection or count
2. confirmation—receipt of a response from an independent third party
3. documentation—vouching for client's documents and records
4. observation—the use of one's senses to assess certain activities
5. inquiries—obtaining written or oral information
6. mechanical accuracy—rechecking computations and transfers of information
7. analytical procedures—using comparisons and relationships

While these categories of evidence can be used by fraud examiners as well, different classification of the types of evidence is often more helpful. Fraud examiners generally classify evidence into four broad types: (1) people, (2) documents, (3) physical evidence, and (4) personal observations.

A. *People as Evidence*

People evidence includes witnesses, victims, complainants, contacts, informants, clients, suspects, police, expert witnesses, or anyone else. People evidence can be direct, such as an eyewitness, or indirect, such as an expert witness. It has the advantage of being able to communicate but has the disadvantage in that testimony can be confused, confounded, or inconsistent. Skilled lawyers can often frustrate inexperienced eyewitnesses or others who serve as witnesses. Because of a natural tendency to want not to be involved, getting the cooperation of witnesses is sometimes difficult.

B. *Documents as Evidence*

Documents are often used to conceal fraud. Documents can be altered, created (counterfeit), forged, or destroyed. One fraud was uncovered, for example, when an examiner noticed a faint photocopy line across the middle of a document. The perpetrator had tried to coverup the theft by creating a new document from two other documents. Documents usually meet the criteria of relevance, competence, and timeliness because they are objective, independent, and easily understood. To properly understand how documents are used in fraud, examiners need to be well versed in accounting and auditing and need to be familiar with a discipline called questioned document examination.

Questioned document examiners are trained in forensic chemistry, microscopy, and photography. They express expert opinions on such matters as (1) the authenticity of documents, (2) the author of the document, (3) alteration of documents, and (4) document preparation. While a fraud examiner need not be an expert in questioned document examination, he or she needs to know the services a questioned document examiner can provide. Examiners also need to know the court rules for documents and how to care for questioned documents.

Good documentary evidence can be ruined because of improper treatment. An examiner has the responsibility of collecting, protecting, identifying, and preserving the questioned document. The examiner should secure both the questioned document and comparison documents for use by forensic document examiners and/or the courts. In caring for questioned documents, the following guidelines should be observed:

1. Carefully mark the document for evidence (probably on the outside of a sealed envelope which contains the document). Include your initials and the date.

2. If possible, use unsealed transparent covers so it can be inspected without direct contact.

3. Don't repair mutilated or torn documents.

4. Use copies of the document during the fraud examination, the original should be handled as little as possible.

5. In order to maintain the chain of custody of evidence, make your own record of all pertinent data: when, where, and how the document was obtained and the contents of the document.

6. Preserve the document with as much care as possible:

   Don't mark or mutilate.

Don't handle more than necessary.

Don't fold.

Don't carry in pocket.

Don't expose the document to heat, moisture or sunlight.

Don't alter the document in any way (including underlining).

Don't leave the document unprotected.

Many documents speak for themselves and need no special interpretation. There are, however, many cases where a document should be examined by trained specialists. The following signs indicate reasons to submit a document to closer scrutiny:

1. abrasions or chemical pen or pencil erasures
2. alterations or substitutions
3. disguised or unnatural writings
4. use of different colored ink
5. charred, mutilated or torn pages
6. pencil or carbon marks along the writing lines
7. existence of lines from photocopying
8. signs of inconsistency or disruption of continuity of content
9. any suspicious appearance or unusual form

A check is an example of a document that might need forensic inspection. If the records of the company indicate that the check was made for $700 and the actual check is payable for $1,700, questioned document experts might be able to determine if the "1" in front of the 700 and the "teen" after seven were added later or written by some person other than the original writer.

With respect to this example, questioned document examiners could in some cases determine if the handwriting was genuine or different; if the entire check was typed on the same machine or written by the same person; if the document was all typed or written on, before, or after the date it bears; and if there have been any additives (typed or handwritten) or alterations to the check. In making these determinations, document specialists have been trained in the following kinds of analyses:

1. handwriting comparisons
2. ink analysis
3. paper analysis
4. alterations
5. folds, staples
6. dating of documents

Of course, "Electronic documents" present their own forensic challenges and methods that do not use any of these forms of analysis. [Computer forensics]

7. damaged document analysis
8. indented writing
9. typing defects
10. typewriter ribbon and printer ribbon analysis
11. electronic image analysis
12. sequence of writing
13. dating of writing

With tools such as microscopy, ultraviolet lights, reagents, chromatography, infrared spectrums, filters and photography, even charred or destroyed documents can be read and interpreted. While it is not the purpose here to make the fraud examiner a trained question document expert, one of the 13 types of analyses—handwriting—will be illustrated.

Every individual (and each mechanical printer for that matter) has its own individual characteristics. In studying handwriting, the following kinds of analyses are made:

1. the basic movements of the handwriting—clockwise, counterclockwise, and straight-line, indicating direction, curvature, shapes, and slopes of the writing motion
2. slant—forward, backward, and in between
3. manner in which letters with loops are curved, and the size, shape, and proportion of the loops
4. peculiarities of the approach strokes and upward strokes in the first letter of a word and in capital letters
5. characteristic initial and terminal strokes, their length and angle in relation to letters and words
6. gaps between letters in specific letter combinations
7. manner in which the capital letters are formed, and the additional hooks or flourishes some writers place at the start or end of these letters
8. relative smoothness, tremor, or hesitation in the writing: Some writing flows smoothly free from hesitation. Other writing shows hesitation in the formation of some letters or defective line quality in the writing as a whole
9. manner in which the writer varies pressure in certain pen strokes, and variations in the weight and width of stroke lines
10. the proportion and alignment of letters, the length or height and size of capital letters compared with lower-case letters
11. manner of crossing the "t"s and the height and slant of the crossing: near the top of the "t" or lower down, straight or at an angle, with a flourish or plain; are words ending in "t" crossed?
12. location and relationship of the dot of the "i" to the location of the letter itself
13. type of ending stroke in words ending in "y," "g," or "s"
14. open or closed letter style as seen in such letters as "a" and "o" and in letters that

Table 6.6
Various Types of Physical Evidence

Alcohol	Alkalis	Alterations
Arsenal Items	Ashes	Blood Stains
Body Fluids	Broken Parts	Bullets
Burns	Casts	Chemicals
Cigarettes	Clothing	Containers
Cords	Debris	Drilling
Drugs	Explosives	Fibers
Fingernail Parts	Fingerprints	Firearms
Footprints	Glass Pieces	Grease
Hair	Hardware	Impressions
Knives	Lethal Clubs	Locks & Keys
Matches	Matchbooks	Oil
Palmprints	Paint	Photographs
Poisons	Rope	Safe Insulation
Shoeprints	Splinters	Soil Samples
Stains	String	Tire Marks
Tool Marks	Tools	Tracks

    combine upward or downward strokes with loops such as "b," "d," "p," and "g"; are the circles of letters open or closed, broad or narrow?

15. separation of letters within a word such as separating a "t" from the remainder of the word, or separating a whole syllable where it should be connected

16. differences in the portions that appear above and below the line in such letters as "f," "g," and "y"

17. relative alignment of all letters, and the uniformity and spacing of letters, words, and lines

18. alignment of lines

19. use and positioning of punctuation

20. lifting the writing instrument from the writing material between words and sentences

Physical Evidence

    Fraud examiners will not use physical evidence as often as documents and people, but understanding the different types of objects that can be used as evidence is still important. These are very valuable to investigators of murders, rapes, and other types of crimes and can be helpful in resolving fraud cases. Each of the objects identified in Table 6.6 can be submitted for forensic analysis. Your role as a fraud examiner is to know what kinds of objects can be used as evidence and when they should be analyzed in detail.

    In broad terms, physical evidence can be classified into four types: (1) objects, such as broken locks, (2) substances, such as grease, (3) traces, such as paint left on tools or equipment, and (4) impressions, such as cutting marks, tire tracks or fingerprints.

To illustrate how physical objects can be used to solve nonviolent crimes, consider the case of the famed detective, William J. Burns (Caesar 1968), who once solved a counterfeit-currency conspiracy by tracking down a single clue to its source. The clue was a four-digit number preceded by a double "xx" mark found imprinted on a burlap covering to a sofa shipped from the United States to Costa Rica, in which were hidden nearly one million counterfeit pesos. By tracing that clue to its source, he gained a great deal of evidence, blew the case wide open, and was instrumental in sending the counterfeiters to Sing Sing State Prison.

Here is what Burns did to solve the crime:

1. Located and called on burlap manufacturers.
2. Learned the significance of the imprinted number on the burlap covering, and how it might help him trace that specific piece of burlap to its purchaser.
3. Found the precise four-digit order number in a pile of old, discarded order forms.
4. Discovered the retail dry goods store that sold that particular piece of burlap.
5. Made inquiries of a retail clerk relative to that specific purchase and to the description of the person who purchased the burlap.
6. Located the purchaser, described to him as a little old lady dressed in black and wearing a shawl. Burns learned later the woman had bought the burlap for her son-in-law.
7. After Burns located her, he took the young retail clerk with him on a pretense call so that the clerk could identify her.
8. Checked out a number of furniture-moving companies to locate one that had moved the old couch containing the pesos to the docks.
9. Questioned a succession of longshoremen at the docks until he found one who remembered loading the sofa, and the undue concern of a dark, handsome man, who constantly urged the longshoreman to handle the sofa with care.
10. Identified the man who was so concerned for the safe shipment of the sofa.
11. Discovered the identity of the man. He had been in the company of a beautiful woman who traveled under her real name. They made a trip to Costa Rica shortly before the shipment of the peso-packed sofa.
12. Learned who had engraved the counterfeit plates used to print the pesos. The engraver turned out to be the son of the lithographer in a plant owned by the two who had traveled to Costa Rica. The chief product of the plant was revolutionary literature linked to a plot to overthrow the Costa Rican government.

Personal Observations as Evidence

Personal observation is the use of the senses to assess certain activities. There may be opportunities for an examiner to exercise sight, hearing, touch, and even smell to evaluate evidence. For example, an examiner may sense extreme nervousness on the part of a suspect when being interviewed; may hear employees talking about a suspicious employee; or may even see boxes stored in a suspect's garage or home. Observation is rarely sufficient evidence by itself. Rather, personal observation corroborates other evidence collected.

Cautions When Collecting Evidence

Fraud examiners must exercise due care when gathering evidence. There are risks involved, including gathering evidence illegally (without adequate search warrants or probable cause), losing or mishandling evidence. The best way to illustrate evidence-gathering risks is to use an example. The following happened at a large, well-known fast food restaurant.

Relying on a single tip, the restaurant's security officer accused one of its managers of embezzlement. The security officer called the police, who hauled the manager away in handcuffs in front of customers and co-workers.

The manager was exonerated and sued the company for malicious prosecution. The case reached the North Carolina Supreme Court, which upheld $200,000 compensatory damages, plus $100,000 punitive damages for the security officer's "reckless and wanton disregard of the plaintiff's rights."

That fraud examiners must exercise caution at all times when collecting evidence cannot be overstated.

lines / minutes of dictation is an interesting ratio for analysis of transcription vendor fraud.

→ Whether billed to the company's (client) or paid to the company's employees can be used in various kinds of comparisons.

7 Analysis of Financial Information

FINANCIAL STATEMENT ANALYSIS

and documentary support.

If financial statements are prepared with integrity, changes in account balances from one period to another should have logical explanations. Frauds are sometimes hidden by manipulating financial statements to hide missing assets or other problems. For example, one company created fictitious financial statements and, over a period of three years, used the statements to borrow $93 million from a large U.S. bank. These financial statements bore no relationship to each other from year to year. If the bank had looked for logical relationships they would have known that the financial statements were false. To offset a theft of cash by top management, another company overstated receivables on the balance sheet by $300 million over a period of seven years. In that company, receivables represented over 90 percent of total assets and increased dramatically during the seven years. Some frauds are large enough to materially affect the financial statements, and a detailed analysis of the statements can identify potential problems.

Using ratios and trend analysis, fraud examiners can identify unusual relationships suggesting errors or irregularities. The examination of relationships between key numbers on the financial statements is referred to as financial statement analysis. External auditors have found that using financial statement analysis to look for unexpected fluctuations in the statements is the single best technique for discovering material errors. *fraud.*

Financial statement analysis provides a good understanding of the entity's performance. While it is most commonly used by investors and creditors in deciding whether to invest in or lend money to a company, it is also useful for managers in making budget, control, and performance evaluation decisions, for regulators who need to evaluate the financial status of entities under their juris-

Table 7.1
Financial Statement Ratios

Current Ratio = $\dfrac{\text{Current Assets}}{\text{Current Liabilities}}$ *Cash Securities receivable Inventory Et.*

Quick Ratio = $\dfrac{\text{Cash + Securities + Receivables}}{\text{Current Liabilities}}$

Cash Ratio = $\dfrac{\text{Cash + Securities}}{\text{Current Liabilities}}$ *+ (other cash equivalents)*

diction, and for fraud examiners who are looking for material errors and irregularities.

This discussion of financial statement analysis includes two elements: (1) analysis of the balance sheet and income statement using ratios and trends, and (2) analysis of changes in cash balances from period to period using a statement of cash flows.

Analyzing the Balance Sheet and Income Statement

Balance sheets and income statements can be analyzed three ways to reveal fraud and other types of errors. First, financial statement data from the current period can be compared with results from prior periods to look for unusual *changes* relationships. Second, financial statement data can be compared with similar information from other companies, or with industry statistics to look for unusual relationships. Third, financial statement data can be associated with nonfinancial data to see if the numbers on the statements make sense.

A. *Comparing Financial Statement Data from Period to Period*

Three techniques can be helpful in comparing financial statement data from period to period: (1) ratio analysis, (2) vertical analysis, and (3) horizontal analysis.

1) Ratio analysis involves computing key ratios to compare significant financial statement relationships from period to period. The most helpful ratios in determining whether financial statements are reasonable are set forth in Table 7.1. Many internal frauds involve the theft of cash or inventory or the manipulation of receivables. All three of these accounts are current (short-term) assets and can be analyzed using the above ratios if the data is available. The second ratio is different from the first in that inventory has been deleted from the numerator. The cash ratio is different from the quick ratio in that receivables have been deleted from the numerator. Since the denominator is the same for all three, the cash ratio is smallest and the current ratio is largest. Significant variations in

Table 7.2
Other Ratios

$$\text{Accounts Receivable Turnover} = \frac{\text{Sales}}{\text{Average Receivables}}$$

$360 ?$

$$\text{Days to Collect Receivables} = \frac{365}{\text{Accounts Receivable Turnover}}$$

$$\text{Inventory Turnover} = \frac{\text{Cost of Goods Sold}}{\text{Average Inventory}}$$

$$\text{Days to Sell Inventory} = \frac{365}{\text{Inventory Turnover}}$$

$$\text{Days to Convert Inventory to Cash} = \frac{\text{Days to Sell Inventory}}{\text{Days to Collect Receivables}}$$

these ratios from period to period can be caused by many factors including changing economic conditions, accounting errors, fraud, or changes in management strategy. The examiner's responsibility is to use these ratios to identify significant, unexplained fluctuations and then determine if those fluctuations have logical explanations. If they do not, someone may be overstating or understating current assets or liabilities to conceal dishonest acts. These ratios only suggest potential problem areas. By themselves, they do not incriminate anyone or prove conclusively that fraud exists. When the current quick or cash ratios suggest a potential problem in either receivables or inventory, five additional ratios can be useful (See Table 7.2).

Unexplained changes in the ratios can signal problems. If, for example, receivable turnover were decreasing and days to collect receivables were increasing, there must be a logical explanation. A recession, financial problems in the industry, or financial problems with specific customers could explain the increase. However, what if these ratios are rapidly changing but there is no logical explanation to the rise? Could it be that cash or short-term securities are being stolen and receivables overstated to make the financial statements balance? And what if inventory turnover were decreasing and days to sell inventory ratio were increasing? Aside from the logical explanations, could it be that inventory is being overstated to increase reported net income? Many times, subunit managers in large organizations who have profit budgets or high expectations will overstate

Table 7.3
Ratios Helpful in Signaling Potential Problems

Debt to Equity Ratio = $\dfrac{\text{Total Liabilities}}{\text{Total Equity}}$

Times Interest Earned = $\dfrac{\text{Net Income}}{\text{Interest Expense}}$

Not the ratios themselves,
but —
1) changes in them
2) comparison to various benchmarks.

Profit Margin Ratio = $\dfrac{\text{Net Income}}{\text{Net Sales}}$

Asset Turnover = $\dfrac{\text{Net Sales}}{\text{Average Total Assets}}$

Return on Equity = $\dfrac{\text{Net Income}}{\text{Average Equity}}$

Earnings Per Share = $\dfrac{\text{Net Income}}{\text{Number of Shares of Stock}}$

receivables or inventories to make their performance look better than it really is.

While the ratios in Table 7.2 are usually most helpful in assisting fraud examiners to identify problem areas, other ratios that can sometimes signal potential problems. The ratios in Table 7.3 are not as sensitive to fraud and the manipulation of accounting records as the current asset ratios, but in cases where very large frauds are committed, they can identify potential problem areas. Anytime there are significant, unexplained fluctuations in any ratio, the cause must be investigated. The question why? should be asked any time there is a change in any key ratio.

Vertical analysis is a technique for analyzing the relationships between line items on an income statement or balance sheet by expressing components as percentages. In vertical analysis of an income statement, net sales is assigned *as* 100 percent. For a balance sheet, total assets is assigned 100 percent. All other items on the statements are then expressed as a percentage of these two numbers *the reference value* (See Table 7.4). *as the reference value*

The vertical analysis of the John Doe Company reveals that cost of goods sold increased from 50 percent of sales in year 1 to 60 percent of sales in year

Table 7.4
Vertical Analysis of Income Statement

John Doe Company
Vertical Analysis of Income Statement
For the Period Ending, December 31, __

	Year 2		Year 1	
Net Sales	$1,000,000	100%	$800,000	100%
Cost of Goods Sold	(600,000)	(60)%	(400,000)	(50)%
Gross Margin				
Expenses	$400,000	40%	400,000	50%
Selling Expenses	(150,000)	(15)%	(120,000)	(15)%
Administrative				
Expenses	(100,000)	(10)%	(88,000)	(11)%
Income Before Taxes	$150,000	15%	$192,000	24%
Income Taxes	(60,000)	(6)%	(80,000)	(10)%
Net Income	$90,000	(9)%	$112,000	14%

Table 7.5
Cost of Goods Sold Calculation

	Beginning Inventory	OK
+	Net Purchases	OK
=	Goods Available for Sale	OK
-	Ending Inventory	Too Low (Stolen)
=	Cost of Goods Sold	Too High

2. While there could be many reasons for the increase, it is possible that someone is pilfering inventory. When inventory is stolen, the ending inventory balance is lower and the cost of goods sold is higher, as shown in Table 7.5. Like ratio analysis, vertical analysis is helpful only if the fraud is large enough to materially affect the financial statement balances.

Horizontal analysis is a technique for analyzing the percentage change in individual income statement or balance sheet items from one year to the next (See Table 7.6). Horizontal analysis supplements ratio and vertical analysis and allows an examiner to determine whether any particular item has changed in an unusual way in relation to the change in net sales or total assets from one period to the next. Like vertical analysis, horizontal analysis quickly points up a potential problem in cost of goods sold. Why did cost of goods sold increase by 50 percent from year 1 to year 2 while sales increased only 25 percent? Could it be that someone is stealing inventory? Could cost of goods sold have been understated last year to make net income look better? Like the other types of financial

Table 7.6
Horizontal Analysis of Income Statement

John Doe Company
Horizontal Analysis of Income Statements
For the Periods Ending December 31, __ & __

	Year 2	Year 1	Dollar Change	% Change
Net Sales	$1,000,000	$800,000	$200,000	25%
Cost of Goods Sold	600,000	400,000	200,000	50%
Gross Margin Expenses	400,000	400,000	0	0%
Selling Expenses	150,000	120,000	30,000	25%
Administrative Expenses	100,000	88,000	12,000	14%
Income Before Taxes	$150,000	$192,000	($42,000)	22%
Income Taxes	60,000	80,000	(20,000)	(25)%
Net Income	$90,000	$112,000	($22,000)	(20)%

statement analysis, horizontal analysis only identifies potential problem areas. It does not incriminate anyone or prove that fraud exists.

Industry Statistics

Similar companies should have financial statements that resemble one another. For example, it would be highly unlikely that General Motors Corporation would have inventory turnovers or days in inventory ratios that are three times as high as those for Chrysler or Ford. Financial analysts and company managers compare the financial statement ratios and results of one company with others in the same industry to assess management skill, operating performance, investment opportunities, liquidity, and solvency. Because comparisons between similar companies are so valuable, industry-wide financial statistics are distributed widely by several publishing companies. Comparing a company's ratios and performance with those for similar companies can also help identify fraud and other significant problems.

Nonfinancial Data

Financial statement data are representations of something that should exist in the real world. If a company reports cash of $5,000, somewhere that cash should be countable. If a company claims that inventory of $10,000 exists, that inventory should be observable. It is easy to fail to associate financial statement data with the real-world assets. However, there should always be analytical relationships between representations in financial statements and physical goods or movements of assets. When searching for fraud, you should be inquisitive and challenge things that appear out of order or out of sequence. For example, inventory does not normally build up over a period of years unless sales are increasing. Accounts receivable should not be increasing unless sales are increasing. If profits are increasing, cash flow from operations should be increasing. If reported sales are rising, the cost of outbound freight should be rising. If purchases are increasing, the cost of inbound freight should be increasing. If manufacturing volume is increasing, you might expect the per-unit cost of labor and material to be decreasing. If manufacturing volume is going up, you should be seeing increases in the dollar amount of scrap sales and discounts on purchases. If inventory is increasing, you should see increases in the costs of warehousing, storage, and handling.

In every business certain analytical relationships should exist. One hotel, for example, discovered that the manager was stealing cash revenues when the cost of laundry increased substantially, indicating increased occupancy, but total revenues did not increase. A small muffler shop realized their accountant was stealing when the percentage of cash sales to total sales decreased by 50 percent. The accountant was pilfering approximately half of the cash receipts.

One large fraud was revealed in the sheet metal division of a large conglomerate. When top management received the operating results of the sheet metal subsidiary, they could not understand how the inventory balance could be so high. Why would inventory increase five-fold in one year? Upon investigation, they found that mid-management had falsified the inventory by preparing fictitious inventory records. During the inventory count subsidiary personnel had prepared inventory tags and delivered them to the auditors who had verified the amount of inventory shown on the tags. After verification, the auditors had deposited the tags in a box in a conference room used during the audit. A manager who wanted to overstate inventory and operating profits had added spurious tags to the box at night. Since there was very little time to fabricate a large number of reasonable tags, some were made to show rolls of sheet metal weighing as much as 50,000 pounds. The manager had also substituted new inventory reconciliation lists to conform with the total of the valid and spurious tags.

The magnitude of the fraud was discovered by the examiners when they performed some analytical tests. First, they converted the purported $30 million of sheet metal stock into cubic feet. Then they determined the volume of the warehouse that was supposed to contain the inventory. At most it could have contained only one-half of the reported amount. Next, they examined the inventory tags and found that some rolls of sheet metal were supposed to weigh 50,000 pounds. None of the fork lifts that were supposed to move the inventory could possibly lift over 3,000 pounds. Finally, the investigators verified the reported inventory purchases and found purchase orders supporting an inventory of about 30 million pounds. Yet, the reported amount was 60 million pounds.

Faced with this evidence, management admitted that they had grossly overstated the value of the inventory to show increased profits and agreed to write the inventory down from $30 million to $7 million. Management had previously forecast increased earnings and, without the overstatement, their earnings would have fallen far short of their target.

Examining financial statement data to see if it makes sense with respect to nonfinancial statement data is one of the best ways to detect fraud. Examiners who ask themselves if reported amounts are too small, too large, too early, too late, too often, and too rare or who look for things that are reported at odd times, by odd people, and using odd procedures are much more likely to detect fraud than those who view the financial statements without sufficient skepticism.

The Statement of Cash Flows

Two basic financial statements, the income statement and balance sheet, have previously been introduced. Generally accepted accounting principles require that a third primary financial statement—the statement of cash flows—also be reported by publicly-held companies. The statement of cash flows identifies sources and uses of cash during a period. The statement is extremely useful for identifying how an entity is funding its operations—whether from investments, earnings or borrowings; and what it is doing with its money—whether it is being distributed to the principals, used to make additional investments, or used in operations. (net income)

Because cash is the asset most often misappropriated, the statement of cash flows is useful for identifying potential fraudulent acts. The statement of cash flows can be viewed as being like a bucket (See Figure 7.1). The bucket represents the cash balance of a company. Into the top of the bucket cash flows into the firm. The three sources of inflows are (1) from operations or earnings, (2) from investments by owners, and (3) from borrowing. Out of holes in the bottom of the bucket cash flows out of the firm. The four outflows are (1) to operations (net losses), (2) to purchases of assets and investments, (3) to pay off loans, and (4) to distribute earnings to owners (dividends). A statement of cash flows can be quite complicated. A simple example will illustrate how it can be used to help detect fraud (See Table 7.7). This statement shows that cash should have increased by $100,000 during the period. The cash flow statement shows that operations brought in cash of $135,000. A net amount of $16,000 was used to make investments, and a net amount of $19,000 was used in financing activities, the payment of dividends to owners, which was partially offset by additional borrowings. Net income was converted to cash inflow from operations by making four adjustments. Depreciation was added to net income because it is an expense that reduces net income but does not reduce cash. It is the purchase of and payment for assets, not their depreciation, that requires cash. The increase in receivables is subtracted because if receivables increased, the cash from some of this period's sales has not yet been collected. Cash is received when receivables

Figure 7.1
Cash Flow Illustration

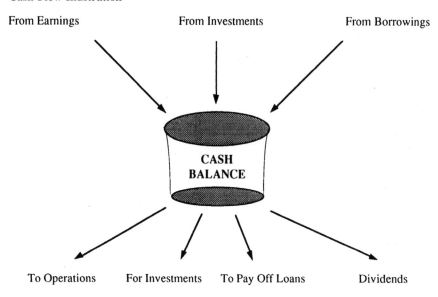

From Earnings   From Investments   From Borrowings

CASH
BALANCE

To Operations   For Investments   To Pay Off Loans   Dividends

are collected, not when sales are made and recognized on the income statement. The decrease in inventories is added back because the sale of inventory results in a cost of goods sold expense that reduces net income. However, since inventories purchased in prior periods were sold (and hence the balance decreased), the inventory sold this period did not require an outlay of cash. It is the purchase of and payment for inventories that require cash, not their sale. Finally, the increase in accounts payable was added because cash has not yet been paid for the expenses incurred. Since the expenses were recognized on the income statement and reduced net income, they must be added back to net income. It is the payment of accounts payable that requires cash, not their incurrence. The effect of these four adjustments is to convert net income, as reported on the income statement, to the net amount of cash received from operations.

The statement of cash flows can be very helpful when detecting fraud. For example, from the simple statement of cash flows for the John Doe Company, questions such as the following may be asked:

Did the cash accounts of the company actually increase by the $100,000, as was expected? If not, could cash have been misappropriated?

Given the company's current level of operations, does it make sense for receivables to go down by $35,000? If sales are increasing, why would receivables decrease?

Does it make sense for the inventory balance to increase by $25,000? Is the inventory actually on hand? Or could inventory have been overstated in order to make revenues or net income look better? Maybe the increase in inventory

Table 7.7
Statement of Cash Flows

John Doe Company
Statement of Cash Flows
For the Period Ended December 31, 19__

Cash Flows From Operations

Net Income	$90,000	
Adjustments to Net Income		
Depreciation Expense	35,000	
Increase in Receivables	(35,000)	
Decrease in Receivables	25,000	
Increase in Accounts		
Payable	20,000	
Net Cash Inflow from Operations		$135,000

Cash Flows From Investing Activities

Sale of Equipment	$6,000	
Purchase of Land	(22,000)	
Net Cash Outflow		
from Investments		($16,000)

Cash Flows From Financing Activities

Payment of Dividends	($34,000)	
Borrowings from Bank	15,000	
Net Cash Outflow		
from Financing		($19,000)
Net Increase in Cash		$100,000

should have been higher. Is it possible that the increase is only $25,000 because someone is stealing inventory?

Why weren't the accounts payable paid? Was it because of some normal occurrence such as cutoff dates or payment periods, or could someone be stealing cash and delaying the payment of debts? And, does it make sense for the accounts payable balance to increase by $20,000 when inventory purchases decreased by $25,000? Certainly that combination would raise questions.

Was the sale of equipment an arms-length transaction? Was only $6,000 received because it was sold to company insiders? Was the fair market value received for the equipment sold?

Why was land purchased? Was it purchased from company insiders at an inflated price? Could it be part of a land swap or related-party transaction?

If cash increased by $100,000, why was $15,000 borrowed? Was there a real need for the money, and if so, why? There should have been ample cash to finance operations; something looks suspicious.

Like other types of financial statement analysis, the statement of cash flows suggests areas of concern. It cannot prove fraud exists or that someone is guilty. The statement is especially useful in detecting fraud in small businesses. In one fraud, for example, an accountant was stealing money instead of paying payroll taxes and other bills. The statement of cash flows highlighted the significant increase in payables. In another fraud, cash receipts were stolen over a period of six years. The statement of cash flows showed significant increases in receivables. The discrepancies went unnoticed.

STATISTICAL SAMPLING

In some cases where fraud is suspected, it may be appropriate to examine a large number of documents to look for intentional errors or other concealment efforts. For example, suppose a target is suspected of improperly endorsing checks or writing checks for incorrect amounts; it may be necessary to look for those checks among thousands of checks. Or, if a receiving clerk is altering receiving reports and stealing inventory, it may be necessary to draw conclusions from all the receiving reports.

In cases where the number of documents to be examined is large, examining every document would be impractical. Statistical sampling is a technique used by fraud examiners and auditors to examine a small part of the sample and still make inferences about the total, unless that part of the sample most likely to contain erroneous documents can be identified in advance. Statistical sampling helps examiners determine the appropriate number of documents to sample and which specific ones to choose.

When using sampling techniques, the objective is to choose a sample representative of the entire population. If, for example, three percent of all items in a population have been altered, the goal is to choose a sample that also contains three percent deviations. The problem is that, as long as only a subset or sample of the population is examined, an examiner can never know for sure the true population characteristics. Although it can never be certain that a sample is representative, the likelihood of a sample's being representative can be increased by the way the examiner selects the sample, designs the tests, and evaluates the results.

Two kinds of problems can make a sample nonrepresentative of a population. The first, called sampling risk, is the inherent risk that the sample will not be representative of the population because of chance. The two ways to reduce sampling risk are to (1) increase the sample size, and (2) use more appropriate methods to select the sample items from the population.

The second problem is called nonsampling risk. It occurs when a sample is drawn that is representative of the population, but it is interpreted incorrectly.

An example of nonsampling risk would be to choose an altered check from a sample of all checks then fail to recognize it as altered. Nonsampling errors occur because of an inability to recognize problems due to boredom, exhaustion, inexperience; or failure to use proper examination techniques, such as handwriting comparisons.

Statistical versus Nonstatistical Sampling

When faced with the requirement of examining a subset of a large population, many examiners select a sample based on some "proven" rule of thumb. They may look at 100 or 200 items because it was a successful sample in a previous audit. Or they may use some rule such as examining every tenth document, or all documents created during the month of June or August, for example. While nonstatistical sampling procedures such as these often work, they are inferior to properly drawn statistical samples. Statistical sampling allows the sampling risk to be quantified. When statistical sampling is used, the examiner can state with a certain degree of confidence that the number of problem items in a population does not exceed a certain percentage. Knowing how much confidence there is in a sample is very useful in deciding whether additional items should be examined or whether it can safely be concluded that fraud does not appear to exist. When examiners use judgmental samples, the only conclusion that can be made is whether problems existed in the sample. Inference from the sample to the population with any degree of accuracy or confidence is impossible.

Sample Selection

There are two steps in both statistical and nonstatistical sampling: sample selection and sample evaluation. For statistical sampling to be valid, every item in the population must have a known chance of being selected. To satisfy this requirement, random sampling is used. With random sampling, every item and combination of items in the population must have an equal probability of being chosen. Examiners usually guarantee that each item has an equal chance of being chosen by using random number tables or a computer random number generator. A random number table is a listing of independent random digits in tabular form to facilitate the selection of random numbers with multiple digits.

In using a random number table, four steps are usually followed. The first step is to identify a number for every item in the population. If prenumbered documents are being examined, the prenumbers are adequate. If there is no numbering system, some method of identification must be devised.

The second step in selecting a random sample is to establish correspondence between the random number table and the population being sampled. This step is accomplished by deciding the number of digits to use in the random number table and their association with the population numbering system. For example, assume an examiner is selecting a sample of 150 checks from a population of

Table 7.8
Random Number Table

Column

(1)	(2)	(3)	(4)	(5)	(6)	(7)
32942	95416	42339	59045	26693	49057	87496
07410	99859	63828	21409	29094	65114	36701
14819	12827	09574	12116	71240	81686	26210
16389	88494	39576	53805	69512	45297	07768
11428	25796	65846	71090	74514	98910	28701
94751	13895	89098	73020	73776	37415	17558
08161	28968	82484	63606	75646	32146	27465
08898	58574	29287	96865	04947	95871	08375
75645	52423	37436	89898	96822	21424	16235
09978	57663	97877	53545	78773	56554	08989
13535	22847	68676	79078	79675	38579	87089
17376	69686	80898	67675	80999	00990	45454
68868	90997	24242	34343	32536	74352	26534
67684	39383	80897	36535	52562	36534	79787
47847	57480	67686	24222	06696	47478	75589

checks with prenumbers 2100 through 8845. Since the check numbers contain four-digits, four digits must be used from the numbers in the random number table (See Table 7.8). If the last four digits of each number are used and the starting point is the top left corner, the first check to be examined would be number 2942 because the first number is 32942 and the last four digits are used.

The third step in drawing a random sample is to select the route through the table. For example, using the top left number as the starting point you could proceed vertically down the left column taking every number, vertically down the left column taking every third number, horizontally across the top taking every number, or along any other route desired. The important point is to establish the rules for the route to be taken before selecting the first number. Once the arbitrary rules are selected, they must be followed throughout the sample selection process. For illustrative purposes, we will proceed horizontally across the table taking the last four digits of every number.

The final step is to select the sample. If a number lies outside the range of checks to be examined, some rule for discards must be established. Most examiners decide before selecting the sample that any numbers outside the population range will be discarded and the next number will be chosen.

If a sample is selected using the rules discussed thus far (top left number as a starting point, proceed horizontally across the table selecting the last four digits of each number and discarding any numbers lying outside the population range), the first three checks selected for the sample would be checks numbered 2942,

5416, and 2339. The fourth number 9045 (taken from the five-digit number 59045) would be discarded and the fourth check examined would be 6693. The next five checks examined would have the numbers 7496, 7410, 3828, 5114, and 6701.

It is very important that the rules for the sample selection be well documented. Documentation leaves a trail that allows both the examiner and others to recheck the sample selection process. In addition, if the sample size needs to be increased or decreased for any reason, the same rules can be followed to change the sample size. Documentation should include the source of the random number table used (book and page number) as well as the rules used to select the sample. A record can be made by copying the pages of random number tables and making the entries chosen. The table should be preserved for possible evidence.

Sample Evaluation

Once the sample is properly selected, it must be evaluated. While there are many ways to evaluate a sample, two are generally used: attribute sampling and variables sampling. Attribute sampling is a statistical method used to estimate the proportion of items in a population containing a characteristic or attribute of interest. A fraud examiner could use attribute sampling, for example, to estimate the percentage of checks that have problem endorsements.

Attribute sampling allows the examiner to estimate the actual occurrence rate, as well as the computed upper and lower deviation rates, with a certain degree of confidence. The occurrence rate is the percentage of items in the sample containing the attribute of interest. Using attribute sampling an examiner might conclude, for example, that the best estimate of the percentage of problem endorsements on checks is 2.5 percent but that he or she is 95 percent confident that the rate is not less than 1 percent (lower deviation rate) or greater than 4 percent (upper deviation rate).

With attribute sampling the purpose is to determine the deviation rate. Variables sampling, on the other hand, is a statistical sampling technique that allows examiners to determine whether the monetary amount of an account balance is materially misstated. Variables sampling is used by financial statement auditors, for example, to determine if the accounts receivable or inventory balances as reported on a client's financial statements are materially misstated. Variables sampling could help an examiner determine if a subunit manager of a large company had overstated an asset to increase net income and his or her bonus.

Discovery Sampling

Attribute sampling is probably more useful in fraud examinations than variables sampling. Even pure attribute sampling, however, can be of limited use. Examiners are seldom interested in the proportion of errors in a population. Instead, they are looking to see if errors exist. Because fraud has such serious

Table 7.9
Discovery Sampling Table

Probability (Percent) of Including at Least One Error in Sample
Rate of Occurrence in the Population (Percent)

Sample Size	.01	.05	.1	.2	.3	.5	1	2
50		2	5	9	14	22	39	64
60	1	3	6	11	16	26	45	70
70	1	3	7	13	19	30	51	76
80	1	4	8	15	21	33	55	80
90	1	4	9	16	24	36	60	84
100	1	5	10	18	26	39	63	87
120	1	6	11	21	30	45	70	91
140	1	7	13	24	34	50	76	94
160	2	8	15	27	38	55	80	96
200	2	10	18	33	45	63	87	98
240	2	11	21	38	51	70	91	99
300	3	14	26	45	59	78	95	99+
340	3	16	29	49	64	82	97	99+
400	4	18	33	55	70	87	98	99+
460	5	21	37	60	75	90	99	99+
500	5	22	39	63	78	92	99	99+
800	8	33	55	80	91	98	99+	99+
1,000	10	39	63	86	95	99	99+	99+
1,500	14	53	78	95	99	99+	99+	99+
2,500	22	71	92	99	99+	99+	99+	99+

consequences, even one error could be critical. Financial statement auditors who want to know whether invoices were initialled, for example, can live with a two or three percent deviation rate.

A special kind of attribute sampling is very useful to fraud examiners when trying to determine whether critical errors exist. Discovery sampling is a sampling design that allows examiners to conclude with a certain percentage confidence level whether any problem endorsements or similar critical errors exist in a population.

Discovery sampling deals with the following kind of questions: If the examiner believes some important kind of error or irregularity might exist in the records, what sample size will the examiner have to audit to have assurance of finding at least one example? It can be commonly used for designing procedures to search for such things as forged checks or other types of fraud (See Table 7.9). For example, if you selected a random sample of 300 invoices from a population and found no errors in the sample, you could conclude from the table at a 78 percent confidence level that the true population error rate does not exceed .5 percent (one-half of one percent). You could also conclude at a 45 percent confidence level that the population error rate does not exceed .2 percent (two-tenths of one percent) and at a 95 percent confidence level that it does not exceed 1 percent.

Since discovery sampling is attribute sampling with a zero expected error rate, the same conclusions could have been reached by using attribute sampling with a 95 percent confidence level and a zero error rate. A 95 percent confidence level table for attributes uses one probability (95 percent) with different sample sizes and different expected error rates. The discovery sampling table uses one expected error rate (zero) with different sample sizes and different populations.

To allow practice using the discovery sampling table, assume that John Doe is suspected of moving funds from certain dormant accounts into his own account. How many confirmations to dormant account investors would you need to send if you wanted to be 95 percent confident that not more than 1 percent of the accounts are in error? To find the answer you look down the 1 percent rate of occurrence column until you find 95 percent. Reading across to the sample size column you find the number 300 which means that 300 confirmations must be sent. If you sent 200 confirmations and didn't find any errors, how confident could you be that the actual error rate of the accounts doesn't exceed 2 percent? This time you start with a sample of 200 and read horizontally across in the 2 percent column. You find that you would be 98 percent confident. Finally, if you sent 200 confirmations and found one error, what you could conclude is that there is a problem. Since the table is built on the expectation of zero errors being found, you would conclude that you are almost 100 percent sure that you have a problem. You can't conclude anything about the frequency of the deviations, but you now know that a problem exists, and that is what you wanted to know.

8 Data Processing

A fraud examiner should have knowledge of computer applications and accounting systems. Many financial statements and accounting records are now prepared from computerized accounting information systems. If, for example, a fraudster makes an accounting entry to conceal a theft of cash, that entry will most likely be input into a computer and processed automatically. In addition, computers can be used to make wire transfers from one account to another, to give authorization, conceal frauds, and obtain information.

NATURE OF DATA PROCESSING

Although the general rules for fraud detection and internal control in a computerized environment are similar to those for manual systems, many specific control and fraud detection procedures also exist. These peculiarities are caused by fundamental differences between automated and manual systems such as the following, which have been articulated by the AICPA (SAS No. 1, 1984).

Transaction Trails

Some computer systems are designed so that a complete transaction trail useful for audit purposes might not exist or may exist for only a short period of time or only in computer-readable form.

Uniform Processing of Transactions

Computer processing uniformly subjects like transactions to the same processing instructions. Consequently, computer processing eliminates the occurrence of clerical errors normally associated with manual processing. Conversely, programming errors (or similar systematic errors in computer hardware or software) will result in all transactions being processed incorrectly when those transactions are processed under the same conditions.

Segregation of Functions

Many internal control procedures once performed by separate individuals in manual systems may be concentrated in systems that use computer processing. Therefore, an individual who has access to the computer may be in a position to perform incompatible functions. As a result, other control procedures may be necessary in computer systems to achieve the control objectives ordinarily accomplished by segregation of functions in manual systems. Other controls may include, for example, adequate segregation of incompatible functions within the computer processing activities; establishment of a control group to prevent or detect processing errors or irregularities; or use of password control procedures to prevent incompatible functions from being performed by individuals who have access to assets and access to records through an on-line terminal.

Potential for Increased Management Supervision

Computer systems offer management a wide variety of analytical tools that may be used to review and supervise the operations of the company. The availability of these additional controls may serve to enhance the entire system of internal accounting control. For example, traditional comparisons of actual operating ratios with those budgeted, as well as reconciliations of accounts, are frequently available for management review on a more timely basis if such information is computerized. Additionally, some programmed applications provide statistics regarding computer operations that may be used to monitor the actual processing of transactions.

Initiation or Subsequent Execution of Transactions by Computer

Certain transactions may be automatically initiated. Or certain procedures required to execute a transaction may be automatically performed by a computer system. The authorization of these procedures may not be documented in the same way as those initiated in a manual accounting system, and management's authorization of those transactions may be implicit in its acceptance of the design of the computer system.

Dependence of Other Controls on Controls over Computer Processing

Computer processing may produce reports and other output used in performing manual control procedures. The effectiveness of these manual control procedures can be dependent on the effectiveness of the controls over the completeness and accuracy of computer processing. For example, the effectiveness of a control procedure that includes a manual review of computer-produced exception listing is dependent on the controls over the production of the listing.

Frauds using computers are generally larger than other types of frauds. With a computer, there is usually no physical possession of the stolen goods, and often a fraudster can rationalize taking larger amounts. As an example, a Chicago bank employee and his accomplices transferred $70 million out of three corporate bank accounts into their own account in another bank. The entire theft took one hour and four minutes and was caught through an accident.

In this section we discuss three aspects of computer systems relevant to fraud examiners: (1) risks associated with data processing and computers, (2) controls for computer systems, and (3) some comments about auditing computer systems. In discussing each of these, we will delineate between risks, controls, and auditing procedures for microcomputers and for large mainframe computers.

The first computers used were large mainframe computers. They were so expensive that they could be justified only in large organizations. In the early 1970s, however, technological advances made possible the production of integrated circuits that contained all central processing unit logic on a single computer chip. This technology revolutionized the computer industry and made smaller computers more powerful and less expensive. Along with these technological breakthroughs, computer software has been developed that has made computers very "user-friendly" or easy to use.

Microcomputers allow end-user computing, meaning that users can create, control, and implement their own data and accounting information. Employees who need data processing no longer have to rely on computer experts to do it for them. Microcomputers can also improve the quality of a user's work, handle complex tasks, eliminate or reduce time-consuming and repetitive tasks, and free users for more creative planning and controlling activities.

While there are many benefits to computers, there are also many risks. Instead of just a few employees having access to computerized data, with end-user computing and microcomputers, nearly everyone in an organization can access and manipulate data. Even hackers working in the privacy of their own homes can access organization systems through telephone lines hooked up to their computers (through modems) and introduce errors and even "viruses" that reproduce themselves and cause serious system problems. Unfortunately, the development of controls for computers always seems to lag behind the technological development.

COMPUTER RISKS

There are a number of specific computer risks that can cause problems. The fraud examiner should be aware of these risks and possible control deficiencies.

Probably the risk of greatest concern to examiners is that the computer will be used to perpetrate fraud, embezzlement, or even extortion. Through the use of a computer, cash or other assets can be intentionally transferred and data can be stolen or manipulated. The potential for unauthorized access to data or alteration thereof may be greater in computerized environments than in manual systems. Decreased human involvement in handling transactions processed by computers can reduce the potential for observing errors and irregularities. In addition, errors or irregularities occurring during the design or modification of application programs might remain undetected for long periods.

Another computer risk is the exposure to copyright litigation from the unauthorized use or duplication of software; from relying on incorrect data; or from violating client confidentiality through careless exposure.

Other computer risks include theft, sabotage, carelessness, disaster, or vandalism. Theft is especially a problem for microcomputers because they are easily transportable. Theft can often result in lost data as well as missing hardware. Vandalism, sabotage, carelessness, and disaster are problems for both microcomputers and large computer installations. A disgruntled or dishonest employee, for example, can quickly vandalize a number of microcomputers or raise havoc with larger computers.

Poor maintenance can lead to a computer risk referred to as downtime, which means that the computer becomes temporarily inoperative. Lost time is a risk that can occur with computers because of duplication of effort, data corruption, or loss or improper documentation.

A risk that is especially common with microcomputers is inefficiency. Logic errors occur because many user-created systems are developed by inexperienced users who are more likely to make errors and less likely to recognize errors that have been made. Inadequate testing of applications can lead to reliance on incorrect data.

MICROCOMPUTER CONTROLS

Because of the large number of risks associated with microcomputers, it is extremely important that controls be implemented and reviewed. Without good controls, it is difficult to know whether a microcomputer error is intentional (fraud) or unintentional (mistake) or even whether an error has occurred. Fraud examiners should be familiar with microcomputer controls for two reasons. First, in looking for fraud opportunities, assessing weaknesses in controls is important. Second, they may be called upon to help strengthen control systems to reduce fraud risks.

Microcomputer controls can be divided into six types: (1) physical controls, (2) access controls, (3) administrative controls, (4) input controls, (5) processing controls, and (6) output controls.

Physical Controls

Microcomputers are easily transportable. Because almost anyone can operate and/or physically move a microcomputer, controls that limit access to equipment are extremely important. Physical controls include locks and/or physical security of computers and rooms and buildings where microcomputers are stored. They also include surveillance equipment such as cameras, security systems to detect unauthorized access, and physical separation of microcomputers from each other and from unauthorized users.

Physical controls also include proper insurance and protection from the environment. Microcomputers can be damaged or ruined by flood, fire, and other natural disasters.

Two other common physical controls include proper maintenance and backup data and programs. Backup files should be stored in fireproof rooms and/or in locations separate from where the microcomputer is kept.

Frauds have sometimes been committed on microcomputers because physical controls were not in place or were not being enforced. For example, employees sometimes leave a computer running and unattended while at lunch or on break. Even if an intruder cannot enter the system, the data can easily be destroyed. Most mainframe applications, however, have automatic shutoffs to prevent such problems.

Access Controls

Access controls include restrictions on the use of the computer itself. These controls range from keys and locks to user-identification safeguards such as passwords. Passwords, which are user-identification codes, limit access to certain data files and programs to those who know the code. Other access controls include data usage logs. These logs identify (1) who has accessed the computer, (2) what information was accessed, and (3) where the computer was accessed. Data usage logs, which can be manual or computer driven, can be reviewed by management for improper access or entry.

Administrative Controls

Administrative controls over microcomputers include the policies, standards, and procedures that are in place to maintain efficiency, and enhance access and physical security. Common administrative controls include proper supervision, proper training, assignment of people, hiring and personnel practices (including adequate background checks), segregation of duties where appropriate, and company policies regarding fraud offenses.

Input Controls

Input controls are computer routines that utilize the computer to check the validity and accuracy of input data. Some computer users refer to input controls as edit programs and the checks they perform as edit checks. There are many different types of input controls and they are known by several different names. The more common include the following:

1. existence checks—for checking entered codes with valid codes on file to make sure they are of the class they are supposed to be
2. format checks—for checking for expected numeric or alphabetic characters
3. mathematical accuracy checks—for checking the calculations performed
4. range checks—for checking whether a number falls within a predetermined limit; for example, a range check on a payroll program might prevent the printing of any check that exceeds $3,000
5. check digit verification—for checking proper relationships within input data; for example, the last digit of a number might be checked to see if it bears the proper relationship to the preceding numbers
6. control totals—for comparing the totals of specific input fields with totals of the same output fields

Processing Controls

While processing input data on a microcomputer, several things could go wrong. Incorrect or unauthorized source data could go undetected. Attempts to correct inaccurate data could fail or they could introduce additional errors. Correct input or file data could be inadvertently distorted through improper operating procedures, computer malfunctions, or program errors of either a deliberate or unintentional nature. There are numerous processing controls. Some of the most common are:

1. Run-to-run control totals involve comparing prior control totals with updated control total and transactions.
2. Programming controls prohibit closed routines and error suspense files. They also verify changes made to programs.
3. Checkpoint controls are mere backup procedures that are available for use.
4. Label controls insure that the proper files are being used.

Output Controls

Output controls are controls over reports, checks, documents, and other printed computer outputs. They are usually performed by users of the output, who review output for reasonableness and proper format. They then reconcile output control totals with corresponding input control totals. Output controls insure that data are only given to authorized personnel and that there are good systems controls.

Computer experts suggest a two-way classification of controls in a large computer-based system. General controls relate to all or many of the computerized activities. Application controls relate to individual computerized applications or programs.

General Mainframe Controls

General controls include such things as plans of organization of the data processing activities, separation of incompatible functions, documentation standards, data security procedures, physical protection of computer facilities, insurance, provisions for backup, hardware controls, and computer security planning.

Separation of Functions

A good computer plan of organization separates the operations activity, which is the day-to-day processing of data on the computer system, from the systems activity. The latter involves the development and maintenance of the computer software including application programs, utility routines, data management systems, and operating systems.

Effective organizational independence in a computer-based system requires a clear division of authority and responsibility among the following functions: (1) application systems analysis and programming, (2) computer operations, (3) systems programming, (4) transaction authorization, (5) file library, and (6) data control. Individuals who have access to computer operations may be in a position to commit or conceal a fraud if incompatible functions are not segregated.

The most important is segregation between programming and computer operations personnel. If a programmer is also permitted to operate the computer, he or she could easily make unauthorized changes in application programs. Likewise, a computer operator who has access to program copies and documentation could also make unauthorized program changes.

Good Documentation

Good documentation is important both to the efficient operation and to the control of a computer-based system. Adequate documentation must be required for projects under development as well as for fully implemented systems. In large systems, three types of documentation are usually necessary. Administrative documentation is the description of the overall standards and procedures for the computer facilities, including authorization for new systems or systems changes, standards for systems analysis, design and programming procedures for file handling, and file library activities. Systems documentation includes narratives, charts, and program listings that describe how the programs work so others will know how to use the computer system. The systems documentation should be organized into a meaningful documentation manual. Operating documentation includes all the information required by a computer operator to run the programs. This includes the equipment configuration used, variable data to be entered on the computer, and descriptions of conditions leading to program halts and related corrective actions.

Data Security Procedures

Data security procedures include those controls that protect the files and programs from unauthorized disclosure or accidental destruction. These controls include such things as requirements for authorization and supervision for removal of tapes or disk packs from file libraries; and protection against fire, dust, excess heat or humidity, and other adverse conditions. Examples of controls that protect against accidentally writing over or erasing files are tape file protection rings (devices that are inserted on tapes that permit writing on the tape), external labels (gummed file identification labels), internal labels (labels written in machine-readable form on the data recording media, and a file backup procedure such as the grandfather-father-son procedure which retains the three most recent master files.

Physical Protection

Physical protections of the computer facilities are the controls that ensure that only authorized individuals have access to files, computer operations, libraries, and other computer-related facilities. Physical protection controls also help prevent damage from accidents or natural disasters.

Hardware Controls

Hardware controls are built into the hardware of the computer system. One hardware control is duplicate circuitry in the arithmetic unit of the central processor that results in duplicate performance of computations and comparisons of the results. Dual reading is a hardware control which reads access media twice and then compares the results of both readings. Dual reading and duplicate circuitry ensure that data are entered and calculated correctly. Another hardware control is an echo check which confirms the accuracy of data transmissions to an output device by comparing a signal sent back to the computer from the output device with the data originally sent.

Computer Security Planning

Computer security planning involves identifying all possible threats or hazards associated with the data processing equipment and operations. The planning assesses vulnerabilities and the likelihood that risks will actually come to pass. The harm or loss that would be suffered if the threat were realized is also assessed. Based on these vulnerabilities, security planning involves preparing a computer security plan that (1) minimizes the likelihood of each threat, (2) minimizes the exposure if the threat is not avoided, and (3) provides for recovery from the damage associated with any threats that are not avoided.

Application Controls

Application controls are those controls that relate to specific processing jobs as they are performed at the computer facility. They involve the data inputs, files, programs, and outputs of a specific computer application, rather than the computer system in general. Their primary purpose is to ensure the accuracy of processed jobs. Common application controls include batch totals, various source data controls, programmed input validation routines, control over errors and exceptions identified by other controls, checkpoint/restart recovery procedures, and on-line data entry controls.

Batch Totals

Batch totals are manually accumulated from source documents prior to input preparation and then compared with machine-generated totals. Their purpose is to ensure that data or records are not lost in processing or transcription. The three common forms of batch totals are financial totals, hash totals, and record counts. A financial total is merely the total of a dollar field in a set of records such as total payroll or total sales. A hash total is a total computed from a field that would usually not be totaled. Examples might include the total of all customer account numbers, the total of all employees' social security numbers, or the total of all check numbers. A record count is the total number of all input documents to be processed.

Source Data Controls

Source data controls include a number of checks on the accuracy and completeness of computer input prior to processing. A common source data control is check digit verification in which all authorized identification numbers contain a redundant digit, called the check digit. For example, in the number 24536, the last digit, 6, could be calculated by subtracting the sum of the first four numbers from the next highest number ending with 0 (20 − 14 $[(2+4+5+3)=14] = 6$). Other numbers such as 23533 or 35678 would fail this test. When check digits are used, the microprocessor within the data entry device must be programmed to perform the check digit test each time an identification number is entered.

Input Validation Routines

Input validation routines are programs that use the computer to check the validity and accuracy of input data. As with microcomputers, these controls are called edit programs and the specific tests they perform are called edit checks. Examples of edit checks include sequence checks that detect whether input data is in the proper numerical or alphabetical sequence, field checks that check on the characters entered to ensure that they are of the proper alpha or numeric type, and validity checks that test identification codes with codes already known to be authorized.

Because most modern data processing systems can be accessed from remote terminals, access controls must restrict physical access not only to the central computer but also to on-line terminals. An example of an on-line access control is an electronic identification number that is assigned to each terminal. The central system then accepts commands only from terminals having authorized identification numbers.

The most common on-line access controls are user codes and passwords. Each authorized user is assigned a user code and a password that must be keyed in to the terminal before access is allowed. To prevent "hackers" from systematically trying millions of passwords and user codes in order to guess the correct ones, three additional controls should be present. First, the system should terminate service to the terminal of any user who is unable to provide a valid user number or password within two or three tries. Second, passwords should be randomly assigned to users rather than being user-selected. (Users often select passwords that relate to their family, home, or some other aspect of their life that can easily be guessed.) Third, if a user who has keyed in the correct user number cannot supply the correct password within a limited time, the user number should be invalidated.

On-Line Entry Controls

On-line data entry controls include all controls over the accuracy and integrity of data entered into the system from on-line terminals. These types of controls usually consist of specialized input validation routines that are unique to an individual system: prompting, which involves displaying a request and then waiting for a correct response before issuing a second request; formatting involves displaying a document format containing blanks for the data items that must be filled in. These and other such common devices are all considered on-line data entry controls.

Output Controls

Output controls are another type of application control. Data control personnel should review all output for reasonableness and proper format. They should also reconcile output control totals with input control totals.

Other Application Controls

A final set of application controls involves procedures for investigating and correcting errors identified by edit programs, batch totals, and other application controls. Procedures for correction and reentry should be prescribed, and individuals should be assigned responsibility to ensure that data are correctly reentered. Procedures should also be in place that identify exceptions which could breach the security of the system. These should be carefully investigated. Fraud examiners are often called to help resolve these discrepancies. If, for example, an application control revealed that a payroll check larger than was authorized was processed, procedures should be in place to ensure that the discrepancy be evaluated. The exception could be an error or unintentional mistake. Or it could be an irregularity or intentional mistake. If fraud examiners are not familiar with computer operations, they may not be helpful in deciding which exceptions merit further investigations, what the various types of exceptions mean, or how deficiencies can be improved. In today's world, fraud examiners should have a working knowledge of computers and data processing controls.

AUDITING DATA PROCESSING ENVIRONMENTS

Since data processing environments offer unique auditing challenges, it is important that fraud examiners understand how computer operations can be audited. Essentially, there are three specialized techniques that enable auditors to use the computer to test data edit routines and other programmed controls in application programs. The three techniques are (1) processing of test data, (2) program tracing, and (3) embedded audit modules.

Processing Test Data

The processing of test data involves the introduction of hypothetical transactions into the computer system to check the completeness and accuracy of the system's processing and control procedures. Test decks can be used to check computer programs before they become operational. Or they can be used to test compliance and completeness once a program is running.

Program Tracing

Program tracing is a technique that enables an examiner to obtain a detailed knowledge of the logic of an application program and test the program's compliance with its control specifications. Using either test or regular data, a trace routine built into the computer system software is activated. This causes the computer to print out, in sequential order, a list of all the application program steps executed during the running of the program.

Embedded Audit Modules

Embedded audit modules are special portions of an application program designed to perform functions of particular use to examiners. Examples are commands to monitor all user numbers and provide an alert when an unauthorized user number is submitted. Another audit module might signal if a check over a prescribed amount is processed. Or it might flag a customer whose record is not authorized to be accessed. Embedded audit modules are on-line signals that send timely messages to examiners as processing takes place, whereas program tracing and the processing of test data must be initiated by the examiner. Properly placed embedded audit modules are probably the most helpful of all data processing audit techniques.

Some fraud examiners might be instrumental in identifying the fraud risks inherent in a company's computer programs, and can help embed appropriate audit modules to detect fraud.

THE COMPUTER AS A FRAUD DETECTION TOOL

A computer can be a powerful fraud detection tool. In addition to the three audit procedures that can help detect fraud or unauthorized use of data, computers facilitate and make feasible otherwise time-consuming evidence-gathering techniques.

There are many automated data bases which can be accessed by computer. Examples of these data bases are NEXIS, which contains newspaper articles from U.S. newspapers, indexed by key words; LEXIS, which contains court records and other legal sources; NAARS, which contains accounting references and financial statement information; and DIALOGUE, which contains indexes from magazines and other periodicals on all topics.

Computers can also be used to gather efficiently large amounts of evidence very quickly. For example, if you were investigating a payroll fraud involving a fictitious employee, you could quickly print out a list of all employees who failed to elect life or medical insurance or other withholdings. Similarly, in the procurement area, the computer could be used to identify suppliers getting an inordinately large amount of business or who are always submitting the latest bids.

9 Proving Illicit Financial Transactions

INTRODUCTION

This section describes various audit and examination techniques to identify and track the secret movement of funds in fraud, corruption, and money-laundering schemes.

Most of the examples are taken from corruption schemes, which provide good illustrations. The same principles apply to other fraud schemes. Company funds can be used to purchase expensive personal items as a form of embezzlement as well as for corrupt gifts; money can be siphoned from a company account by cash or check for the benefit of the owners as well as to bribe another; hidden interests can be taken in related transactions to earn fraudulent profits, or can be given as a means of a pay-off. The illegal objectives may differ, but the means are the same, and relatively limited in number.

We begin by reviewing how the most common schemes operate, followed by the techniques to unravel them.

MAKING ILLEGAL PAYMENTS AND TRANSFERS

There are certain traditional methods of concealing, which fall into a common pattern, as described below.

Corrupt Gifts and Favors

Gifts given with corrupt intent have included everything from a box of expensive cigars (as an initial step) to a 50-acre horse farm. Favored items include expensive wine and liquor, clothes, and jewelry for the recipient or other family members, particularly on such occasions as birthdays, anniversaries, and holidays, which provide natural covers for such payments. Savings bonds are also popular, probably because they can be purchased at a discount off face value.

Providing prostitutes, call girls or other sexual favors is also common, as are lavish paid vacations and the free use of resort facilities, such as beachfront condos or hunting lodges. Businesses often make gifts of their own inventory or services to cut costs; a contractor, for example, may provide free home improvements or materials.

Gifts or other favors provide an easy and safe way to initiate a corrupt relationship: the parties can test each other without being too obvious. They are, however, an impractical medium of exchange if the relationship flourishes. The parties then usually turn to currency.

Cash Payments

Cash is probably the favored method of making illicit payments. In relatively small amounts, it is difficult to trace directly. Its utility diminishes as larger sums are required. Significant amounts are often difficult to generate, at least without drawing attention to the transactions. The use of currency in major transactions may itself be incriminating.

Checks and Other Financial Instruments

Because of the above considerations, as well as for convenience and security, illicit payments are often made by normal business check, cashier's check or wire transfer, and are disguised on the books of the payers as legitimate business expenses. Such payments may be made directly or through an intermediary (the "bagman"), or through a series of such persons, entities or accounts.

Hidden Interests

Rather than simply hand over money to the recipient, the payer may suggest the illicit funds be invested into some joint venture or other profit-making enterprise, in which the recipient has an undisclosed interest. The recipient's interest may be concealed through a straw or nominee, or hidden in a trust or other business entity, or merely included by an undocumented, verbal agreement. Such arrangements are often very difficult to detect. And even if identified, proof of corrupt intent may be hard to demonstrate, particularly if the intended recipient produces some evidence of payment for the interest.

Other Methods

There are a number of other common methods of making illicit payments or transfers.

Loans

Three types of loans, purported or actual, frequently turn up in corruption and fraud cases.

1. A prior outright payment may be described as an innocent loan. Such claims can be tested by the following:
   - Was the alleged loan documented at the time it was made?
   - Was a promissory note executed?
   - Was the loan repaid on schedule? If not, was any schedule established to repay the loan?
   - Was normal interest charged?
   - Was there a legitimate purpose or need for the loan?
   - If the loan was allegedly secured, was a chattel mortgage or financing statement filed?
   - Did the loan appear on the financial statements of the parties?
   - If the loan was not repaid, did the lender deduct it as a bad debt on her or his income taxes?
2. The recipient may receive a legitimate loan, made by a third party bank or other institution, with the payments made or guaranteed by the payer. The latter is a common method in more sophisticated schemes.
3. The payer may extend an actual loan to the recipient, which is to be repaid, but which is made interest free, at favorable terms, or under other circumstances which indicate it was a "thing of value" given and received with corrupt intent.

Payment of Credit Card Bills

The recipient's transportation, vacations, and entertainment expenses may be paid for with the payer's credit card, or the recipient may forward his or her own credit card bills to the payer for payment. In some instances the payer simply lets the recipient carry and use the payer's card.

Transfers at Other Than Fair Market Value

The corrupt payer may sell or lease property to the recipient at far less than its market value, or may agree to buy or rent property from the recipient at an inflated price. For example, the payer may purchase—in a fully disclosed and documented transaction—the recipient's vacation home, for $200,000, when in fact its fair market value is only $100,000. A variation on this technique is the phantom sale. The recipient "sells" an asset to the payer, but in fact retains title or at least the use of the property.

Promises of Subsequent Employment

A more subtle method is to promise the intended recipient lucrative employment with the payer or inflated retirement and separation benefits. The spouse or other relative of the recipient may also be employed often at an inflated salary and with little actual responsibilities. Here the relationship or "payment" may be open, but the intent disputed.

CONCEALING ILLEGAL PAYMENTS AND TRANSFERS

Typical schemes and devices which are utilized to conceal embezzlement, corrupt payments, and other illicit transfers fall into two categories: "On-Book" and "Off-Book" schemes.

On-Book Schemes

On-book schemes occur after the point of receipt of funds. Here illicit funds are drawn from the regular bank accounts and recorded on books and records, disguised as a legitimate trade payable, salary payment, or other business expense.

Such payments are often made by regular business check, often payable to a sham business, or through an intermediary. The check may also be cashed by the payer, with the currency given to the recipient or used to create a slush fund for illegal purposes. Direct cash withdrawals are difficult to explain and deduct, if in significant amounts. Relatively small amounts of cash are often generated by fictitious charges to travel, entertainment or miscellaneous accounts.

The following is an example of a simple on-book scheme:

Orion Corporation manufactures paper and is anxious to secure more business. To this end, they put a buyer for one of their customers on their payroll as a "consultant." Each month Orion mails a regular company check equal to two percent of the sales for that month to a post office box in the name of Design Consultants, Inc., a shell company set up by the buyer. The buyer endorses the check with a Design Consultant stamp and deposits it into a bank account in the company's name, on which his wife, using her maiden name, is the authorized signature.

Orion raises its price by an amount sufficient to cover the kickback (and perhaps a little bit more). The payments are recorded on its books and records as a consulting fee and deducted as a normal business expense. In order to obtain the tax benefits, at the end of each year a Form 1099 (Miscellaneous Income Statement) is issued by Orion to Design Consultants and to the IRS, reporting the total fees paid during the year.

On-book schemes are simple to use, convenient, and offer at least a minimum amount of protection, particularly in areas in which such payments are not normally suspected. In some instances where the tax consequences are severe, or where the only source of funds available to make the payments is the regular receipts of the payer's business (as is often the case with small companies involved in kickback schemes), this method is dictated by necessity.

There are a number of obvious disadvantages to on-book schemes: they create an audit trail and leave incriminating evidence in the company's normal accounts and records. The parties are often sloppy and careless in covering the transactions, particularly if the scheme has survived for some time without detection. Documentation is often incomplete, inconsistent, and perhaps omitted entirely. The parties may neglect to file the appropriate tax forms or they may treat the payments differently on their returns: one party may disclose the payments, the other may not.

The payer in an on-book scheme is sometimes reluctant to make her or his bank account information and books and records available to an examiner. Such schemes should be suspected if a previously cooperative payer balks at making records available, particularly if the circumstances suggest that the source of funds for such payments is probably limited to normal business receipts.

Overbilling Schemes

A variation of the direct on-book scheme requires the assistance of a third-party contractor or supplier. The illicit payment is added to a legitimate business expense or trade payable, and then the cooperative third party forwards the excess payment directly to the intended recipient or returns it, usually in cash, to the payer for distribution. In similar fashion, rebate payments or kickbacks may be demanded from contractors, suppliers or even employees, and used by the principal to fund illegal payments, create a slush fund, or generate tax-free income.

Overbilling schemes are more difficult to detect than direct on-book payments, as the payer's record will reflect only the apparently routine trade payables and business expenses which, at least in major part, can be documented. The examiner confronted with such a scheme must not only identify which contractor or supplier is providing such a service, but must then obtain and examine the books and records of the supplier to find what may be relatively small increments to legitimate charges.

Persons employing an overbilling scheme are generally more confident that they will avoid detection. They will often offer to make accounts and records available to the examiner to demonstrate innocence. There are, however, drawbacks to this approach. Such schemes necessarily involve an extra conspirator (and therefore another potential witness, with records). They may be more expensive, since the conduit usually demands a fee. Below is an example of a simple overbilling scheme:

Orion Corporation has come under new and more sophisticated management who want to replace the "consulting" payments to the purchasing agent with a better-insulated scheme. An agreement is reached with a subcontractor, the White Company, under which Orion will increase its price for its services by 15 percent, five percent to go to the purchasing agent, five percent to go to Orion's manager, and five percent to be retained by the subcontractor, all as tax-free cash.

The White Company invoices Orion at the new, 15 percent-higher price. The subcontractor then charges an amount equal to the overpayments to fictitious travel and entertainment expenses, cashes the "reimbursement" checks, and distributes the proceeds.

Off-Book Schemes

Off-book refers to those schemes in which the funds used for illegal payments or transfers are not drawn from regular, known bank accounts. The payments do not appear anywhere on the books and records. In relatively small amounts, such payments may come directly from the pocket of the payer, from her or his personal accounts, or may be borrowed from other ventures. In larger schemes, the funds are usually generated by unrecorded sales or by failing to record legitimate rebates from suppliers. Off-book schemes are often employed by businesses with significant cash sales. The simplest example is a bar or restaurant owner who accumulates an untraceable cash hoard (and evades taxes) by reporting only a part of the cash receipts. A more complex off-book scheme is illustrated below:

The Metalloy Corporation repairs military jet aircraft engines. Engines which cannot be repaired are so certified by a government inspector who works on the premises, and they become scrap.

Management of Metalloy devised a scheme whereby they would pay the inspector to falsely certify that engines in good working condition were in fact irreparable and had only scrap value. Metalloy could then sell the engines for large profits.

The "scrap" engines were transferred to a local warehouse. A separate company was organized offshore to secretly acquire the engines for resale in Europe. Proceeds of such sales were deposited in a numbered Swiss bank account, and funds were withdrawn in cash from that account by Metalloy company employees, who transported them to the United States for direct distribution to the government inspectors. No record of the improper payments to the government inspectors appeared anywhere on Metalloy's records, nor did their accounts or books reflect the sale of the scrap engines in Europe. Record of such sales by the offshore company, and the related banking transactions, were beyond the subpoena power of the United States. Inventory records were falsified to indicate the "scrap" engines were still in storage or had been cannibalized for spare parts.

The principal advantage of off-book schemes is their secrecy. Even a full audit of the suspect's accounts and books will usually reveal nothing amiss. For this reason, persons who employ such schemes are often quite willing—even eager—to show the examiner their books and records and to be fully cooperative. This does not mean that such payments cannot be detected and traced. It means only that the techniques for doing so are entirely different from those for on-book schemes, generally involving examination in the field to identify potential sources of unreported sales and cash funds.

The major disadvantage of off-book schemes for most businesses is the difficulty of generating significant off-book funds. This usually requires access to offshore or large cash transactions, which many companies lack.

Use of On-Book and Off-Book Schemes

The discussion above reveals a very basic but important principle which merits repeating: the type of scheme employed—on-book or off-book—depends primarily on the source and type of funds available. If funds are limited to normal business receipts, which must be deposited in regular accounts and used to pay legitimate business expenses, the illicit payments most likely come out of such accounts as well. A payer who has the potential to generate cash or other unrecorded income may opt for an off-book arrangement, particularly if making extremely sensitive payments, operating in a heavily regulated industry, or otherwise subject to intense audits.

THE CORRUPTION INDEX

With the above as background, we now turn to the first steps in the examination process: how to detect the existence of an illicit payment.

Unfortunately, as experienced fraud examiners know all too well, most fraud and corruption cases do not start with hot leads to secret payments, or a roster of givers and takers, or even the assurance that the suspected wrongs actually occurred. The examiner needs an effective means to evaluate the allegations, identify the suspects, generate leads and get the case started. Often this is accomplished through the collection and analysis of very basic information, called here the corruption index.

The corruption index lists the most common and recurring signs of fraud and corruption, the abnormal behavior and situations which suggest hidden motives and interests. No single indicator is conclusive. Look for clusters and patterns of behavior, particularly conduct which appears to be contrary to normal practice.

The Corrupt Recipient (or Embezzler)

A person who is taking payoffs or embezzling funds often exhibits the following characteristics:

The Big Spender

Many corrupt recipients or embezzlers are caught because they spend ostentatiously or live beyond their means. Their new affluence is often explained by the claim that they spend every penny of their legitimate income or are heavily in debt. Others spend their money less conspicuously, often paying off debts or paying down mortgages; this requires closer study to detect.

The Gift Taker

An official who regularly accepts gifts, particularly those that seem questionable, is often one who is susceptible to larger payments.

The "Odd Couple"

Corrupt payers and recipients often appear to have very friendly social relationships, which extend beyond normal business hours and contacts. Frequent lunches and dinners, joint business trips, and other after-hours contact—particularly between parties who do not appear to have much in common—may be a sign of deeper and more troublesome ties between the parties.

The Rule Breaker

A person committing fraud will often bend, break, or ignore standard operating procedures or rules. Be particularly alert for someone who inserts himself or herself into areas in which he or she is not normally involved, or attempts to assert authority or make decisions normally made by others. The common signals include poor quality, late deliveries, or high prices, and complaints from subordinates. Finally, look for higher prices, extra payments or commissions approved by the suspect: these may be the source of kickback funds.

The Unappreciated Workaholic

Some hardworking and honest employees and public servants go bad because they become bitter about their lack of advancement, recognition, or material success. This leads them to rationalize the acceptance of illegal payments, particularly if these start as small gifts and favors from counterparts in the private sector or other companies who earn two or three times as much for doing essentially the same work.

The above conditions may coincide with the "burn-out" phenomenon, when the employee's enthusiasm and attention to work drastically deteriorate. Here the damage done by corruption is the most severe, as the recipient may sell out completely. This condition is often signaled by physical deterioration, poor work habits, negligence, shortened work hours, frequent absences or alcohol or drug abuse.

An internal fraud or embezzlement may be indicated by the presence of an employee with access to company assets who refuses to take time off, declines promotions, and consistently works early and late. This may indicate he or she fears a replacement or co-worker will detect the wrongdoing. (It could also indicate a highly motivated, valued employee; remember, no single indicator is conclusive.) To be safe, however, many companies and agencies enforce a mandatory vacation policy and regular job changes in sensitive areas.

The "Middle-Aged Crazy"

Divorce and the financial pressures associated herewith, the "mid-life crisis," and the corresponding need to boost self-esteem through a more lavish lifestyle have led to irresistible temptations in numerous cases.

The Three "Bs"

An old cliche—with just enough truth to survive—is that the cause for some corruption and embezzlement among male workers are the "three Bs": "booze, babes, and bets." Today one would also have to add drugs. Cocaine addiction by white-collar employees, and the fraudulent conduct it spawns, is an increasingly severe problem.

Genuine Need

Occasionally, legitimate financial pressures, such as the illness of the family members, can induce participation in an illegal scheme. In such circumstances, the corrupt relationship often begins with "loans" or some other face-saving device.

The Corrupt Payer

Typical signs of a corrupt payer include:

The Gift Bearer

The businessman who routinely offers inappropriate gifts, provides lavish business entertainment, or otherwise tries to ingratiate himself with his counterpart is frequently the one who will offer still more valuable inducements under the table.

The Sleaze Factor

Unlike the typical corrupt recipient, who may be known as a diligent and honest employee, the payer is frequently a person with a generally poor reputation for integrity, both personally and in business, who may be widely reputed in the industry to be involved in payoffs or other fraudulent activities, or have a criminal record.

The Too-Successful Bidder

A supplier who is consistently awarded work without any apparent competitive advantage may be providing under-the-table incentives.

Poor Quality, Higher Prices

Particularly after the corrupt relationship is sealed, the quality of product and service provided by the payer may deteriorate, and prices may increase. In certain highly competitive industries, however, payoffs may be used primarily as a means of getting a foot in the door, and subsequent service and quality may be adequate.

The One Man Operation

In certain industries, small closely held companies, which do not have SEC reporting requirements, stringent internal audit reviews, or the sales resources available to larger companies, are more prone to resort to payoffs than their larger corporate competitors. Also be alert for the use of independent sales representatives, "consultants" or other middle men: these are a favored way to funnel and conceal illegal payments.

METHODS OF PROVING ILLICIT TRANSFERS

There are but two ways to identify and trace illicit funds: from the point of payment or from the point of receipt. The choice of which to use—or both—depends on the circumstances: the availability of records at either end, whether one person is taking from many, or vice versa, and the size and complexity of the organizations involved. Money which may be impossible to find from the payer's end may be relatively easy to identify among the recipient's accounts. Naturally, one chooses the method which appears to be the easiest; or uses both, if sufficient resources are available. As a general proposition, suspected on-book schemes are best approached from the point of payment. Off-book or other cash schemes are easiest caught at the suspected point of receipt.

Examination from the Point of Payment

Usually some sort of business organization or other entity is involved in originating illegal payments. Depending on the size and complexity of the enterprise, this may significantly complicate the search. Many examiners confronted with a corporate subject are unsure how to proceed, what to ask of whom, what documents to acquire, and what to do with them. This usually results in considerable delay and wasted effort.

The business profile is designed to overcome these difficulties and begin the examination process. It identifies prospective witnesses and targets, relevant documents and transactions, and provides leads as to whether an on-book or off-book scheme is being used. The profile is divided into six categories of information, which is usually readily available from interviews or documentary sources.

The Business Profile

1. How is the business organized, legally and structurally?

    This information helps determine what records are available (corporate or partnership) and what steps are necessary to obtain them (sole proprietorship records may be protected by the Fifth Amendment; corporate and partnership records are usually not).

2. Who are the key personnel associated with the enterprise?

    This helps to identify potential witnesses and informants, as well as possible suspects. Key positions include:

a. the owners of the business

b. the persons directly involved in the suspect transactions, including secretarial and clerical staff, present and former

c. the bookkeeper, outside accountants and tax preparers

d. outside consultants, sales representatives, and independent contractors (a popular conduit for payoffs)

e. competitors (these are often eager witnesses who can identify leads to sources of off-book funds such as customers and rebate practices)

3. What is the money-flow pattern involved in the suspect transaction?

It is most important to identify the source of the enterprise's funds and relevant expenditures, particularly those related to the suspect transactions. Information regarding the source of funds should provide leads regarding whether an on-book or off-book scheme and the location of off-book accounts. Expenditures related to the suspect transactions may cover on book payments.

a. Determine all sources of funds through the following questions:

1) What goods or services does the business provide?
2) Who are its customers or clients?
3) How is the business paid (cash, check)?
4) What other sources of funds are available, such as rebates from suppliers and shippers, proceeds of insurance claims, liquidation sales, sale of assets, and loans?

b. Identify all expenditures associated with the suspect transactions through the following:

1) What disbursements are made to third parties, such as commissioned sales agents, consultants, subcontractors, suppliers, and shippers?

2) Did the business have any extraordinary expenses during the suspect time period, such as extra commissions, or advertising allowances to assist the customer in meeting its advertising expenses or inventory losses?

3) How are the expenses and disbursements paid (cash or check, and from what accounts)?

4) Does the business maintain an account or fund used to pay miscellaneous expenses? If so, where is it located, who keeps the records, and who signs the checks or authorizes payments?

5) How are travel and entertainment expenses reimbursed, and from what account?

6) What is the company's practice with respect to business gifts; what gifts were given to the suspect recipients, who were they paid for, and what records are maintained regarding them?

4. Where are the suspected bank accounts?

Find out where the suspect deposits her or his receipts. This can usually quickly be determined from the bank stamp on deposited checks. Identify all accounts by bank, account number, and authorized signature.

5. What is the financial condition of the suspect?

This data may provide evidence of a motive for the crime, or the fruits thereof.

6. What is the suspect's record-keeping system?

How are the receipts, expenses, and disbursements documented? Where are the records kept?

Sources of Information for the Business Profile

Principals, Employees, and Records of Suspect. Persons suspected of committing fraud are often willing to be interviewed, particularly if they are confident that the payments are well hidden. Interviews should also be conducted with other key employees (including the accountants) involved in the suspect transactions, particularly those who have since left the company. Use the business profile as a guide to questioning. Obtain copies of business brochures, annual reports, financial statements, loan and line of credit applications, business tax returns, and related workpapers.

Customers and Competitors. In a kickback case, the "customer" (agency) is the employer of the person taking payoffs and the victim of the crime. He or she can provide valuable information about the suspect business's operation, particularly cancelled checks. This will identify the payer's regular bank account. The customer may also have invoices and shipping documents, which may identify the location of inventory and provide other useful leads to off-book funds.

Banks and Lending Institutions. The business's banker may have credit applications, financial statements, and loan files helpful to the examiner as well as bank account information. Of course, this information may not be available without a subpoena.

Business Reporting Companies. Dunn & Bradstreet and other commercial reporting companies disseminate basic information about the size, structure, sales, and employees of businesses. Information about larger companies may also be found in Standard & Poors and other business directories.

Other Sources of Information. Telephone toll records, mail covers, and even surveillances may provide information regarding a firm's customers, contractors, and suppliers. Public filings and state records may also provide basic information about the company's principals and organization.

Proving On-Book Payments

We now turn to the investigative steps to identify and trace payments in the most common on-book schemes: fictitious payables, payments to ghost employees, and overbilling schemes.

Fictitious Payable Schemes

If possible, obtain the following records from the entity suspected of making illegal payments:

1. bank account information

    a. all records of payments: cancelled checks, wire transfer receipts, receipts for the purchase of cashier's checks and money orders, and withdrawal slips

    b. check registers

    c. account statements

2. sales backup documentation

    a. purchase orders

    b. invoices

    c. documents showing receipt of goods ordered

3. accounting books and records

    a. cash disbursements journals

    b. cash receipts journals

    c. ledgers

The most important of the above information is the bank account information. Begin by examining the checks, check register, and/or the cash disbursement journal for payments which fall into the following categories:

1. Payables and expenses charged to the account on which the illicit payments are suspected. If it is suspected that kickbacks were paid on sales to the ABC Corporation, look at the payables and expenses charged to that account;

2. Payments for services, such as sales commissions or consulting fees, which do not require the delivery of goods and relatively little documentation to obtain payment;

3. Anomalous charges for the business, such as the payment for design fees by a company engaged in business which would not normally require such services.

After this preliminary examination, focus on the most suspect payments, noting in particular:

1. the endorsement on the check

    This may be by signature, or more commonly, by a stamp in the name of the business payee. Obviously, note the identity of the endorser: it frequently happens that the corrupt recipients have endorsed checks in their own name.

2. the location where the check was negotiated

    If not obvious in the endorsement, identify the bank where the deposit was made. The depository bank's stamp will appear on the back of the check (along with the stamp of the Federal Reserve Bank which forwarded it for collection and the stamp of the bank on which the check was drawn). The geographical location of the depository bank is an important lead to connect the check to the suspected recipient. And of course the identity of the depository bank is critical in order to know where to get the recipient's bank account information.

3. checks with a second endorsement

    A check payable to a business if endorsed by that business and then endorsed personally (permitting the check to be cashed or deposited in a personal account) is a typical indication of a phony payable; likewise a check payable to a third party endorsed over to the issuer of the check.

4. checks payable to a business which were cashed and not deposited

Generally a "For Deposit Only" stamp appears on the backs of checks that are deposited. Most banks have a code stamp to indicate the check was cashed. These codes vary, and can be obtained from the bank where the check was negotiated.

5. checks which fall into an unexplained pattern

For example, checks drawn once a month in an amount equal to some percentage of the sales against which they are charged, and not otherwise explained, may indicate a kickback.

If examination of the checks themselves does not yield any clear leads, the next step is to compare the various records of payment with the backup documentation. Note particularly the following circumstances:

1. The absence of documentation to support a particular payment; examples include no invoice appearing in the files for a payment to a supplier or contractor, no receipt to indicate that materials paid for were actually delivered, or no consultant's work product to substantiate consulting fees paid.

2. Discrepancies between the payment information and the backup documentation, such as a check payable to a supplier in an amount different from the invoice, or a check payable to a person or entity different from that identified on the invoice.

3. Anomalies in the backup documentation, such as invoices from several suppliers in different names with have the same business address, or signed by the same person; or returned to a post office box number.

4. Unnumbered or sequentially numbered invoices (such as invoices 101, 102, 103) dated 30 days apart. It is highly unlikely that a legitimate business would not be issuing invoices in the interim.

5. Alterations on or photocopies of the backup papers. Copies may be made in order to conceal alterations made on the originals.

6. Location and other information on the invoices which may tend to tie them to the suspected recipient.

If the above steps still do not yield any suspect payments, return to the check registers and cash disbursement journals to look for discrepancies between the entries therein and the checks or backup documentation, or the absence thereof. Finally, the register and journals may indicate the purpose of payments made by wire, cashier's check or cash.

Once a suspect payment has been isolated, begin the tracing process. Remember the phony payable may go directly to the recipient to be deposited in a shell account. It may also go through an intermediary account, person or entity, or be converted to cash by the payer. The cash is often given to the recipient.

In those instances where the individual recipient is not apparent from the face of the check, as in checks payable to a business entity, do the following:

1. Examine the back of the check and note where the check was deposited, and the account number, if available. The account number may appear as part of the stamped or written endorsement; otherwise it will not appear on the check. If the check is not endorsed, the bank will still be able to locate the account to which it was deposited through internal records.

2. If possible, obtain the records of the account where the check was deposited. The signature card and the monthly account statement will show the nominal account holder. The signature card will also show the persons authorized to sign on the account, as well as their social security numbers or tax identification numbers. In the case of business accounts, the bank should also have a copy of the corporate resolution or partnership agreement authorizing the account.

3. If the identity of the individual recipient is still not apparent, check the public filings required of business entities to determine ownership. Corporate documents (articles of incorporation, annual reports, and some other basic documents) and limited partnership agreements are usually filed with the secretary of state. Limited partnerships may also be filed in some jurisdictions at the county level. The fictitious name index, business license files, telephone billing records, and even utility billing records can also lead to the identity of the principals.

4. If the original check is missing or has been destroyed, a microfilm copy may possibly be obtained from the bank on which the check was drawn. The bank where the check was deposited will also have a microfilm copy of the check, but unless the exact date of deposit and the identity of the depository bank are known, it will be impossible to locate it.

5. Payments by wire transfer or cashier's check can also be traced to the recipient. A wire transfer from an account appears on that account statement as a debit memo (often abbreviated as DM). Wire transfer requests should show the name of the purchaser, the payee, and the bank and account number to which the funds were transferred. The sender receives a copy of this request, and the bank also maintains a copy, usually filed by date. Funds may also be wired by Western Union, which maintains records identifying the sender and recipient. The bank's retained copy of a cashier's check will identify the payee. The bank also keeps the negotiated check when it is returned for payment. The check will contain the endorsement and show where it was negotiated. Banks usually file cashier's checks by number, making it necessary to know the approximate date checks were issued in order to link them to the purchasers. Look for a cashier's check or wire transfer on the dates of suspect cash withdrawals, checks to cash, or checks to the issuing bank. Remember, however, that such instruments can be purchased for cash from any bank, not only where the payer's account is located.

6. If the trail described above leads to an intermediary, the entire process must be repeated. Attempt to obtain the intermediary's bank records, particularly his checks and other disbursements. If unavailable, attempt to obtain such records from the bank. Of course, the latter alternative is by far the least desirable. It will take considerable work and effort, usually working from the account statements, to identify suspect payments. The bank must then locate them on their microfilm records.

Ghost Employee Schemes

Illicit funds may be generated or funneled through phony salary payments to fictitious or former employees, or by making extra payments to presently salaried employees. These are then either returned to the payer or passed on to the recipient.

In these instances obtain the following records from the suspect company:

1. payroll and employee lists
2. personnel files, employment applications, tax withholding forms (documents with social security numbers)
3. payroll checks

Attempt to identify the ghost through the following steps:

1. Compare a list of all current and former employees from the personnel office to the payroll list. Note discrepancies. Determine whether any employees have not executed tax withholding forms, or have not elected any health benefits or other optional withdrawals. The absence of such elections is often an indicator that the employee does not exist.
2. Verify the employee's claimed social security number. A fictitious employee may inadvertently be given a social security number which does not exist.
3. A regular employee's normal salary may also be inflated or, more commonly, travel and expense reimbursements may be padded to generate illicit payments. Look for unusual disbursements from the accounts where such checks are deposited.

Once a suspect's paycheck has been identified, the process of tracing it to its ultimate destination is similar to that described above for phony payables. Determine whether the check was cashed or deposited, note the endorsement, the bank and account where the check was deposited, and whether there are any second endorsements which may transfer the check to the ultimate recipient. Cashed checks may contain identifying information under the endorsement (usually a driver's license number), which may aid in identifying illegible endorsements.

If the ultimate recipient is not apparent from the above analyses, and the check was deposited, obtain the account signature cards and monthly account statements from the depository bank if possible, as well as all documents pertaining to the account from the account holder. Follow the steps described above to trace disbursements out of that account. If the check was cashed, use the techniques described below to attempt to trace the cash proceeds.

Overbilling Schemes

As described above, illicit funds may be added to legitimate payments for goods or services provided by actual suppliers, subcontractors, engineers, and agents. The additional amounts are passed on by the supplier or returned (usually in cash) to the payer for distribution. Of course, these schemes differ from normal, disclosed rebate programs (which may also be used as a source of funds for illegal payments) by virtue of their secrecy.

The same records required for tracing phony payables, described above—bank account information, backup documentation, and accounting records—from both the original payer and intermediary. Note the following indicators of suspect payments to the intermediary:

1. Notations on invoices or other billing documents breaking out "extra" or special charges, particularly those which require no delivery of goods for payment;
2. Discrepancies between the purchase order or invoice amounts and the amount of payment. Particularly note invoices which appear to have been altered or copied; and
3. Unusually large amounts appearing on particular bills, or bills which break a consistent pattern of amounts, schedule, or purpose.

Disbursements from the intermediary may be covered in the same ways as in other on-book schemes: phony payables; direct cash withdrawals or disbursements charged to miscellaneous accounts, travel or entertainment, and so on. The tracing process is the same as in any on-book schemes. Remember that the overbilling entity will usually add its own fee for providing such services, and that therefore the illicit disbursements coming from its account may not be in the same amount as the additional payments made to the firm.

Proving Off-Book Payments

Identifying and tracing off-book payments is usually more difficult than on-book schemes. Success generally depends on identifying the source of the funds or accounts (from which payments can be traced), turning an inside witness or focusing on the point of receipt.

The source of off-book funds may be located through:

1. indirect evidence of unrecorded sales on the suspect company's books and records
   The suspect company's books and records may reflect unusual costs and expenses which are not associated with the enterprise's known sales or business; examples include rental payments for an undisclosed warehouse, shipping documents reflecting deliveries to an unlisted customer, and commissions paid to sales agents in a region where sales are not reported. The same principle applies to service companies. A sales representative may show travel and entertainment expenses associated with a location or client not reflected on the regular books.
2. unbalanced ratios of costs of sales
   The cost of producing and selling a particular item usually bears some fixed relationship to the revenue it generates. The amount of raw material, labor, or man hours used to produce an item usually is fairly constant. The same is true with respect to utility usage and transportation costs. If twice as much raw material is being ordered

as is needed to produce the reported sales (and the extra is not located in inventory), this indicates possible unrecorded transactions.

Analytical techniques are used frequently to obtain circumstantial evidence of unreported sales and off-book funds in cash retail businesses. A bar may record 50 liquor sales a night but liquor costs may indicate twice the sales. In one actual case, clever examiners were able to prove falsification of sales data of such a business by showing through utility records and statistics that the number of toilet flushes on a daily basis (based on water consumption figures) indicated a customer traffic far greater than that indicated by the reported sales.

Of course, inventory shortages may also indicate unreported sales. However, the suspect enterprise will usually either not accurately record its inventory in the first place, or will falsify their books and records to conceal any discrepancies.

3. investigation in the marketplace

Customers of the suspect business, whose payments may have been diverted to off-book accounts, may have records reflecting such sales and the bank and account to which the funds were deposited. Competitors may identify previously undisclosed customers and other helpful information.

Payments In Cash

The following techniques may be used to prove cash payments circumstantially or corroborate testimony of such payments.

1. Match evidence of cash withdrawals or disbursements by the payer with corresponding deposits, expenditures or visits to a safe deposit box by the recipient.

2. Look for the purchase of cashier's checks, traveler's checks or wire transfers, payable to the recipient, at or shortly after cash withdrawals or disbursements. Also look for a correlation between cash-generating transactions and Western Union money wires, Express Mail, Federal Express or other private mail deliveries which are sometimes used to send cash.

3. Unexplained or unusual cash disbursements or withdrawals—particularly from a business which does not normally deal in cash—may themselves indicate illicit transactions. To be effective, the examiner must identify and rebut all legitimate explanations, which usually requires an intensive interview of the payer.

4. Focus the investigation on the suspected recipient, as discussed below.

Examination from the Point of Receipt

Often the only practical approach to identifying and tracing illicit funds is to focus on the suspected recipient, particularly if the person making the payments is unknown, the payments are in cash or from off-book funds, or one person is suspected of taking from many.

The techniques described below can be used to locate hidden assets and trace the proceeds of almost any type of illegal activity, from tax evasion to fraud and corruption to drug dealing. They are based on the simple and almost invariably true principle that significant dirty money will eventually show up, directly or indirectly, in the accounts, assets, and activities of the recipient.

The first step is to prepare the financial/behavioral profile of the target. This is in essence a detailed financial statement, with certain modifications and additions, which shows what the suspect owns, owes, earns, and spends over a period of time. The profile may yield evidence of illegal income or hidden assets by showing that the suspect's expenditures exceeded known sources of income. Both of these approaches are discussed in detail below. The information provided by the profile will assist in tracing the illicit payments directly or circumstantially through the methods discussed below.

The Financial Profile

Step Number 1: Identify all significant assets held by the suspect. Assets typically held by individuals include:

• residence
• rental real estate
• bank account balances
• brokerage accounts, stocks and bonds
• automobiles
• home furnishings
• jewelry
• clothing and other personal property
• collectibles
• pensions
• cash value of insurance
• boats, airplanes, and recreational vehicles

For each significant asset, try to determine:

1. When was the asset acquired?
2. From whom?
3. What was its cost (not fair market value)?
4. How was it paid for (cash, check, cashier's check)?
5. What was the source of funds to acquire it?
6. What documentation exists of the purchase, and where?

Step Number 2: Identify all significant liabilities. Typical liabilities include:

• mortgage (first, second, line of credit)
• other loans

- credit cards and installment purchases
- taxes and other bills
- alimony and child support

For each significant liability determine:

1. What was the original amount of the liability?
2. What is the present balance due?
3. When was the liability incurred?
4. What was the purpose of the debt?
5. How were the proceeds used, or where were they deposited?
6. What security, if any, was given for the debt?
7. What documentation exists of the transaction, and where?
8. Was the debt written off as a bad loan for tax purposes?
9. Who was the creditor or lender?

Step Number 3: Identify all sources of income during the relevant time period. Income includes money or other things of value received in exchange for services or goods. Income is not included in assets. Typical items of income include:

- salary
- commission and fees
- rental income
- dividends and interest on bank accounts and investments
- proceeds of the sale of assets, insurance proceeds, disability payments, court settlements and awards, and inheritances

Loan proceeds are not included as income, but are rather treated as an asset, which is offset by a corresponding liability.

As to each item of income, inquire:

1. What was the total amount during a given period?
2. What was the source?
3. How was it paid (cash, check, other)?
4. When was the income received?
5. Where was it deposited?
6. How was it spent?
7. What documentation exists (e.g., W–2 or 1099 forms)?
8. Where is it located?

Step Number 4: Identify all significant expenses incurred during the relevant period. An expense is any payment for consumables, for personal or business reasons, over a relevant time period. Expenses are not included in liabilities unless they are still owed. Common expenses include:

- rental and mortgage payments
- utilities
- food and other incidentals
- transportation costs
- insurance payments
- clothing and other necessities
- interest on loans and mortgages
- credit card payments
- travel and entertainment
- health costs

For each major expense item, determine:

1. What was the total amount of the expense?
2. For what was it incurred?
3. How was it paid (cash, check, credit card, etc.)?
4. Where were the funds obtained to pay the expense?
5. What documentation (receipts, bills, etc.) exists and where?

The Behavioral Profile

The financial profile will identify illicit funds deposited to accounts or expended in significant amounts. It will not catch relatively small currency transactions, particularly if spent on concealed activities, consumables, or on unusual one-time expenses, such as medical bills. The financial profile may give inaccurate or false negative readings unless such activities are identified. These types of expenditures are best understood through the preparation of a behavioral profile. Be alert during the interviews and review of documents for signs that the suspect has:

- drug or alcohol addiction
- gambling habit or debts
- loan shark or other private debts
- extramarital relationships
- extraordinary medical expenses
- significant, regular cash expenses on entertainment and travel

The behavioral profile may also provide evidence of possible motive for the crime, such as large debts, as well as additional evidence of illicit funds. This is accomplished by showing that the suspect spent significant amounts of cash with no corresponding cash withdrawals from disclosed bank accounts.

Sources of Information for the Financial/Behavioral Profile

The Suspect Recipient. An interview should usually be requested with the suspect. Use the financial/behavioral profile as a guide. Pin down the suspect's income, assets, and accounts, and have him or her state explicitly that she or he had no other sources. This is to prevent later fabrications and additions.

If the witness claims to have legitimate sources of large sums of currency, determine the following:

1. What was the source of the cash?
2. What was the amount of cash on hand at the starting point of the investigation, at the end of each year thereafter, and on the date of the interview?
3. Where was the cash kept?
4. Why was the cash not deposited in a financial institution or invested?
5. Who knew about the cash?
6. What records of the cash exist?
7. What were the denominations?
8. When and for what was any of the cash spent?
9. Will the suspect consent to an inventory of the remaining cash during the interview? If not, why not? If so, the cash should be counted at least twice in the presence of another examiner. A list of serial and series numbers should be made.

If the target claims that suspect funds were legitimate loan proceeds, ask:

1. Who was the lender?
2. When was the loan made?
3. What was the amount of the loan?
4. What was the purpose of the loan?
5. Was the loan repaid?
6. How was the loan documented?

Don't forget your powers of observation at the interview. The suspect may wear expensive jewelry, watches, clothing, or other indications of substantial wealth. An alert examiner in one case was able to identify the tailor shop label on an expensive suit worn by the suspect, which led to helpful information.

A famous New York City civil trial lawyer claimed to be able to discover hidden assets of an opposing party by unexpectedly asking the witness on deposition to produce his wallet and empty his pockets. The tactic could produce credit cards, bank identification cards, receipts, keys to a safe deposit box, an undisclosed automobile or properties, or other items.

Finally, attempt to interview the suspect's spouse, but do so separately.

Third Party Witnesses. Business colleagues, personal associates, bankers, brokers, real estate agents, accountants and tax preparers, ex-wives, ex-husbands, and girlfriends or boyfriends all are potential sources. Suspects often boast to their close associates of new wealth, or entertain them lavishly. Casual remarks by a suspect to a colleague, repeated to an examiner, have unravelled a suspect when intensive audits have failed.

Follow the financial/behavioral profile format to the extent feasible. Of course, no single third-party witness is likely to have all this information, but a complete picture may be assembled from bits and pieces provided by a number of sources.

Bank Account Records. The suspect's bank account records are probably the single most important source for the financial profile. In almost every case, illicit funds in any significant amount will at least pass through the suspect's accounts, leaving a record and leads to other accounts, assets, and income.

Obtain the following from the suspect for all open and closed accounts:

1. monthly account statements
2. cancelled checks
3. check registers
4. deposit slips
5. certificates of deposit
6. year-end tax summaries

The bank, with authorization or subpoena, can produce the following for all open and closed accounts of the suspect:

1. account signature cards
2. monthly account statements (copies)
3. certificates of deposit
4. year-end tax summaries

The bank will also have microfiche copies of the suspect's checks for at least the previous five years, and items deposited to the account for at least the previous two years. These are often difficult and expensive to retrieve, and should be requested (front and back) only as necessary.

Bank Record Retention Requirements. The Bank Secrecy Act requires financial institutions to keep certain records of customer's transactions.

U.S. Treasury Regulations, implementing the Bank Secrecy Act, provide, in part, that an original, microfilm, or other copy or reproduction of most demand deposits (checking account) and savings account records must be retained for five years. The records must include:

1. signature cards
2. statements, ledger cards, or other records disclosing all transactions; that is, deposits and withdrawals
3. copies of both sides of customers' checks, bank drafts, money orders, and cashier's checks drawn on the bank or issued and payable by it

In addition, banks must retain for a two-year period all records necessary to:

1. Reconstruct a customer's checking account. The records must include copies of customer's deposit tickets.
2. Trace and supply a description of a check deposited to a customer's checking account.

All of the above requirements apply only to checks written or deposits made in excess of $100. Most banks, however, find it cheaper to microfilm all such records, including checks and deposits of less than $100, rather than sort their records.

The Bank Secrecy Act also requires financial institutions to retain a record of any extension of credit over $5,000 as well as each transfer of $10,000 or more outside the United States.

HOW TO ANALYZE BANK ACCOUNT RECORDS

Identify Significant Deposits to Accounts

Start by reviewing the monthly account statements:

- Note whether there are unusually high monthly balances: this may be useful as circumstantial evidence of illicit funds even if the individual deposits cannot be identified.
- Identify unusually large deposits, deposits in even numbers or on regular dates, or deposits which cannot be connected to legitimate sources of income. Legitimate deposits can be determined by comparing the dates and amounts to company payroll information.
- If possible, obtain copies of the suspect deposit items from the bank. These will usually be microfilm copies of deposited checks, or deposit slips or other internal bank records indicating that deposits were in currency.

Remember that the banks are required to keep deposit items on microfilm for only two years. If a copy of the deposited check is unavailable, the bank teller proof sheet should also identify the source of the deposit and whether it was in currency. The deposit slip will also show whether the deposit was in check or currency; if in check, it may show the ABA code number identifying the bank on which the deposited check was drawn.

Deposits of wire transfers may be shown on the account statement as a credit memo (CM). Copies of the wire transfer request, which will show the source of funds, are maintained by the bank, often filed by date. Copies of wire transfers received from offshore banks may be filed separately.

Examine Checks Written on Account

Of importance equal to or greater than that of the deposits to the suspect's account are the checks written on it. Checks may identify other bank accounts, credit cards, the purchase or location of major assets (through, for example, the payment of real estate taxes, broker's fees, and utility payments), and loans, which may provide valuable leads through the loan applications and attached financial statements. If feasible, all checks, large or small, should be examined; a $25 check for a utility hookup may identify a $300,000 hidden condo.

A useful technique is to list the information from the suspect's checks on spread sheets. List the checks by number and date on the left with the payee, amount, and purpose, if known, of the check to the right. This exercise will show the suspect's routine monthly or annual expenditures, useful for computing the comparative net worth, explained below. The absence of a check for a particular month may indicate a cash payment, which in turn may indicate possible undisclosed cash income.

Examine the back of checks payable to cash to note where the check was cashed. This is identified by the depository bank's stamp. It may provide a lead to another bank account.

Loan Files

Loan files generally consist of the application, the collateral register, and the payment records. The application often contains a financial statement, or its equivalent, on which the suspect may identify other accounts and assets more candidly than in an interview, since the suspect may be eager to impress the loan officer with his solvency. The file may also contain tax returns, credit agency reports, and notes of interviews by the loan officer. The security for the loan, if any, may be a hidden asset. (Con men often use bogus or stolen securities or overvalued properties to collateralize loans to get cash.) Loan payment records may also reflect accelerated payments or large pay-downs on the balance, indicating sudden wealth. And, of course, the loan proceeds may have been used to finance an asset, the down payment for which came from illegal funds.

Safe Deposit Box Records

The safe deposit box rental agreement will show the date the box was first rented (which may correspond with the time the scheme commenced), the identity of the renter and deputy (a person authorized to enter the box while the renter is living), and any special instructions. The entry log (maintained by the bank and showing dates and times of visits to the box) may show visits which correlate with other evidence of currency payments. This may be used to corroborate testimony of such payments from a co-conspirator.

The bank records will not show the contents of the box. The examiner may request permission to inventory the box with the suspect present, carefully noting and describing the exact contents such as legal description on deeds, or policy numbers of insurance policies.

Currency Transaction Reports

Currency Transaction Reports (Treasury Department Form 4789) are required to be filed by banks and certain other financial institutions whenever there is a currency transaction (deposit, withdrawal, exchange, a cashing of checks) of $10,000 or more. The CTR will reflect the identity, address, and social security number of the person making the cash transaction, its total amount, and certain other information. Some organizations are exempt from the filing requirement, including certain high volume cash businesses, government agencies, and payroll account holders.

Bank Collection Department Records

The bank's collection department, which is normally involved in collecting amounts due on installment contracts and notes, can also be used to collect personal checks (usually in large amounts and with special instructions), thus circumventing the normal record-keeping associated with checking accounts. Such a transaction will not be reflected on the suspect's regular checking account statements, but will appear in the collection department records. A copy of the check will also be microfilmed.

Mortgage Loan Files

Mortgage loan files often contain the most detailed financial statements submitted by the suspect. The loan file should also identify the title company which handled the closing, the home owner's insurance carrier, the closing attorney, and perhaps the real estate broker. The title company files often contain copies of the cashier's checks used for the down payment, which may identify new accounts. The home owner's insurance policy may contain a rider that lists individually the home owner's valuable assets, such as jewelry or furs, perhaps with appraisals and purchase receipts.

The closing attorney will have many of the same materials as found in the title company files. The real estate broker may keep copies of personal checks used to make deposits, and be able to provide information about other real estate transactions by the suspects. Also, don't forget to look for accelerated or lump sum payments on the mortgage balance.

Stock Brokerage Records

Many stock brokerage houses now offer the same type of services as banks: check-writing privileges, credit cards, loans (against the value of securities held), as well as their normal securities business. All records pertaining to the suspect should be requested.

The examiner is primarily interested in the source of funds used to purchase securities or deposited to a cash account. These transactions are reflected on the suspect's monthly account statements, which are somewhat more complex than equivalent bank statements, but can be interpreted with the help of explanatory material on the statement or an employee of the firm. Receipts for the purchase of stock and deposit receipts should reflect whether the payment was in currency or check and the ABA code of the bank on which the check was drawn.

Checks issued by the brokerage to the suspect from the proceeds of sale of stock should also be examined, as these may be deposited directly to new accounts or endorsed over and paid directly to third parties for the purchase of assets.

OTHER RECORDS

Tax Returns and Related Documents

Personal tax returns are usually not obtainable from the Internal Revenue Service for use in nontax criminal investigations (unless the criminal case is an adjunct to a tax case), and the suspect may refuse to produce his or her copies under the Fifth Amendment privilege. A supposedly cooperative suspect, however, may elect to produce tax returns and backup records voluntarily, or copies may be obtained, by subpoena, from the suspect's accountant or tax preparer. Corporate tax returns are not privileged and may be subpoenaed directly from the business.

Tax returns make interesting reading. Even if the suspect is not reporting illicit funds (which many do, disguised as commissions or other legitimate income, particularly in commercial bribery schemes), the returns and attached schedules may provide indirect evidence of illicit payments, such as profits or losses from previously undisclosed business ventures, or interest and dividends on hidden CDs and bank accounts. The returns may also show deductions and expenses, such as real estate taxes or mortgage interest, which may lead to previously unknown funds or assets. Even dishonest people claim tax deductions if possible.

Credit Reporting Agency Records

Credit agency records, which include identifying and employment information, credit history, existing credit lines, and payment record, are available only by court order. Identifying information, limited to the consumer's name and present and former places of employment, may be obtained under provisions of the Fair Credit Reporting Act of 1971.

Telephone Toll Records

Long-distance toll charges may reflect contacts with real estate brokers or sellers, identify charge calls from vacation spots, or provide other leads to assets and expenditures.

Most telephone companies keep their long distance toll records for only six months. Generally records of local calls are not available, although in some metropolitan areas, such as Washington, D.C., certain calls may be recorded as long distance or local, depending on the type of service elected by the customer. Remember that long-distance service is now provided by a variety of companies, which may require separate inquiries.

Credit Card Account Records

Credit card receipts will track the travels of the defendant, and, of course, record his or her expenditures. An extremely high balance on the cards may itself indicate hidden income, and even modest charges may provide leads to identifying hidden assets. For example, charges for boating supplies purchased at a marina would suggest further investigation to determine whether the suspect owns an expensive motorboat.

TRACING ILLICIT DOLLARS DIRECTLY TO THEIR SOURCE

The financial profile should reveal the assets, accounts, and expenditures of the suspect; the next step is to trace the underlying funds to their source. The examination generally proceeds in reverse order to the acquisition process: from the asset to the account from which the funds were drawn, to the source of deposit to the account, until the ultimate payer is identified.

Identifying Funds Used to Acquire Assets

Real estate brokers and sellers of other major assets sometime make a copy of the check received in payment. If not, invoices and receipts may reflect the mode of payment—check, cash or credit card. If by check, the date of the transaction should be sufficient to obtain a microfiche copy of the purchaser's check deposited to the seller's account.

Cash purchases of real estate, automobiles, and certain other major assets in an amount of $10,000 or more are required to be reported to the IRS by the seller on Form 8300, similar to the Currency Transaction Reports required to be filed by financial institutions. Copies of checks used to make credit card payments can, if appropriate, be subpoenaed from the credit card company.

Identifying the Source of Deposits

Deposits by Check or Wire Transfer

The microfiche copies of checks deposited to the suspect's account usually reflect on their face the account holder, the account, and bank on which they are drawn.

If the account holder or bank identification on a check is obliterated, the ABA code in the upper right corner and the imprinted account number on the lower edge will identify the bank and account number. The deposit receipt may reflect the ABA identification number for the bank from which the check was drawn. Teller proofs and other internal bank documents may also be used to identify the deposited check. From these records, the paying bank will be able to locate a copy of the check on its microfilm, then the original can be subpoenaed from the payer. The purchaser of a cashier's check or the remitter of a wire transfer may also be identified through internal bank records, whether paid for in cash or by check, if the approximate date of purchase is known. The records may also show the account to which the funds were charged.

In many instances, checks paid to a suspect in a corruption or fraud case are drawn on intermediary or shell accounts, requiring additional steps to identify the ultimate source. This is done simply by obtaining the signature card and account statements for the shell account, which should identify the name of the account holder, and then checking the fictitious name indices and other sources to identify the principals. If further tracing is required, the same steps described above are utilized.

Currency Deposits

As noted, currency deposits of $10,000 or more must be recorded in a Currency Transaction Report, form 4789, which identifies the depositor. Currency deposits may also be matched to withdrawals or payments by the suspect payer, providing at least a circumstantial link.

Of course, the suspect should be asked the source of cash deposits in an interview. A pattern of significant cash expenditures or deposits, with no corresponding cash withdrawals or other apparent legitimate source, is itself an indicator of hidden income. Absent an explanation from the suspect or other evidence indicating illegal activity, these funds may be presumed to be illicit.

A final method of proving the receipt of hidden payments indirectly is to show that the suspect has more funds at his or her disposal than can legitimately be accounted for, through the techniques described below.

CIRCUMSTANTIAL PROOF OF ILLICIT INCOME

The net worth method, or comparative net worth analysis, is used to prove illicit income circumstantially by showing that the suspect's assets or expenditures for a given period exceed that which can be accounted for from admitted sources of income. The technique is most useful when the recipient is taking currency or other payments which can't be traced directly, and when the amount of illicit income greatly exceeds his or her legitimate income. Net worth evidence is also useful to corroborate testimony of hidden illicit payments.

The steps outlined below will enable the prosecution to prove with a high degree of certainty that the suspect has undisclosed income. In many cases, however, a very rough net worth analysis may be sufficient to demonstrate that the suspect is living far beyond her or his means—the payroll clerk who lives in a half-million-dollar mansion—which can then be used to provide "probable cause" or leads for further investigation.

There are two basic methods of net worth computation: the asset method and the expenditures or sources and application of funds method. The asset method should be used when the suspect has invested illegal funds to accumulate wealth and acquire assets, causing net worth (value of assets over liabilities) to increase year to year. The expenditures method is best used when the suspect spends his ill-gotten gains on lavish living, travel, and entertainment, which would not be reflected in an increase in net worth.

Begin both methods by assembling the financial profile. Identify all major assets and liabilities, sources of income, and other funds, including loan proceeds and sale of assets and major expenses owned or acquired during the relevant period. The increases in the suspect's net worth, or the level of expenditures, is then compared to the legitimate funds available. The difference, if any, may be inferred to come from illicit or at least undisclosed sources.

Special attention should be paid to the following matters in preparing the comparative net worth analysis:

1. All assets should be valued at cost, not fair market value. Subsequent appreciation or depreciation of assets is ignored.

2. The amount of funds available to the suspect from legitimate sources should be estimated or computed generously. The amount of living expenses (particularly hard-to-document living costs such as food and entertainment) should be estimated low, or eliminated entirely. Any doubts should be resolved in favor of the suspect. Assuming that the comparative net worth still shows substantial unexplained funds, the result will be an even more convincing demonstration of the existence of illicit sources.

3. Attempt to interview the suspect, in order to identify all alleged sources of funds and to negate defenses that he or she may raise later.

Computing the Comparative Net Worth—Asset Method

1. Establish the starting point, generally the year before the suspect's illegal activities begin. This will be referred to as "year one" in the following computations.

Table 9.1
Formula to Determine Opening Net Worth

Assets at Cost		Liabilities	
Residence	$100,000	Mortgage Balance	$90,000
Stocks and Bonds	30,000	Automobile Loan	
Automobile	20,000	Balance	10,000
TOTAL	$150,000	TOTAL	$100,000
	Assets	$150,000	
	Liabilities	100,000	
	Net Worth	$50,000	

Table 9.2
Formula to Determine Year Two Net Worth

Assets at Cost		Liabilities	
Residence	$100,000	Mortgage Balance	$50,000
Stocks and Bonds	30,000	Automobile Loan	
Automobile	20,000	Balance	0
C.D.	50,000		
TOTAL	$200,000	TOTAL	$50,000
	Assets	$200,000	
	Liabilities	50,000	
	Net Worth	$150,000	

2. Compute the suspect's net worth at the end of year one. Identify all assets held by the suspect (valued at cost), including assets which were acquired earlier, and the amount of current liabilities.

   The difference between the value of the asset and the liabilities is the suspect's net worth at year one, or opening net worth (See Table 9.1).

3. Compute the suspect's net worth for year two, using the same method (See Table 9.2).

   Note that in the example the suspect's net worth increased by $100,000 during year two. To determine the source of such increase, do the following:

4. Determine the suspect's known income, during year two, and subtract known expenses for year two. (See Table 9.3).

   The difference between the suspect's income and expenses equals the increase (or decrease) in net worth from year one to year two which can be attributed to known sources. Here, it is $20,000.

5. Subtract the increase in net worth from known sources from the total increase in net worth to determine the amount from unknown sources (See Table 9.4).

Table 9.3
Formula to Determine Net Worth after Expenses

Income		Expenses	
Salary	$30,000	Mortgage Payments	$20,000
Commissions	20,000	Living Expenses	10,000
TOTAL	$50,000	TOTAL	$30,000

Table 9.4
Formula to Determine Income from Unknown Sources

Total Increase in Net Worth	$100,000
Increase attributed to Known Sources	20,000
Dollars from Unknown Sources	$80,000

Table 9.5
Asset Method Formula

	ASSETS
less	liabilities
equals	NET WORTH
less	prior year's net worth
equals	NET WORTH INCREASE
plus	living expenses
equals	INCOME (or EXPENDITURES)
less	funds from known sources
equals	FUNDS FROM UNKNOWN SOURCES

6. Repeat the above steps for subsequent years as necessary. The procedure is greatly simplified through use of the worksheet (See Table 9.5 and Figure 9.1).

Expenditures Method

1. Establish the suspect's known expenditures for the relevant year. Expenditures include the use or application of funds for any purpose, including deposits to bank accounts, purchase of major assets, travel and entertainment expenses, and payment of loan and credit card debts.

2. Identify all sources of funds available to the suspect, including loans and gifts, as well as cash on hand from previous years.

3. The difference between the amount of the suspect's expenditures and known income is the amount attributed to unknown sources. (See Table 9.6 and 9.7).

Figure 9.1
Formula for Comparative Net Worth—Asset Method

Assets	End Year One	End Year Two	End Year Three

Liabilities			

TOTAL LIABILITIES			
Net Worth			
Change in Net Worth			
Plus Total Expenses			
TOTAL			
Less Known Income			
Equals Income from Unknown Sources			

Rebutting Defenses to the Comparative Net Worth Analysis

Circumstantial evidence of excess income is often met with the defense that the extra funds came from cash accumulated earlier or other legitimate sources, such as loans from relatives. The examiner must carefully determine the amount of cash on hand at the beginning of the relevant period (through amounts listed on financial statements or claimed in interviews) and take other steps to negate these defenses, including:

1. Obtain a financial history of the suspect and spouse, through interviews and other means, showing dates and places of employment, salary and bonuses, and any other related income.

2. Determine whether the spouse had any separate source of funds which were used to purchase jointly-held assets, deposited in joint accounts, etc. If so, the spouse must be included in the financial profile calculations.

3. Claims of a substantial prior cash hoard may be rebutted by showing that the suspect lived penuriously, borrowed money, made installment purchases, incurred large debts, was delinquent on his accounts, had a poor credit rating, or filed for bankruptcy. Claims that cash came from family or other private loans may be rebutted by showing that the alleged lender was incapable of generating the amounts supposedly lent, the

Table 9.6
Example of Expenditures Method

Suspect:	Year 1	Year 2
Application of Funds:		
Increase in Bank Balance	$2,000	$10,000
Down Payment on Residence	---	10,000
Purchase of Automobile	10,000	---
Mortgage Payments	8,000	20,000
Credit Card Payments	5,000	10,000
Other Expenses	15,000	30,000
TOTAL	$40,000	$80,000
Less: Known Sources of Funds		
Cash on Hand	1,000	---
Salary	30,000	35,000
Interest Earned on Savings Account	1,000	5,000
Loan Proceeds	8,000	===
TOTAL	$40,000	$40,000
Funds from Unknown or Illegal Sources	0	$40,000

Table 9.7
Formula for Expenditures Method

	EXPENDITURES (APPLICATION OF FUNDS)
less	known sources of funds
equals	FUNDS FROM UNKNOWN SOURCES

absence of any documentation reflecting the source of the alleged loan (no bank account withdrawals), and the absence of other sources of funds available to the lender.

THE BASICS OF MONEY LAUNDERING

An examiner tracing illicit funds may find an apparently legitimate source at the end of the trail: a prosperous cash retail business, a profitable real estate transaction, or offshore "loans" or investments. This is the realm of money laundering. Although it can be used to conceal and "clean" the proceeds of virtually any type of illegal activity (whether distributed in cash or otherwise), money laundering is usually associated with narcotics trafficking and the large sums of currency it generates.

A distinction must be made between money-hiding and money-moving schemes, intended merely to conceal the source or existence of dirty money, and true money-laundering schemes. The latter both hides the actual source and provides an apparently legitimate explanation for the funds. Technically, money laundering refers only to the second situation, although the term is often used incorrectly to describe both.

Money-Hiding Methods

The most common money-hiding methods include the following:

1. The illegally acquired funds may simply be hoarded, or spent or deposited inconspicuously. Discretion and moderation are, however, not typical virtues of narcotics dealers or other major white-collar criminals. Large currency transactions draw attention, and those of $10,000 or more trigger federal reporting requirements. Eventually the major criminal will be forced to use financial institutions or adopt other measures, as follows.

2. Funds may be deposited in or transferred through financial institutions, by engaging in multiple transactions under the $10,000 reporting limit. This includes multiple deposits, currency exchanges (replacing small denomination bills with larger ones), or the purchase of cashier's checks, bank checks, or money orders. Multiple deposits may be made in different accounts at the same institution, or by couriers at various banks. Funds may be converted to cashier's checks and then hoarded, or deposited to other accounts, from which the funds may be wire transferred out of the country. This method—known as "smurfing"—is extremely common, particularly with cocaine traffickers.

3. Fictitious accounts may be established using phony social security or tax identification numbers. Fictitious accounts are usually used to move large sums in short periods, then closed and opened elsewhere. They are often used in collusion with dishonest bank employees.

4. The launderer may open an account under the guise of a business exempt from the reporting requirements, such as a restaurant or retail sales business, or actually acquire such a business and make deposits through its accounts.

5. The launderer may corrupt bank officials to ignore the filing requirements, facilitate the use of fictitious accounts, or falsely certify a business as an exempt account. These schemes usually involve payments of a small percentage of the laundered funds.

6. Finally, the launderer may smuggle the illicit currency directly out of the country, often by private aircraft. Transportation in amounts of $10,000 or more are supposed to be reported on a customs form, but of course this is ignored. Currency removed from the United States in this manner may be used to pay suppliers, or returned to the United States via sham "loans" or investments, as described below.

Money-Laundering Methods

All money-laundering schemes are some form or variation of one of the three following basic schemes.

1. The use of a legitimate business enterprise as a front to conceal and commingle illicit dollars. Ideally, the business is one which deals primarily in cash, has relatively fixed costs (such as a movie theatre or massage parlor), and is exempt from bank currency-reporting requirements. Bars and restaurants, which meet two of the three criteria (their costs fluctuate with sales), and also provide a ready location for illicit sales and clandestine meetings, are probably the most common fronts. This method of laundering is usually an accounting exercise. The illegal dollars are not physically mixed with legitimate receipts. Instead accounting and tax records are simply falsified to attribute more income to the enterprise and indirectly its owners.

2. Manipulated Buy-Sell Transactions. Real estate or other commercial transactions can be manipulated to hide the use of illicit funds. A buyer and seller may agree to convey property worth $2 million at market for a stated price of $1 million, with the balance paid under the table. When the property is sold (perhaps after substantial improvements, also paid for with dirty money), at market or higher, the "profits" provide a source of apparently legitimate income. The same principle can be used to generate false profits in other commercial transactions, particularly between related entities.

3. Offshore Transactions. Money moved offshore surreptitiously or through banking channels may be returned to its owner as a sham loan, investment, or payment for supposed goods and services. Documentation to prove the illicit source of the funds and true nature of the transaction is beyond the subpoena power of the United States, and if a bank-secrecy jurisdiction is involved, unavailable through treaty arrangements. Money repatriated in this manner not only comes back clean, but tax-free, and if "interest" is paid on the sham loan, may even provide additional tax deductions.

Proving Money-Laundering Schemes

Although money laundering is now itself a crime (as a result of the Money Laundering Control Act of 1986, 18 USC 1956), it is usually detected as a result of the investigation of the underlying offenses. Effective investigation measures have included visual and electronic surveillance, sting and undercover operations. Below is an outline of Bank Secrecy Act reporting requirements, followed by various techniques and approaches to identify and prove money-laundering schemes.

Federal Reporting Requirements

1. Currency Transaction Reports (CTR), IRS Form 4789. The Bank Secrecy Act and the Treasury regulations require domestic financial institutions to report all currency transactions of $10,000 or more on IRS form 4789 within 15 days. Failure to file a CTR can constitute a criminal offense under the Bank Secrecy Act. Some business and transactions—retail stores, high-cash-volume businesses, government agencies

and payroll withdrawals—are exempt. Transactions with other domestic banks are also excepted, but transactions of $10,000 or more with foreign banks must be reported. The forms must be retained for five years.

2. Report of International Monetary Instruments, Customs Form 4790 (CMIR). Any person who physically transports, mails or ships currency or other defined monetary instruments in an aggregate amount in excess of $10,000 outside the United States must file a form 4790, with the Customs Service. As used here, monetary instrument means bearer instruments; those that can be readily negotiated by the bearer, such as endorsed traveler's checks, money orders, and bank checks. Certain exceptions, many of which apply to banks, exist.

3. Report of Cash Payments Over $10,000 Received in a Trade or Business, IRS Form 8300. Any person engaged in a trade or business who, in the course of such business, receives more than $10,000 in a single or related transaction must file a form 8300 within 15 days with the IRS. Financial institutions which are required to file a CTR (Form 4789) and certain businesses, such as stockbrokers and currency exchanges, are exempted. Automobile dealerships, boat and airplane vendors, jewelers, pawn-brokers, and other businesses attractive to the criminal element are covered. Casinos must file on form 8362. Nevada casinos, which make equivalent reports to state authorities, are exempt.

4. Foreign Bank Account Reports, Treasury Form 90–22.1 (FBAR). U.S. citizens and resident aliens are required to report annually a financial interest in or signature authority over a foreign financial account with a balance that reaches $10,000 or more.

Examination Techniques

Suspected Front Businesses. Laundering schemes conducted through a front business are best proven through the cooperation of an insider, such as the business's accountant or tax preparer, or by infiltrating an agent. Indirect methods of proving laundering activity include the following.

1. Ratio Analyses and Sampling Techniques. Overreporting revenues of a front business to launder funds may result in an imbalance of the normal ratio of costs to sales: costs will appear unduly low compared to reported revenues. (This is why the ideal laundering operation would have relatively fixed costs against sales.) Surveillance of the suspect enterprise may provide additional evidence that revenues are being underreported, by showing low customer traffic. Surveillance may also permit sampling procedures, a standard audit method, wherein a count of the number of customers or sales during a given period is used to extrapolate total sales.

2. Flow Chart Techniques. A laundering operation may also be revealed by flow chart techniques. Enterprises used to launder funds will generally have common ownership or other connections, usually under the control of the targets. Therefore, corporate and other business filings and records showing the principals in the suspect businesses should be obtained and patterns of ownership noted. Financial and bank records can then be subpoenaed to trace the flow of funds between the enterprises.

Manipulated Buy-Sell Transactions. Again, an inside witness is a valuable asset. An independent appraisal or comparative sales data may establish that real property was sold substantially below market. The techniques described above to trace illicit funds and find hidden assets may be employed to find the under-the-table payments. Also look for false pricing schemes involving subsidiaries or other related entities to the suspect business.

Offshore Transactions. Most sophisticated traffickers use banks or business fronts in countries which have strict bank secrecy laws and no treaty relationship with the United States.

In such cases there is virtually no way to obtain documentation of offshore transactions. Jurisdiction may be obtained, however, over a foreign bank which transacts business in the United States, and a subpoena served on the local branch. The bank may still refuse to produce the requested papers, citing its home country's secrecy laws which may make such disclosures a criminal offense. Contempt sanctions may then be sought, or the suspect, if within the jurisdiction of the United States, may be ordered by the court to sign a consent directive directing the foreign bank to release the requested records. Some foreign jurisdiction will honor such consents, others will not, requiring further legal efforts—of uncertain utility because of the different sovereigns involved—to attempt to compel production.

10   Evaluating Fraud Risks

Much fraud evidence is circumstantial. Early clues can include symptoms such as changed lifestyles or behavior, suspicious documentation, or complaints from customers or suspicion by fellow employees.

In its early stages, internal fraud may surface first through environmental and personal clues. Good fraud examiners will be alert to these factors and make appropriate inquiry where they exist. These environmental and personal characteristics and situations are called red flags. While the presence of red flags does not necessarily indicate fraud, they are nonetheless present in almost every case. Red flags can also signal a higher risk for most frauds when management is involved. Some examples include increased uncollectible receivables, loss of customers, obsolete inventory, rapidly changing outside auditors or management, and restrictive loan agreements. These frauds usually take the form of misstating financial statements to hide losses or gloss over "temporarily" bad situations. As an example, one real estate company was a legitimate business until interest rates rose, sales of condominiums slackened, and its cash position became critically bad. When faced with the prospects of losing their business, they turned to investor fraud to try to "make it through the rough times." They misstated their financial statements and company assets and sold limited partnerships to individuals. The sales were made mainly to retired people, and financed by taking out second mortgages on the investors' homes. With promises such as "the company will pay the second mortgage, give you a new car to drive, and pay you ten percent interest on the money (equity) you are not using anyway," elderly investors placed approximately $39 million in the company. The company was misrepresented as having $20 million in assets when in reality it had significantly less. This fraud might not have occurred had the business continued to be profitable; who knows?

Similarly, high personal debts or expensive personal habits are often present.

While the red flag approach can be helpful, sometimes personal characteristics are difficult to observe.

INTERNAL CONTROL AND THE EVALUATION OF CONTROLS

For many frauds, especially internal theft and embezzlement, three personal factors are often present: (1) some kind of pressure, such as a perceived financial need, (2) some perceived opportunity to commit and conceal the fraud, and (3) a way to rationalize the behavior as consistent with one's own level of integrity (Albrecht et al. 1982). For example, a perpetrator might justify a fraud because he has debts beyond his ability to pay, he is the warehouse foreman and internal controls are weak, and he is only "temporarily borrowing" the money and will pay it back when his financial condition improves. Companies can prevent or reduce the incidence of fraud by working on any or all three of these areas: that is, they can help employees reduce or deal with pressures, they can prevent fraud opportunities, and they can watch for rationalizations expressed by employees.

Many traditional techniques to prevent fraud concentrate almost exclusively on opportunity. And, although there are many ways to reduce perceived opportunities, companies usually rely exclusively on an internal control system to do the job. There is no question that a good internal control system that is rigorously enforced can prevent many frauds committed by one person (collusion by two or more people can usually circumvent most internal controls). For a solo fraud to occur, internal controls usually must be overridden, inadequate, or absent. A good understanding of controls and control systems is essential for fraud examiners because controls work both to prevent and detect fraud. Examining weaknesses in internal controls allows examiners to see where opportunities exist to commit and conceal fraud.

An internal control system consists of the policies and procedures designed to provide management with reasonable assurance that their goals and objectives will be met. One of the major purposes of the internal control system is to safeguard the assets and records of a business against fraud, errors, and misuse. The effectiveness of internal controls depends on the competence and dependability of the people using them. For example, a control requiring the counting of inventory by two individuals is only effective if the employees understand the instructions for counting and if they exercise care in completing the count. The control could be inadequate if the employees decide to overstate the count to cover up a theft of inventory by one or both of them, or the control could be overridden by management's instructions to employees to increase the count in order to improve reported earnings.

Internal Control Structure

There are three major elements of a good internal control structure: (1) the overall control environment, (2) the accounting system, and (3) the specific

Table 10.1
Internal Control Structure

Control Environment	Accounting System	Control Procedures
1. Management Philosophy & Style	1. Validity	1. Separation of Duties
	2. Authorization	2. Proper Procedures for Authorization
2. Organizational Structure	3. Completeness	
		3. Adequate Documents and Records
3. Audit Committee	4. Valuation	
4. Communication Methods	5. Classification	
	6. Timing	4. Physical Control Over Assets and Records
5. Internal Audit Function		
		5. Independent Checks on Performance
6. Personnel Policies and Procedures		

control procedures (See Table 10.1). If this internal control structure is in place and working, the chances of fraud occurring undetected are greatly reduced. Fraud examiners must be familiar with each of the components of the internal control structure so they can evaluate it and look for weaknesses.

Overall Control Environment

For fraud to be minimized, top management must set the proper tone. Unless management sets an example and articulates what is acceptable and unacceptable, fraud will be more likely to occur. Management sends the most important signals in an organization. If employees see management being dishonest with customers, cheating on taxes or expense reimbursements, or rationalizing other improper behavior, they will usually justify dishonest acts of their own. Because management's attitude is so critical, fraud examiners must get some sense of their attitude about control. In one company, for example, where top management switched from an attitude of "we want to know when someone is prosecuted for committing fraud" to "we want to know when and why someone who committed fraud is not prosecuted," dishonest acts decreased substantially. Psychologists generally agree that the two most important elements of teaching honesty to others are (1) properly modeling honest behavior (setting a good example), and (2) properly labeling actions as acceptable or unacceptable (codes of conduct, training, and enforcement of policy).

Like management philosophy, organization and structure are overriding elements of good control. If responsibility and authority are clearly defined, internal fraud is less likely to occur. Fraud is also more likely to occur where confusion about assignments and overly complex organizational structures exist. Only in a clearly defined organizational structure can employees, auditors, and fraud examiners perceive how control-related policies and procedures are to be carried out.

An independent audit committee has evolved as one of the most important control elements in organizations. The audit committee is a subcommittee of the board of directors and has the responsibility of dealing with both internal and external auditors, as well as with corporate security in most organizations. The audit committee's existence is critical because it can act as a sounding board for ethical concerns raised by fraud examiners, auditors, and security personnel. Because the committee is a subgroup of the board of directors, it has leverage over top management and can frequently make sure that honest policies are followed and clearly articulated. Legally, audit committees and boards of directors have the responsibility to make sure that corporations act in an ethical manner. Any company whose stock is listed on the New York Stock Exchange is required to have an audit committee composed of outside directors. In addition to their direct audit responsibilities, these committees are usually given oversight responsibilities for the financial reporting process, including the internal control structure and compliance with applicable laws and regulations.

A good structure must include both formal and informal ways to communicate authority, responsibility, and other control-related matters. Communication methods include the system of memos, operating plans, employee job descriptions, policy documents, and codes of conduct statements. When management has methods to communicate control matters it deems important, goal congruence can exist between top management and others in the organization.

Management control methods include all systems of monitoring the activities of others. These control methods include such things as the budgeting process, the reporting process, investigation of variances from budget, and other activities which allow management to monitor and take appropriate corrective action. These methods enable managers to detect some frauds before they become larger.

The internal audit function is established to monitor the effectiveness and efficiency of all other control-related policies and procedures. Internal audit is generally considered the "eyes and ears" of top management and the audit committee. In order for internal audit to be effective, it must be independent of operating management and have direct reporting responsibility to the audit committee of the board of directors. Because internal auditors spend considerable time and effort examining the activities within a company, they can provide a very good defense mechanism against fraud. Unfortunately, some statistics show that internal auditors uncover only about 20 percent of frauds while over one-third are revealed by anonymous tips (Albrecht et al. 1982). These statistics can be improved considerably where internal auditors receive adequate training in fraud prevention and detection.

Personnel Policies and Procedures

Personnel policies and procedures are the most important elements of a good internal control system. If employees are well screened before being hired and are trustworthy and competent, other controls can be less effective and fraud will still be minimized. Honest, efficient employees can compensate for a lack of other controls and can maintain an air of integrity. Incompetent or dishonest employees can override controls and create an environment where fraud can occur and remain undetected.

Notwithstanding the critical importance of good personnel policies and procedures, it should be remembered that nearly every person is capable of committing fraud. Otherwise honest employees, faced with high pressure and high perceived opportunity, can rationalize a dishonest act. A most common comment when a fraud is committed is usually, ''I can't believe it. He (she) was my most trusted employee.'' Fraud can be reduced (but not eliminated) by hiring honest people and having good personnel policies and procedures.

Another element of personnel policies and procedures is the way in which employees are treated. If employees feel needed, fulfilled, and satisfied with their work, they are less inclined to be dishonest. Many frauds are committed by employees who feel that they were treated unfairly, did not receive proper compensation or promotions, had a supervisor who was difficult to deal with, feared being terminated, or were bored with their jobs. Assessing the attitudes of employees is a critical step in evaluating the effectiveness of an internal control system.

The final element of the control environment is the external influences. Often, activities and pressures from the outside can work to either increase or decrease internal fraud. Examples of outside influences include the Securities and Exchange Commission, which requires periodic reports of most companies, the Internal Revenue Service, which requires reporting, and industry regulators who exercise oversights and require periodic reports. Examples of outside influences that may work to increase fraud include difficult conditions in the economy or industry, heavy competition, delayed paying of receivables by customers, or decreased demand for products or services. When individuals have invested all their personal resources in a firm, many times they will commit fraud to keep the company going.

The Accounting System

A company's accounting system is established to record, classify, and summarize data about its economic transactions and to maintain accountability for assets and liabilities. A good accounting system must satisfy the elements of validity, authorization, completeness valuation, classification, timing and posting, and summarization. First, the system must have controls to insure that fictitious or nonexistent transactions are not entered, that all recorded transactions are valid. Second, it must not allow fraudulent or unauthorized transactions to be recorded. Such transactions could allow company assets to be stolen, wasted, or destroyed. Third, it must insure that all proper transactions are included. Omission of transactions could lead to improper financial statements and a lack of accountability for assets. Fourth, the accounting system must have controls to insure that all transactions are properly valued. A system that allows calculation errors or improper valuation of assets or liabilities would result in accounts and financial statements that are meaningless. Fifth, controls must be present to insure that transactions are properly classified. If employees are allowed to enter expenditures into the wrong accounts, for example, fraud can be easily concealed. Sixth, transactions must be recorded at the proper time. If transactions can be recorded before or after they have taken place, financial statements can be misstated. This increases the likelihood of failing to record transactions or recording transactions in improper amounts. Finally, transactions must be properly posted and summarized or subsidiary records and ledgers will not be in balance. Unbalanced ledgers and subsidiary records allow perpetrators to conceal thefts easily by overstating or understating specific balances.

Control Procedures

The final category of a good internal control structure is the specific control procedures that must be in place. While these procedures are usually examined much more closely than the control environment and accounting system by auditors and others, they are no more important.

If a control system is to have integrity, there must be a segregation between the functions of authorization, custody, operation, and record keeping. Without adequate segregation of authorization from custody and record keeping, the likelihood of error or fraud is significantly increased. For example, a potential for fraud exists if one individual authorizes purchases of merchandise and services and also approves checks for payment. Custody of assets should be segregated from record keeping. If the custodian of assets also performs the record keeping function, no control exists for comparing the physical existence of assets with the quantity of assets recorded.

Every transaction must be properly authorized if controls are to be satisfactory. If individuals in an organization could acquire and expend assets at will, internal fraud would be very easy to perpetrate. Proper authorization means that management establishes policies and procedures that must be followed by others. An example of authorization is a policy that states that any expenditure over $500 must have the approval of a division manager.

Having proper documents and records is a control technique that serves two primary purposes. First, good documentation serves as a communication medium. Second, documents provide an audit trail. As a communication medium, good documentation facilitates the processing of transactions. Procedures manuals outline documentation to be used for communication of authorizations and processing. Standard documents such as sales invoices facilitate the approval function. Devices such as prenumbering provide assurance that only authorized transactions are processed. A major documentation aid that facilitates the preparation of financial statements is the chart of accounts. This chart standardizes the information-gathering and -accumulation process.

Documentation also provides an audit trail for use as an independent check. Both internal and external auditors use audit trails as reference points in the performance of their duties. The audit trail serves as a vehicle for controlling and following transactions as they pass through the accounting system.

Physical control over assets and records helps to prohibit their unauthorized use. Internal control techniques for safeguarding assets revolve around custodial responsibility. This entails the establishment of physical precautions to safeguard assets. Providing proper safeguards reduces opportunities to misappropriate assets. Each entity needs a comprehensive security program that includes locks, fences, gates, cages, storerooms, secured warehouses, safes, and other safeguards to protect corporate assets.

The last control procedure is independent checks on performance. Independent checks incorporate internal and external audit functions as well as the internal checks created by a proper segregation of duties. The critical characteristic of an independent check is the true independence of the reviewing party. For this reason the internal auditor usually reports to the audit committee of the board of directors.

There are many ways to independently check performance. Using internal auditors is one of the most common. Other methods include mandatory vacations, where another employee performs the vacationing person's duties, periodic rotations or transfers, and the preparation of bank reconciliations by someone independent of the accounting function.

Evaluating Internal Controls

In addition to understanding internal controls, fraud examiners must also be able to evaluate their effectiveness and identify weaknesses. While there are many ways to evaluate controls, one of the most effective is to use the following three-step procedure:

1. Consider the types of errors and frauds that could occur.
2. Determine the control procedures and structure that would prevent or detect such errors and frauds.
3. Determine whether those controls are in place and are being followed satisfactorily.

Considering the types of errors or frauds that could occur in processing transactions is a formidable task. In order to make it more manageable, transactions can be classified by function, operating unit, or cycle. Then, internal control objectives for each of those functions, units or cycles can be identified. Finally, controls that satisfy the control objectives can be identified and examined.

As an example, the following twelve categories might be identified for a business:

1. sales and accounts receivable
2. cash receipts
3. purchases and accounts payable
4. cash disbursements
5. cash balances
6. payroll
7. inventories and cost of sales
8. securities
9. property, plant and equipment acquisitions, and deposits
10. other assets and liabilities
11. journal entries and general ledger
12. external financial reporting

For each of these areas, an examiner would determine whether sufficient controls are in place to provide the necessary reasonable assurance that internal fraud will be difficult to accomplish. The key question to be considered is whether the essential control procedures would be likely to prevent or detect a significant error or fraud. This evaluation process may not only identify essential control procedures which need to be added, it may also reveal that some existing procedures are not essential in meeting control objectives and can be deleted.

Once a decision is made about the adequacy of prescribed controls, the next step is to determine whether the control procedures are functioning as intended. In many organizations there is a significant difference between the control system as it is supposed to be working (formal system) and the control system as it is actually working (informal system). In fact, a common contributing factor to fraud is not the lack of internal controls but the lack of compliance with existing internal controls.

The Cash Receipt Example

As an example of the kind of evaluation that is necessary to assess the adequacy of controls, consider the class of transactions that encompass cash receipts. The functions of handling checks and currency and keeping records of cash receipts need to be segregated if all the control objects are to be met. Adequate segregation of duties reduces the possibility of undetected errors by providing a check over the receipt of cash. Ideally, the person who handles cash receipts should not have the authority to prepare or sign checks, have access to the accounting records, nor be involved in reconciling bank accounts. If such segregation is impracticable, there should be alternative procedures to ensure that discrepancies come to light.

The functions that must be segregated in the cash receipts cycle include:

1. opening of mail and listing of checks
2. handling of receipts or currency
3. preparation of bank deposits
4. maintenance of cash receipts journal
5. initiation of wire transfers
6. maintenance of accounts receivable ledger
7. reconciliation of bank accounts
8. authorization of write-offs of receivables
9. collection of past due accounts

The authorization objective would be satisfied by insuring that the opening and the closing of all bank accounts are authorized by the board of directors or persons designated by the board. Control is strengthened by insuring that appropriate individuals are assigned the authority and responsibility for making deposits and wire transfers and that appropriate individuals are assigned the responsibility for handling currency.

Documents and record controls would insure that appropriate procedures are in place to accomplish the following:

1. That all cash receipts (checks and cash) are recorded in the accounting records.
2. That all cash receipts in the accounting records have actually been received.
3. That all cash receipts transactions are recorded in the appropriate accounts.
4. That all cash receipts are recorded in the proper period.
5. That all cash receipts are classified correctly.
6. That all cash receipts are summarized correctly.
7. That all cash receipts are posted correctly.

Physical access controls would ensure that access to cash receipts is limited to those who are authorized to handle such receipts. Personnel should not have access to blank credit memo forms, blank checks, check-signing machines, or accounting records. In addition, they should not have authority to sign checks, issue checks, write off accounts receivables, or reconcile bank accounts.

The independent control for cash receipts would require periodic counts of cash on a surprise basis, as well as monthly reconciliation of bank accounts by employees who have no other involvement in functions related to cash receipts or cash disbursements. Independent checks on cash receipts would also involve periodic job rotations of key people, mandatory vacations, and reviews by both independent and internal auditors.

In addition to internal controls, opportunities can be reduced by making sure that internal controls are followed, by watching for fraud symptoms, and by monitoring employees. Most frauds have symptoms that, if recognized, would reveal the fraud. Don't let these symptoms go unexplained:

1. missing documents
2. second endorsements on checks
3. unusual endorsements
4. unexplained adjustments to inventory balances
5. unexplained adjustments to accounts receivables
6. stale items in bank reconciliations
7. old outstanding checks
8. customer complaints
9. unusual patterns of deposits in transit

ENVIRONMENTAL RED FLAGS

Some organizations have significantly more fraud than do others. Environment could be critical to reducing fraud risks. Some of the more common environmental red flags are identified below.

Poor Management Philosophy

There are several noted cases of how top management's example of dishonesty filtered through an organization until many employees were being dishonest. In the large Equity Funding fraud, for example, when top management's fraud was finally discovered, many employees used that as an opportunity to cheat on their expense accounts or credit cards.

Red flags involving management's attitudes include ambivalence about dishonest acts, autocratic management, low trust of employees, short-range planning, management by crisis, a political reward system, negative feedback, poor promotion opportunities, poorly defined business ethics, hostile working relationships, high turnover and/or absenteeism, low company loyalty, and a reactive management philosophy. Many frauds occur, for example, where an autocratic management arbitrarily sets budgets for lower level managers to meet. When these budgets are unattainable, the managers have a choice to either cheat or fail. When their jobs, reputations, and careers are at stake, cheating is sometimes easier than failing.

Personality traits of managers associated with frauds include wheeler-dealers, a management that is feared, impulsive, too numbers-oriented, and insensitive to people. Obviously, the contrast is a management that is friendly, calm, and generous with their time, self-confident, and goal oriented.

A company's attitude toward fraud starts at the top. If management ignores the fraud problem, the company will probably be unsuccessful in dealing with fraud. If top management is supportive and concerned, fraud can be significantly reduced.

Prosecuting a fraud offender is often expensive and time-consuming. As a result, many organizations will take the easy route of simply terminating an embezzler and not filing charges. Management must recognize, however, that while not prosecuting may be the most economical decision in the short run, it only sends a signal that the organization does not deal harshly with criminals. Prosecuting even small offenders sends a signal that fraud will not be tolerated. If the criminal justice system is reluctant to cooperate because of the nonviolent nature and "insignificance" of the crime, dealing firmly with criminals is very important.

The second indication of management's attitude about fraud is the willingness to acknowledge that fraud may exist. Fraud cannot be reduced if the problem is denied.

Poor Financial Position

Obviously an organization that is continually struggling to meet expenses, buy inventory, and meet payroll is at greater risk to commit fraud. When employees are insecure about their jobs or the company's fate, they may be less reluctant to take advantage of company resources. The existence of cash-flow problems is a red flag that should not be ignored.

Low Employee Loyalty

Fraud often occurs when a perceived opportunity is combined with a way to rationalize the dishonest act. When employees lack loyalty to an organization, they don't feel so inhibited about taking advantage of the company. With high loyalty, the offender may feel that he or she has a stake in the business; with low loyalty there is a feeling of stealing from "them."

There are many factors that lead to low employee loyalty. Some reasons (such as personal problems) cannot be observed or addressed. Others, especially work-related reasons, are often obvious. Perceived inequities at the work place, for example, can often lead to decreased employee loyalty. If an employee is passed over for a promotion, he or she might embezzle because of a feeling of being wronged. It is easier to view fraud as compensation for injustice.

Some of the most frequently identified reasons why employees have used fraud to "correct" injustices are the following:

- being passed over for a raise
- being assigned undesirable jobs
- being subjected to disciplinary action

- feeling that pay is inadequate
- favoritism to other employees
- resentment toward superiors
- frustration with job
- boredom

Some of these may, in fact, not be justified. But it is the perception rather than the reality that motivates the perpetrator's actions.

Confusion about Ethics

Computer fraud was problematic when computers were first introduced because laws concerning their legality were not well articulated. Many judges and juries did not understand computers. There was significant confusion about whether an act was fraudulent. Similarly, confusion in an organization can lead to an increase in fraud. For example, if there is confusion among procurement personnel about what types of gifts are acceptable, increasingly large gifts might be accepted until they turn into outright bribes or kickbacks. If there is confusion about the confidentiality of information, leaks might escalate. The purpose of a corporate code of conduct, policy statements regarding gift receiving and giving, security badges allowing access to certain kinds of operating units, and security policies and memoranda is to eliminate confusion about what is acceptable. Absence of a clearly defined code of conduct, executive disclosure statements, and policy statements are red flags that should alert fraud examiners. Some companies have established detailed employee-awareness programs involving periodic posters, small-group education sessions, videos, and other education efforts. These programs inform employees what is acceptable and how they are hurt if someone is dishonest. Awareness programs help employees understand that fraud hurts everyone. Sometimes these programs involve such themes such "fraud takes a bite out of everyone's check." The whole purpose is to reduce confusion among employees.

Improper Background Checks

A serious red flag is the lack of proper background checks or the failure to exercise due care when hiring new employees. Because many companies are still reluctant and even prohibited from disclosing negative information about former employees, it is critical that proper screening take place. Proper screening has the following benefits:

1. Results in more honest employees.
2. Acts as a deterrent to employee dishonesty.
3. Protects innocent employees from false accusations or suspicion.

Table 10.2
Examples of Problem Employees

Type of Problem	Number of Applicants	% of Total
Previous Arrests	82	16
Unstable Work Record	30	6
Wanted Short-Term Job	10	2
Fired from Previous Job	15	3
Major Employee Theft	64	13
Personal/Domestic Problems	11	2
Health Defects	15	3
Mental Problems	31	6
Drug Users	16	3
Other Problems (Temper, etc.)	30	6

4. Eliminates problem employees such as substance-abusers, job-hoppers, accident-prone individuals and serial thieves.

5. Eliminates poor security risks.

6. Permits honest employees to work in harmony with their colleagues.

As examples of the kinds of problem employees that can be eliminated with thorough background investigations, three companies kept records of their employees screened during one year (Albrecht et al. 1982) (See Table 10.2). Hiring problem employees presents many difficulties in addition to an increased risk of fraud. Hiring drug dealers or individuals with uncontrollable tempers can result in other problems. If, for example, an employee gets high on drugs purchased at work and kills someone in an automobile accident while returning home, victims may be able to recover from the employee's company because the company allowed drugs to be sold on their premises. Similarly, if an employee with an uncontrollable temper injures a fellow employee, the injured employee may be able to recover from the company because of inadequate screening of employees.

Lack of Employee Support (Assistance) Programs

A second element usually present in internal fraud is some kind of pressure felt by the employee. These pressures are usually of a "nonsharable" financial nature and are often embarrassing to the employee. If, for example, an employee needs to borrow money to finance the purchase of a home, there are legitimate channels for arranging the loan. On the other hand, if an employee has made bad investment decisions, or spent beyond his or her means, additional borrowing is often not an alternative. And, because publicly admitting failure is often perceived as a show of weakness on the part of the employee, fraud is sometimes seen as the only remaining alternative.

There are two ways organizations can help their employees deal with such pressures. The first is a formally established employee-assistance program that confidentially counsels with employees about their problems. These programs are commonly found in large organizations but are usually limited to substance-abuse problems. If these programs are expanded to provide financial counseling to employees, much of the perceived financial problems could be addressed. Employees could seek help with such problems as gambling, stock market spec-ulation, and the need for money to cover other obligations.

A second way of assisting employees with stress is to have an open-door policy or free informal communication lines within the organization. If employees have a good relationship with their managers and can talk freely, managers may understand their pressures before they become acute. Certainly managers cannot interfere in an employee's personal life. However, keeping senses alert, watching for distress signals, and being available to talk can go a long way in reducing fraud pressures.

History of Fraud-Related Problems

Fraud recurs where opportunity exists. Repeated fraud is a red flag that signals other problems: inadequate controls, confusion about what is acceptable, or a poor prosecution policy. Empirically, one of the best environmental predictors of future frauds is the number of past frauds.

Other Environmental Conditions

There are other general environmental conditions that raise red flags signalling a higher probability of fraud. Some of these are near-term mergers or acquisitions, regulatory problems, related-party transactions, rapid turnover of employees, too much trust in key employees, and lack of physical security. In addition, some other environmental red flags are industry-specific. Often a red flag is not the existence of a condition as much as a change in conditions.

Fraud examiners should be constantly alert to red flags and take appropriate action when they exist. And, they should leverage their knowledge by educating management, auditors, and others involved about increased risks. Management and fellow employees are sometimes in the best position to observe red flags. They are the ones who best know the potential perpetrators and can best observe their behavior. It is no coincidence that most frauds are detected through tips from fellow employees rather than by auditors and others who come in contact with perpetrators only for brief periods.

PERSONAL RED FLAGS

There are three types of personal or employee-specific red flags: (1) personal financial factors, (2) personal habits, and (3) personal feelings. Fraud examiners must be alert to all three, as discussed below.

Financial Factors

It has been estimated that a majority of all internal frauds are initially motivated by a financial need. However, once the theft occurs and the financial need is met, embezzlers rarely cease their dishonest activity. Usually they will continue to steal. Rarely will they hoard the proceeds. Instead they will change their lifestyles and spending habits. Fraud examiners should know that employees with serious financial problems are in a high-risk category and are more likely than others to turn to fraud as a solution to their problems.

An illustration of how financial losses or high debts can create pressures to commit fraud is the case of a grain-elevator owner in Iowa. Raymond K. was the local boy who made good. He started out driving a coal truck, bought into an elevator, and made it a thriving business. He really struck it rich when he profited from trading grain on the commodities market. He built a lavish house, complete with an indoor swimming pool, a sauna, and a three-car garage. He worked hard, sometimes from 5 A.M. to 11 P.M. during harvest, and was generous, always extending credit to farmers in a bind. He attended a church and even sent the pastor and his wife on a trip to the Holy Land.

All was fine until his finances took a turn for the worse. He apparently lost a lot of money playing the commodities market, developed cash problems, and went deeply into debt. He turned to embezzlement to cover his losses. His fraud received national notoriety when he drove seven miles outside of his hometown and committed suicide.

While high debt and financial problems are the most common personal financial red flags, fraud often occurs when employees live beyond their means. This in turn develops additional financial problems. Living beyond one's means can exhibit itself in taking expensive vacations, incurring high social expenditures such as joining exclusive clubs, purchasing recreational vehicles such as boats, cottages, cabins, airplanes or expensive automobiles, buying expensive personal items such as jewelry, designer suits or other apparel, and flaunting or bragging about money.

Personal Habits

Sometimes employees become engulfed by habits that require so much money that, in and of themselves, they can motivate fraud. Examples of these habits include extensive stock market or speculative investments, gambling, maintaining a second household because of divorce, relationships with others outside of the family, and heavy use of alcohol or drugs. To appreciate the kind of pressures that these kinds of habits can place on employees, consider the following excerpts from the diaries of reformed gambling addicts:

1. Terry A.: "When I was at the blackjack table, my wife could have been home dying from cancer, and I could not have cared less."
2. Thomas J.: "Gambling was the ultimate experience for me—better than sex, better than any drug. I had withdrawal tortures just like a heroin junkie."
3. Ronald P.: "I degraded myself in every way possible. I embezzled from my own company; I conned my six-year old out of his allowance."
4. Archie K.: "After I woke up from an appendectomy, I sneaked out of the hospital, cashed a bogus check, and headed for my bookie. I was still bleeding from the operation."

Personal Feelings

Some frauds are motivated more by emotional than financial pressures. Examples of these feelings are a sense of community, family, or social expectations to succeed financially, perception of being treated unfairly or inadequately by one's employer, resentment of superiors, frustration with the job, peer-group pressures within the company, or an insatiable desire for self-enrichment or personal gain.

Many of these feelings are created by the working environment. In addition, however, fraud examiners should constantly be alert for verbalizations and hints of these types of feelings. One fraud was discovered, for example, when fellow employees worried about another who constantly talked of being financially successful. He was always encompassed by feelings that if he did not succeed financially, he was a failure. His strong desires to "be rich" were of concern, and so his area was reviewed carefully. They discovered that he had been stealing by using a fictitious company supposedly providing services to his employer.

In addition to personal financial factors, personal habits, and personal feelings, other personal red flags include abruptly changed behavior, consistent rationalization of contradictory behavior, and a strong desire to beat the system. As with the other red flags, existence of these factors does not indicate that fraud exists. Rather, it raises a flag or signal for further inquiry.

IV Investigation

11 Introduction to Fraud Examination

Fraud is defined by Black's Law Dictionary as a generic term, "embracing all multifarious means which human ingenuity can devise, and which are resorted to by one individual to get an advantage over another by false suggestions or suppression of truth, and includes all surprise, trick, cunning, or dissembling, and any unfair way by which another is cheated."

With such a broad definition, we commit fraud if we steal from our employer under the guise of a fiduciary relationship, and we commit fraud when we lie to our spouses, friends, and co-workers. The law, however, deals more with the former than the latter; in order to be actionable, a fraud must meet the test of materiality and damages: frauds of a more serious nature.

The professional examination of fraud issues commences with several axioms:

1. Fraud, by its nature, is hidden. No absolute assurance can be given that fraud does or does not exist.

2. To find the proof that fraud has not occurred, one must endeavor also to prove it has occurred.

3. To find the proof that fraud has occurred, one must endeavor to prove also that it has not occurred.

4. The final determination as to whether fraud exists is the responsibility of the courts and juries, not the fraud examiner.

No absolute assurance can be given that fraud exists or does not exist, because fraud remains concealed until some event or transgression uncovers its possible existence. Indeed, once the possible existence of fraud is discovered, other frauds can be used to conceal it. For these reasons, a fraud examiner may not express any opinion that any enterprise is free of fraud.

Auditors will find familiar ground in the second two axioms. In order to try and prove that financial statements are reasonably stated, tests are normally conducted in an attempt to prove they are not. To prove cash is in balance, for example, a test is conducted (counting the cash) in an attempt to find an error, omission, or defalcation. Auditors call this concept "negative assurance."

Similarly, fraud examiners must begin with a proposition: that fraud has been committed, or conversely, that it has not. The methodology for proving those two mirror images is exactly the same: the interviews of potential witnesses, the gathering of documentary and other physical evidence, and the interrogation of the suspect or target of the examination to support or refute either proposition. For examination purposes, it theoretically should not matter which approach is taken, as long as the examination methodology is consistently applied. In each case, the same witnesses are interviewed, the same suspect is interrogated, and the same records and other evidence are gathered. The conclusions, therefore, regardless of the approach, should be the same.

The last axiom is that the final determination of what constitutes fraud belongs to the judge and jury. Guilt or innocence, insofar as this manual is concerned, refers to the examiner's theory of guilt or innocence; it is necessary to make such presumptions when conducting fraud examinations. These theories, however, are just that, something for the examiner to test, and not absolute indicators of culpability. The examiner should, therefore, not express these theories during his or her work; to do so could lead to charges of bias, libel, or slander.

THEORY OF FRAUD EXAMINATION

Each fraud examination begins with the proportion that all cases will end with litigation. In order to solve a case without all the evidence, it is necessary for the examiner to make certain assumptions, like the scientist who postulates a theory based on observation and then tests it. In the case of complex fraud examinations, use of the case theory approach is almost indispensable. It involves:

1. analyzing the available data
2. creating a hypothesis
3. testing the hypothesis
4. refining and amending the hypothesis

Put another way, the case theory approach begins with the assumption, based on the known facts, of what might have occurred. Then that assumption is tested to determine whether it is provable. If so, the assumption is correct.

It is absolutely vital for the examiner to employ the case theory approach early in an examination, and stick to the approach throughout. An example will illustrate the concept. An anonymous letter is received indicating a purchasing manager for Bailey Book Corporation, Linda Reed Collins, is "too close" to a buyer for Orion Corporation, James Nagel. The letter does not directly state, but rather implies, that there may be payoffs. If that is correct, a case theory approach to determining if payoffs exist would follow this reasoning.

If Nagel is making payoffs to Collins, one or more of the following conditions would probably be present:

1. Collins would have the capability of approving purchases from Orion.

2. The purchases from Orion would probably be higher than the prevailing market price in order to cover the cost of the kickbacks.

3. Collins, the buyer, may have a close relationship to the supplier, Nagel.

4. Collins may have conspicuously spent any ill-gotten gains, or may have financial problems.

In order to test the theory of the above example, it would be necessary for the examiner to develop specific investigative or examination steps, called leads. In the above case, these leads might include a review of purchases from Orion Corporation and a comparison to other industry vendors; reviews of purchasing procedures to determine if Collins has the ultimate decision over the vendor selection; interviews of Collins' co-workers to determine any financial problems, or excessive spending habits. If the examiner tests his or her theory and develops information that refutes the theory, then at least reasonable assurance indicates that nothing material is amiss. Conversely, testing the theory can come up with good information on which to base further action.

Predication, as it relates to the examination of fraud, means the basis upon which the examination is undertaken. More specifically, predication is the totality of circumstances that would lead a reasonable, prudent, and professionally trained person to suspect that a fraud has occurred, is occurring, or will occur. In the case of an anonymous letter alleging fraud on the part of an employee, the letter would be predication for the examination. In the case of a routine audit that uncovered suspicious payments, the audit would be the predication. Unlike routine audits, fraud examinations are not conducted without predication. There should be a good reason for conducting an examination; unfounded suspicion is usually insufficient.

The type of predication as well as its strength can vary from case to case. The important point is that some reason must exist to conduct a fraud examination. The failure to have adequate predication for conducting an examination may lead to charges of invasion of privacy, harassment, unfair labor practices, or other torts.

Investigative Objectives in Fraud Cases

Because investigations of fraud often involve an extensive array of information to digest, it is easy for the fraud examiner to lose sight of the objectives. One of the characteristics which most distinguishes investigation of white-collar crime from that of common crimes is the necessity for the investigator to establish the intent and underlying motives of the subject by placing together jig-saw puzzle pieces of apparently legitimate activities to add up to a picture of illegitimacy—rather than by a simple showing of one event which by itself flatly demonstrates wrongful intent. (Edelhertz 1977: 123)

Elements of White-Collar Offenses

While it is not possible or necessary to list all variations of white-collar crime and fraud, all have common elements (Edelhertz 1977: 124):

1. intent—to commit a wrongful act or to achieve a purpose inconsistent with law or public policy
2. disguise of purpose—falsities and misrepresentations employed to accomplish the scheme
3. reliance—by the offender on the ignorance or carelessness of the victim
4. voluntary victim action—to assist the offender
5. concealment—of the crime

Intent must be shown in most all criminal fraud matters. Intent is rarely self-evident, but must rather be proven through a pattern of activity. Some of the more common ways to show intent include proof that the individual:

1. had no legitimate motive for the activities;
2. repeatedly engaged in the same or similar activity of an apparent wrongful nature;
3. made conflicting statements;
4. made admissions;
5. acted to impede the investigation of the offense;
6. made statements he or she clearly knew to be false.

Misrepresentation is usually shown by the facts that:

1. The representation was made. This can be accomplished by interviewing victims and examining documents.
2. The representation was false, by either omission or commission.

Proof that the victim assisted the offender is usually not difficult to obtain from the victim. It is important for the fraud examiner to ascertain the exact circumstances of the fraud from the victim, clearly drawing out what set of facts made the fraud possible. In the case of employee thefts, for example, the victim (the company) entrusted the care of assets to the target, and that fiduciary capacity must be established.

Concealment is a cornerstone of fraud. As opposed to traditional crimes in which there is no effort to conceal, concealment addresses those aspects of the execution of a fraud which are undertaken to keep the victim ignorant. Some of the acts in fraud schemes designed to conceal include:

1. Crimes too small to be recognized as crimes by the victim: In embezzlement cases, for example, the amounts of money taken at any one time are usually small in relation to the total assets of the company. By showing a continuing pattern of thefts, the concealment aspect can be shown.
2. Creating complex financial trails: The more obscure the act, the greater the likelihood that it will not be detected. The theft is normally accompanied in some fraud cases by fraudulent invoices and journal entries. Proof of concealment in these cases can be often proven by the fact that the entries made had no business purpose other than to conceal.

Collection, Organization, and Analysis of Evidence

The proof in most complex white-collar cases proceeds usually through basic stages:

1. Build the circumstantial case through interviews of cooperative witnesses and the available documentation.
2. Use the circumstantial evidence to identify and turn an inside witness who can provide direct evidence against the defendants.
3. Seal the case, identify and rebut defenses, and prove intent through examination of the subject or target.

Interviews are as important in so called "paper" cases as in any other, if not more so. Indeed, major fraud and corruption cases have been made through interviews alone, without the issuance of a single subpoena. The intensity of the interviewing process is critical: some examiners may fail to obtain necessary information because they fail to interview enough witnesses, or to ask enough questions, or get enough detail.

Interviews usually proceed from the outer circle of honest, disinterested witnesses inward to the co-conspirators and ultimately to the target; from the circumstantial to the direct. Start with the complaining witness, exhaust his or her knowledge of the facts, and the reasons—factual or speculative—for suspicions. Proceed in the same manner with other outer-circle witnesses.

Take the time and effort at the outset of the case to become familiar with any special terminology involved in the case, as well as the business methods and organizational structures involved. Always ask the early witnesses to identify all other witnesses and documents which may be pertinent to the case.

In a fraud case, pin down the subject's representations; in a corruption investigation, establish the norm and evidence of the breach. Ask whether the witnesses are aware of other, similar transactions involving the suspects, which may yield "similar act" evidence admissible to prove intent, common scheme or plan or absence of mistake. Also be alert for the strategically placed witness—the disgruntled ex-employee, the former partner, spouse or girlfriend—who may provide invaluable assistance.

Stage One: Building the Circumstantial Case

As used here, circumstantial evidence means all proof other than direct admissions of wrongdoing by the subject or a co-conspirator. In a fraud case, it is the proof of the defendants' representations, evidence of their falsity and intent; in a corruption case, it is evidence of the standard behavior, the defendant's breach, and the illegal payments. The circumstantial case may also include similar-act evidence to show common scheme or plan, lack of mistake or accident, modus operandi, and most commonly, intent.

The circumstantial evidence may be all that is available. It must be complete (no gaps in the proof), consistent (all evidence tending to prove a single point), and exclude all explanations other than guilt. Collecting this type of evidence is far more difficult than many examiners and prosecutors realize. Anticipate defenses and plug holes in the proof before trial, when it will be too late. The idea, prevalent among inexperienced examiners and prosecutors, that weak points can be handled by "argument" has resulted in many lost cases and red faces. One extra corroborative fact is worth a thousand words of argument.

Many complex cases bog down and lose direction in the circumstantial stage when the examiner becomes overwhelmed by the mass of accumulated detail and documents. To avoid getting bogged down:

1. "Keep your eye on the ball." Remember the importance of the case theory. Know exactly what you are trying to prove and keep it in focus at all times: If you lose track of your objectives, review and reorganize the evidence, update chronologies, chart relationships, to regain your bearings and refocus your efforts. You should always be trying to prove (or disprove) something—even if you are merely guessing—never merely collecting information.

2. Simplify the case. If the case starts to sink under its own weight, look for a less demanding legal theory, break the case down into smaller components (e.g., prove one set of charges against one set of defendants before pursuing the other), or look for an informant or inside witness. The objective in every complex case is to reduce it to its essentials and make it as simple and clear as possible.

3. Look for alternative approaches. For example, if unable to prove illegal payments for the point of payment, focus on the point of receipt. Always try to find and follow the path of least resistance.

Stage Two: Obtaining Direct Evidence

In many cases cooperation from a co-conspirator or other insider is a necessity, either because the case is so complicated as to be otherwise unmanageable, or because a key element—such as cash payments in a corruption case or the full extent of wrongdoing or intent in a fraud case—cannot be proven circumstantially. In fact, in some cases, the objective of the circumstantial stage is not so much to obtain evidence to convict the ultimate defendant, but to identify and turn an inside witness.

Ideally, the least culpable witness should be approached first. In a corruption case, this may be the "bag man," a subordinate, or, if the only choice is the payer or taker, usually the payer. The jury will react negatively if they perceive that the witness is more culpable than the defendant.

A decision must also be made as to how to convince the witness to assist. Ideally, to preserve the witness's credibility, the fewer concessions the better. Immunity may be given only with the consent of the courts.

Remember that even the most self-incriminating testimony of a co-conspirator must be corroborated. Testimony from the insider should mesh with and augment the circumstantial evidence, not replace it. The credibility of a turned witness can become the central issue in the case; it distracts the jury from the strength of the circumstantial evidence. If nonessential testimony from a co-conspirator cannot be corroborated, don't use it.

Be aware that a cooperating, culpable witness in a white-collar case often minimizes his or her role to avoid embarrassment, even if protected from the legal consequences, and is prone to describe himself or herself more as an observer than as a participant in the crime. This is very damaging to credibility, and must be overcome before trial for the witness to prevail as believable.

Stage Three: Seal the Case Through Examination of the Target

Circumstantial evidence may be explained away, direct testimony impeached or rebutted. The best witness against the suspect may be himself or herself. His or her admissions may provide otherwise missing elements, and "false exculpatories," lies offered in an attempt to explain or justify conduct, may be the best evidence of intent. False denials of cash deposits in a corruption case may indicate an illicit source; false explanations for fraudulent representations may help prove the original misstatements were intentional.

Remember that to be effective impeachment must show real, not apparent or explainable, contradictions, and focus on central, not tangential or trivial, points. Much attempted impeachment fails because the prosecution overreaches, or has not laid a sufficient foundation to show that the defendant's statements were knowingly false.

Qualities of Fraud Examiner

Fraud examiners should have unique abilities. In addition to technical skills, the successful examiner has the ability to lawfully elicit facts from numerous witnesses in a fair, impartial, and accurate manner, and to report the results of the examination accurately and completely. The ability to ascertain the facts and to report them accurately are of equal importance.

Allan Pinkerton, one of the first successful private investigators, stated his idea of what qualities a detective should possess: "The detective must possess certain qualifications of prudence, secrecy, inventiveness, persistency, personal courage, and above all other things, honesty; while he must add to these the same quality of reaching out and becoming possessed of that almost boundless information which will permit of the immediate and effective application of his detective talent in whatever degree that may be possessed" (Buckwalter 1984: 35).

The ability to deal effectively with people is paramount to fraud examiners. The examiner typically meets people for a short period of time and with a specific purpose: to obtain information. Ideally, the examiner has the personality to attract and motivate people. There are a number of people-oriented skills the investigator must possess:

Attitude

The examiner's attitude toward others affects their attitude toward him or her. A hostile attitude in the examiner will produce anxiety on the part of the interviewee, thereby causing the person being interviewed to become withdrawn and protective, even if there is no reason to do so. Contrary to lore, the successful investigator is rarely "tough," except when the need arises and these actions have been carefully planned.

Showing Interest in Others

Buckwalter says, "The secret is for each private investigator to be the kind of person others will want to deal with" (Buckwalter 1984: 37). For each guilty person an examiner encounters, he or she will deal with many innocent witnesses. Those innocent witnesses, and the examiner's ability to draw them out, are indispensable tools of the trade.

Establishing Rapport with Strangers

Because an examiner deals with people from all walks of life, the ability to establish rapport with strangers is paramount. The examiner should not try to conduct an interview without first creating that initial receptivity.

Adapting to Differing Personalities and Circumstances

Since no two people are alike, it is necessary for the fraud examiner to be able to communicate in the language of the interviewee. A college graduate will not be questioned exactly the same way as a ninth-grade dropout; someone with a technical vocabulary will not offer the same answers as a person with an artistic background. As each case differs, so will the examiner's approach.

Communication

There are four basic objectives that must be considered in any investigation (Buckwalter 1984: 41). Fraud examiners must:

1. Be able to communicate on the other person's own level and to make known just what is wanted from that person; in interviewing, that would be the disclosure of whatever relevant information the interviewee has.

2. Be sure that they are clearly and accurately understood by the interviewee (or person).

3. Get the interviewee (or other party) to communicate with them. In the case of an investigative interview, the interviewee must clearly make known just what he knows about the matter.

4. Be sure that they clearly and accurately understand what the interviewee is saying.

To Buckwalter's list must be added the technical ability to understand financial concepts, and the ability to draw inferences from them. A unique feature of fraud cases is that, unlike traditional property crimes, the identity of the perpetrator is usually known. In a bank robbery, for example, the issue is not whether a crime was committed, but rather who committed the crime. In fraud cases, the issue is usually not the identity of the individual, but whether or not that individual's conduct constitutes fraud.

It is also important that the examiner be able to simplify financial concepts for the benefit of others. Fraud cases frequently involve concepts that appear complicated; but in reality, most are simple.

12 Documenting Cases

INTRODUCTION

A fraud examiner will obtain a great deal of evidence in the form of documents. It is critical that the examiner understand the relevance of this evidence, as well as how it should be preserved and presented. Many examiners may pay too much attention to documents. It is easy to get bogged down in detail when examining records and to lose sight of a simple fact: Documents do not make cases; witnesses do. The documents make or break the witness. So-called "paper cases" often confuse and bore the jury. You should keep in mind always that documents can either help or hurt your case, depending on what documents are presented as well as how they are presented. The idea is to make sure all relevant documents are included, and all irrelevant documents eliminated. Certain basic procedures in handling evidence are necessary for the evidence in question to be accepted by the courts. These procedures include:

1. proof that the evidence is relevant and material
2. proper identification of the item
3. proof of the chain of custody of the document

Early in a case, the relevance of documents cannot be easily determined. For that reason, it is recommended that all documents possible be obtained; if they are not needed, they can always be returned. Here are a few general rules regarding the collection of documents (Edelhertz 1977: 162):

1. Obtain original documents where feasible. Make working copies for your review, and keep the originals segregated.
2. Do not touch originals any more than necessary; they may later be needed for forensic analysis.

3. Maintain a good filing system for the documents. This is especially critical where large volumes of documents are obtained. Losing a key document is an unpardonable sin, and may cause mortal damage to your case. Voluminous documents can be sequentially stamped for easy reference.

CHAIN OF CUSTODY

From the moment evidence is received, its chain of custody must be maintained in order for it to be accepted by the court. Simply put, this means a record must be made when the item is received by the fraud examiner, and a record must be made any time the evidence leaves the care, custody, or control of the examiner. This is best handled by a memorandum of interview with the custodian of the records when the evidence is received. The memorandum should state (1) what items were received, (2) when they were received, (3) from whom they were received, and (4) where they are maintained. If the item is later turned over to someone else, a record should be made, preferably in memorandum form:

"On June 15, 1988, the following items of original evidence were turned over to John Stone, St. Augustine, Florida, Police Department:

1. original employment application of Linda Reed Collins

2. schedule of purchases from Orion Corporation

3. copy of check to Orion Corporation 9/15/90

All evidence received should be uniquely marked so it can later be identified. The preferred way is to initial and date the item; however, this can pose problems in the case of original business records received voluntarily. In these situations, a small tick mark or other nondescript identifier can be used. If it is not practical to mark the original document, it should be placed in a sealed envelope, which should then be initialled and dated.

OBTAINING DOCUMENTARY EVIDENCE

There are three principal methods for obtaining documentary evidence. Subpoenas are ordinarily issued by the court or grand jury. A subpoena *duces tecum* calls for the production of documents and records, whereas a regular subpoena is used for witnesses. If the examiner is not an agent of the grand jury or the court, obtaining documents by subpoena is not possible. Subpoenas can call for the production of documents at a grand jury or deposition at a specified time. A forthwith subpoena means that the records should be produced instantly. A forthwith subpoena is usually served by surprise, and reserved for those instances where it is thought the records will be secreted, altered or destroyed.

Search warrants are issued by a judge upon presentation of probable cause to believe the records are being used or have been used in the commission of a crime. An affidavit is usually used to support the request for the search warrant. The affidavit must describe in detail the reason(s) the warrant is requested, along with the place the evidence is thought to be kept. Courts do not lightly issue search warrants, as the Fourth Amendment to the Constitution protects individuals against unreasonable searches and seizures. Search warrants are almost never used in civil cases. Although there are provisions in the law for warrantless searches, they should be avoided at all costs by the examiner. Searches can be conducted by voluntary consent.

Documents can be obtained by voluntary consent, and this is the preferred method. The consent can be oral or written. In the cases of obtaining information from possible adverse witnesses, or from the target of the examination, it is recommended that the consent be in writing.

TYPES OF EVIDENCE

Evidence generally falls into one of two categories, either direct or circumstantial (Kramer 1988: 25). Direct evidence is that which shows *prima facie* the facts at issue. What constitutes direct evidence depends on the factors involved. For example, in the case of kickbacks, direct evidence might be a check from the person making the kickback directly to the target.

Circumstantial evidence is that which would indirectly show culpability. For example, in the case of a kickback allegation, cash deposits of unknown origin deposited to the account of the target around the time of the suspect transaction could be circumstantial evidence.

ORGANIZATION OF EVIDENCE

One of the single biggest problems in fraud cases is keeping track of the amount of paper they can generate. It is absolutely essential that the documents obtained be properly organized early on in an examination, and be continuously reorganized as the case progresses. Remember, early in the case it is usually difficult to ascertain the relevance of the evidence. Good organization in complex cases usually includes the following:

1. Segregate documents by either witness or transaction. Chronological organization is the least preferable method. The idea is to have the witness introduce the document, not you.

2. Make a "key document" file for easy access to the most relevant documents. Periodically review the key document files, moving the less important ones to back-up files in order to keep only the most relevant paper in the main files.

3. Establish a database early on in the case of volumes of information. The database should include, at a minimum:

    a. date of the document

    b. individual from whom the document was obtained

   c. date the document was obtained

   d. brief description of the document

   e. subject to whom the document pertains

   This data base may be kept manually or it can be computerized and accessed by key words.

In the case of voluminous evidence, an evidence control log can be maintained.

A chronology of events should be commenced early in the case. The purpose of the chronology is to establish the chain of events leading to the proof. The chronology may or may not be made a part of the formal report; at a minimum, it can be used for analysis of the case and kept in a working paper binder.

Remember to keep the chronology brief, and include only the information necessary to prove your case. By making the chronology too detailed, you are defeating its purpose. The chronology should be revised as necessary by adding new information and deleting the irrelevant.

CHARTING TECHNIQUES

Link Network Diagrams

Link networks show the relationships between persons, organizations, and events. Different symbols are used to represent different entities, e.g., a square for an organization, a circle for a person, triangle for an event, and so on. It doesn't matter what symbols you use, but be consistent. Confirmed connections between entities can be represented by a solid line, or enclosure within another symbol; speculative or presumed relationships can be shown by broken lines. The graphic should be clear and simple, otherwise, their purpose is defeated. Don't cross lines if possible. An example of how charting can simplify relationships follows.

Smith is vice president of ABC Corporation and president of DEF Corporation, a subsidiary of ABC. DEF is general partner in two limited partnerships. Jones and Green are limited partners in the First Partnership, Brown and Black are limited partners in the Second Partnership. Black is also a general partner in the Third Partnership. Smith may also have an interest in the First Partnership.

Time Flow Diagrams

These charts show the relation of significant events, in the order they occurred (See Figure 12.1).

Matrices

A matrix is a grid which shows the relationship or points of contact between a number of entities. Known contacts can be differentiated from presumed by

Figure 12.1
Time Flow Diagrams

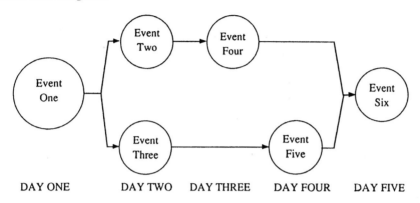

DAY ONE   DAY TWO   DAY THREE   DAY FOUR   DAY FIVE

Figure 12.2
Matrix Example

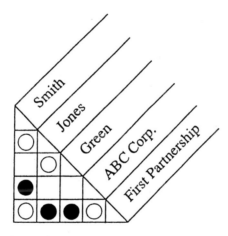

use of different marks, such as a dot or o (See Figure 12.2). A matrix is a useful preliminary step in complex cases to identify the relative status of the parties by showing the number of contacts of each. The proper relationship can then be presented graphically with the most important figure displayed most prominently(See Figure 12.3). It which can then be represented in chart form (See Figure 12.4). A matrix can be used to identify the direction and frequency of telephone traffic between suspect parties (See Figure 12.5).

SUMMARIES OF WITNESS STATEMENTS

Voluminous testimony or witness statements should be reduced to summary form to permit quick review and to identify inconsistent statements. To quickly

Figure 12.3
Link Network Example

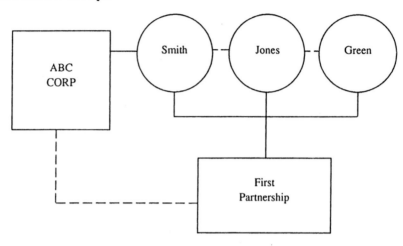

Figure 12.4
Matrix Example

	450-1011	550-2022	650-3033	750-4044	850-5055	Total To
450-1011	X	1	3			4
550-2022		X	2	2		4
650-3033	8	8	X	8	9	32
750-4044	1		1	X		2
850-5055			8		X	18
	9	8	14	10	9	

Total To

identify pertinent passages, indicate very briefly the topic being covered at any point, as well as a synopsis of the statement.

Keep the synopsis as succinct as possible. Too much detail will make the summary almost as bulky as the original and impair its utility. The examiner or

Figure 12.5
Link Network Example

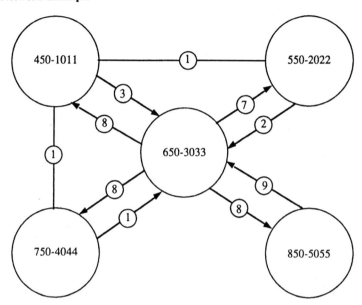

someone familiar with the facts and issues in the case should prepare the summary; not, as is often the case, an assistant who does not know what may or may not be relevant. The summary can also be a useful source of information for its chronology.

Another indispensable aid is the "To Do" List. The list, which must be updated frequently, should be kept in a stenographer's pad or other permanent ring binder to allow a cumulative record. In a very complex case, the list can be broken down between long- and short-term objectives; that which must be done eventually (e.g., prove elements of a particular count) and that which should be done tomorrow. However organized, some sort of list must be kept, as important points will otherwise be forgotten in the lengthy case.

BUSINESS AND INDIVIDUAL RECORDS

As stated previously, originals of documents should be obtained wherever possible. In the case of business enterprises (especially if they are legitimate), it may be difficult or impossible to obtain the originals. If it is possible to obtain them, by all means get them, and give copies back, along with the pledge to return the originals when the case is completed and adjudicated. If the originals cannot be obtained, settle for copies. If necessary, furnish the record custodian a receipt for the property.

The exact records obtained will vary from case to case, but where appropriate, basic business records often include:

1. organization of the business, such as articles of incorporation
2. financial statements and tax returns
3. customer lists
4. business diaries, address and telephone lists
5. travel and entertainment expense records
6. business telephone toll records
7. personnel records, including employment applications
8. bank account records, deposit slips and cancelled checks
9. relevant contracts or agreements
10. computer programs and/or diskettes

Originals of individual records are usually easier to obtain than originals of business records. Some of the more relevant records usually include the following:

1. bank account records, deposit slips, and cancelled checks
2. financial statements and tax returns
3. credit card statements and payment records
4. telephone toll records

13   Interview Techniques

INTRODUCTION

An interview can be best defined as a structured question-and-answer session designed to elicit specific information. For the fraud examiner, there is nothing more important than the ability to conduct good interviews. It is as important as—if not more important than—any technical ability to examine documents, prepare schedules, or conduct audits.

Interview relates to obtaining information from witnesses; interrogation's primary purpose is to elicit a confession. Interviewing carries with it a positive connotation, interrogation a more negative meaning. The line between interview and interrogation is often fluid. An examiner may commence an interview which turns into an interrogation at some point. Conversely, an interrogation can be commenced, only to reveal that the target appears to be innocent; in which case the interrogation turns into an interview.

The primary purpose of the interview is to obtain information. More specifically, interviews gather information to develop evidence in an alleged offense. Prior to commencing interviews, one or more of the following conditions is usually present:

1. An offense may have been committed, but the facts concerning its commission have yet to be established.
2. There may be a complainant or victim, perhaps an individual, corporation, or governmental entity.
3. There may be some physical evidence of the offense.
4. There may be rumor, innuendo, or intelligence information concerning a specific subject.

The interview is the process for developing the above information, to separate the wheat from the chaff. It is important that the fraud examiner obtain the following from the interview:

1. information which establishes or refutes the essential elements of the offense
2. leads for developing the case and gathering evidence
3. the cooperation of victims and witnesses in recounting their experiences in court
4. information concerning the background and personal and economic motives of those to be considered as witnesses at the trial

TYPES OF WITNESSES

There are three types of witnesses that will be encountered by the examiner: the cooperative witness, the neutral witness, and the adverse witness.

Cooperative Witness

The cooperative witness is one who is more than happy to be interviewed and more than happy to cooperate. The disadvantage of these witnesses is that they are frequently friends of the victim, and sometimes in their zeal are difficult to control. In addition, they tend to mix fact and opinion, and may furnish irrelevant information.

Witnesses can be cooperative for a variety of reasons and to different degrees. Some of the reasons include the possibility of gain as a result of information furnished. Some people are friendly by nature, and will tell you most anything. Others feel the excitement or ego-satisfaction of being involved in an important case. Many others have been watching too much television and want to "play detective."

"Playing detective" is a good technique to master in obtaining information; it is essentially a role reversal. You ask the witness: "Mr. Jones if you were looking into this matter, where would you go? Who would you talk to? What documents would you look at?" It is an excellent way to deffuse the witness and get the lead information you want.

As with the case of adverse witnesses, it is necessary for the examiner to pin down the facts from the cooperative witness. All too often, the witness may be so prejudiced as to render himself or herself useless, save for information to get additional leads.

Neutral Witness

Neutral witnesses tend to furnish the best information. They have nothing to gain or lose, and as a result, their information is usually free of bias. Normally, these witnesses are willing to cooperate, but may not know what is relevant or important to the examiner.

Adverse Witness

The adverse witness presents the greatest challenge to the examiner. The witness may be adverse for a number of reasons: he or she may be a friend or colleague of the target, or perhaps the witness is culpable.

In some cases, it is best that only one interviewer be present during the interview of an adverse witness; certainly no more than two people should be present. The interview should be conducted with a high degree of formality—no first names and a minimum of small talk.

Unlike the interview of a cooperative or neutral witness, the questions to an adverse witness should not be in a predictable order. To do so lets the witness anticipate the questions and prepare his or her answers. This does not imply that the witness should be asked questions in a thoughtless order—only that the witness not know what the order is.

As a general rule, questions necessary to lay a foundation for later impeachment of the witness should be asked early in the interview before their significance becomes apparent. In addition, identifying information should be asked early in the interview before the witness possibly becomes hostile or defensive. There are two basic approaches to interviewing the adverse witness:

1. Get the witness talking, while he or she is uncooperative. This is usually done by asking innocuous questions.
2. Attempt to turn the witness and obtain truthful testimony. Adverse witnesses usually respond only under the following conditions:
a. When the evidence implicating them is clear and convincing.
b. The witness is provided an out for his or her behavior.
c. When there are sufficient rewards or punishments for cooperation; or failing to do so.

It is possible that the adverse witness may agree to an interview but refuse to discuss certain relevant topics. If so, don't attempt to move too quickly to the sensitive issues. The key with many adverse witnesses is to keep them talking. Sooner or later, you may get the information you need.

Once the examiner has gotten into the relevant subject matter, care should be taken not to reveal, by questioning or tone of voice, what is expected of the witness. In order to get the needed information, it is imperative that you keep the witness's cooperation.

One common reason you may encounter an adverse witness is that the witness is close to the target. Although it is not always possible to predict when a witness will be hostile, family, friends, and co-conspirators of the target can be expected to be uncooperative. You may be able to diffuse the problems associated therewith by taking the target's side. Try to impress the witness with your neutrality by inviting the witness to provide evidence that would disprove the charges.

Do not reveal the limits of your knowledge; the witness usually thinks you know more than you do anyway. It is best to slip in a fact every now and then so the witness is impressed with how well you know the case. This will make deception less likely.

PLANNING THE INTERVIEW

Proper planning enhances the probability of a successful interview. Prior to conducting the interview, the examiner should have a clear notion of what principal points should be covered. All documents and related material should be reviewed prior to conducting the interview to refresh the examiner's memory. Documents that should be reviewed by the witness should be segregated for easy reference. Under nearly all circumstances only one witness should be interviewed at one time. Two or more witnesses present not only presents an unwieldy interview, but the testimony of one witness will invariably influence the other. In general, only one examiner is needed on information-gathering interviews with neutral or cooperative witnesses. Two examiners should be used on interviews of adverse witnesses, co-conspirators, and the target.

Time and Place

In the case of cooperative witnesses, a time and place for the interview should be scheduled in advance. The preferred location is the home or business of the witness, for the following reasons:

1. The witness is more likely to have papers and documents available for production, should they be needed in the interview. The witness may also be in a position to call on family members or co-workers who may be conveniently nearby.
2. It will probably be more convenient to the witness, making cooperation more likely.
3. The witness may be more comfortable in his or her own surroundings. In the case of adverse witnesses, it is suggested that the witness be interviewed by surprise. The principle reason is to avoid giving the witness time to contact the target, an attorney, or other persons relevant to the inquiry. Of course, by so doing, the examiner risks that the witness will not be available, or will chose not to be interviewed. However, in most cases, if you give the adverse witness a chance to think it over for a few hours or days, he or she will decline to be interviewed. The surprise interview should be conducted at a time least likely to antagonize the witness.

Information to Be Obtained

Although the information to be obtained from the witness will vary significantly from case to case, there should be common elements to all interviews, namely, the aim to obtain evidence regarding the target of the examination. It is generally best to obtain information in a chronological order, from when the witness first met the target, up through the present time. Information should include:

 1. name, address, and employment of witness, along with contact numbers
 2. witness's connection to target
 3. meetings with target
 4. representations of target
 5. documents furnished to witness by target
 6. other potential witnesses
 7. witness's opinion of target
 8. financial losses suffered by witness, if any
 9. background information on target
10. other relevant information

Key Steps

The amount of preparation varies from interview to interview, and the exact steps will depend on the situation. Many may not require the elaborate preparation herein described, but proper organization can pay large rewards.

1. Collect all documents available to the witness in one file. Make copies for separate files if necessary.
2. If not already done, organize the contents logically. In the case of large files, break down and/or reorganize the contents. If the facts are complicated, make a summary of key points. Flow chart as necessary.
3. Read the file carefully before you conduct the interview. In all cases, it is absolutely imperative that you be prepared before conducting any interview.
4. Have a clear objective of what you want to find out, and stick to it. In all situations, you should have developed a case theory which you will attempt to prove or disprove.
5. Decide the structure of the interview. A typical complicated interview is usually organized by one or more of the following methods:

a. Chronologically: The witness is questioned about the relevant events in the order in which they occurred, from beginning to end. This is by far the easiest and most common method of organizing the interview.
b. According to the documents: If the transactions are well documented, this can be an effective method for organizing the questioning. Of course, the documents themselves must then be organized in some logical way, such as chronologically.
c. By transaction or event: If the events or transactions have little significance chronologically, the examination may be organized according to the transaction. These should be listed in the interview before it is begun

Tape Recordings

If it is desirable to record the interview there are two ways to do so, openly or surreptitiously. If state laws prohibit secret tape recordings, do not tape the conversation. If the law allows surreptitious tapings, it is best to turn the recorder on out of the presence of the witness, and state for the record the date, time, who is being recorded, and who is recording the conversation. When in doubt about the lawfulness of surreptitious recording, seek legal advice. If the taping is made openly, the date and time should be announced at the front of the tape, and the witness should be asked if he or she is aware the interview is being recorded. Recording devices generally inhibit witnesses. If a recording is made, the best information will normally be obtained when the recorder is out of sight.

Writing Down Questions

It is generally a bad idea to write questions in advance. There are several reasons: First, you probably will be guided by what is on paper rather than let the interview follow its natural course. Larry King, the talk show host, says his best interviews occur when he doesn't know anything about the subject; he never takes notes. Let the interview flow naturally. Second, it is possible that the person being interviewed will see your questions well in advance of your asking them and have time to prepare his or her answers before you ask the question. If you must write down several points you know need to be covered.

PARTS OF THE INTERVIEW

Introduction

A number of interviewers have trouble with how to approach the witness. Interviews should have three specific parts: the introduction, the body of the interview, and the close. The introduction is especially critical because it gets you on the right foot. The introduction should usually be the same: start with your name, and state your purpose in contacting the witness. No matter how potentially hostile the witness, you should always be polite and professional. It is necessary only to state the purpose of the contact in a general way, the less wordy the better:

Right: Mr. Jones, my name is Loren D. Bridges. I am conducting an examination in connection with possible losses at Bailey Book Corporation. May I speak to you for a few moments?

Wrong: Mr. Jones, my name is Loren D. Bridges. I am investigating Linda Reed Collins and I need to talk to you.

The key in the introduction is to get the potential witness to say that he or she will talk to you. Next is to keep the interview going, by taking the lead and beginning to ask questions. But do so gently, and without appearing to threaten the witness. If you have never met the witness before, proceed from the general to the specific. Start by asking his correct name for your records. Get the interviewee to spell it for you. Get the witness's address and telephone number. What you are trying to accomplish is to get the witness in the frame of mind to answer questions. If the witness perceives you as a threat, this will close off any reasonable avenue for you to get the information voluntarily.

Don't rush into the subject matter, as many witnesses are apprehensive. Give assurances, if necessary, that the witness will not be unduly embarrassed or inconvenienced by cooperating, and that providing truthful information has no legal liability.

It is common during the introduction for the witness to ask you to clarify who you are and why you are contacting him or her.

Witness: Why are you contacting me?

Examiner: I am conducting an examination of the purchasing policies at Bailey Book Corporation, and I thought you might be able to help me.

Reluctant or hostile witnesses may try to turn your interview into their interview. Here are the more common responses during the introduction:

Witness: Why should I talk to you? I don't want to be involved.

Examiner: You certainly are not required to talk to me. I am just seeking some information on a serious matter, which may or may not result in legal action. By speaking informally with me now, it may save you the trouble of having to testify later, depending on the information you have. Is that O.K.?

or

Witness: I don't want to answer any questions at this time, without first talking to my lawyer.

Examiner: You certainly don't have to talk to me, with or without your lawyer, but you're not required to have one present. Let's do it this way. I'll ask a few simple questions, and you can stop anytime you feel uncomfortable.

Body of the Interview

The body of the interview should proceed from the general to the specific, and address the age-old questions of who, what, when, where, why, and how. It is especially important in the interview not to cast aspersions on the target; keep your comments in check, and simply ask the questions. Do not give your opinions. More investigators get sued over making statements than anything else; there is no legal liability in asking questions, no matter how embarrassing the questions might be.

Some examiners try to keep their questions to just facts. There is nothing wrong with soliciting opinions as long as they are labeled as such. You can even ask the witnesses' opinion on the guilt or innocence of the target. Most people have reasons for their opinions, and by soliciting them, you can often get the reasons.

During the body of the interview, let the witnesses tell their own story in their own words. Some patience is required, as witnesses frequently ramble somewhat in the beginning, where the outline of the case is still fuzzy. When the witness finishes, go over the facts in greater detail, according to the structure you have already chosen.

Since most interviews go from the general to the specific, go over the general scope of knowledge first and then go back over it again in as much detail as necessary. Always press for detail, and proceed to the next topic only when you are convinced the witness's knowledge is exhausted on the current topic. Details are the key to witness corroboration, and witnesses are the underpinnings of all cases, criminal and civil.

Many if not most interviews in fraud cases will be about what someone "said." Witnesses have a natural tendency to mix fact and opinion, and relate conversations in terms of what was "talked about." You must separate the two, and find out as closely as possible what actually happened, and what was the actual conversation (verbatim if possible). You can do so by the proper phrasing of questions:

Wrong: What did you and Mr. Smith talk about?

Right: What did Mr. Smith say to you? What did you say to him?

In conversations, try to find out how long it took, so you can determine if you have a full account of the conversation. If the meeting lasted all day and you only have a few minutes of conversation, there are details missing.

In the case of documents, it is usually a good idea to have the witness review and examine them carefully. It often provides additional leads. If you show the document to a witness, determine whether he or she can authenticate it at trial.

Questions about record-keeping procedures in business crimes can be invaluable in understanding the flow of paperwork, and identifying other witnesses who may be able to provide testimony. You must have a thorough understanding of business or special terminology used in the case. Do not be afraid to ask stupid questions.

Close

When closing the interview, the examiner should go over the key points discussed during the body of the interview. The purpose of doing so is to make sure the examiner has gotten the facts straight, and that the witness agrees with the summary. At this time, the examiner should also ask three important questions:

1. Is there anything else I may have forgotten to ask?
   Probably the number-one reason interviewers don't get the answers they are looking

for is that they simply forgot to ask the questions. This question is a catchall designed to give the opportunity to the witness to play detective.

2. Is there anyone else you think I should speak to?
   This question is designed to elicit additional leads. There is nothing wrong with telling the witness that you will not reveal their name to the person they suggest; however, do not promise confidentiality.

3. Is there anything else you would like to say?
   The final question is to give the witness one last chance to say anything he or she wishes. Reluctant witnesses may use the opportunity to defend the target. This is fine; it is much better to find the weaknesses in your case, if any, before it goes to court.

There is nothing wrong with asking the witness not to discuss the case with others, although non-law-enforcement personnel cannot enforce this request. Usually, it is best to give a reason, such as prejudicing the other witnesses or ruining an innocent person's reputation. Do not, however, believe that you can control the witnesses' behavior. In the case of friends and colleagues of the target, you should always assume that they will tell the target immediately after you leave. For this reason, if you fear that the witness may compromise your case, don't conduct the interview. Above all, don't threaten the witness if he or she talks about the case.

INTERVIEWER DEMEANOR

Interview demeanor goes much beyond simply being polite and professional. The interviewer's personal style has as much to do with the success of obtaining information as anything else. The interviewer should adapt a style that shows him or her as natural as possible; what works for another interviewer may not work for you. As stated previously, the tough style doesn't usually work. It is much better to be friendly and disarming.

Remember, every professional contact you make reflects on you and your employer, agency, or your own firm. Under no circumstances should the interviewer accept even the smallest gratuity; not that such would influence your work, but that the hint of any impropriety cannot help your case and can conceivably hurt it.

Here are other suggestions regarding interview demeanor:

1. Never talk down to the person you are interviewing, and don't assume that the person is less intelligent than you. Any hint of condescension or disrespect can quickly turn a cooperative witness into an uncooperative one.

2. Never use language which disparages the intelligence or competence of the interviewee, even if you may think he or she acted foolishly.

3. Be sensitive to the personal concerns of the victim or witness, especially when these involve perceptions of how the interviewee may be treated because of sex, race, religion, or ethnic background.

4. Be businesslike. Conduct the interview in a professional manner. The investigator should be friendly but not familiar. Certain pleasantries should be exchanged, but not to the point of imitating a social event.

5. Do not become authoritarian or attempt to dominate the interview. Never lose your temper with a witness, no matter how recalcitrant.

6. Always be sympathetic and respectful to victims. Do not suggest the victim is in a position because of his or her own fault or stupidity.

7. Give careful thought to the language you use to make sure it is consistent with your approach and understandable to the interviewee. Avoid jargon.

8. End every interview by thanking the interviewee.

OBSTACLES TO INTERVIEWING

There are a number of reasons why someone is reluctant to be interviewed. It is up to the examiner to recognize these reasons and overcome the obstacles they present.

First, victims of fraud are especially sensitive to the fact that they have been defrauded. No one likes to think they have been stupid. For that reason, many people are reluctant to come forth with information. This can be overcome by a sensitive interviewer.

Second, both private and governmental enterprises operate on a basis of public trust and confidence. Businesses are especially sensitive to embarrassment and public scorn because of their activities. Being involved in a fraud may not only cause a financial loss, but losses in stature, prestige, and the ability to conduct business. These objections can sometimes be overcome by pleas to the moral sense of right and wrong.

Third, if a witness has previously denied knowledge, or has furnished false information, he or she generally is very reluctant to admit it. The key to overcoming these denials is to give the interviewee an out; normally it will be taken.

Example: Mr. Jones, I know when we talked before that you denied knowing Mr. Smith. You probably forgot about meeting him. Can we start afresh?

Finally, witnesses have very little to gain by cooperating in an investigation, and some have much to lose. Most of the time, these objections can be overcome by gently persuading the witness that you may be saving the witness trouble. If the case gets into litigation, the witness may be called to testify before a jury, judge, or grand jury. You are assisting them in that you are doing the preliminary work; and if the information is not vital to the case, you can save them some effort.

COMMON MISTAKES IN INTERVIEWING

In most cases, if the witness is approached too soon, you will not have developed sufficient incentives for cooperation if needed. Take time to analyze what could go wrong before you decide to do the interview. Decide in advance what concessions you are prepared to make and think them through. Don't give up anything you don't have to.

Trying to turn an adverse witness with threats rarely works, and often creates special problems in presenting the case. Overbearing tactics should be avoided at all costs. On the other hand, you must obviously follow through and ask all relevant questions, and not promise the witness unduly lenient treatment, as this often results in incorrect information.

There are several interview techniques that must always be kept in mind: (1) Provide a face-saving device for the reluctant witness; (2) do not inadvertently signal to the witness that you cannot be trusted; and (3) convince the witness of the strength of any evidence implicating him or her.

SPECIFIC INTERVIEW TECHNIQUES

Don't Call It an Investigation

Witnesses are easily intimidated by the shadings of various words. Except in the case of the target, the word "investigation" should generally be avoided. This is because it carries with it an especially official air, and the witness becomes much more careful about what is being said. Your job is to draw out the witness, not close him or her off.

The best terminology to use is often the words "inquiry" or "examination." The words "special audit" or "audit" may also be substituted when appropriate.

Good Guy—Bad Guy

The so-called "good guy—bad guy" technique of handling adverse witnesses has been around a long time. Its premise is to have one investigator attack the witness while the other defends him or her. In this technique, the adverse witness seeks refuge in the good guy. The bad guy leaves the room, and the witness confesses to the good guy. The effectiveness of this technique is dubious at best, and should be a last resort if used at all. It may work with some, but the average fraud offender is a con, and sensitive to being conned.

Playing Detective

As stated previously, playing detective is a useful technique in obtaining information. The witness reverses roles with the examiner.

Example: Mr. Jones, if you were looking into this matter, what would you do?

This serves two purposes: First, it diffuses any problem with vindictiveness that the witness may feel you have toward the target. That in turn will break down the witness's defenses. Second, you may obtain leads that cannot be obtained by any other manner.

Voice Vacuums

You can gain a lot of ground in some cases by letting your question hang, and not immediately following up. It creates the so-called pregnant pause or uncomfortable silence that makes some people want to pick up the conversation and continue talking.

Breaking Down the Story

Normally, the truth is obtained not by an abrupt confession but by a gradual process of getting the story from the mouth of the witness, and then pointing out the inconsistencies therein. The witness concedes a small inconsistency in the facts, then makes larger and larger admissions. In many cases, the witness never admits changing a story. You simply start out with a lie and end up with the truth.

Providing a Graceful Exit

Some of the most heinous admissions have been made by defendants because someone seemed to have a sympathetic ear. In one case, a kidnap/murder suspect confessed because the investigator took the defendant's side by stating he understood why someone would want to kill the victim. If the witness provides an excuse for her or his behavior, accept it and ask her or him to amplify on it. Do not register animosity, disapproval, or disgust at the witness's story.

In the case of all witnesses, you must also exit gracefully, so the door is open if you need additional cooperation in the future.

Give the Witness Something

You may not have to give very much to an adverse witness.

Example: Mr. Jones, I promise I will help you in any way I can by telling of your cooperation in this matter. I assure you it will not be unnoticed.

Note that you have only promised that you would fairly present the facts, which is what you would have done anyway.

Drawing Out Admissions

Commonly, reluctant witnesses need to be drawn out. Do not move too quickly into critical areas that the witness doesn't want to discuss. Confront the witness with contrary evidence only after you have pinned down a concrete story. Draw out admissions by being objective about the evidence, without implying that the witness is lying. It is essential that the witness believes there is no doubt in your mind about the facts. Be polite but not overbearing, and be confident about your position, as the witness will perceive it.

Talking with Lawyers Present

It is not necessary that most witnesses have an attorney present during the interview, especially if it appears the witness has no culpability. From an interview standpoint, it is not desirable for an attorney to be present, and usually you can persuade the witness not to have an attorney present by simply stating that fact. This does not mean that you should deny this right. If the witness insists, the attorney should be present only with the agreement that he or she will act as an observer. It is you who should control your own interview.

SUMMARY

In all interviews, there are specific objectives that should be achieved. If you have obtained the following goals, your interview should be successful:

Get Detailed, Explicit Information

Rumor and opinion, while a basis for a beginning, are not sufficient. If the only thing the witness has is opinion or hearsay, there is little chance of its having any relevance other than to develop leads.

Obtain All Relevant Documents

The examiner should be sure that all documents are fully explored and that the witness can attest to their authenticity. If the documents cannot be obtained for possible evidence, it is important that they be fully described.

Determine the Motives of the Witnesses

Most witnesses have their own motives for furnishing information. The examiner should ensure that these motives are fully understood in order to avoid problems in litigation.

Establish Rapport

Once the interview of a witness is concluded, make sure that the door is left open in case additional information is needed from the witness. Even in the case of adverse or hostile witnesses, the examiner should endeavor to leave the interview on a positive note.

Obtain All Possible Leads

The examiner's interview is not complete unless and until he or she learns of other persons or documents that might aid in the understanding of the case. In the words of one seasoned FBI agent, "Our job is to obtain leads, not solve the case. If you cover enough leads, the case will solve itself."

14   Evaluating Deception

INTRODUCTION

Almost everyone lies. There are two reasons: to receive rewards, or to avoid punishment. Evaluating deception is one of the more challenging arts for any investigator or examiner. Most experienced examiners can relate several stories of being deceived by a witness or target of an investigation. It would, of course, be easy to detect deception if there were any absolute indicators of deception, but there are not. There are simply clues that when taken together give a good indication.

Fundamental to the evaluation of deception is the concept that lying produces emotion in most people (psychopaths and the mentally ill excepted), and that this emotion in some cases can be detected by both verbal and nonverbal clues. The indicators, then, are not clues to deception but clues to stress. It is up to the examiner to determine whether this stress is created by the lie or by some other event, related or unrelated. It is a difficult job at best.

In detecting deception during an interview or interrogation, the examiner must remember that the interviewee or target may already be under stress because of the situation. This does not necessarily mean he or she is lying, of course. Darting eyes, shallow breathing, stuttering, or any of the other classic stress signs may be exhibited because the witness is afraid of the situation, not because he or she is fearful of being caught in a lie. For this reason, it is necessary for the examiner to carefully assess the normal behavior of the individual before assessing any clues to deception. Assessing the norm is sometimes called calibrating the witness.

The best way to calibrate a witness is through the use of nonthreatening questions, about background information, place of employment, and the like. If the witness displays general nervousness or other verbal and nonverbal clues during this phase of the questioning, subsequent indicators may not be reliable. The key is to observe changes in behavior when pertinent questions are asked.

TYPES OF LIARS

Psychologists have categorized liars into six groups. A panic liar is one who lies because of the consequences of confession. He or she is afraid of embarrassment to loved ones and suspicion is a serious blow to his or her ego. He or she believes that confession would only make matters worse. An occupational liar is someone who has lied for years. This person is a practical liar and lies when lying has a higher payoff than telling the truth. A tournament liar loves to lie and is excited by the challenge of not being detected. This person views an interview as another contest and wants to win. The fourth type of liar is the sadistic liar. This person lies because it is the only weapon remaining with which to fight. This person realizes that he or she will probably be caught but will not give anyone the satisfaction of hearing him or her confess. He or she wants family and friends to believe that the law is punishing an innocent person. An ethnological liar is one who was taught not to be a "squealer." This person loves to be interrogated and has adopted a creed, either personal or shared, that he or she will never reveal the truth. The creeds of underworld gangs make their members ethnological liars.

All five of these liars can usually be brought to confession by a skilled examiner. The most difficult type, however, is the psychopathic liar. He or she shows no regret for his dishonest actions and no manifestation of guilt. This person is a good actor and can usually fool most investigators and can even fool polygraph and other lie-detector tests. A psychopathic liar has usually been involved in dishonest actions before.

FACTORS CONCERNING DECEPTION EMOTION

The emotion caused by deception, according to Ekman, is dependent on a number of factors (Ekman 1986: 39). For example, "white" lies cause less stress than lies of significance, primarily because white lies are usually told to prevent hurt feelings. Guilt over deception will be greatest when:

1. the lie is totally self-serving
2. the person being lied to is unwilling to participate in the lie (i.e., the lie is not expected)
3. the lie is scorned or looked upon negatively
4. the liar has little experience
5. the liar and the person being lied to have the same social values
6. the liar and the person being lied to are personally acquainted
7. the person being lied to is not easily deceived
8. the stakes are high

VERBAL CLUES

Verbal clues to deception include not only the spoken word, but gestures of acknowledgement, such as a nod of the head. When a deceptive person avoids a truthful answer by supplying evasive answers, he or she does so as in attempt to reduce the inner conflict created by not telling the truth.

Methods of Responding to the Question

Many clues to deception can be found in the way the respondent answers the question. Truthful people tend to be direct; untruthful people tend to be circumspect about their answers.

Length of Time before Giving Response

In general, truthful persons answer questions quickly; untruthful persons take their time in giving a response. There may be an awkward silence, or the respondent may use a delaying tactic, such as "who me?" or "why would I do that?"

Repetition of Question

Repeating the question is another means for the deceiver to gain time to frame his or her answer. The question may be repeated verbatim, or the respondent may frame the answer with a request to repeat the question. Example: "What did you say, again?" or "Are you asking me if I took kickbacks?" A truthful subject usually does not have to contemplate his or her answer.

Fragmented or Incomplete Sentences

A liar will often speak in fragmented or incomplete sentences. This is usually because he or she has commenced the answer, then thought better of it. Statements such as "I . . . I . . . can't think . . . it seems to me" can be clues to lying. Many liars will speak half-truths as well, and add qualifiers, such as "to the best of my memory" or "if I recall correctly."

Being Overly Polite

Most people, when wrongly accused, don't take the accusation lightly. Anger is a common response to an unjust accusation, as well as answering the statement with a terse "no." Untruthful subjects are more likely to be polite to the accuser, using flattering terms such as "sir" or "ma'am." The suspect who has been accused and is untruthful will often say, "Sir, no offense to you, but I didn't do it."

Oaths

Untruthful persons will frequently recite oaths, such as "I swear to God I didn't do it" or "I swear on my father's grave." Most truthful people do not need to swear or affirm; they are vehement in their denials. Some people who use words like "frankly" or "to tell the truth" often are neither being frank nor are they telling the truth.

Clarity of Response

Truthful people tend to be very clear in their responses, while untruthful persons tend to mumble, talk softly, and diffuse their answers. Such responses are to avoid the stress caused by an untruthful response; the liar is hedging. In that way, if caught in a lie, the earlier "soft" response may aid in diffusing the lie.

Use of Words

The words used by truthful and untruthful subjects can be very revealing. As a general rule, truthful subjects have no trouble denying the allegation in specific terms, while an untruthful one will have problems with the wording used. A truthful subject might say, for example, "I did not steal that money," while an untruthful one might say, "I did not borrow it." Untruthful suspects also tend to deny specific instances. Example: "I did not take the $7,500 in kickbacks." That may be a truthful answer; perhaps the amount was $8,000.

Assertiveness

Truthful persons are assertive about their innocence. Untruthful ones are not as assertive unless they are very practiced liars. Truthful people will respond directly without waiver or qualification; untruthful people tend to respond indirectly with waivers and qualifications. If someone gets assertive when accused, that can be a reliable indicator of truthfulness.

Inconsistencies

Inconsistent statements made by the witness are one of the best indicators of untruthfulness; liars usually get caught up in their own web of deceit. In the interview or interrogation, if an interviewee gives contradictory information, there can be two explanations: the person was mistaken or lying.

Slips of Tongue

Liars, as Freud discovered, quite often slip up and reveal themselves through a slip of the tongue. An example would be a witness who referred to Mr. Black when he really intended to say Mr. Brown. Could Mr. Black, then, be the truth and Mr. Brown be the lie?

Tirades

Sometimes people who are deceptive leak more than a word or two, as in the slip of the tongue. The information doesn't slip out, it pours out. Ekman believes this may be a result of the internal stress generated from the lie "leaking" out. Tirades may be in direct proportion to the stress generated in the lie, and occur at a time of anger or other strong emotion.

Indirect Speech

Liars without much experience quite often try to conceal their lie by the way in which the answer is framed.

Question: Did you take any money from Mr. Smith?

Answer: I saw him on the morning of the 24th. We went to breakfast together, and he was telling me about this new diet he was trying. He was working out with weights the other day.

Pauses

Pauses in speech patterns may be one of the more reliable clues to deception. Pauses in speech that are too long, too frequent, or which occur at inappropriate places should be evaluated closely by the examiner.

Voice Pitch

Anger or fear is often marked with an increase in voice pitch. The subject could be angry because he or she is being unjustly accused, or fearful because of the possibility of being caught in a lie. In one experiment, nurses were positioned in a room near a television screen. Although they were watching gruesome and grisly accidents and operating room scenes, they were instructed to tell the interviewer (who could not see the screen) that they were watching a beautiful field of flowers. At the time of the deception, most of the nurses had a measurable increase in the pitch of their voices.

Speed of Speech

Persons who are nervous or upset frequently increase the speed of their speech; words tend to run together and the conversation can be disjointed. A pattern of increased speed of speech during the relevant portion of the questioning could indicate deception.

NONVERBAL CLUES

Like verbal clues, nonverbal clues are caused by increased stress. Nonverbal clues include patterns in body movement as well as certain facial expressions.

Emblems

Emblems are expressions made with the body, whose meanings are clearly understood. The universal "thumbs up sign" is an emblem, as is the circled finger and thumb to indicate "okay." Other examples would include a broad wink to show the remarks are to be taken in jest, as well as a shrug of the shoulders. Emblems are always performed deliberately.

In some cases involving deception, the motion of an emblem may stop abruptly before it is completed; someone, for example, may start to turn his or her palms up and then think better of it. This could be because the witness has decided to be deceptive about his or her true feelings, and this is an outward expression.

Illustrators

Illustrators are motions, primarily by the hands, to illustrate a point—jabbing your finger in the air, for example. Some ethnic groups tend to use illustrators more than others. Illustrators that appear deliberate, out of place, or otherwise discordant may be signs of deception.

Manipulators

Manipulators are the habitual behavior of touching one self. Manifestations include grooming the hair, wringing the hands, and picking imaginary lint from a coat. Manipulators may last a short time, or may go on for several minutes. Props, such as cigarettes, pencils, and so on can be used in the manipulation. Social scientists have documented that body movements, fidgeting, and other behavior occur with stress. As stress increases, so do the manipulators. However, other evidence suggests that people also increase their use of manipulators when they are totally relaxed, possibly out of boredom.

Breathing, sweating, and heart rate are controlled by the autonomic nervous system, and are prone to change under stress. These are exactly the changes observed and measured by the polygraph.

Breathing

Breathing, although an involuntary movement, is very much affected by stress. Many persons under prolonged periods of stress hyperventilate. Of course, this stress may have nothing to do with lying. But an increase in breathing rate or volume may indicate deception.

Sweating

Sweating is another uncontrollable body function. Perspiration occurs with heat as well as with emotion. Studies indicate that the rate of perspiration is not the same for all emotions, such as fear and anger. Excessive sweating could very well indicate an involuntary reflex with deception.

Frequent Swallowing

A dry mouth frequently accompanies deep emotion. Often the witness is not aware of increased efforts at swallowing. All of us have had an experience where our mouths went dry, perhaps before or during a speaking engagement. Around the time of the critical question, increased swallowing or throat clearing might indicate deception.

Microexpressions

Microexpressions are those made for an instant. In some cases, deceptive persons react without being conscious of the movements. They usually last less than a quarter of a second. What happens is that someone is caught off guard about the felt emotion, and the emotion "leaks" before the person becomes aware of it. An example would be a sad expression that quickly turns to a smile. Microexpressions are hard for novices to detect, but experiments have shown that with training some people can learn to recognize them. The microexpression is usually an attempt to conceal a feeling, and could be an indicator of deception.

Facial Muscles

People can control certain facial muscles at will, but other muscles are quite difficult to control. It is easy, for example, to force a smile. But the forced smile can also be detected even by novices who notice something "isn't right" about the smile. What usually isn't right is that muscles above the eyes, called reliable facial muscles, are not controlled, but the muscles involving the mouth are. The muscles above the eyes control certain eye movements, along with movement of the eyebrows. These muscles are difficult for even experienced actors and actresses to train, and can be used with some success in detecting deception.

Eyes

The eyes probably convey as much emotion as any other part of the anatomy. Blinking, pupil dilation, and tears are some of the signs indicating emotion in the eyes.

Rapid blinking can signal emotional stress in the eyes. Conversely, the absence of blinking may indicate the subject has "tuned out" the interrogator or interviewer.

Pupil dilation is an autonomic response and beyond the control of the subject. Of course, the most common reason for a change in pupils is because of the light source. Studies have also shown, however, that the pupil will respond to felt emotion.

Experienced actors know how to cry: they think of something in their life that was particularly sad, and they concentrate on that emotion. Trying to cry at appropriate times, and conversely, trying to hold back tears could be a sign of deception.

Face

Many people believe, with some truth, that lies most frequently show up in the face and eyes. The face can contain two messages: what the liar is trying to show as well as what he or she is trying to conceal. Reddening or blanching of the face is supposed to be a sign of embarrassment and cannot be controlled. Such signs may indicate strong emotion.

PRECAUTIONS

There are several precautions that must be considered in evaluating deception. The most significant, of course, is that many verbal and nonverbal clues signal only emotion, not deception. It is the overall balance of the clues that is most helpful in determining if someone is lying.

Examiners must be careful when trying to evaluate deception in any person with a psychiatric history or psychopathic traits. Such persons exhibit very few helpful clues that help to evaluate deception.

Legitimate or illegitimate use of drugs can negate any possibility of accurate evaluation of deceptive traits. Sedatives prescribed to reduce nervous tension can be especially difficult, in that they produce behavior symptoms of withdrawal and disinterest. Other drugs may produce similar unreliable symptoms. An individual withdrawing from the use of medications can be fidgety, sweaty, and shaky. Examiners should be cautious when evaluating deception of any person using drugs.

As a general rule, the more intelligent the witness, the more reliable his or her behavior symptoms. The intelligent person will respond more reliably to issues of right and wrong. Persons with strong moral backgrounds will experience more internal conflict in deceptive situations, and hence will have generally stronger reactions. Young people, who see themselves largely as unaccountable for their behavior, will have less reliable symptoms of deception.

Victims of violent crimes often exhibit stress symptoms as a result of being victimized. They frequently suffer from extreme anxiety and therefore their stress signals are unreliable. Other individuals who are highly emotional for reasons not having to do with the offense under investigation can also send unreliable signals. The examiner should not confuse guilt with high emotion.

AIDS IN EVALUATING DECEPTION

There are a number of aids that have been historically used to evaluate deception. Two of these aids work on the autonomic nervous system (ANS). The theory, again, is that lying produces stress, and that the ANS can measure the by-products of this stress.

Use of the polygraph, which was severely restricted with the Polygraph Protection Act of 1988, is one of the oldest scientific aids using the ANS theory. It is an instrument that measures minute changes in breathing, galvanic skin response (perspiration), and blood pressure. The instrument is calibrated to the individual through asking a series of control questions designed to elicit response to nonthreatening questions (i.e, where the individual went to school) and then is used to measure their responses to the pertinent questions.

It has been said that the polygraph instrument is only as good as the expert administering it. Industry experts claim reliability rates in excess of 80 percent; however, these reports must be viewed with some skepticism. In a "60 Minutes" episode several years ago, investigative reporters invented a theft of a camera from a business, and hired polygraphers to determine the "thief." A reporter, posing as the business manager, told three different polygraphers that he suspected three different people. In each case, the polygraphers concluded (after administering the polygraph) that the "thief" was the person whom the business owner "suspected."

As the name implies, voice-stress analyzers work under the theory that stress can be detected in the voice. There are a number of manufacturers of these devices, but all employ the same technology. A device measures minute changes in the pitch and timbre of the human voice over time. When the voice pitch changes, a light goes off, indicating to the observer stress in the voice. Although these devices do indeed measure changes in the voice, they may be of marginal value in detecting deception. Their use was also restricted by the Polygraph Protection Act of 1988.

A number of companies offer so-called "pencil and paper honesty tests" to determine the test-taker's propensity to honest conduct. These devices cannot be used to test a specific falsehood, but rather an attitude toward telling lies and stealing. The theory is that the liar and thief has the attitude that he or she lives in a dishonest world, and that others around are dishonest. The truthful person, in turn, sees the world as basically honest, and dishonest behavior as aberrant behavior. Most of these tests are used for pre-employment screening, but have been attacked by some ethnic groups as being racially biased. Their accuracy is claimed, by the test designers, to be at least as good as the polygraph for pre-employment screening.

DRAWING CONCLUSIONS

In evaluating signs of deception, it is easy to draw the wrong inferences. Ekman (1986) believes it is easier to verify a truthful subject than to discover an untruthful one. It must be understood and repeated that no one sign is an indicator of deception. Three things must be kept in mind when drawing conclusions:

1. Look for changes in normal behavior. Those changes can best be measured by calibrating the witness.
2. Evaluate indicators on the basis of when they occur and how often they occur. Reliable behavioral changes of deception should occur immediately around the time the pertinent questions are being asked.
3. No one behavior should be isolated and a conclusion drawn. All should be considered together.

15   Interrogation

INTRODUCTION

An interrogation is an interview of a suspect conducted for the main purpose of obtaining a confession. There are, however, other objectives. The three principal purposes to the interrogation are (1) to obtain an admission of guilt, and, in the absence thereof, (2) to identify and neutralize defenses the target may raise; (3) to obtain information that can be used to impeach the suspect. If the suspect is indicted and tried, his out-of-court statements may, under certain circumstances, be used against him or her in court.

No matter what the skill level of the examiner, many (if not most) guilty suspects may not confess during the interrogation. This is especially true for fraud perpetrators, who tend to be above average in intelligence, and who have usually plotted their defense before ever committing the crime. It must be remembered, however, that information that can be used to impeach the suspect's honesty is almost as useful as a confession.

Some of the tactics used in interrogation are similar to those used to interview the adverse witness; however, the objectives can be different. In the case of the adverse witness, the examiner is attempting to turn the witness. In the case of the guilty suspect, the examiner is looking for a confession, or for impeachment information.

The choice of when to interrogate a suspect is important. Normally, the interrogation should be conducted when:

1. As much information as possible has been developed from sources other than the suspect.
2. There is some evidence that can be obtained or explanation given only by the suspect.
3. The interrogator can reasonably control the place, time, and subject matter of the interrogation.

As a general rule, the suspect is the last interview conducted in an investigation or examination. Since the purpose of the interrogation is to elicit a legally binding confession, the examiner's preparations are key. You cannot be too prepared for an interrogation, as your case may rest substantially on the confession or the lack thereof.

In preparing, the examiner should use most of the basic steps employed for interviews: collect and review all pertinent documents and prior statements, organize the evidence, and decide the objectives to be pursued. In addition, the examiner should review the legal elements developed in the case to insure there are no gaps in the proof. Then, the case should be evaluated as to whether or not sufficient evidence exists to prevail in litigation without the confession of the target. Pay particular attention to evidence which only the suspect can provide. Can he or she make seemingly exculpable admissions that would help in the case? Can you develop information on his or her defenses?

PRELIMINARIES

Scheduling the Interrogation

The suspect is usually questioned late in the examination, after information regarding him or her is clearly known. In some cases, however, it might be advisable to talk to the suspect earlier, especially if he or she knows of the investigation. This is usually helpful in developing information regarding assets, bank accounts, and other similar matters. However, if insufficient investigation has been conducted, it is not a wise idea to confront the suspect for the purposes of an admission.

In most cases, the suspect is aware of the investigation; he or she has probably been so advised by witnesses you have already interviewed. As a general rule, it is best not to let the suspect know the interrogation has been scheduled; it will simply permit him or her to develop exculpatory answers to the questions and make obtaining a confession more difficult.

Interview Room

In most situations, the examiner will not be in a position to control the location of the interrogation; therefore, the following suggestions may not be applicable in all cases. The key point is to establish an environment to control the interrogation with a minimum of distraction.

The location established for the interrogation should be as quiet and private as possible. There should be a minimum of distractions and physical objects, thus enabling the examiner to conduct the interrogation and have the full attention of the suspect.

The examiner should never lock the interview room, or create any other physical impediments to the suspect's leaving the room if he or she desires. This will help avoid any claims by the target that the interrogation was conducted against his or her will. The room should typically be free of large objects or drapes which would lead the suspect to feel that the room conceals someone overhearing the conversation.

Ideally, the interview room should be as bare as possible. There should be no photographs, paintings, other objects on which the suspect can focus his or her attention during the interrogation. Even small objects such as paper clips and pencils should be out of reach of the suspect, so as not to give the suspect something to play with during the interrogation.

Contrary to popular television lore, the interrogator does not shine a bright light in the face of the suspect. Lighting should be adequate without being harsh. The illumination of the person's facial features is desirable, but, not to the point where claims of harassment can be made.

Telephones, radios, excessive noise from air conditioning and ventilation should be minimized. Such distractions work against the concentration of the person being interrogated.

The suspect should not be allowed to sit behind a desk, or have any other physical barriers between him or her and the examiner. The purpose for not having barriers is to allow the examiner a full view of the body posture and language of the suspect, and to prohibit the security of a physical barrier. The suspect and the examiner should be separated by about four to five feet; enough so the examiner is not in the face of the person being interrogated, but close enough so that he or she can speak in a normal tone of voice. The chairs should be straight backed, not chairs in which one can fully relax.

Note Taking

Note taking during interrogation should be kept to an absolute minimum. In some cases, taking notes cannot be altogether avoided. But the examiner should not take notes in a manner that suggests the legal significance of the person's problems. If the person mentions a name or other key information, the examiner can duly note the information, but no obvious gestures should be made.

Presence of Counsel

It is much more difficult to elicit a confession with someone else present. For that reason, the presence of the suspect's attorney will reduce the probability of confession. Under no circumstances should the examiner let himself or herself be placed in the position of seeming to deny either the right to consult with an attorney or having the attorney present during the interrogation.

If it appears that the case can be successfully brought without of the suspect's confession, the examiner should consider eliminating the interrogation if the suspect insists on an attorney being present. Since the probability of a confession is greatly reduced when the attorney is in attendance, the examiner risks giving up a great deal of information about the case without getting anything valuable in return.

Others Present

Under certain conditions, employees may have the right to union or similar representation during interviews and interrogation. Some suspects may wish to bring a boss, friend, or spouse. Interrogations should generally not be conducted with anyone other than the target present. The reasons are twofold: as with attorneys present, confessions are harder to get with an advocate of the suspect present. Second, the examiner risks disclosing significant information to third parties; legal liability could attach.

TECHNIQUES IN INTERROGATION

The following techniques are recommended in situations where the guilt of the individual is reasonably known, and the purpose of the interrogation is to elicit a confession of guilt. Not all of these steps will work in all instances. Indeed, this material is meant only to be a guide.

Commence the interrogation by introducing yourself and the purpose of the interrogation (do not call it an interrogation with the target). Your introduction should be general about the purpose.

Wrong: Mrs. Collins, my name is Loren D. Bridges, with the Bailey Book Corporation. I need to interrogate you about taking kickbacks from Jim Nagel.

Right: Mrs. Collins, my name is Loren D. Bridges, with Bailey Book Corporation. I need to ask you some questions about some contract matters.

Before confronting the suspect, obtain background information. Background questions get the suspect used to answering questions. Such questions also permit you to obtain lead information if the suspects refuses to cooperate later. Carefully observe the suspect's behavior while asking nonthreatening questions.

Confront the target directly and observe his or her reaction. Vehement denial of the allegation by the suspect could be a sign of innocence. If the target is passive, it could be an indication of guilt. The confrontation should be direct and without qualification. Example: "Mrs. Collins, I have conducted an extensive investigation which indicates that you have been taking kickbacks."

Give the suspect a morally accepted excuse for the behavior. If he or she seems to accept the explanation, or is passive (even if no confession results), it can be an indication of guilt. Example: "Mrs. Collins, I want you to know that I think I understand how this matter happened. I know you didn't do it for yourself; you have had some very serious marital and financial problems. Faced with the same situation, I may have done the same thing."

If the suspect continues to deny guilt (which is probable), cut off the other denials and lay out the evidence, without naming names of witnesses. Then return to the morally accepted rationalization for the behavior. Example: "Mrs. Collins, I know you say you didn't do it, but, unfortunately, the evidence indicates the contrary. I have talked to several witnesses and examined a lot of evidence. Your denying it will not make it go away. My question is why? Did you need the money? Was your husband giving you a hard time? Whatever it is, I need to know so we can get this matter resolved."

If the suspect keeps objecting, continue to offer alternate explanations for his or her behavior. Then ask the same question regarding guilt in a nonoffensive way. Example: "Mrs. Collins, I know what you are saying, but, again, this will not go away by your denying the truth. Besides, there is not that much money involved. I have seen people in a lot worse shape than you. Were you given money all the time, or just on a few occasions?"

Try to get the suspect to offer an explanation of his or her behavior. It is common for targets to make partial admissions. If that happens, it is usually only a matter of time before the full admission is made. Example: "Mrs. Collins, you need to talk to me about this. Remember, I am not your enemy, I am just doing a job. I know a lot about you, and I know you are under a lot of strain. If you will talk to me and tell me the truth, I will try to help. The first thing I need to know is if this happened all the time, or on just a few occasions?"

Continue to keep the target talking. As previously stated, once any admission is made, a full confession usually follows. Get the confession orally, and try to get all the details. Assure the suspect that he or she is doing the right thing. Example: "Tell me about it, one at a time. It is the only way I can help. Believe me, it is much better for you to tell someone who knows the situation, rather than a complete stranger."

Reduce the oral confession to writing. Try to be low-key about the written confession, and make sure you include the target's reason for committing the offense. Example: "Mrs. Collins, I need to get this down in writing. The main reason is so there will not be any misunderstandings about what happened or why. I want to make sure we include the fact that you didn't mean to hurt anyone, and you meant to pay the money back later."

Close the interrogation on a positive note, in case additional cooperation is needed in the future. If the confessor perceives you as someone not out to injure him or her, cooperation will be a lot easier. Example: "Mrs. Collins, I know this was difficult for you, but believe me, you did the right thing. Things usually go easier on people who have the courage to admit their mistakes. I will assure you that I will make your cooperation known to the proper people."

The above example is only a guide. Not all steps will be used in all instances. It is important to remember that the basics of interrogation include (1) the positive confrontation, and (2) giving the target an "out" or rationalization for his or her behavior. People in trouble need a safe harbor, and it is up to you to provide it in order to be successful. In most cases an interrogator will do well to verbally maximize the sympathy and minimize the crime.

INTERROGATOR QUALIFICATIONS

There is no one characteristic that distinguishes a successful from an unsuccessful interrogator. The key is to be professional without being distant. Under no circumstances should the examiner create the impression that he or she is out to get the suspect, or that the sole purpose is to obtain a confession. It is much better to show the suspect, through conversation and demeanor, that the examiner is seeking only the truth. After all, that is why you are there.

The successful interrogator's personality will reflect his or her personal background. In conveying aspects of your personality, you should attempt to look at yourself through the suspect's eyes, and try to create the right impression: someone who is caring, helpful, honest, and approachable. Here are other helpful hints:

1. Treat the suspect with decency and respect, regardless of the offense or your true feelings.

2. If the target lies, do not scold or reprimand him or her. It is better to conceal any reaction of resentment or surprise. If the suspect later admits a falsehood, acknowledge it in a manner that is not condescending.

3. Recognize that there is good in everyone, no matter how slight.

4. The examiner should dress appropriately. This helps create an impression of authority and formality.

Persuasion is a form of communication wherein the listener's attitudes, beliefs, and perceptions are changed. It is necessary for the successful interrogator to be persuasive.

Credibility is based on sincerity, knowledge, and demeanor. Whether real or not, sincerity can be displayed behaviorally through good eye contact, the use of open-handed gestures, a forward posture, and open facial expressions. Verbally, sincerity is portrayed by talking slowly and using careful, deliberate statements.

It is vital that the interrogator be aware of the suspect's attitudes, to be able to size him up. It is especially important to have a good idea of what consequences are being avoided through the use of deception and an estimate of the anxiety tolerance of the individual.

Identifying the consequences the target is avoiding is easier said than done. It may be that the suspect simply wants to avoid losing a job, or there may be a more complex motive, such as the loss of esteem common in fraud cases.

The degree of anxiety tolerated by a suspect is usually indicated during the confrontation phase of the interrogation. For example, a truthful suspect denies the allegations vehemently; the untruthful one uses weak denials.

PSYCHOLOGY OF CONFESSIONS

Offenders can generally be classified into two types, the emotional offender and the nonemotional offender. An emotional offender is one who ordinarily experiences feelings of remorse, guilt or mental anguish. In short, he or she has a strong conscience. Such offenders are best dealt with by a sympathetic approach, with the examiner sensitive to the suspect. The emotional offender reacts with strong emotion when confronted; the nonemotional offender does not.

The most effective way to deal with nonemotional offenders is on the basis of facts. This approach means appealing to common sense on the basis of overwhelming evidence of guilt.

Reducing Anxiety through Behavior

Anxiety can be reduced in a deceptive individual through both verbal and nonverbal responses. As the suspect denies the truth, the stronger the denial, the more stress it creates. If the suspect tells the truth, full responsibility is accepted and anxiety over being untruthful is relieved. If the suspect denies guilt through omissions (an implied truth), it produces some anxiety. Evasion often leaves an out, but at some level of anxiety. Outright denial produces the maximum stress.

Nonverbal attempts to reduce anxiety usually manifest themselves through body movements or through physical activity. If the suspect fidgets or moves when the tough questions are asked, he or she is attempting to relieve anxiety.

Reducing Anxiety Cognitively

Cognitive measures to reduce anxiety are called defense mechanisms. They operate within an individual by denying or distorting reality. There are two principal defense mechanisms, rationalization and projection.

Rationalization is the defense mechanism of redescribing what was done in such a way as to avoid the consequences of certain behavior. It is common for fraud offenders (and more specifically embezzlers) to rationalize that they have "borrowed" the funds in question rather than stealing them.

During projection, the suspect shifts the blame for his or her own thoughts or actions onto another person, place or thing. An example would be an employee who acknowledged that he or she stole because of not being paid enough.

Why Persons Confess

With the understanding that individuals deceive to avoid the consequences of telling the truth, people confess for the mirror image of the same reasons: to avoid the consequences of telling a lie. In other words, most people will not confess if the perceived benefits of lying are greater than the perceived benefits of telling the truth. The goal of the interrogator is to decrease the suspect's perception of the negative consequences of confessing while at the same time increasing the anxiety associated with not telling the truth.

OVERCOMING OBJECTIONS TO CONFESSIONS

As a general rule, a target will not confess while denying guilt. Rather than argue with someone who is denying guilt, a more effective technique is to attempt to neutralize the objections by reducing the perceived consequences of confessing. According to Inbau (1986: 341), there are several beliefs held by the perpetrator that reduce the perceived consequences of his or her behavior:

1. denial of responsibility (blame alcohol, drugs, amnesia, or stress)
2. denial of injury (the company wasn't hurt)
3. denial of the victim (they got what they deserved)
4. condemning the condemner (everyone steals)
5. appeal to higher loyalties (target stole for family)

It is perfectly acceptable for the examiner to use one or more of these techniques to neutralize the objections to the confession. By far the most effective technique in eliciting confessions is to give the suspect an acceptable excuse for his or her behavior.

Wrong: Mr. Smith, the reason you stole this money is because you are a thief.

Right: Mr. Smith, I can easily see why you took this money. First of all, everyone has taken something in their lives. Second, you didn't take it for yourself, you took it for your family. And third, you didn't take enough to really matter to the company.

In the above example, you have given the suspect several rational reasons for his behavior. These techniques, if properly employed, will more likely result in a confession of guilt.

The fraud examiner should not expect immediate confessions of guilt. It takes patience and persistence to ask someone to confess to a crime or other offense. To expect anyone to voluntarily give up property or liberty without some soul-searching is asking a lot. It usually takes time for the suspect to come around.

If the suspect senses impatience on the part of the interrogator, the suspect will usually react by expecting that the end of the interrogation is near. If the examiner's impatience results in anger, the chances are the interrogation will not result in a confession. Even if it does, the confession might be considered as being obtained through the use of threats, and be invalid. Because of the tedious nature of the interrogation, it is common for all interrogators to lose a sense of patience, and want to give up. In the words of Inbau (1986: 196),

"Never conclude an interrogation at the time when you feel discouraged and ready to give up, but continue for a little while longer—if only for 10 or 15 minutes." Many guilty subjects have later remarked that they were ready to confess just as the interrogator gave up.

LEGAL ASPECTS OF CONFESSIONS

There are several legal aspects of the interrogation process that the fraud examiner must know. Failure to observe proper legal procedures when obtaining a confession might render it unusable, and indeed, may place the entire case in jeopardy. In addition, a confession obtained under certain conditions may even expose you and/or your company to civil liability.

Voluntariness

All confessions must be voluntary. No threats, force, or intimidation should be used in obtaining the confession. In a criminal case, use of physical force, pain, or other harm will invalidate the confession, and it cannot therefore be introduced into evidence. Indeed, it can be brought out by the defense in establishing misconduct on the part of the plaintiff.

The promise of immunity or leniency will similarly create problems for the confession, and should be avoided at all costs. There is no prohibition against telling the confessor that his or her cooperation will be made known for possible consideration.

Trickery and Deceit

The use of trickery and deceit to obtain confessions has generally been held constitutional by the Supreme Court for use by the police. In one case, the interrogators falsely told the suspect that his accomplice had confessed (Frazier v. Cupp, 394 U.S. 731). The court said: "The fact that the police misrepresented the statements that (the suspected accomplice) had made is, while relevant, insufficient in our view to make this otherwise voluntary confession inadmissible. These cases must be decided by viewing the totality of the circumstances."

The law is less clear in the situation of private police, but the measure is the "totality of the circumstances." It is safe to say that the use of trickery and deceit in obtaining confessions is generally not necessary, even though it may be legal. If deception is used, the examiner must be prepared to defend that tactic.

Defamation

It is common during the interrogation for the interrogator to accuse the suspect of the offense, even if the interrogator has no hard evidence of this fact. Some could construe this as a form of trickery and deceit; however, a larger issue is that of slander or defamation of character.

Case law normally holds that no slander or other form of defamation occurs when an interrogator directly accuses a suspect of committing an offense, even if it turns out that the suspect was totally innocent. However, two conditions must be present. First, the accusation must be made in private, so that no third party is present (attorneys or others with a legitimate common interest are exempt); and second, there can be no "publication" of the remarks to others. If the accusation is made for the sole reason of inflicting emotional harm to the accused, then the accused may recover damages as a result.

Admissibility

In order for a confession to be legally admissible, there are two general requirements. First, the confession must have been made voluntarily. Second, the interrogator must have reasonable belief that the information obtained in the confession is trustworthy. The reason for these common-law requirements is to avoid extracted confessions, when the interrogator had knowledge that the confession was probably not true.

Under federal and most state laws, an additional requirement has been read into the common-law test of voluntariness and trustworthiness: the confession must have been obtained by "civilized" interrogation procedures. The test for that civilized procedure varies from case to case.

In short, through the understanding of the psychology of offenders and the underlying laws, the fraud examiner may obtain a valid confession of guilt, which greatly enhances the probability of a successful case.

As a general rule, Miranda warnings are not required for suspects who are not going to be placed in custody immediately following the interrogation.

SIGNED STATEMENTS

Introduction

Signed statements are normally taken (1) from witnesses, if there is reasonable suspicion by the examiner that the witness will attempt to change his or her testimony at a later date; or (2) in the case of all oral confessions of guilt or culpability.

All signed statements, whether from a witness or the target of the examination, should be prepared and executed immediately following the interview or interrogation. Most all witnesses, if given the opportunity of reflection, will not sign a statement at a later time. If the confessor or witness refuses to sign a statement, any oral statements made during the course of the interview are still admissible, but proof may be more difficult.

Parts of a Signed Statement

The signed statement can be divided into three distinct parts: the introduction, the body, and the close.

Introduction

The introduction of the signed statement should identify the witness and use language indicating the statement was given voluntarily. If Miranda warnings are given, those should be so indicated in the introduction.

Example #1: I, Linda Reed Collins, furnish the following free and voluntary statement to Loren D. Bridges and Tonya Vincent, who have identified themselves to me as investigators for Bailey Book Corporation. No threats or promises of any kind have been made to induce this statement.

Example #2: I, Linda Reed Collins, furnish the following free and voluntary statement to Loren D. Bridges, who has identified himself to me as a fraud examiner for Bailey Book Corporation. I have been advised of my constitutional rights regarding self-incrimination. No threats or promises of any kind have been made to induce this statement.

Body

The body of the signed statement should contain a narrative of the information, preferably in chronological form. Some examiners may prefer the question and answer format; however, a short narrative is usually best. The narrative should stand on its own; that is, the reader should be able to reasonably deduce the witness's involvement in the matter without referring to other documents.

In the case of a confession, it is preferable that the admission of guilt be detailed early in the written statement. Example: "I freely admit that I have accepted gratuities and other considerations."

The effect of placing the confession early in the written statement is primarily for the reader's benefit; it draws attention to the fact that the statement is an admission of guilt.

The body of the statement should also contain an "excuse clause," which is the target's explanation for his or her behavior. This clause makes signing the statement more palatable to the confessing suspect, and can be used as a reason for signing the statement. The clause should not state that there was no "intent" to commit fraud, as this is a required element in most criminal cases.

There should be no attempt to make the statement long. In the first place, the suspect may get impatient and refuse to sign. Second, it is necessary to get only enough detail to validate the confession. The statement should contain some facts known only to the confesser, so those statements can be verified as necessary. Usually, two or three handwritten pages is sufficient for the confession.

Close

The close of the statement should include language that the statement has been read, and that other pages in the confession have been initialed (if there are

Figure 15.1
Example of Signed Statement Closing

"I have read this statement consisting of this page and one other typewritten page. I have initialed the other page, and now sign my name because this statement is true and correct to the best of my knowledge and belief."

Signature	Date

Witness	Date

Witness	Date

corrections, the close should indicate that these have also been initialed). Finally, the close should have language to the effect that the declarant has signed the statement because it is true. The statement should be signed and witnessed (See Figure 15.1).

Key Points in Signed Statements

Handwriting of Declarant

There is no requirement that the signed statement be holographic (i.e., in the handwriting of the declarant). As a matter of fact, it is usually easier if the statement is prepared by the examiner, using the same general wording the declarant uses. Handwritten statements by the examiner are perfectly acceptable as well; there is no need that the statement be typed or taken down stenographically. The presence of a stenographer is frequently inhibiting to the statement process.

The reason to write the statement for the declarant is a practical one: it is much more efficient. The examiner should know how to take one and get the essential elements better than the declarant. There is, of course, no objection to the statement's being written by the declarant; but in the case of confessions and statements, the rule is that the closer in time that the statement is taken after the confession, the greater the likelihood the subject will sign it.

Wording of Statements

During the interview or interrogation process, the interrogator has elicited a confession by primarily using "soft words" to describe the offense, "take" as opposed to "steal." When drafting the statement, the examiner now should be as accurate as possible in the wording of the written confession, and include the fact that the confessor committed the offense knowingly and willingly. Example:

"I was aware at the time I began taking money from Nagel that such conduct was illegal and violated Bailey Book policy."

Then counter that statement with the "excuse clause." Example: "I committed these offenses because I was in a severe financial bind. I am truly sorry for my conduct, and would like to do anything I can to make up for it."

In wording statements, it is best to be as precise as possible. However, if there is any chance that the information might be incorrect, be sure that is made clear in the statement. Example: "The total amount of money I have received is approximately $150,000, which has been paid to me by Nagel since January, 1989."

Intentional Errors

In some cases, examiners insert intentional errors in statements. Examples of those errors would be nondescript items, such as a spelling error or an incomplete sentence. When the declarant reads back the statement, the errors are corrected and initialed by the declarant. Then, if an argument ensues later about whether the declarant read the statement, his or her initials by the intentional error will help to refute this defense.

Reading and Signing

The statement should be read by the declarant after it is completed. It is a good idea to save the entire statement until it is finished before giving it to the declarant to read and sign. The reason is that not too much time should be given to the declarant to reflect on the decision to tell the truth. Each page of the statement should be initialed and dated by the declarant and the person taking the statement.

In some cases, it might be a good idea to save the close of the statement for the declarant to attest in his or her own writing. When the statement is presented to the declarant for reading, it should be signed immediately, without any undue delay. The language for requesting the signature is important; it should be declaratory.

Wrong: Would you sign this statement, please?
Right: Please sign here.

Witnesses

Witnesses are not actually required for a signed statement to be valid; only one person attesting to the authenticity of the signature is needed. However, two persons witnessing the statement is a good idea. If the declarant balks at witnesses being present, it is acceptable for the interrogator alone to attest to the signature. Keep in mind that oral statements are as binding as written ones, although greater weight might be given to the written statement. Having a statement in writing gives the psychological benefit to the interrogator.

More Than One Written Statement

The examiner should refrain from taking more than one signed statement from the declarant on the same offense. Two statements of varied facts on the same offense create obvious problems for the prosecution, and reduce or eliminate the credibility of the statement. If it is later determined that there are serious flaws or omissions in the original statement, it is a better idea to make an addendum to the original statement detailing the facts omitted or misstated.

Confessions to More Than One Offense

In some cases, multiple unrelated offenses might be involved. It is preferable where the multiple offenses are not closely related that a different statement for each offense be made. This is because there may be two or more trials involved in which case facts from the first crime might not be admissible at the second. In addition, the statement should not include references to any prior arrests or convictions, as this information is usually not allowed into evidence because it is prejudicial to the jury.

It is a good idea to preserve and keep all notes taken during any interview, and especially concerning a confession. This is to aid in any cross-examination regarding the validity of the signed statement. Stenographic notes, if a stenographer is used, should also be maintained.

The signed confession is not the end of the examination. Unless already done, any fact that can be substantiated by the confession should be verified. Just as targets can be unreliable, so can the information they furnish. It is of little value to take a statement from a witness of dubious credibility, only to find out later that the information is false. This is especially true if the bulk of the evidence lies with the confession.

16 Public Records

INTRODUCTION

A great deal of information of value to the fraud examiner can be obtained from public records. Public agencies, federal, state, and local, maintain much information in accordance with laws. Private agencies such as credit bureaus and associations maintain information as a means of livelihood. Whether such information is available for review by the fraud examiner depends on the laws governing dissemination of information, as well as the particular policy of the organization.

The importance of public information cannot be overemphasized. By one private investigator's estimate, more than half of the information obtained by the profession is from records easily available to the public. The secret, of course, is knowing where to look.

Generally, this section does not address whether particular records are open to the public. That determination must normally be made by the respective agency or source.

FEDERAL AGENCIES

Department of Defense

The Department of Defense maintains records on all military personnel (by branch of service). In addition, intelligence records are kept on persons or organizations that may be a threat to national security in order to furnish information on these persons to the proper federal law enforcement agencies (i.e., the FBI and CIA).

Department of Health and Human Services

The Department of Health and Human Services; Alcohol, Drug Abuse, and Mental Health Administration is responsible for federal efforts to reduce problems caused by substance abuse and mental health procedures.

The Food and Drug Administration is responsible for protecting the health of citizens against impure and unsafe drugs, foods, cosmetics, and other health hazards. The Social Security Administration administers the national contributory program on social insurance through the collection of monies from contributors and the disbursement of funds to recipients. The Health Care Financing Administration oversees Medicare and Medicaid programs, and works with state and county agencies, as well as third parties, such as Blue Cross/Blue Shield.

Department of Justice (DOJ)

DOJ represents the citizen in enforcing the federal criminal laws and related activities. The department is involved in law enforcement, crime prevention and detection, as well as prosecution and rehabilitation of offenders. The Justice Department operates local offices of the United States Attorney and U.S. Marshal. It is responsible for the following agencies:

Federal Bureau of Investigation (FBI)

The FBI is the principal investigative arm of the Department of Justice. All federal criminal matters not specifically assigned to another agency fall within the FBI's jurisdiction. The FBI also investigates cases involved in national security that occur within the United States, as well as certain civil and security cases. The FBI maintains the National Crime Information Center (NCIC), the fingerprint records of all citizens on file, and the Interstate Identification Index (III).

Bureau of Prisons

The Bureau of Prisons operates the nationwide system of federal prisons, correctional institutions, and community treatment facilities. It also maintains files and records on persons who are or have been incarcerated in federal facilities or parole or probation programs.

Immigration and Naturalization Service (INS)

INS maintains and administers the laws relating to the admission, exclusion, deportation, and current residency status of persons who are not citizens of the United States.

Drug Enforcement Administration (DEA)

DEA enforces the controlled substances laws by monitoring persons involved in illicit drug trafficking. In addition to its own cases, the DEA disseminates intelligence information to a variety of foreign governments, as well as state and local law enforcement agencies.

Department of the Treasury

The Treasury Department performs four principal functions: it formulates economic, financial, tax, and fiscal policies; it serves as the financial agent for the government; it assists federal law enforcement; and it manufactures currency and coin.

Bureau of Alcohol, Tobacco, and Firearms enforces firearms and explosives laws, and regulates production and distribution of alcohol and tobacco products.

The U.S. Customs Service collects revenues from imports as well as enforcing import and export laws; it handles the seizure of contraband, the processing of persons, cargo, and mail in and out of the United States, as well as the detection and apprehension of persons engaged in violation of customs laws.

Internal Revenue Service enforces internal revenue laws except those relating to alcohol, firearms, tobacco, and explosives. The service also works with other federal agencies in determining, assessing, and collecting taxes. It also assists in the investigation and prosecution of those who evade taxes.

The U.S. Secret Service is primarily responsible for those persons committing criminal offenses involving coin, currency, and securities, as well as interstate credit card rings and certain computer crimes. The service is also responsible for the protection of the President, Vice President, and other dignitaries.

U.S. Postal Service

The Postal Service, a quasi-government corporation, has complete responsibility for the U.S. mails, including protecting citizens from loss or theft, and prosecuting those who violate postal laws. Postal inspectors work major fraud cases involving use of the mails, and share jurisdiction with other federal, state, and local agencies.

Veterans Administration (VA)

VA is responsible for administering the needs of the veterans and their dependents. They maintain records on medical compensation, education, rehabilitation, insurance, and equal opportunity. Military service records are kept by the VA.

Central Intelligence Agency (CIA)

CIA is an executive office of the President. It generally investigates security matters outside the United States, whereas the FBI has investigative jurisdiction for security within the United States. The CIA maintains files on certain persons making application for employment in governmental agencies, as well as all U.S. citizens employed in foreign countries.

Department of State

The State Department maintains records on passport matters, and on visas for U.S. citizens traveling abroad. Its Division of the Office of Security maintains an index of all persons investigated for passport fraud. The Passport Office maintains an index of passport applications.

Department of Labor

The Labor Department maintains a master index of claimants for workers' compensation benefits under the Federal Employees Compensation Act (FECA). These benefits are provided for civil employees and officers of the United States who are injured in the performance of their duties.

Department of Commerce

The Department of Commerce has information on international trade, social and economic statistics, patents, trademarks, ocean studies, domestic economic development, and some information on minority business.

Federal Government Personnel Lists

Four different federal publications maintain personnel data: (1) the United States Government Organization Manual; (2) the Federal Register, (3) the Book of States, and (4) the Congressional Directory.

STATE AND LOCAL AGENCIES

State Attorneys General usually enforce all state laws, both civil and criminal, in cooperation with local agencies. Often, state Attorneys General have investigative arms, such as the state Bureau of Investigation.

The Comptrollers' offices, known sometimes as Budget Bureaus, administer state monies, collect a variety of taxes, and investigate violations of local tax laws.

Normally, the State Corrections Departments supervise the states' prison systems, and maintain records of those who have been or are incarcerated, or are on probation or parole.

Alcoholic Beverage Control (ABC) Boards normally license and investigate violations of businesses and individuals involved in the sale of alcoholic beverages.

The state director of the Selective Service System maintains a master list of all Selective Service registrants who were residents of the state at the time of registration. A local Selective Service Board maintains the individual applicant's records.

The functions of counties and municipalities vary widely. In general, local actions such as lawsuits, criminal convictions, and local tax records are available. See the information below for a more complete description.

LAW ENFORCEMENT RECORDS

In general, law enforcement records that do not lead to arrest and conviction are not available to the public. Often, fraud examiners will have relationships with law enforcement officials that will lead to the sharing of information on a specific case.

National Crime Information Center (NCIC)

NCIC is a database maintained by the FBI, and available to all federal, state, and local law enforcement agencies. It contains information on stolen and suspect vehicles, license plates, articles, securities, boats and planes; stolen and missing firearms; missing persons; and persons for whom there is an outstanding warrant. Some states have similar database systems. In order to access most databases such as the NCIC and the Interstate Identification Index (below), it is necessary to have a date of birth or other identifying number such as a social security number. Because of the database size, it is not possible to access information with a name only. These records are restricted to law enforcement.

Interstate Identification Index (III)

III is an outgrowth of the NCIC, and is maintained by the FBI for the benefit of federal, state, and local law enforcement. Its records are not open to the public. The III is a database of arrest and criminal records. Although criminal convictions are usually public information, arrest records are not.

Federal Criminal Records

In order to locate a criminal record without accessing the III, it is necessary to know the legal jurisdiction in which the conviction occurred. On the federal level, the convictions are maintained by the clerk of the criminal court. Records of convictions are usually open to the public.

State and Local Criminal Records

As with the federal system, state and local arrest records are maintained by the clerk of the court for the jurisdiction in which the conviction occurred. If the investigator is in doubt about what particular clerk's office maintains the records, the local police or sheriff's office can usually be of assistance. State and local criminal records are usually open to the public. In addition, trial records (if the proceedings were transcribed) are normally public information, as are all evidence and other matters introduced into open court.

CIVIL LAWSUITS

Civil lawsuits, both federal and local, are maintained by the clerk of the court in the jurisdiction where the suit was adjudicated. Of particular assistance to fraud examiners are depositions taken in civil litigation. Civil litigation is invariably over monetary damages, and a great deal of financial information can be gleaned in the review of depositions.

BUSINESS RECORDS

Corporate Records

All corporations must file documents in the state in which the incorporation occurred. If the incorporation occurs in one state (such as Delaware) and business is conducted in another state, the corporation normally will have to file documents as a "foreign corporation" in the state where business is conducted. The information required on corporations varies somewhat by jurisdiction, but usually the articles of incorporation, annual reports on franchise taxes, and in some cases bylaws are available. This information can be valuable in tracing corporate ownership. Corporation documents will reflect names of the incorporators, the registered agent in the state (normally the attorney who prepared the documents), and the initial board of directors and officers. In a limited number of cases, financial statements are filed. If a company is publicly held, its financial statements and records of significant events must be filed with the Securities and Exchange Commission.

Partnerships

Partnership records may or may not be a matter of record in the state where the partnership was formed. In the case of general partnerships (one in which the partners share in all profits and losses), there is normally no requirement to file agreements with licensing authorities.

Limited partnerships, in which the partner's liability is limited to his or her investment, are normally filed in the state in which the limited partnership is formed. A Certificate of Limited Partnership will usually list the general partners, the limited partners, the capital contributions of the partners, the agreements regarding the divisions of profit and loss, and the powers and duties of the various partners. Limited partnerships are the norm in real estate, oil and gas, and other investment ventures.

Trusts

A trust is a legal entity in which certain person(s) or entities, known as the trustee, hold and administer property on behalf of others (the beneficiaries). Commonly, trusts are used as vehicles for managing land transactions and other assets. Registration of trusts is required by some states; however, the beneficiaries of the trust are not always named.

Assumed Name Indexes

An assumed or fictitious name is used when one business or person conducts business in another name, such as a trade name. In most circumstances, an Assumed Name Certificate or Fictitious Name Certificate is filed in the county or city in which the business was organized. Although mostly used for legitimate purposes, the Assumed Name Certificates can be used to hide the true nature of the business and principals. Typically, such records are filed by business name and cross indexed by the business owner.

Better Business Bureau

Better Business Bureaus maintain information for one of three reasons: first, the bureau has received a prior request for information; second, a business or industry has volunteered information; or third, a complaint has been lodged against the business. The information contained in such files is usually limited.

Chambers of Commerce

Chambers of Commerce normally exist to promote the local area. They maintain information on commercial and industrial establishments within their areas, as well as information on trade and industry. Many publish extensive lists of business firms within the area, as well as officers of the companies listed.

Uniform Commercial Code (UCC) Filings

Filings under the UCC are made at the state and county level, and contain information regarding chattel mortgages (non-real-estate transactions). The UCC filings will normally reflect loans to individuals or businesses on equipment, furniture, automobiles, and other personal property.

Bankruptcy Records

Bankruptcy records are kept by the clerk of the federal court in which the bankruptcy was filed. Such records contain the names of creditors and the amounts owed, as well as financial statements. Testimony of the bankrupt in proceedings is normally given under a grant of immunity; therefore, those records may be sealed and not available for review.

REAL ESTATE RECORDS

Real estate records are usually found in the county in which the land is located. There are two general ways to trace real estate records. The land-ownership records are found at the county land office, which is sometimes referred to as the recorder of deeds. This office maintains the deeds and title certificates. The second way is through the property tax records, which are maintained at the tax assessor's office in the county where the property is located.

Property records indicating taxes paid or assessed are normally indexed by the address or legal description of the property. They also may be cross-indexed by the owner's name.

The county land records can be indexed by the name of the seller (grantor) and the buyer (grantee) in the grantor/grantee index. These records are excellent for determining changes in ownership of land. Sometimes the records in the county are computerized, and may contain information regarding the mortgage-holders or others who have a financial interest in the property.

Tax and land records will sometimes reveal the identity of the sellers, the broker, and others involved (such as the attorney who handled the transaction), and may have copies of cancelled checks and other supporting documents. Because of the complexity of some county systems, title companies and real estate brokers may be of assistance.

In the case of land sold under "contract for deed," the buyer does not receive title to the land until it is paid for, so county records may be of no value. Many real estate records are cumbersome, and contain errors and omissions.

CREDIT RECORDS

Credit records are maintained for both individuals and mercantile companies. There are essentially two types of credit-reporting agencies. The first is known as a file-based credit-reporting agency, which develops its information from credit files and public records. The other type is known as an investigative credit-reporting agency, which gathers most of its information through interviews.

The Fair Credit Reporting Act

The Fair Credit Reporting Act was passed into federal law effective in 1971. Its purpose is to regulate the activities and record-keeping of mercantile credit, insurance, employment investigation agencies and bureaus. Every organization engaged in activities affecting interstate commerce is thus within the reach of the act.

In its broadest sense, the act requires persons who will be subjected to investigation of their background, character, habits, and associates by consumer reporting agencies to be informed of that fact. A consumer reporting agency is generally an organization like a credit bureau; however, it can include any organization that provides such information to third parties:

A consumer reporting agency is generally an organization like a credit bureau or a mercantile reporting agency. However, it can include any organization that provides information to third persons about the background, character, reputation, lifestyle, or habits of an individual. The assumption is that such information has not come from direct and personal dealings between the agency or organization and the person about whom it is providing the information. Thus, a former employer, when queried by a current employer about an individual who was at one time employed, could become a consumer reporting agency. For that it must, in addition to the direct data it possessed about the individual's employment, also provide information it had acquired from others when it first employed the individual in question. (Walsh 1988: 13)

The key to being defined as a "consumer reporting agency" is whether or not information is furnished to a "third party." If furnished to "third party," the information probably falls under the Fair Credit Reporting Act.

If adverse action is taken against an employee as the result of a third-party inquiry, the employee must be given notice thereof. However, the employer is not obligated to tell the employee what specific information was contained in the third-party report; the employee may obtain that information directly from the third-party agency.

In the case of an employee investigated by in-house personnel, no notification is required of the employer. However, should the employer, by omission or commission, fall under the definition of a consumer reporting agency, the employer may have to open its files to the affected individual. This exposure can best be overcome by not releasing any information regarding an employee that was obtained from a third-party source. In short, the fraud examiner must be very circumspect in utilizing credit information, as its use may create a legal liability.

Credit bureaus are used primarily by retail organizations, and typically maintain the following information:

1. consumer information, such as address, age, family members, employers, income levels, length of employment, the extent of other obligations

2. account information, such as payment schedules, items purchased, defaults (if any), and buying habits

3. marketing information, such as customers broken down by age, sex, income levels, and other classifications

4. information on current and former employees

Credit bureaus rely on information supplied by organizations granting credit. In a typical situation, the potential creditor calls the credit bureau (or makes an on-line request) for information. The creditor receives information regarding other credit histories of the individual, such as payment schedules, delinquencies, and related information.

The credit bureau also gathers information on public record, such as bankruptcies, judgments, divorces, criminal convictions, and registered chattel mortgages. Information is regularly updated at the request of the consumer or by request of the credit grantor. Following are examples of three of the larger consumer credit agencies.

Consumer Credit Agencies

Credit Data is a subdivision of TRW, Inc., based in Redondo Beach, California. All of its information is computerized, and accessible by remote terminals. Data may also be accessed by telephone and letter. All Credit Data clients are required to supply credit information every 30 days. Information is released only to credit grantors and certain governmental agencies. Credit Data only supplies all available information, both positive and negative.

Retail Credit Company, located in Atlanta, Georgia, has over 300 branch offices and employs several thousand investigative personnel. Its business is to supply personal-history information on life insurance, and provide credit reports on individuals.

Credit Index, Inc., is a computerized credit database offered by the Hooper Holmes Bureau. It contains only negative information, such as slow credit, liens, judgments, and so forth.

FINANCIAL AND BUSINESS PUBLICATIONS

Business publications offer a wide range of information to the fraud examiner. Although a complete listing is beyond the scope of this book, Standard and Poor's, Moody, and Dun and Bradstreet contain a great deal of data on business enterprises.

Corporations

Standard and Poor's Corporation Records includes compilations of corporate data, such as corporate background, capitalization, earnings, balance sheet information, and stock information. S&P also publishes a reference list on corporate personnel entitled *Register of Corporations, Directors and Executives*. Dun and

Bradstreet publishes a *Reference Book on Corporate Management* which contains information on corporate officers and directors.

Dun's Marketing Services publishes the *Million Dollar Directory*, which contains information on more than 50,000 U.S. businesses with a net worth in excess of $500,000. The information is listed alphabetically, geographically, and by product classification.

Manufacturers

Information on manufacturing organization can be obtained from the *Thomas Register of American Manufacturers*. In addition to an alphabetical listing, the register also carries information on products manufactured.

Retail Stores

Fairchild's *Financial Manual of Retail Stores* is a wealth of information about retail chains, including officers, directors, business activities, revenues, stockholders' equity, income, assets, and liabilities.

Banking

Polk's *World Bank Directory* lists data on banks in the United States, Canada, Mexico, and the Caribbean. It is published by R. L. Polk and Co., Nashville.

The *Rand McNally International Banker's Directory* gives information on banks, as well as on the Federal Reserve System. The directory includes check-routing numbers by city and area, as well as financial information on all banks. It also includes automated bank clearing house information and data on bank holding companies.

Business Credit Ratings

The largest source of business credit ratings is Dun and Bradstreet. It lists the names, financial information, and credit ratings of retailers, manufacturers, and wholesalers in the United States. Subscribers to their services can obtain specific information on the credit of firms.

OTHER RECORDS AND INFORMATION SOURCES

Motor Vehicle Records

All states have an agency responsible for the registration of motor vehicles. In most cases, the same agency, usually the Department of Motor Vehicles, is also responsible for maintaining driver's license information. Driver and vehicle registration information usually provides information on operator's licenses, certificates of title, motor or serial numbers, license plates, and data on vehicle ownership.

Social Security Records

The Social Security Administration, headquartered in Baltimore, is responsible for the issuance of social security numbers. Records on social security paid by an individual or business are not available for review by the public.

If a social security number is known, it might lead to helpful information regarding the location in which the card was issued. Since many people apply for a social security number at a young age, this in turn can lead to locating the place of birth of an individual. There are nine digits in the social security number. With the exception of the 700 series, the first three digits reflect the state of issue. The last six digits are individual identifiers. (See Table 16.1).

Medical Records

In general, medical records of individuals are unavailable to the public. The State Board of Health usually contains public information on medical malpractice cases. County coroners maintain records on autopsies and post-mortem examinations in fatal accidents, homicides, and suicides.

The Medical Information Bureau is an unincorporated membership association of more than 700 life insurance companies. Its purpose is to supply potential insurers with data on medical problems of the insured. Its files contain over ten million entries. The entries come primarily from companies who turn down individuals for insurance coverage because of health problems.

Newspapers

Newspapers are a valuable source of information for the fraud examiner. Many newspapers maintain morgues of past issues that contain a wide range of public information. Some papers maintain this information for a year or more. Databases such as Nexis and The Source maintain entire texts of information from major newspapers that can be accessed by key words.

Student Records

Records of students in grammar and high schools as well as secondary schools are generally restricted. If available, they can supply information on parents, such as employment.

Investigative Databases

Investigative databases are maintained by private corporations. Many contain public record information such as motor vehicle registrations, arrest records,

Table 16.1
Social Security Listings by State

Initial Numbers	State of Issuance
001-003	New Hampshire
004-007	Maine
008-009	Vermont
010-034	Massachusetts
035-039	Rhode Island
040-049	Connecticut
050-134	New York
135-158	New Jersey
159-211	Pennsylvania
212-220	Maryland
221-222	Delaware
223-231	Virginia
232-236	West Virginia
237-246, 232 with middle digits 30	North Carolina
247-251	South Carolina
252-260	Georgia
261-267, 589-595	Florida
268-302	Ohio
303-317	Indiana
318-361	Illinois
362-386	Michigan
387-399	Wisconsin
400-407	Kentucky
408-415	Tennessee
416-424	Alabama
425-428, 588 allocated not in use	Mississippi (also 587)
429-432	Arkansas
433-439	Louisiana
440-448	Oklahoma
449-467, 627,645	Texas
468-477	Minnesota
478-485	Iowa
486-500	Missouri
501-502	North Dakota
503-504	South Dakota
505-508	Nebraska
509-515	Kansas
516-517	Montana
518-519	Idaho
520	Wyoming
521-524	Colorado
525, 648-649 allocated not in use	New Mexico (also 585)
526-527, 600-601	Arizona
528-529, 646-647 allocated not in use	Utah
530	Nevada
531-539	Washington
540-544	Oregon
545-573, 602-626	California

credit records, and real estate filings. Others contain newspaper and magazine articles.

SEC Filings

The SEC maintains records of corporations with stocks and securities sold to the public. These are probably the most extensive public sources of information on such businesses, and often include the following:

- financial statements
- identities of officers and directors
- identification of owners of more than 10% of stock
- descriptions of registrant's properties and businesses
- significant provisions of the securities to be offered
- events of interest to potential investors
- identification of accountants or attorneys
- history of business operations

Utility Records

Many cities and other jurisdictions make available subscribers to utility services, by both name and location. Such information is usually up-to-date, and can provide the examiner with locations of witnesses.

Bureau of Vital Statistics

The Bureau of Vital Statistics (sometimes called the Marriage License Bureau) can be a state or local agency. In most cases, birth and death information is maintained in addition to marriages and divorces. Divorce information can also be obtained locally, from the court where the divorce was granted.

Voter Registrations

Registered voters are normally kept on record with a county agency, such as the Board of Elections. Precinct books can determine how long a person has resided in any area.

Census Information

General information only can be collected from the Bureau of the Census. They collect information on the population in such areas as the economic, medical, and personal health. No information can be released on individuals, and census personnel can be criminally charged for releasing information.

Associations

The Encyclopedia of Associations, published by the Gale Research Company of Detroit, lists national organizations of the United States under 17 different categories. Some of the information available includes trade and business organizations, scientific and medical associations, and technical organizations. Gale also publishes the Encyclopedia of Business Information Sources, which lists organizations that provide handbooks, periodicals, and the like.

SUMMARY

This section is not meant to be a complete listing of public information sources, as such a listing would fill several books. Suffice it to say that there is no substitute for looking at public records in the early stages of any fraud examination. In so doing, the fraud examiner can save much time, trouble, and perhaps duplication of effort. Again, the secret is knowing where to look.

17   Report Writing

INTRODUCTION

Writing reports of fraud investigations is one of the most demanding and important tasks of a fraud examiner. Often, the written report is the only evidence of the work performed. Cases are frequently won or lost on the strength of the report. There are several other reasons why a written report is so important:

1. Properly done, the report conveys to the litigator all the evidence needed to evaluate the legal status of the case.
2. The written report adds credibility to the examination and the examiner.
3. The report forces the fraud examiner to consider his or her actions before and during the interview, so that the objectives of the investigation can be best accomplished.
4. The report omits immaterial information so that the facts of the case can be clearly and completely understood.

Buckwalter (1984: 206) writes: "Obviously, a satisfactory report can only be based on a satisfactory investigation. Unfortunately, a very satisfactory investigation can be completely ruined by a totally unacceptable report."

CHARACTERISTICS OF GOOD REPORT WRITING

Accuracy

Each official contact during the course of a fraud examination should be recorded on a memorandum of interview on a timely basis. Although no attempt should be made to recapitulate testimony word for word, it is recommended that, for accuracy, all facts of possible relevance be included in the memorandum of interview.

Dates and supporting information should be reconfirmed with the interviewee to ensure their accuracy. Reconfirmation acts as a precautionary measure to make certain all facts are accurate before the report is written, not after. Attachments to the report, if any, should be fully and completely described. In the words of Buckwalter (1984: 208), "Inaccuracies and careless errors are inexcusable, and can render a report useless."

Clarity

Investigative reports should strive to convey the proper message in the clearest possible language. If necessary, the interviewee can be quoted, provided the quotation does not distort the context of the memorandum of interview. Language used in the report should be used to convey only the facts, not to editorialize and give judgments. Complex or technical terms should be used in the proper context, and where necessary, their meanings should be explained. Do not use jargon, as the report is quite often read by persons who are not familiar with unusual or technical terminology.

Impartiality

In ascertaining the facts, it is necessary that the fraud examiner report them without bias. "Everything relevant should be included regardless of which side it favors or what it proves or disproves" (Buckwalter 1984: 208).

Relevance

The fraud examiner should ensure that only matters relevant to the examination are included in the details of the report. In almost every investigation, much information is gathered whose relevance is not immediately known. In such cases, any doubt should be resolved in favor of including the information. The examiner should make every effort to determine, at the outset, what information will be needed during the interview, and attempt to include only this information. Irrelevant information confuses and complicates the written report, and leaves the examiner open to criticism of his or her methodology.

Timeliness

Upon completion of the examination, a written record should be made in a timely manner. It is highly recommended that all interviews be reduced to writing as soon as practicable following the interview. The main reason timeliness is so important is to ensure the accuracy of witness testimony. The longer the examiner waits to record the interview, the more will be forgotten. Once all investigation has been completed, a final or interim report, whichever is appropriate, should be prepared in a timely fashion.

Opinions

Except for expert opinion on matters involving accounting or other related bodies of expertise, no opinion of any kind should be included in the report. The examiner should be especially careful not to include any statement of opinion as to the integrity or veracity of any witness, even if the examiner is convinced that the witness is being untruthful. The truthfulness or lack thereof can be demonstrated through conflicting statements from the witness or suspect.

THE WRITTEN REPORT

Written reports vary widely in style and format. In the absence of an established system of report writing, fraud examiners may wish to consider adapting the format below.

Cover Page

The cover page of a report typically includes all pertinent data gathered during the course of an examination. A recommended format would include the following:

File Number

There are several ways to construct file numbers. One is to assign the first two digits to the year the case was opened, followed by the numerical sequence of the case. For example, the first case for 1991 would be 91–0001. A second way to assign the number is by the type of investigation and the numerical sequence of the case. If 817 were a kickback investigation, the first case, regardless of year, would be 817–101. There are numerous combinations; the importance is for each case to have a unique and logical identifying number.

Case Description

This section lists the type of case, such as embezzlement, kickbacks, conflict of interest and so forth.

Employee Status

This information can be used for gathering employment-related information on the subject(s) of the examination. If the subject is employed by your company, a block can be checked so indicating this information for later statistical analysis.

Investigator

The lead investigator/examiner should be listed on the cover sheet. If more than one examiner is assigned, the names of each can be listed.

Date of Report

The date of the report is the actual date it was finally completed and typed.

Case Status

The status of the case can be divided into three different classifications:

Pending: The case is still under examination and further reports will be issued. In most cases, pending reports will be issued when the examination is expected to be lengthy, and an interim report is needed.

Inactive: The inactive status is normally used after all examination has been completed and referred to legal or law enforcement authorities for action.

Closed: The closed status is used when the final disposition legal or administrative) has been completed.

Report Number

In the case of multiple reports on the same examination, the report number (i.e., report 1 of 1, 1 of 2, etc.) should be indicated.

Type of Inquiry

This information is used to determine the type of matter under examination. Three choices are available: civil, criminal, and administrative. The matter under examination can also be a combination of the preceding. That is, an employee committing a criminal fraud may be also civilly liable, and administrative action (in the form of dismissal) may be taken against the employee.

Referrals

When a report is disseminated to an outside agency (attorney, law enforcement or the like), the name of the person to whom the report is disseminated, along with the date, should be supplied.

Synopsis

A final synopsis of the examination should be included on the cover page of the report. The synopsis should be brief (not more than one paragraph) and contain only the most relevant information uncovered during the examination. If a confession was obtained, the synopsis should so state.

Financial Data

This part of the report cover page should contain all costs associated with the case, including investigative/examination expenses, as well as projected losses as a result of the fraud. Information on losses should be supported in the body of the report.

Final Disposition

Once a case has been closed, the final-disposition portion of the report cover should be filled out. It should include relevant data concerning fines, prison sentences or probation. If an earlier report has been submitted which includes all data except for the final disposition, then this block can be used to summarize information for closing the case.

Predication

The predication of a report is the basis under which the investigation commenced. The recommended form for predication is a memorandum setting forth why the investigation was commenced. Example: "On May 18, 1991, an investigation into the above captioned matter was authorized and commenced, predicated on the contents of the letter."

The predication becomes important to establish that there was a reason to investigate. Failing to include predication in a report leaves the examiner vulnerable to allegations that the investigation was conducted for some other purpose, such as race, sex, or employment discrimination.

Witness Statements

Each witness interviewed should be recorded on a memorandum of interview. When the final report is assembled, witnesses who have provided no relevant information can be excluded from the formal report, as appropriate. Each witness should be recorded on a separate memorandum, even though the memorandum might be short. If this approach is followed, a request by the courts or others for a particular witness's statement can be fulfilled without providing the entire report. The memoranda of interview should include the following:

Details

This part of the memorandum contains all relevant information concerning the interview. The first paragraph should contain, at a minimum:

1. That the interview was voluntary.
2. That you provided your identity.
3. That you stated the nature of the inquiry.
4. The date the interview was conducted.
5. How the interview was conducted; i.e., in person or on the telephone.
6. Whether the interview was recorded.

If documents or copies thereof are obtained as a result of the interview, those documents should be attached to the memorandum, and fully described and summarized in the memorandum.

Cover Letter

A cover letter to the requester of the investigation is typically included with the report. The purpose of the cover letter is to:

1. Accompany the report.
2. Set forth a succinct summary of witness testimony.
3. Provide details on the location of potential witnesses.
4. Set forth the apparent violation of law, if any, that the report addresses.

The cover letter does not need to include all witness summaries, only those that are pertinent to the matter at hand.

Working Papers

Working papers, if developed, should also be summarized and described in memorandum form, and if necessary, enclosed as attachments to the report. It is a good idea to keep papers to a minimum in the report itself, and enclose the remainder only if needed. If working papers are enclosed with the report, they should be so described in the cover letter to the report.

MISTAKES TO AVOID IN WRITING FRAUD REPORTS

Conclusions

One of the most significant mistakes made by examiners is the stating of conclusions or opinions in the written report. Under no circumstances should conclusions be made, as they may come back to haunt the examiner in litigation. The opposing counsel's main tactic is usually to try to impeach whatever testimony is given, and to show that the examiner is biased. The conclusions of the investigation should be self-evident. If not, the report has not been properly prepared.

Opinions

Like conclusions, opinions have no place in the report. Under no circumstances should an opinion be written concerning the guilt or innocence of any person or party, as this is the purview of the courts; it is up to the jury to decide guilt or innocence.

Evidence

There are strict legal rules regarding the handling of evidence and the chain of custody thereof. Simply put, all problems with maintenance of evidence can be addressed by writing a memorandum any time evidence comes into or leaves the hands of the fraud examiner. Because of the nature of fraud cases, most evidence will be in the form of documents. If the examiner is operating under a lawful order of the courts that compels a custodian of records to furnish original documents, they should be copied, preferably in the presence of the custodian, before being removed from the premises. A receipt describing the items taken should be furnished to the custodian.

If not operating under a court directive (or in the cases of certain federal authorities, under an administrative subpoena), and the records are being provided voluntarily by the custodian, the examiner may, at his or her discretion, retain copies instead of originals. Some of the considerations in obtaining voluntary documents are:

1. whether it appears likely the originals may be lost, stolen, or destroyed when needed for trial

2. the importance of the originals to the examination

3. if the release of the original documents would be seriously disruptive to the conducting of normal business affairs

In all cases where records are voluntarily provided by a custodian, good judgment must prevail. They are, after all, being provided voluntarily. If the originals are not later available, all is not necessarily lost, because the copies will usually suffice under the "best evidence" rule.

Copies of documents provided should be initialed and dated. In the case of originals, they should be initialed and dated without defacing the document. After the originals have served their purpose (such as upon the conclusion of a trial), they are normally returned to the custodian. Alternative ways to mark original documents include small tickmarks and such techniques as ultraviolet pens. The main point is to mark the document in some distinct way in case you later have to identify it. All evidence, whether or not documentary in nature, should be located in a secure area, and that location should be described in the memorandum. When it leaves that area for some other area, it should be noted in a memorandum. For the fraud examiner to lose his or her case because of the mishandling of evidence is inexcusable. Don't take short cuts with evidence.

Magnetic, Photographic, or Electronic Recordings

There are two types of recordings: those made with consent of the individual and those without. In the case of recordings made with the consent of the individual, the examiner should state for the record that the recording is made with consent. For audio/video recordings made without consent, the examiner should predicate the recording (out of the range of the individual) with the date, time, and the name of the person being recorded. Any recordings, like all evidence, should be maintained until the conclusion of the case in a secure fashion, with a memorandum describing same.

INVESTIGATIVE NOTES

Some courts have held that investigative notes are producible as evidence. You should endeavor to take notes during an interview, but not to the extent that it impedes the process. Just use an amount of notes sufficient to get all the necessary details. Initial and date your own notes and maintain them as evidence in a secure file. You may have to produce them later.

DISCOVERY OF INVESTIGATIVE REPORTS

There is no privilege, per se, for investigative reports and notes, or for any fraud examination, forensic audit or similar services. There are exceptions:

1. If the examiner is conducting an investigation at the request of an attorney in anticipation of litigation, the report is considered in most courts as an attorney/client work product.
2. If the investigation is being conducted by a public authority, such as the police, federal agents, the courts or grand jury, or the like, the report can be considered privileged.

If the examination is being conducted under the authority of the lawyer/client/court privilege, each page should be marked "PRIVILEGED AND CONFIDENTIAL."

INFORMANT AND SOURCE INFORMATION

Under no circumstances whatsoever should the name of a confidential source or informant be disclosed in the report, nor anywhere else in writing. It is recommended that the source or informant be referred to by symbol number. For example, sources could be referred to as S-1, S-2, etc., while informants could carry the designations I-1, I-2, and so on.

Each source or informant contact should be documented on a memorandum of interview, but always referring to the source or informant by his/her symbol number. A statement should be made concerning the reliability of the individual source. The following reporting language is recommended: "A source of known reliability and in a position to furnish relevant information (hereinafter referred to as S-1) advised as follows:" or "A source of unknown reliability but in a position to furnish relevant information (hereinafter referred to as S-1) advised as follows:" or "An informant of unknown reliably or relevance (hereinafter referred to as I-1) furnished the following information."

Do not pay an informant or source without obtaining a receipt. Some informants might balk, but it is your security, so make this a rigid rule. Ensure that your payment is noted in the body of the memorandum of interview. Example: "A source of known reliability and in a position to furnish reliable information (herein after referred to as I–1) was paid $500 on May 1, 1989. I-1 stated as follows:''

The identities of informants should be fully documented and retained in a secure file, available only on a need-to-know basis.

If the examiner has pledged confidentiality to any person for information furnished, that oath must be kept. There are extreme perils for promising confidentiality: you might violate a court order and be sent to jail.

INDEX

A good report contains an index. If there are a limited number of memoranda of interview, the index may be omitted; otherwise it is a good idea. The index should be in chronological order rather than alphabetical, so the reader of the report may easily follow the development of the case.

Glossary of White-Collar Crime Terms

Abuse of Trust: the misuse of one's position and/or of privileged information gained by virtue of that position in order to acquire for oneself (or for another in whom one has an interest) money, property, or some privilege to which one is not entitled. Abuse of trust often involves as well a violation of fiduciary duty.

The victims of such abuses are those who rely to their detriment (i.e., who have been harmed by placing their trust in) the individual or group which misuses a trusted position.

The abuse of trust can occur in many areas, but it arises most frequently in the following four white-collar crime areas:

1. *banking*—where abuse of trust can involve self-dealing in connection with loans or credit to oneself, one's friends or business associates
2. *securities*—where insider information may be used for personal benefit at the expense of clients, stockholders, and others
3. *commercial bribery*—where the procurement and competitive bidding processes may be manipulated
4. *embezzlement and fiduciary violations*—where trustees and others may misuse property or funds in their custody

Remedies for abuses of trust include criminal, civil, and regulatory remedies, enforceable under federal and state law. *See also* Banking Violations, Commercial Bribery, Competitive Procurement Frauds, Embezzlement and Fiduciary Violations, Insider Self-Dealing, Securities Fraud

Advance Fee Schemes: schemes in which assurances of some future benefit are made, with full compensation to the promisor/perpetrator, who has no intention of performing, but rather is interested in obtaining the partial payment requested as a service fee or an advance good faith deposit (often called a "returnable" deposit).

Typical victims of advance fee schemes are businessmen who cannot obtain customary banking or credit sources. They thus pay "deposits" or "fees" to others to arrange loans or credit for them. These frauds are customarily prosecuted under the federal mail fraud statute and state larceny and fraud statutes. Investigated frequently by the postal service.

Antitrust Offenses: combinations in restraint of trade, price fixing or other schemes to unlawfully drive competitors out of business; and/or agreements among competitors to share business according to some agreed formula (such as bid-rigging conspiracies and discriminatory pricing agreements); and/or domination of a business area by one or a few enterprises. Victims of antitrust offenses are businessmen, and purchasers of goods or services who pay higher prices.

Antitrust offenses constitute violations of both federal and state criminal and civil laws. Check with local prosecutors, state attorneys-general, U.S. Department of Justice and regional offices of the U.S. Federal Trade Commission. *See also* Competitive Procurement Fraud, Price-Fixing, Restraint of Trade

Auto Repair Fraud: a form of consumer fraud involving maintenance services to automobiles.

Auto repair frauds fall into several categories:

1. overcharging for labor or parts or use of shoddy or substandard parts
2. failure to perform promised services or repairs
3. charging for services not performed or parts not used
4. performing services or repairs that are unnecessary or unwanted

Remedies usually involve state fraud or larceny laws, state and local licensing laws, etc. Many law enforcement agencies have adopted proactive detection techniques, such as the use of decoy vehicles. *See also* Consumer Fraud, Repair Fraud

Bait and Switch: a form of consumer fraud involving misleading advertising. The substance of the bait and switch is where a store may advertise a "bargain" which may be an inducement (i.e., "bait") to lure a customer to the store where he or she is presented with similar but higher-priced items (i.e., the "switch"). Thus the advertisement does not constitute a bona fide offer for sale of the merchandise in question. This may be because (1) the advertised item is not available on the premises or is available in unreasonably short supply; or (2) acts are undertaken to prevent the customer from purchasing the advertised item in favor of higher-priced merchandise (i.e., by downgrading or "knocking" the advertised goods). Such sales tactics only sometimes are sufficiently blatant to support criminal fraud prosecutions. More frequently they are dealt with through civil remedies invoked by local consumer protection offices and district attorneys (where they have civil jurisdiction), consumer divisions of state attorneys general offices, and the U.S. Federal Trade Commission. *See also* False and Misleading Advertising

Banking Violations: violations by insiders or by customers of banks, savings and loan associations, or credit unions. Insider violations generally involve embezzlements or self-dealing (where insiders lend money to themselves or to businesses in which they have an interest), or take bribes or special favors to make loans or to refrain from collecting loans. Violations by outsiders would include false financial statements to induce a bank to make a loan, the use of fraudulent collateral, check-kiting, and similar offenses.

Victims are depositors and shareholders, bank stockholders, creditors, the federal government as the insurer of deposits, and surety companies that bond bank employees and officials.

These violations are prosecuted under federal and state statutes for embezzlement, false entries in books and records of banks (including computerized records), and misapplications. Violations in state-chartered institutions are often federally prosecuted because deposits are federally insured. *See also* Abuse of Trust, Check-Kiting, Collateral Frauds, Commercial Bribery, Insider Self-Dealing

Bankruptcy Fraud: frauds involving financial insolvency.

Victims of bankruptcy frauds are usually creditors and suppliers of the failed or failing business, although silent partners and stockholders can also be victimized by managers of the business who operate fraudulently. There are two major types of bankruptcy fraud:

1. *the scam* or planned bankruptcy, in which the assets, credit and viability of a business are purposely and systematically milked to obtain cash which is hidden by scam operators.

2. *fraudulent concealments* or diversions of assets in anticipation of insolvency so they cannot be sold for the benefit of creditors (i.e., squirreling away assets when bankruptcy appears imminent)

Planned thefts and fencing activities may be associated with either type of bankruptcy fraud as a means by which assets can be diverted and converted to cash.

Bankruptcy fraud is primarily a federal violation. Some forms of bankruptcy fraud, such as scams would also be violations of state fraud and larceny laws.

Bid-Rigging: see Competitive Procurement Fraud

Boiler Room: a technique used to promote fraudulent sales of securities, charitable solicitations, etc.

The "boiler room" technique involves the use of telephone solicitors, who might operate locally or by use of long distance lines; they call lists of victims, soliciting them to buy. The telephone sales persons work on high commissions using preplanned sales pitches. Their services, particularly in charitable solicitations, are sometimes sold to otherwise legitimate enterprises—which rarely see very much of the collections. The technique depends primarily upon glib misrepresentations.

The use of this technique exposes the perpetrators to criminal prosecution under federal wire fraud and mail fraud laws and under fraud and nonregistration provisions of the Securities Acts administered by the U.S. Securities and Exchange Commission. It also exposes the users to criminal or civil action in state and local jurisdictions under state fraud statutes, state "blue-sky laws" regulating securities sales, and local and state laws requiring licensing and filing of information in connection with charitable solicitations. *See also* Charity and Religious Frauds, Securities Fraud

Business Opportunity Schemes: one of the most prevalent and varied forms of fraud, in which victims are offered the opportunity to make a living, or to supplement their income, by going into business for themselves (full or part-time), by purchasing franchises or equipment to manufacture some item, sell merchandise, or perform some service.

Victims are generally individuals with some small pool of money they have saved and to whom the prospect of the promised independence and/or income is attractive.

Such schemes range from being total shams to being opportunities whose promised returns are highly illusory.

The operators of these schemes have essentially one goal, which is to acquire the money of subscriber or investor victims. Work-at-home merchandising schemes (knitting machines, raising minks, etc.) or the sale of distributorships (cosmetics, special rug-cleaning processes, etc.) are common examples of the kinds of situations involved in the business opportunity fraud. The opportunity presented by the fraud operator often includes the promise of "guaranteed" markets for the goods or services to be produced. Often the schemes induce the victim to enlist other victims, creating a pyramid scheme.

These schemes are generally prosecuted under federal mail fraud laws, and state laws which proscribe larceny or false pretenses. Check with U.S. Postal Inspector, U.S. Federal Trade Commission, state attorneys general offices, and local prosecutors. *See also* Franchising Frauds, Pyramid Schemes, Self-Improvement Schemes, Work-at-Home Schemes

Chain-Referral Schemes: any scheme in which the victim is induced to part with money or property on the representation that he or she will make money through inducing others to buy into the same deal.

First-tier victims usually believe that those whom they involve in the scheme (second-tier victims) will themselves make money; but since second-tier victims can only make money by involving third-tier victims, and so on, the scheme must eventually collapse. Generally only the fraud operators who manage the scheme make money on it; few first- or second-tier victims (especially if they are honest) have a sufficient number of victimizable friends and acquaintances to come out whole.

One common type of chain-referral scheme is the chain-letter; more sophisticated is the "pyramid scheme," in which (for example) the victim is sold a franchise to sell both merchandise and other franchises, with the promise of profits on merchandise sold and commissions, or "overrides," on merchandise sold by any second- or later-tier victim who buys a franchise. The profits appear, therefore, to bein selling franchises rather than in selling merchandise. These schemes ultimately collapse of their own weight.

Chain-referral schemes are criminally prosecuted under federal mail fraud statutes and state fraud laws. Civil actions have been undertaken by the U.S. Federal Trade Commission, state attorneys general offices, and local prosecutors. *See also* Merchandising Frauds, Pyramid Schemes

Charity and Religious Frauds: frauds arising out of the fund-raising activities of charitable and/or religious groups.

Almost anyone can be the victim of such frauds, often without knowing it, but even where the victim may later suspect the fraud, his or her individual loss may be so small that there is little desire to pursue the matter. Three types of fraud situations are observed in this area:

1. *the bogus charity or religious group*—where money is solicited for a nonexistent organization or cause, or for a charitable front created for the sole purpose of soliciting funds which will end up in the collectors' pockets

2. *misrepresentation of association with a charity or religious group*—where money is solicited on behalf of a legitimate organization or cause by those who have no ties to such organization or cause, and no intention of giving to the group

3. *misrepresentation of the benefits or uses of contributions*—those solicited for donations to a legitimate charity or religious organization are not aware that most of the money collected reverts not to the charitable cause but rather is used to cover the cost of professional fund-raisers and/or administrative overhead expenses. (This is a gray area, since professional fund-raisers perform a legitimate service for which they may properly and legitimately be compensated.)

In some instances charitable organizations themselves are the victims of con men who use them as a front, keeping the lion's share of the collections, as in the case of boiler room operations (see "Boiler Rooms," above). In other instances the solicitation falls into a gray area where otherwise legitimate charities and causes will cover up the fact that most of the monies collected go to salaries, fund-raisers, etc. Depending on how blatant the operation is, or where in the gray area a con falls, there may be federal criminal violations (i.e., mail fraud or wire fraud), violations of state fraud statutes, violations of local licensing laws dealing with charitable solicitations, or of state laws requiring filing of information with state agencies and full disclosure as to funds collected, costs of solicitation, and monies provided charitable beneficiaries. *See also* Boiler Room

Check-Kiting: any of a variety of frauds against banks which depend for success upon the time it takes to clear checks.

The most common form of check-kiting involves the opening of two or more accounts. Balances are built up in each by deposits from the others. Checks are circulated between accounts, with no money taken out of any account, until at least one of the banks develops confidence in the depositor. Then the depositor takes money out of that bank, depending on the circulation of checks between the two or more banks, and the several days it takes to clear checks (especially between different cities), to prevent detection.

Banks are victims of check-kites. When first discovered, check-kites appear far more costly than when all transactions are analyzed, since hundreds of thousands of dollars in checks may be circulated to steal only a few thousand dollars. In some instances, however, massive amounts have been stolen. In many instances businessmen employ check-kites when they cannot get loans from banks to tide themselves over a temporary business situation, and intend to (and often do) put the money back into the accounts before the check-kite is discovered. In such instances the bank has been fraudulently induced to unwittingly grant what amounts to an interest-free loan.

Check-kites are generally prosecuted under federal laws dealing with mail fraud and banking fraud. Local law enforcement investigations should carefully consider signs of check-kites in cases investigated, since they may play a part in other, broader fraud schemes. *See also* Banking Violations

Collateral Frauds: frauds involving the holding, taking or offering of collateral pursuant to a financial transaction.

In many instances these will be banking transactions (see ''Banking Violations'' above). Beyond this, however, such frauds may be encountered in connection with any transaction in which security is provided, such as security for private loans, nonexistent accounts receivable sold or pledged to factors. In some cases collateral used as security may not belong to the person offering it. It could be stolen, e.g. stolen securities; or borrowed, or already subject to an undisclosed lien or other encumbrance; or there can be some gross misrepresentation as to its value.

Collateral frauds may be violations of federal banking laws, the mail fraud statute, or state fraud laws. They may be elements in banking or corporate violations involving self-dealing, as where a bank officer makes a loan knowing the collateral is bad. Collateral frauds may also be involved in organized crime activities, e.g., obtaining proceeds of stolen securities not by an attempted sale which would precipitate discovery when title was transferred, but by their use as collateral for loans. *See also* Banking Violations

Commercial Bribery: a form of insider fraud or abuse of trust in which an employee or officer of a private enterprise or government entity is given a bribe or some other valuable consideration to induce the employee or official to make a purchase or grant a contract or some special privilege (such as a zoning variance or license).

Commercial bribery is a violation of specific statutes in a large number of states, and falls within the proscriptions of more general criminal statutes in other jurisdictions. It may violate numerous federal statutes, depending on the manner in which it is executed.

Competitive Procurement Fraud: unlawful manipulation of the public or private contracting process.

Victims are competitors not participating in the fraud, the public or private entity soliciting bids (which are believed to be competitive), and customers or constituents of those entities who do not realize benefits that would be derived from a truly competitive procurement process.

Three main forms of competitive procurement frauds are:

1. *bid-rigging*—form of illegal anti-competitive conduct in which bidders in a competitive procurement collusively set their bids so as to deprive the bid solicitor of a competitive process. The effect is an administered bidding process in which the winner and the terms and prices of the goods and services involved in the procurement are set by the conspirators rather than by the "competitive" process. Parties to the conspiracy are thus able to divide among themselves a relevant set of procurement contracts and to fix prices for goods and services at the same time.

2. *bid-fixing*—a form of illegal manipulation of the procurement process whereby one bidding party is provided with inside information (by the bid solicitor or an agent thereof) which enables said bidder to gain an unfair advantage over other bidders

3. *bribery/kickbacks*—situations in which procurement contracts are let on the basis of the payment of bribes and kickbacks to procurement officials rather than on the basis of competitive procurement guidelines

Competitive procurement frauds are prosecuted under federal and state criminal laws proscribing mail fraud, criminal conspiracy, bribery or kickbacks. Proof in these cases usually involves (1) the most painstaking analysis of bidding patterns, (2) examination of relationships between bids to the entity whose defrauding is being investigated and bids by the same bidders to other entities for possible broader patterns of trade-offs, and (3) close scrutiny of performance on the jobs done pursuant to contracts. *See also* Commercial Bribery, False Claims, Kickbacks, Public/Official Corruption

Computer Fraud: frauds arising out of the increasing use of the computer to maintain business and governmental records, such as those relating to inventories, accounts payable and receivable, customer and payroll records.

Often the thief or fraud artist is the computer system operator or someone with access to the computer's memory system. The frauds are usually related to embezzlement or theft, but can involve data destruction, alteration, and manipulation.

Consumer Fraud: frauds of the marketplace involving seller misrepresentations to buyers. Victims are consumers of all kinds, individual and institutional, public and private.

Common forms of consumer fraud include:

1. selling of useless goods or services, represented as beneficial; e.g., "miracle" face creams
2. misrepresentation of product performance, benefits or safety
3. false and misleading advertising
4. failure to service items after sale, including reneging on warranties
5. repair fraud
6. hidden charges with respect to financing, necessary follow-up services, etc.
7. weights and measures violations

See also Bait and Switch, False and Misleading Advertising, Merchandising Frauds, Repair Fraud, Weight and Measures Frauds

Coupon Redemption Frauds: frauds which involve cheating manufacturers or merchandisers who promote sales of their products by offering coupons which return part of the purchase price when the products are purchased.

Many manufacturers, primarily in the food business, place coupons in newspaper and magazine ads offering, for example, "15 cents off" if the product is purchased. The grocery store is supposed to redeem the coupon, and will customarily receive a service charge of about five cents for handling the transaction. Frauds are committed against the manufacturers by amassing large numbers of coupons and submitting them to manufacturers without any bona fide purchases of the products.

The modus operandi of this type of fraud involves two basic steps: (1) collecting coupons, and (2) processing for redemption. Collecting coupons may be done by going through large numbers of old newspapers and magazines; sometimes this is done by trash-collection or waste-disposal companies as a side venture. Processing for collection requires the collaboration of retail merchants, and is most efficiently done with the cooperation of officials of food retail chains, frequently without the knowledge of their companies.

These frauds have involved organized criminal syndicates. They have usually been federally prosecuted under the mail fraud statute, though they could be prosecuted under numerous state fraud statutes.

Credit Card Frauds: frauds arising out of the application for, extension and use of credit cards.

Victims are the issuers of the credit cards. Common credit card abuses include:

1. use of stolen credit cards
2. false statements in application for credit card, including application under a false name

3. buying with no intention to ever pay, by use of a credit card which was originally legitimately obtained

Credit card cases are usually referred to prosecutive agencies by credit card company investigators, who have completed major portions of the investigation. Prosecution can be undertaken under the federal mail fraud statute, and under state fraud, larceny, and forgery laws.

Credit-Rating Schemes: frauds arising out of the application for, extension and use of credit.

Victims are generally the providers of credit. Common credit-related schemes include:

1. sale of good credit ratings to high risk applicants
2. false statements in application for credit
3. creation of false credit accounts for purpose of theft

The modus operandi of such schemes varies widely. In recent periods employees of credit-rating organizations have altered credit ratings for payment, sometimes using computer techniques; false financial statements are a most common method. On a smaller scale is a fraud which operates like shoplifting, opening a charge account with false information in order to purchase and take away goods simultaneously with opening the accounts.

Cases involving sales of credit ratings and alteration of computerized rating sare commonly prosecuted under the federal mail fraud statute, since they have been nationwide in scope. They would also be prosecutable under state laws proscribing fraud, false pretenses, and larceny. *See also* Loan or Lending Frauds

Debt Consolidation or Adjustment Swindles: swindles perpetrated against people who are heavily in debt, and against their creditors, by purporting to provide a service which will systematically organize the marshalling of the debtor's assets and income to repay all creditors over a period of time, with creditors refraining from pressing for immediate payment of all sums due.

Some such services are provided by legitimate private agencies, and provision is made for such processes in non-bankruptcy proceedings in federal bankruptcy courts.

The modus operandi of this fraud is often to use heavy TV and newspaper advertising to lure debtors into signing up. The fraud operators then take their fee, usually a heavy percentage of the total debt, in advance. Sometimes they talk creditors into waiting for their money; in other instances they falsely tell the debtors they have done so. They then take debtors' assets, and a portion of their weekly or monthly earnings, paying themselves first, then (usually only after they have their entire "fee") doling out the remainder to creditors. Frequently creditors receive little or nothing, and the debtors are left minus their fees and still in debt.

These schemes have been prosecuted under the federal mail fraud law, state general fraud, larceny, and false pretenses statutes.

Directory Advertising Schemes: frauds arising from the selling of printed mass advertising services.

These schemes are of two basic kinds: (1) impersonation schemes, in which con men send bills to business enterprises which look like those customarily received, e.g., from the phone company for "yellow page" advertising, with directions to make checks payable to entities which look like legitimate payees of such bills; and (2) schemes in which it is promised that advertising will appear in a publication distributed to potential customers but where, in fact, distribution will be limited to the advertisers themselves, if the directory is printed at all.

These cases have been federally prosecuted under the mail fraud statute and can be prosecuted under state general fraud laws, larceny, and false pretenses statutes.

Embezzlement and Fiduciary Frauds: the conversion to one's own use or benefit of the money or property of another over which one has custody, to which one is entrusted, or over which one exerts a fiduciary's control.

These crimes are prosecuted under specific statutes, such as those dealing with embezzlement, banking misapplications, etc., the federal mail fraud statute, federal and state laws regulating brokers and investment services, and state general fraud or larceny statutes.

Victims are institutions, businesses in general, pension funds, and beneficiaries of estates being managed by fiduciaries. *See also* Abuse of Trust, Banking Violations, Insider Self-Dealing, Loan or Lending Frauds

Employment Agency Frauds: fraudulent solicitations of money or fees in order to find employment for, to guarantee the employment of, or to improve the employability of another.

Victims are generally individuals seeking jobs or hoping to improve skills in order to obtain better-paying employment opportunities. Variations of employment-related frauds include:

1. *phony job agencies*—where an agency solicits advance fees in order to find employment for the victim, when in fact the service is neither performed nor intended to be provided

2. *job-training frauds*—where money is received from victims to train them for specific employment and (1) the training is not supplied; (2) guaranteed job opportunities on completion of training are not supplied; or (3) the training is misrepresented as being "certified" or "recognized" by employers when it is not and does not qualify victim for anticipated employment

These frauds are prosecutable under the federal mail fraud statute and state general fraud statutes. Substantial recoveries have been made for victims of such frauds by the U.S. Federal Trade Commission.

Energy Crisis Frauds: frauds arising out of the sale of goods or services related to energy or fuel use, saving, and production.

Victims are generally individual consumers interested in stretching their dollars spent on energy sources and/or saving energy. Energy schemes include the following types of frauds:

1. *merchandise schemes*—sale of worthless or bogus items which do not deliver the specific benefits promised or the degree of benefit promised, such as carburetor gadgets to save gasoline or phony solar-heating systems. Often these frauds occur because of the novelty of the items involved, combined with the naivete of the victims.

2. *weights and measures violations*—short-weighing or measuring of fuels to customers; for example, manipulation of gas-pump measuring devices, or misrepresentation of fuel, e.g., changing of octane ratings on fuel pumps

3. *discriminatory allocation of fuel* by distributors to sub-distributors and retailers, in consideration of commercial bribes to distributors' executives or special payments to companies with the power to make distribution in the form of under-the-table payments or required purchases of other items—useful or not needed—in violation of anti-trust or other laws

These cases can be prosecuted under special state statutes, such as those dealing with weights and measures, or violations of specific administrative regulations promulgated to deal with energy crises, and (in appropriate situations) as commercial bribery or antitrust violations. *See also* Antitrust Offenses, Commercial Bribery, Merchandising Schemes, Weights and Measures Violations

False and Misleading Advertising: use of untrue or deceptive promotional techniques resulting in consumer fraud.

Victims are consumers relying to their detriment on the false or misrepresented advertising or promotion. The following kinds of practices are prominent among those which fall under the heading of false and misleading advertising:

1. advertising as a "sale" item an item at the regular or higher price

2. misrepresentations concerning the size, weight, volume or utility of an item

3. falsely claiming an attribute which a good or service does not in fact possess

4. misstatement of the true costs of a good or service through the use of confusing payment provisions or otherwise

These violations are prosecutable under the federal mail fraud statute, state general fraud statutes, and specific statutes dealing with false advertising.

Administrative and other civil remedies are frequently invoked against these offenses, and local consumer protection offices provide mediation remedies, since these offenses frequently fall into grey areas with respect to wrongful intent. *See also* Bait and Switch, Consumer Fraud

False Claims: fraudulent written claims for payment for goods or services not provided as claimed, to public or private entities. False claims may involve activities such as:

1. presentation of a bogus claim or claimant, e.g., the ghost payroll situation
2. misrepresentation of the qualifications of an otherwise ineligible claim or claimant, such as welfare fraud
3. false representation of the extent of payment or benefits to which claimant is entitled, like overtime-pay frauds
4. claims for reimbursement for goods and services allegedly provided to nonexistent recipients, e.g., Medicaid fraud, by service providers

The false claim will carry all the trappings of a legitimate claim and is most successfully undertaken by an individual(s) with a thoroughgoing knowledge of the system being defrauded. The false claim is one of the basic implementing tools of the white-collar thief and can run the gamut from the elaborate computerized creation of fictitious claimants to the simple manipulation of numbers on a time card. False claims will sometimes involve the cooperation of executives or officials of the private or governmental entity to which such claims are submitted.

Violations are prosecuted under both general and specific fraud statutes, for example, that dealing specifically with false claims submitted to the federal government, larceny, and false pretenses statutes. Such violations are also generally a basis for civil action, whether or not the proof is sufficient to meet the criminal standard of proof. *See also* Commercial Bribery, Frauds Against Government Programs, Ghost Payroll, Medicaid/Medicare Fraud, Overtime Pay Fraud, Welfare Fraud

False Statements: the concealment or misrepresentation of a fact material to the decision-making process of an entity, with the result that the entity accepts the false statement.

The false statement is often the means by which a fraudulent scheme to obtain money or benefit is effected either because (among other things):

1. the false statement constitutes the underlying documentation for a false claim; or
2. the false statement impedes discovery of the fraudulent scheme; i.e., covers up the fraud. These statements often provide the opportunity for conditioning the victim to unquestioningly accept and approve a false claim.

On the federal level, false statement prosecutions under 18 U.S.C. 1001 and 1014 have been a major weapon against white-collar crime directed at the federal government. Even where such statutes are not present as part of the arsenal of state statutes, their use for the purposes outlined above will be valuable in showing the manner and means by which frauds were perpetrated, in prosecutions under state general fraud, larceny, and false pretenses statutes. *See also* False Claims, Frauds Against Government Programs, Ghost Payrolls

Franchising Frauds: frauds arising out of business-opportunity situations in which individuals invest time, talents, and money to obtain a business enterprise, relying on others (i.e., the franchiser) to supply at prearranged rates specified goods and services, such as necessary business structures, the goods to be sold or materials with which goods can be made, advertising, and an exclusive territorial market or market area for the franchisee's output.

Victims generally invest their major assets in what are fraudulent franchise opportunities.

Frauds in franchises generally arise because one or more of the following occurs:

1. Franchisor has no intention of performing on any of his obligations; i.e., the "franchise" is a complete ruse to acquire victim-franchisee's initial investment monies.
2. Franchisor fails to provide promised goods or services essential to success of franchise.
3. Franchisor makes success for franchisee either difficult or impossible by extending too many franchises in a given locale or market area.
4. Franchisor has misrepresented the market or demand for goods/services central to the franchise, or has misrepresented the level of skills needed to realize franchise profitability.

Number 1 is outright fraud, while numbers 2–4 represent variations ranging from fraud to shady dealing, to failure to fulfill contractual obligations.

Franchise frauds are federally prosecuted under the federal mail fraud statute, and under state statutes proscribing frauds, larceny, or false pretenses. In some instances, where success does not depend on the victim's own labor, the franchise agreement may be considered a "security," and enforcement may be possible under securities acts in the jurisdiction of the U.S. Securities and Exchange Commission or state securities regulatory agencies. *See also* Business-Opportunity Schemes, Chain-Referral Schemes

Frauds Against Government Benefit Programs: unlawful application for and receipt of money, property or benefit from public programs designed to confer money, property or benefit under specific guidelines.

Victims are federal, state, and local governments, their taxpayers, and qualified, intended beneficiaries of such programs.

Typical kinds of frauds suffered by government programs include:

1. *misrepresentations of applicants' qualifications* concerning program eligibility, for example, food stamps received by ineligible persons
2. *false billing/vouchering* in which public programs make good on false claims for services not rendered or for nonexistent beneficiaries, such as physician's claims under Medicaid programs for patients not treated, or for specific treatments not provided

3. *inflated billing/vouchering/claiming*, by which public programs are charged more than allowable costs, such as housing fraud where cost of construction is inflated so that builder/owner receives more than total cost of land and buildings and avoids making investment required by law and administrative guidelines

4. *embezzlement*, by which employees or officials of public programs convert funds, property or benefits to their own use (often via their custodial, fiduciary or programmatic relationship to the program), e.g. licensed dispensers of food stamps converting funds to their own use

5. *misuse of properly obtained funds, etc.* in which money, property or benefit conferred under very specific guidelines concerning end use are received and utilized for unauthorized ends; e.g., receipt of federal loan funds (such as student educational loans) with failure to use such for specified purposes

These frauds are prosecutable under specific enforcement sections of statutes setting up government programs, as well as statutes proscribing false claims, false statements, and conspiracy. They will also be violations of general fraud and larceny statutes on the state level. *See also* Embezzlement and Fiduciary Funds, False Claims, False Statements, Medicaid/Medicare Fraud, Welfare Fraud

Funeral Frauds: class of guilt-inducement frauds relying for success on the emotional stress of victims who have lost or are about to lose loved ones through death. Victims are the relatives or friends of deceased or terminally ill persons.

Funeral-related frauds often take the form of consumer and merchandising frauds and generally involve one or more of the following practices:

1. Relying on the guilt or anxiety of bereaved relatives. Victims are persuaded to contract for unnecessary or unduly elaborate funeral services or merchandise.

2. Billing for funeral expenses to include charges for services not performed (here fraud artist relies on victims' anxiety or guilt to preclude memory of whether service was performed or not and/or to preclude victim's challenge of the bill for payment).

3. Services or goods in connection with burial are represented as legally required, when in fact they are not.

4. Contracts are made for future provision of goods or services in connection with funeral and burial arrangements which fraud operator does not intend or has no capacity to provide; e.g., sale of nonexistent cemetery plots.

Since many such abuses fall into gray areas of consumer fraud and misrepresentation, state attorneys general and consumer protection agencies often undertake to provide civil mediation remedies. In addition, the U.S. Federal Trade Commission has expressed considerable interest in fraudulent activities in this area. *See also* Consumer Fraud, Guilt-Inducement Fraud, Merchandising Fraud

Ghost Payrolls: form of false claim in which fictitious employees are added to a payroll and payments to these employees revert to the payroll manipulator(s). Fictitious employees are commonly referred to as "ghosts."

Victims are generally public and private entities responsible for honoring payroll claims. Often the ghost payroll is used to defraud government programs designed to provide employment for the unemployed or disadvantaged. This is closely related to welfare and unemployment-insurance frauds. This device can also be used in cost-plus contracts to cheat governmental entities, or by managers of subunits in private enterprises to steal from their parent organizations.

A variation on the ghost payroll is the overtime-pay fraud in which false claims are made with respect to overtime work by bona fide employees.

Prosecution on the federal level would be under mail fraud, conspiracy, false claim, and false statement statutes. On the state level, such prosecution would be under general fraud, false pretenses, and larceny statutes. *See also* False Claims, Frauds Against Government Programs

Guilt Inducement Frauds: frauds perpetrated via the tactic of inducing guilt or anxiety in the victim concerning his or her relationship or obligations to another person who is significant to victim (i.e., a child, parent, spouse).

Victims are individuals who, susceptible to the guilt or anxiety induced by the fraud operator, are persuaded to part with money or property in the belief that the questioned transaction will atone for any "shortcomings" or fulfill "obligations" they have toward another.

Because guilt inducement is a major tactic used to secure voluntary victim action, it cuts across many fraud areas. A few examples of the dynamics of such frauds are noted below:

1. Encyclopedia salesmen induce victims to enter into purchase contracts for books having suggested to victim that imminent scholastic failure of children can be expected if such purchase is not made. Here a merchandising fraud is consummated by the offender's capacity to induce parental anxiety in victims.

2. Children of deceased are persuaded to purchase elaborate and unnecessary funeral arrangements construed by the fraud operator to constitute a "decent" burial. The implication in such funeral frauds is that failure to buy the most expensive items, or close checking of the details of bills, are tantamount to lack of affection or respect for the deceased.

3. Unnecessary and imprudent expenditures for life insurance are made by many wage-earners to whom it is suggested that failure to subscribe to such policies constituted a failure toward one's spouse and family.

4. Self-improvement merchandise and facilities are marketed to victims on the basis of such guilt inducements as "you owe it to your spouse to be as (lovely, manly, successful, etc.) as you can be" or "you can only be a failure if you fail to take advantage of opportunities to improve your (looks, job, speaking ability)."

Depending on the level and quantity of misrepresentations involved in such frauds, remedies will range from criminal prosecutions (mail fraud, state general fraud statutes, etc.) to regulatory or administrative measures at federal, state, and local levels to enjoin deceptive practices, and compel reimbursement of victims. *See also* Funeral Frauds, Self-Improvement Frauds

Home-Repair or -Improvement Frauds: frauds arising out of the provision of goods and services in connection with the repair, maintenance or general improvement of housing units.

Victims are generally homeowners but may also include public agencies or programs which subsidize and/or underwrite home purchase and ownership. Home repair or improvement frauds include the following practices:

1. shoddy or incompetent workmanship
2. sale of overpriced or unfit materials or services for home-repair projects
3. failure to provide services or goods paid for by customer
4. submission of false claims for materials or work not provided
5. misrepresentation of the need for particular materials or services to be performed
6. misrepresentations or concealment of the costs of credit, or of the nature of liens securing the payment obligations

The victim may be told that the home is in violation of building codes or in a condition substandard to the rest of the neighborhood, endangering the value of the home or the safety of the victim's family.

These violations are prosecutable under a broad range of statutes including mail fraud, statutes aimed at fraud against the federal government, state general fraud statutes, local licensing laws, including those regulating door-to-door solicitations. This is a major area for administrative and mediational activities on the part of attorneys-general offices and municipal consumer-protection offices. *See also* Consumer Fraud, Merchandising Frauds, Repair Fraud

Insider Self-Dealing: benefiting oneself or others in whom one has an interest by trading on privileged information or position. Insider self-dealing is a major cause in bank failure.

Typical violative situations include those where a corporate officer or director trades in the stock of his company on the basis of inside information as to prospective profits or losses; bank officers lending money to themselves or businesses in which they have an interest; corporate executives or purchasing officials setting up suppliers of goods and services to contract with their companies, etc. For nature of enforcement remedies, *see also* Abuse of Trust, Banking Violations, Commercial Bribery, Securities Violations

Insider Trading: the use of nonpublic information to make beneficial stock trades. For example, a stockbroker receives confidential information that a company is introducing a revolutionary product. The broker then acquires stock in the company. The news is then released to the public, causing the stock price to go up. Thereafter, the broker sells his stock for a gain.

Insurance Fraud: fraud perpetrated by or against insurance companies. Victims may be the clients or stockholders of insurance companies or the insurer itself. Insurance fraud breaks down into the following categories and subclasses:

1. Frauds perpetrated by insurers against clients/stockholders include the following deliberate and intentional practices.
   a. failure to provide coverage promised and paid for when claim is made
   b. failure to compensate or reimburse properly on claims
   c. manipulation of risk classes and high-risk policy-holder categories
   d. embezzlement or abuse of trust in management of premium funds and other assets of insurance companies
   e. twisting—illegal sales practices in which insurer persuades customers to cancel current policies and purchase new ones from it
2. Types of frauds perpetrated by insureds against insurance providers:
   a. filing of bogus claims for compensation or reimbursement; multiple claims for same loss from different insurers
   b. inflating reimbursable costs on claim statements
   c. payment of bribes or kickbacks to local agents to retain coverage or coverage in improper risk category
   d. failure to disclose information or false statements made in application for insurance

Cases are often developed by insurance company investigators or state insurance departments and referred to investigative and prosecutive agencies. Federal prosecutions are generally under the mail fraud statute; state and local prosecutions under general fraud laws, larceny statutes, etc. Where the frauds are committed against insurers, assistance may be obtained from the Insurance Crime Prevention Institute (ICPI), Westport, Connecticut. *See also* Abuse of Trust, False Claims

Investment Frauds: frauds in which victims, induced by the prospect of capital growth and high rates of return, invest money in imprudent, illusory or totally bogus projects or businesses.

Investment frauds generally victimize those with a pool of liquid or convertible assets, ranging from retirees or near-retirement-age people, widows or widowers, to high-income professionals and businessmen. Hallmarks of many such frauds are:

1. higher than average promised rates of return
2. developmental nature of investment object, i.e., project or business is not a mature entity
3. sales made by strangers, e.g. through boiler rooms
4. generalized definition of nature and scope of project, lack of detailed plans by which progress might be observed

5. object or site of investment geographically remote or distant from investors

6. failure to fully disclose facts material to investor prior to commitment of money

7. nonregistration with U.S. Securities and Exchange Commission and comparable state regulatory agencies

8. promise of special advantages, e.g., tax shelters

Examples of such frauds are numerous and are generally violations of special statutes, such as the federal Securities Acts enforced by the U.S. Securities and Exchange Commission, state securities regulatory laws enforced by state agencies, the mail fraud statute, and state general fraud, larceny, and false pretenses statutes. Where land frauds are involved, the U.S. Department of Housing and Urban Development and state agencies which require full-disclosure filings will have enforcement jurisdiction. In this area of enforcement, state and local investigatory and prosecutive agencies can anticipate major support and assistance from federal agencies which have overlapping or parallel enforcement interests. *See also* Land Fraud, Ponzi Schemes, Pyramid Schemes, Securities Fraud

Land Fraud: a type of investment fraud which involves sale of land, based on extensive misrepresentations as to value, quality, facilities, state of development.

Victims are usually individuals buying land for retirement, investment, or both simultaneously. Land frauds usually consist of one or more of the following practices. The sale of land or of interest in land:

1. to which seller has no present title or claim of right; i.e., seller cannot properly transfer title or interest to buyer as represented at the time of sale

2. about which a misrepresentation or failure to disclose a material fact has occurred

3. at inflated or unjustified prices based on misrepresentations to purchaser

4. on the promise of future performance or development which the seller neither intends to provide nor can reasonably expect to occur

Misrepresentations usually involve presence of utilities, water, roads, recreational facilities, credit terms, etc. Such frauds have been perpetrated for decades, and resulted in numerous successful prosecutions on both federal and local prosecutive levels, as well as in extensive civil actions by regulatory agencies which have resulted in both extensive restitution to victims and options to cancel improvident purchases. Federal prosecutions are undertaken with the mail fraud statute, and it may be anticipated that there will be increasing prosecutions for failure to comply with recently enacted registration and disclosure laws under the jurisdiction of the U.S. Department of Housing and Urban Development; there are parallel state registration and disclosure laws. Local prosecutions have been undertaken under general fraud laws, false advertising, and larceny statutes. There is substantial federal-state-local cooperation in this enforcement area. *See also* Investment Fraud

Landlord-Tenant Frauds: unlawful practices involving the leasing or renting of property. Common fraud practices by landlords include:

1. keeping two sets of books, i.e., tax violations
2. schemes to avoid return of security deposits
3. rental of property to which one has no title claim of right
4. deliberate and persistent violations of safety and health regulations, and failure to provide heat, services, etc.

These white-collar crimes are usually misdemeanors, and violations of local ordinances. Frauds such as schemes to cheat tenants out of their security deposits should be prosecutable under state's general fraud laws.

Loan or Lending Fraud: unlawful practices arising out of the lending or borrowing of money. Victims may be financial institutions, the stockholders of financial institutions, or borrowers.

Loan frauds generally involve either the failure to disclose information relevant to the extension or granting of a loan or the provision of false information, or both. When perpetrated by the lender, loan frauds may take the form of:

1. lending to oneself through ghost accounts
2. lending to friends or entities in which one has an interest
3. commercial bribery, approving loans to those who would not qualify as borrowers, i.e., in exchange for kickbacks or other considerations
4. advance fee schemes, by which borrowers remit money to secure a loan which is not forthcoming or for which no payment was necessary

When perpetrated by borrowers, loan frauds may take the form of:

1. false statements, by which a loan to one who is not entitled is fraudulently obtained
2. improper use of legitimately obtained loans, where improper use was intended at the time the loan application was made
3. larceny by false pretenses, by which loan is obtained with no intention of repayment

A separate and important dimension of loan fraud involves the misuse or misrepresentation of items of collateral and collateral accounts.

These frauds are prosecutable under federal statutes proscribing mail fraud, banking frauds, securities frauds, program frauds (such as those involving construction or repair loans which are federally guaranteed). They are also prosecutable under general state fraud laws, false pretenses statutes, and larceny statutes. *See also* Abuse of Trust, Banking Violations, Collateral Frauds, False Statements

Medicaid/Medicare Fraud: fraudulent practices arising in connection with the receipt or provision of health-care services under government-financed programs.

Such frauds are nearly always perpetrated by health-care providers (both professionals and facility operators) against the government(s) financing the programs and/or the intended beneficiaries of such programs. Specific Medicaid/ Medicare fraud practices include:

1. *pingponging*—referring patients to other doctors in a clinic in order to claim reimbursements for the "consultation" rather than for bona fide patient treatment or observation
2. *upgrading*—billing for services not provided
3. *steering*—sending patients to a particular pharmacy, medical lab, etc., for required prescriptions or services, and receiving kickbacks therefrom
4. *shorting*—delivering less medication, e.g., pills, than prescribed while charging for full amount
5. *procurement abuses*—establishment of supply/purchase arrangements with firms which pay kickbacks to health care facilities or which are owned by those controlling the facility itself
6. *false claims*—submission of claims for which payment from government for patients who do not exist, or were never seen or treated

These violations are prosecutable under federal fraud statutes, including mail fraud, false claim, and false statement statutes, as well as specific statutes in legislation authorizing such programs. Since many such programs are administered through state agencies and involve use of state funds, state general fraud, false pretenses, and larceny states will also be applicable. *See also* Competitive Procurement Abuse, False Claims, Frauds against Government Benefit Programs, Kickbacks

Medical Frauds: unlawful activities arising out of the provision and sale of bogus, highly questionable or dangerous medical services, cures, or medications.

Victims are often individuals who have been given little hope of recovery or improvement by traditional medical establishments and desperately seek any promise of ameliorating their condition. Also victimized are persons who are poorly informed and thus vulnerable to claims made by medical fraud artists, often in such areas as beauty treatments and cosmetics. Medical frauds generally include one or more of the following abuses:

1. *quackery*—false representation of oneself as a legally trained and licensed health-care professional
2. *fake cures*—sale of bogus or highly questionable "cures" for specific illnesses or diseases
3. *misrepresentations of medication*—misrepresentations as to the therapeutic value of medications, and/or omissions made regarding known side effects of medications
4. *misrepresentations of treatment*—false statements made with regard to the therapeutic value of a particular treatment protocol, with regard to its degree of "acceptance" or

bona fide medical practice; and/or omissions of material information concerning known side effects of treatment that would affect patient's choice of treatment program

Such frauds may operate through misrepresentations made to victims themselves, as well as to regulatory agencies such as the U.S. Food and Drug Administration. In the latter case the misrepresentations may involve the nature of test results or the methodology or procedures involved in conducting such tests.

Federal enforcement has been dominant in this field, through the mail fraud prosecutions, Food and Drug Administration efforts, and U.S. Federal Trade Commission proceedings. Local quacks should, however, be open to prosecution or control under general fraud statutes, larceny and false pretenses statutes, and vigorous exercise of licensing powers with respect to health and beauty services.

Merchandising Frauds: an umbrella term for a broad variety of consumer frauds involving misrepresentations inducing the victims to purchase merchandise, which either is not as represented or which in fact will never be delivered to them. The frauds usually involve one or more of the following aspects:

1. representation that the item is sold at lower than usual price, whereas it is in fact sold at the usual retail price or higher
2. misrepresentation as to the quality or utility of the merchandise
3. misrepresentation as to the ultimate price, or credit terms
4. misleading information as to warranties, cancellation of transaction, returnability of merchandise, and validity of "money-back guarantees"
5. solicitation of money with no intention to deliver the merchandise promised
6. "Bait and Switch" frauds

Victims customarily buy from door-to-door salesmen or are entrapped when they respond to newspaper, magazine, radio or TV advertisements. Examples of such frauds include door-to-door magazine subscriptions sales, hearing-aid frauds, bulk sales of items falsely represented to be at wholesale prices (i.e., freezer food sales), and false sales (where items sold are falsely represented to be priced at less than regular prices, or sold pursuant to closeout of a business or replacement of inventory).

Enforcement with respect to these frauds has been successfully undertaken at federal, state, and local levels. Laws invoked have included federal mail and wire fraud statutes, the U.S. Federal Trade Commission Act, general state fraud and false advertising statutes, and local licensing laws governing door-to-door sales and solicitations. *See also* Consumer Fraud

Nursing Home Abuses: a variety of frauds perpetrated by individuals who provide institutional nursing and convalescent care to patients, particularly the aged.

Victims of such frauds are the patients of such facilities, their families, and/or governmental entities who subsidize the cost of care provided to eligible patients. Forms of nursing home fraud abuses include:

1. unlawful conversion or attachment of patients' assets
2. false claims to patient, family or government entity regarding services delivered
3. false statements in license application or renewal
4. maintenance of fraudulent records as to general or overhead costs of operation of facilities, as a basis for false claims to governmental entities
5. receipt of kickbacks from facility suppliers
6. employment of inadequate or unqualified staff in violation of licensing guidelines

These frauds are prosecutable under federal false claim and false statement statutes, and state fraud laws. They generally require careful and painstaking audits to separate out extensive self-dealing, kickback arrangements, and concealments through sophisticated accounting techniques, etc. *See also* Competitive Procurement Abuses, Embezzlement and Fiduciary Frauds, False Claims, Frauds Against Government Programs, Medicaid/Medicare Fraud

Patent Fraud: a form of self-improvement scheme which most closely resembles vanity publishing frauds.

In patent frauds, individuals are solicited through newspaper or other advertisements to send "patentable" ideas or gadgets to fraud operator for "evaluation by experts." The "evaluation" of course usually involves a fee, or at least "further processing" of the submission may involve a fee; thus an advance fee situation evolves. The fraud operator generally has neither the intention nor the capacity to develop or process a patentable item. For further information on remedies, etc., *see also* Advance Fee Schemes, Self-Improvement Schemes, Vanity Publishing Schemes

Pension Frauds and Abuses: thefts and fraudulent conversions of pension fund assets by trustees, employers or employees.

—*Frauds perpetuated by trustees*: violators of fiduciary duty in management of pension fund monies through:

1. poor investments tied to self-dealing or commercial bribery
2. embezzlement

Such frauds victimizes those who have contributed to the fund as much as those intending to benefit from it.

—*Fraud perpetuated by employees*: accrual of abnormal overtime, etc., to form an inflated base period on which pension payment level is to be established (very often in local public-sector-employment situations). Victims are other employees whose potential benefits are reduced by fraud of their peers or bankruptcy of fund, as well as employer-contributors to the pension plan. Victims are employees who have relied on promised future benefits.

Prosecutions in this white-collar crime area have shown patterns of questionable union-employer agreements to permit widespread trustee fraud. Major violations have been prosecuted under the federal mail fraud statute, and this area is considered one in which there are major white-collar crime/organized crime interrelationships. *See also* Abuse of Trust, Embezzlement and Fiduciary Frauds, Commercial Bribery, False Claims

Pigeon Drop or Pocketbook Drop: one of a large variety of street con games regularly perpetrated on gullible victims. It is a scheme in which the victim is persuaded to withdraw a large sum of cash from a bank account in order to show good faith or financial responsibility regarding the sharing of a "discovered" cache of money with two other persons (who are con artists). In the course of the con, both the "discovered" money and the victim's "good faith" money disappear, as do the con artists.

Victims may be anyone, since perpetrators of this fraud have a remarkable ability to disarm their victims. Keys to the pigeon drop con are:

1. The con artists do not appear to be associated or know each other in any way.
2. A pocketbook, envelope, etc., is "found" by one of the confederates, and it contains a sizable amount of money, no owner ID, and the suggestion that the money is illicitly generated, such as a gambler's proceeds.
3. An agreement to share the money is made with the victim showing "good faith" (i.e., putting up money) by those involved. (Alternately, a deal is made for all to put up money in a pool to be held by victim.)
4. A switch is made while the victim is distracted, and his or her money is stolen by one of the confederates.

Street cons of this type are generally prosecuted under state fraud, false pretenses, and larceny statutes. Police in most jurisdictions have had experience with one or more such street con games.

Pollution and Environmental Protection Violations: many abuses in the environmental area involve more than violations of specific environmental/pollution control statutes and orders. White-collar crime abuses in this area consist primarily of the making or submitting of false statements concerning the degree of compliance with statutes and regulations for pollution control; and in order to cover up violations or lack of compliance with environmental standards. Falsification of test or sample data designed to measure compliance with standards represents another form of white-collar violation in this area. *See also* False Statements

Ponzi Schemes: a general class of frauds in which the fraud operator uses money invested by later investor/victims to pay a high rate of return instead of making investments represented to them. Such schemes must inevitably collapse because it is mathematically impossible to continue them indefinitely. The length of time they can continue will depend upon the promised rate of return to investors, the amount of money the fraud operator takes out for himself or herself, and the costs of inducing victims to part with their money (e.g., sales commissions). Many such frauds have cheated victims of millions of dollars; some have operated over a period of years.

Ponzi elements are to be found in many varieties of investment frauds, under different guises and in different variations, such as long-term investments and short-term business financing.

These schemes have been federally prosecuted under the mail fraud statute, and as securities violations investigated by the U.S. Securities and Exchange Commission. On the state level they would be violations of general fraud, false pretenses, and larceny statutes. *See also* Investment Schemes

Price-Fixing: illegal combinations by sellers to administer the price of a good or service, depriving customers of a competitive marketplace, restraining competition, and maintaining an artificial price structure.

Victims are customers of such combinations who are deprived of freely determined prices for the goods and services they purchase. Secondary victims may be competitors of the firms participating in the price-fixing agreement.

Often when one thinks of price-fixing, one thinks of a large nationwide conspiracy between industrial giants. While this is part of the problem, it is equally probable that many price-fixing arrangements occur at the local level. For example, in Virginia the practice of a local bar association that set the price for title searches was held to be unlawful. In other locally prosecuted cases, druggists have been punished for fixing prices on prescription drugs.

Price-fixing violations are most often the subject of federal enforcement efforts, but are also proscribed by many state antitrust statutes. *See also* Antitrust Offenses, Restraint of Trade

Procurement and Contracting Abuses: see Competitive Procurement Abuses

Public/Official Corruption: white-collar crime that generally falls into the category of abuse of trusttype violations involving commercial bribery, collusion with bid-rigging, avoidance of the competitive process in connection with the purchase of goods and services by governmental entities, self-dealing in connection with governmental purchases or grants of franchise to use public property and real estate variances.

Most public corruption has its parallel in the private sector. Thus conflict of interest is the public equivalent of insider self-dealing; and there is little distinction between public and commercial bribery situations particularly where they overlap, such as in the government procurement area.

These violations are federally prosecuted under federal mail fraud and organized crime statutes. On the local level there are numerous statutory provisions for prosecution involving bribery, taking of kickbacks, and perjury. *See also* Abuse of Trust, Commercial Bribery, Competitive Procurement Frauds, Frauds Against Governmental Programs

Pyramid Scheme: the commercial version of the chain-letter scheme, used by fraud operators in the selling of phony distributorships, franchises, and business-opportunity plans. *See also* Chain-Referral Schemes, Franchising Frauds, Investment Frauds

Referral-Sales Schemes: *see* Chain-Referral Schemes, Merchandising Schemes

Repair Fraud: a form of consumer fraud involving repairs or maintenance services performed on consumer goods. Such white-collar crime schemes generally involve:

1. overcharging for services performed
2. charging for services and parts not used
3. performing services or repairs not wanted or needed
4. failing to perform services or repairs promised

This is a major area for proactive investigations, particularly decoy techniques. Where a sufficient pattern of deliberate violations has been developed, or the decoy technique successfully implemented, there have been convictions under state general fraud laws. *See also* Consumer Fraud

Restraint of Trade: actions, combinations or schemes which interfere with unfettered marketplace transactions. Examples are: price-fixing, bribery and kickbacks for commercial advantage, interference with competitive bidding processes, dictation of price structure to customers or dealers, exclusive buying arrangements.

While the best-known statutes in this area are federal, many abuses occur in local jurisdictions and are subject to state or local remedies, especially when interstate commerce is not involved. Many organized crime activities, aimed at monopolizing local markets to provide certain services or merchandise, may also involve restraints of trade, and state antitrust statutes should be reviewed to determine their applicability in such situations. *See also* Commercial Bribery, Competitive Procurement Abuses, Price-Fixing

Scam: *see* Bankruptcy Fraud

Securities Fraud: fraudulent activities involving the sale, transfer, or purchase of securities or of money interests in the business activities of others.

Victims are generally securities investors who are not aware of the full facts regarding transactions they enter. Abuses cover a broad range; for example, situations where:

1. Businesses or promoters seek to raise capital unlawfully or without proper registration and oversight.
2. Securities of no value are sold, or are misrepresented to be worth far more than their actual value.

3. Purchasers are not advised of all facts regarding securities, and/or of failure to file appropriate disclosures with federal and state regulatory agencies.

4. Insiders use special knowledge to trade in securities to the disadvantage of the general public, which lacks such knowledge.

5. Broker-dealers and investment advisers act for their own benefit rather than for the benefit of their clients.

6. False information is provided to security holders and the investing public in financial statements published or filed with securities regulatory agencies, or by payments to financial writers or publications.

7. Manipulation of the price of securities by purchases and sales occurs in stock exchange or over-the-counter markets.

8. There has been a failure to file registration or other reports with federal and state regulatory agencies.

Securities violations potentially exist wherever investors rely on others to manage and conduct the business in which an investment is made. It is not necessary that there be any formal certificates such as stocks and bonds. Any form of investment agreement is potentially a security. *See also* Advance Fee Schemes, Boiler Rooms, False Statements, Insider Self-Dealing, Investment Frauds

Self-Improvement Schemes: frauds which appeal to victims' desires to improve themselves personally or financially, by the acquisition of social or employment skills.

Schemes in this category tend to run on a continuum from improving purely personal/social skills and attributes to those tied to an individual's employment opportunities. On the personal end of the scale are the dance studio or charm school schemes; on the employment end of the scale are fraudulent job-training schemes and advance-fee employment agencies.

Somewhere in the middle are modeling agencies which purport to improve the person and his or her other employment prospects; also courses on improving one's image or ability to communicate with others. Some business-opportunity schemes which hold out the prospect of financial improvement plus "being a respected community businessman" also fall into this category by appealing to victim's desire to improve his or her finances and lifestyle.

These abuses have been prosecuted under mail fraud and state fraud statutes, curbed by the U.S. Federal Trade Commission, and have also been the subject of enforcement efforts based on state and local legislation, licensing codes, and other codes governing the operation of schools or educational settings. *See also* Business-Opportunity Schemes, Employment Agency Frauds, Talent Agency Frauds, Vanity Publishing

Sewer Service: a term of art used to describe the kinds of activity noted below.

Many merchandising, home repair, and other frauds rely on the use of litigation for ultimate collections of proceeds of the fraud. Likewise, many enterprises which are not, strictly speaking, fraudulent, such as those which sell much overpriced merchandise on credit, similarly depend upon litigation or the threat of litigation to squeeze money from victims.

In both these situations devices are often adopted to fraudulently deprive victims of the opportunity to defend against such litigation—usually by not informing them that litigation has been initiated against them (for example, dropping the summons or subpoena "down the sewer"). This is accomplished, usually, by false affidavits, filed in court, that a summons and complaint were served on the victim.

Such violations have been federally prosecuted for violation of the 1966 Civil Rights Act, but state violations are clearly present where false affidavits are filed in court.

Short Weighting or Loading: purposeful shorting of the volume or quantity of a cargo, accompanied by a false claim (invoice) demanding payment for the full amount.

Such frauds are easiest to perpetrate where the cargo is of such nature or bulk that it is difficult for the receiver to detect shortages. The reverse of the short weighting/loading fraud is often used as a modus operandi for diversions (thefts) of cargo. In this situation a transport vehicle is purposefully overloaded; the overage is not recorded (false statement by omission); and the overloaded amount forms the basis of kickbacks to the scheme operators by the recipients of the shipments (often fences of stolen goods). Manipulation of the size or volume of loads must always be accompanied by false claims or false statements, since accompanying documentation or invoices do not reflect the fraudulent changes in the load size.

This violation involves either a false claim to a customer or a plain and simple theft from the shipper. Since insiders are frequently involved, it will often involve commercial bribery, kickbacks, etc., as well as federal violations involving interstate shipment of stolen property. *See also* Weights and Measures Violations

Talent Agency Schemes: *see* Self-Improvement Frauds, Vanity Publishing Schemes

Tax and Revenue Violations: perpetrated with the intent to deprive a taxing authority of revenues to which it is entitled or of information it needs in order to make a judgment regarding revenues to which it is entitled, or to avoid admission of involvement in illicit, though profitable, business activities.

Tax frauds may be perpetrated through the filing of false returns, as in personal income tax frauds; through the bribery of public officials, as may occur in property tax assessment frauds; or in the failure to file appropriately, as with an organized crime-figure who may not be concerned with avoiding tax liability but rather with revealing the sources of his taxable income. Many white-collar crimes obligate the offender to commit tax fraud because of illicitly obtained monies he or she does not wish to report, i.e., assets due to bribes, larcenies, kickbacks, or embezzlement proceeds. Common crimes, especially of a business nature, also result in tax violations, e.g., bookmaking, fencing of stolen goods (both income and sales tax abuses).

Tax avoidance through false statements may be a component of otherwise legitimate business enterprises, especially in areas of business and occupation taxes, inventory taxes, and sales taxes. Individuals and businesses will also seek to avoid or evade excise taxes; e.g., on cigarettes, or substitution of low-taxed home heating oil for higher-taxed diesel fuel for trucks.

Tax violations are usually prosecuted under special federal, state and local tax statutes.

Vanity Publishing Schemes: schemes which involve eliciting fees from individuals on the promise of promoting their creative "talents" (real or imaginary), or assisting them in the development of said talent.

Such frauds rely upon the vanity of the victim (i.e., his or her belief that she/he has a creative talent that has not as yet been discovered). Generally these schemes relate to creative endeavors in which clear performance standards regarding the talent are not available and are often a matter of taste, such as literary publishing or song writing.

The scheme operator will imply a promise of national advertising, book reviews, distribution, special marketing services, but not so concretely that he or she can be held to any implied promise. The victims usually invest heavily and lose both their money and their hopes. They are left with a few copies of a printed and scored song arrangement, or a number of copies of books which established book-review publications have not troubled to look at because of their publishing source.

It should be kept in mind that there is a legitimate private publishing market. General principles of fraud analysis should be applied to determine whether or not the line has been crossed in ways which make misrepresentations fraudulent. *See also* Self-Improvement Schemes, Talent Agency Schemes

Weights and Measures Violations: abusive practices involving the cheating of customers by failure to deliver prescribed quantities or amounts of desired goods. These violations usually involve false statements or claims in which the victim has relied on seller's representation of the delivered quantity in remitting higher payment, for example:

1. gas pump meter manipulation to show more gas pumped than received by customer
2. butcher's thumb on the meat scale
3. odometer rollbacks in auto sales

These frauds are most successful where one victim cannot easily verify weights or measuring devices, or where victim has no reason to question the seller's claim or statement, such as when products sold are bottled or packaged.

These abuses are usually detected on inspection by local agencies' personnel, and prosecuted or enforced as violations of local ordinances. Purposeful, intentional, and continued activities of this kind should be considered as possibilities for violations of general fraud, false pretenses, and larceny statutes. *See also* Short Weighting or Loading

Welfare Fraud: abuses associated with government income- and family-subsidy programs.

Government welfare programs are always exploited by a small number of applicants who apply for benefits to which they are not entitled, or continue to claim eligibility when they no longer meet the established criteria for such aid.

Receipt of monies from claimants by officials processing welfare claims represents another dimension of this fraud area. Such monies may be solicited as kickbacks in exchange for inflated claims filed; as bribes to certify claimants who are ineligible or to avoid reporting claimants' ineligibility, or as extortion for processing claims to which recipient is fully eligible. In some cases nonexistent recipients ("ghosts") may be created to fraudulently siphon money out of such programs.

These violations are enforced under specific provisions of welfare legislation and under general fraud statutes. Where federal funds are involved, there may be overlapping federal/state enforcement jurisdiction. *See also* Frauds Against Government Benefit Programs

Work-at-Home Schemes: *see* Business-Opportunity Schemes, Franchise Frauds, Self-Improvement Frauds

References

Adler, Fred. 1975. *Sisters in Crime*. New York: McGraw-Hill.

Adler, Jerry. 1977. "Employee Thievery: A $6 Billion Hand in the Till." *New York Sunday News Magazine* (September 11): 6t.

Akers, Ronald. 1977. *Deviant Behavior: A Social Learning Approach*. 2d ed. Belmont, MA: Wadsworth.

Albrecht, W. Steve, Marshall B. Romney, David J. Cherrington, I. Reed Payne, and Allan J. Roe. 1982. *How to Detect and Prevent Business Fraud*. Englewood Cliffs, NJ: Prentice-Hall.

Benson, Michael L. 1985. "Denying the Guilty Mind: Accounting for Involvement in White-Collar Crime." *Criminology* 23: 585–607.

Blumberg, Abraham S. 1984. "The Practice of Law as a Confidence Game: Organization Cooptation of a Profession." In *Criminal Justice: Law and Politics*, 2d ed., ed. George Cole, 123–26. Monterey, CA: Brooks/Cole.

Bowker, Lee. 1981. "Crime and the Use of Prisons in the United States: A Time Series Analysis." *Crime and Delinquency* 27: 206–12.

Braithwaite, John. 1979. "An Exploratory Study of Used Car Fraud." In *Two Faces of Deviance*, ed. Paul R. Wilson and John Braithwaite. Queensland, Australia: University of Queensland.

———. 1982. "Enforced Self-Regulation: A New Strategy for Corporate Crime Control." *Michigan Law Review* 80: 1466–1502.

———. 1984. *Corporate Crime in the Pharmaceutical Industry*. London: Routledge and Kegan Paul.

Brenner, S. N. and E. A. Molander. 1977. "Is the Ethics of Business Changing?" *Harvard Business Review* 55 (January-February): 59–70.

Broy, Anthony. 1974. "The Big Business Rip-Off." *Finance* (November): 42–45.

Buckwalter, Art. 1984. *Investigative Methods*. Woburn, MA: Butterworth.

Caeser, G. 1968. *The Biography of William J. Burns*. Englewood Cliffs, NJ: Prentice-Hall.

Cameron, Mary Owen. 1964. *The Booster and the Snitch*. New York: Free Press.

Chambliss, William. 1967. "Types of Deviance and the Effectiveness of Legal Sanctions." *Wisconsin Law Review* (Summer): 703–19.

Clarke, John, and Richard Hollinger. 1983. *Theft by Employees in Work Organizations.* Washington, DC: U.S. Government Printing Office.

Clinard, Marshall B., and Peter Yeager. 1980. *Corporate Crime.* New York: Free Press.

Comer, James. 1985. "Black Violence and Public Policy." In *American Violence and Public Policy.* New Haven, CT: Yale University: 63–86.

Cressey, Donald R. 1953. *Other People's Money: The Social Psychology of Embezzlement.* New York: Free Press.

Dalton, Katharina. 1971. *The Premenstrual Syndrome.* Springfield, IL: Charles C. Thomas.

Dunford, Franklyn, and Delbert Elliott. 1983. "Identifying Career Criminal Using Self-Reporting Data." *Journal of Research in Crime and Delinquency* 21: 57–86.

Durkheim, Émile. 1951. *Suicide.* Trans. John A. Spaulding and George Simpson. New York: Free Press.

Edlehertz, Herbert. 1970. *The Nature, Impact and Prosecution of White-Collar Crime.* Washington, DC: U.S. Government Printing Office.

———. 1977. *The Investigation of White-Collar Crime.* Washington, DC: U.S. Department of Justice Law Enforcement Assistance Administration.

Ekman, Paul. 1986. *Telling Lies.* New York: Berkley.

Elliott, Delbert, and Suzanne Ageton. 1980. "Reconciling Race and Class Differences in Self-Reported and Official Estimates of Delinquency." *American Sociological Review* 45: 95–110.

———, David Huizinga, and Suzanne Ageton. 1985. *Explaining Delinquency and Drug Abuse.* Beverly Hills, CA: Sage.

Fedora, Orestes, and Shawn Fedora. 1982. "Some Neuropsychological and Psychophysiological Aspects of Psychopathic and Nonpsychopathic Criminals." In *Laterality and Psychopathology,* ed. P. Flor-Henry and J. Gruzeliar. New York: Elsevier North-Holland Biomedical Press.

Franklin, Alice P. 1976. "Internal Theft in a Retail Organization." Ph.D. dissertation, Ohio State University, Columbus, Ohio.

Glazer, Daniel. 1978. *Crime in Our Changing Society.* New York: Holt Rinehart and Winston.

Gluek, Sheldon, and Eleonor Glueck. 1974. *Of Delinquency and Crime.* Springfield, IL: Charles C. Thomas.

Green, Gary S. 1990. *Occupational Crime.* Chicago: Nelson-Hall.

Greenberg, David. 1975. "The Incapacitative Effects of Imprisonment: Some Estimates." *Law & Society Review* 9: 541–80.

Greenwood, Peter. 1982. *Selective Incapacitation.* Santa Monica, CA: Rand Corporation.

Gross, Edward. 1979. "Organizations as Criminal Actors." In *Two Faces of Deviance,* ed. Paul R. Wilson and John Braithwaite. Queensland, Australia: University of Queensland.

Henderson, Charles. 1901. *Introduction to the Study of the Dependent, Defective and Delinquent Classes* 2d ed. Boston: D.C. Heath.

Hirschi, Travis. 1969. *Causes of Delinquency.* Berkeley, CA: University of California.

———. 1973. "Procedural Rules and the Study of Deviant Behavior." *Social Problems* 21: 159–73.

Hopkins, Andrew. 1980. "Controlling Corporate Deviance." *Criminology* 18: 198–214.

Inbau, Fred E., John E. Reid, and Joseph Buckley. 1986. *Criminal Interrogation and Confessions.* Baltimore, MD: Williams & Wilkins.

Johnston, Michael. 1982. *Political Corruption and Public Policy in America.* Belmont, MA: Wadsworth.

Kramer, Ronald. 1978. "Corporate Crime: An Organizational Perspective." In. *White Collar and Economic Crime*, ed. Peter M. Wickman and Timothy E. Dailey, 75–94. Lexington, MA: Lexington Books.

Kramer, W. Michael. 1988. *Investigative Techniques in Complex Financial Crimes.* Washington, DC: National Institute on Economic Crime.

Loeffler, Robert. 1974. *Report of the Trustee of Equity Funding Corporation of America Pursuant to Section 167(3) of the Bankruptcy Act.* United States Bankruptcy Court, Los Angeles (November).

Mabbott, J. D. 1939. "Punishment." *Mind* 49: 152–67.

Mannheim, Hermann. 1955. "Lombroso and His Place in Modern Criminology." In *Group Problems in Crime and Punishment,* ed. Hermann Mannheim, London: Routledge and Kegan Paul: 69–84.

Manson Donald. 1984. *Tracking Offenders.* Washington, D.C.: Bureau of Justice Statistics.

Martinson, D. Lipton, and J. Wilks. 1975. *The Effectiveness of Correctional Treatment: A Survey of Treatment Evaluation Studies.* New York: Praeger.

Martinson, Robert. 1974. "What Works—Questions and Answers About Prison Reform." *Public Interest* 35: 22–54.

Merton, Robert. 1968. *Social Theory and Social Structure.* 2d ed. New York: Free Press.

Newman, Graeme. 1983. *Just and Painful.* New York: Macmillan.

Parisi, Nicolette. 1984. "Theories of Corporate Criminal Liability." In *Corporations as Criminals,* ed. Ellen Hochstedler, 73–75. Beverly Hills, CA: Sage.

Petersilia, John, Susan Turner, and Joyce Peterson. 1986. *Prison versus Probation in California: Implications for Crime and Offender Recidivism.* Santa Monica, CA: Rand Corporation.

Phillips, David. 1983. "The Impact of Mass Media Violence on U.S. Homicides." *American Sociological Review* 48: 560–68.

Pollack, Harriet, and Alexander B. Smith. 1983. "White-Collar Versus Street Crime Sentencing Disparity: How Judges See the Problem." *Judicature* 67: 175–82.

Rennie, Ysabel. 1978. *The Search for Criminal Man.* Lexington, MA: Lexington Books.

Rensberger, Boyce. 1976. "Few Doctors Ever Report Colleagues' Incompetence." *New York Times* (January 29):1.

Shapiro, Susan. 1985. "The Road Not Taken: The Elusive Path to Criminal Prosecution for White-Collar Offenders." *Law & Society Review* 19: 179–217.

Siegel, Larry J. 1989. *Criminology.* 3d ed. St. Paul: West.

Sykes, Gresham, and David Matza. 1957. "Techniques of Neutralization: A Theory of Delinquency." *American Sociological Review* 22: 664–70.

Thornton, Mary. 1984. "Computer Crime." *Washington Post* (May 20): A1t.

Tittle, Charles. 1988. "Two Empirical Regularities (Maybe) in Search of an Exploration: Commentary on the Age/Crime Debate." *Criminology* 26: 75–85.

Tittle, Charles, Wayne Villemez, and Douglas Smith. 1978. "The Myth of Social Class and Criminality: An Empirical Assessment of the Empirical Evidence." *American Sociological Review* 43: 643–56.

U.S. Congress. House. Committee on the Judiciary House of Representatives. *Rules of Criminal Procedures for the United States District Courts.* Washington, D.C.: U.S. Government Printing Office, 1985.

Vaughan, Diane. 1982. "Toward Understanding Unlawful Organizational Behavior." *Michigan Law Review* 80: 1377–1402.

Wheeler, Stanton, David Weisburd, and Nancy Bode. 1982. "Sentencing the White-Collar Offender: Rhetoric and Reality." *American Sociological Review* 47: 641–59.

———, David Weisburd, Elin Waring, and Nancy Bode. 1988. "White-Collar Crime and Criminal." *American Criminal Law Review* 25: 331–57.

Whitman, H. 1953."Why Some Doctors Should Be in Jail." *Collier's* (October 30): 23–27.

Wilson, James. 1975. *Thinking About Crime*. New York: Basic Books.

———, and Richard Herrnstein. 1985. *Crime and Human Nature*. New York: Simon and Shuster.

Winans, R. Foster. 1984. *Trading Secrets*. New York: St. Martins.

Wolfgang, Marvin E. 1960. "Cesare Lombroso." In *Pioneers in Criminology*, ed. Hermann Mannheim, 168–227. London: Stevens.

———, Robert Figlio, and Thorsten Sellin. 1972. *Delinquency in a Birth Cohort*. Chicago: University of Chicago.

Yeudall, L. T. 1977. *Childhood Experiences as Causes of Criminal Behavior*. (Senate of Canada, Issue no. 1) Thirteenth Parliament: Ottawa, Canada.

Index

About the Author

JOSEPH T. WELLS, CFE, CPA, is Chairman of the Board of the National
Association of Certified Fraud Examiners in Austin, Texas.

ISBN 0-89930-639-X

HARDCOVER BAR CODE